CASES IN ORGANIZATIONAL BEHAVIOUR

FIRST EDITION

CASES IN ORGANIZATIONAL BEHAVIOUR

FIRST EDITION

Tupper Cawsey
Wilfrid Laurier University

Gene Deszca
Wilfrid Laurier University

Toronto Montréal Boston Burr Ridge IL Dubuque IA Madison WI New York San Francisco
St Louis Bangkok Bogatá Caracas Kuala Lumpur Lisbon London Madrid Mexico City
Milan New Delhi Santiago Seoul Singapore Sydney Taipei

Cases in Organizational Behaviour
First Edition

ISBN: 0-07-088783-7

1 2 3 4 5 6 7 8 9 10 TRI 0 9 8 7 6 5

Printed and bound in Canada

Vice President, Editorial and Media Technology: Patrick Ferrier
Sponsoring Editor: Kim Brewster
Senior Marketing Manager: Kelly Smyth
Developmental Editor: Darren Hick
Senior Production Coordinator: Madeleine Harrington
Supervising Editor: Anne Nellis
Senior Editorial Coordinator: Christine Lomas
Copy Editor: Kelli Howey
Cover Design: Greg Devitt
Interior Designer: Michelle Losier
Cover Image Credit: Coneyl Jay/Getty Images
Composition: Lynda Powell
Printer: Tri-Graphic Printing

Library and Archives Canada Cataloguing in Publication

Cawsey, Thomas F. (Thomas Frederick), 1943-
Cases in organizational behaviour / Tupper Cawsey, Gene Deszca.— 1st ed.

Includes bibliographical references.
ISBN 0-07-088783-7

1. Organizational behavior — Case studies. I. Deszca, Gene II. Title.

HD58.7.C395 2004 658 C2004-905817-7

We would like to dedicate this book to the managers who invited us into their organizations and encouraged us to document the challenges faced by business today.

T. C.

G. D.

about the authors

Tupper Cawsey is Professor of Business Administration at Wilfrid Laurier University. He has been Associate Dean of Business at Laurier, MBA Program Director, Director of the Laurier Institute, and Area Coordinator of Management and Organizational Behaviour. Dr. Cawsey was recognized in 2001 as one of Canada's top five business professors with the Leaders in Management Education Award, sponsored by Bell Nexxia, PricewaterhouseCoopers, and the National Post. He is a recipient of the 1994 David Bradford Educator Award and the 1990 Wilfrid Laurier University Outstanding Teacher Award. Dr. Cawsey is chairperson of the Board of Directors of Lutherwood CODA, a not-for-profit organization in Kitchener-Waterloo. His consulting and research interests focus on the management of organizational change and on managerial careers. He has written widely in these areas.

Gene Deszca is Professor of Business Administration, a past Director of the MBA program, and a former Area Coordinator of Management and Organizational Behaviour at Wilfrid Laurier University. He has published and/or presented more than 100 papers, monographs, and technical papers. Two recent examples are the co-authored pieces "Driving Loyalty through Time-to-Value" and "Managing the New-Product Development Process: Best-in-Class Principles and Leading Practices" (with H. Noori and H. Munro). Current consulting and research involves organizational change, career processes of knowledge workers, and the development of high-performance organizations. He has been instrumental in the development of the Society of Management Accountants of Canada's post-university professional accreditation programs, and is a member of their national Board of Directors.

CASE CONTRIBUTORS

Tony Atkinson, *University of Waterloo*
Glenn Brophey, *Nipissing University*
Celeste Brotheridge, *University of Regina*
Tupper Cawsey, *Wilfrid Laurier University*
Nina Cole, *Ryerson University*
Daniel Coleman, *University of New Brunswick*
Gene Deszca, *Wilfrid Laurier University*
Bob Ellis, *Wilfrid Laurier University*
Ken Harling, *Wilfrid Laurier University*

David Hemsworth, *Nipissing University*
Elizabeth Husby, *University of Manitoba*
Rosemary McGowan, *Brescia College, University of Western Ontario*
John Melnyk, *University of Winnipeg*
Gary Mischke, *University of Manitoba*
Shripad Pendse, *Saint Mary's University*
Lindsay Sawyer, *University of Winnipeg*
Robert Sexty, *Memorial University*
Andrew Templer, *University of Windsor*
James Tolliver, *University of New Brunswick*
Michael Wade, *York University*
Laurier Institute
Lisa Carson
Kevin Doucette
Michelle Linton
M. Lohbihler
Don Morrison
Jazz Samra

CASE TEACHING RESOURCES[1]

Organizations

Case Association (Eastern Case Writers): http://caseweb.org

North American Case Research Association (NACRA): www.nacra.net/

Society for Case Research & Annual Case Writer's Workshop: www.sfcr.org/

Western Case Writers Association: newton.uor.edu/FacultyFolder/JSpee/wca/main.htm

World Association for Case Research & Application: www.wacra.org/

Suppliers and Publishers of Case Resources

Academy of Management 2001 Meeting Cases: http://web.bentley.edu/empl/c/lchin/nacra/aom2001.htm

CaseNet—South-Western Publishing: http://casenet.thomsonlearning.com/casenet_global_fr.html

CasePlace.org: www.caseplace.org

Case Studies for Politics: www.york.ac.uk/depts/poli/casestud/

Darden (UVa) Case Collection: www.darden.edu/case/collection/

---

[1]From the North American Case Research Association (NACRA)

Electronic Hallway—Cases in Public, Non-Profit, & Health Administration: www.hallway.org/

European Case Clearing House: www.ecch.cranfield.ac.uk/

Global View Interactive Cases: www.globalview.org/

HBS (Harvard) Case Collection: www.hbsp.harvard.edu/products/cases/index.html (when at this site, click also on Harvard Business Online for Educators)

i-Case Interactive Cases: www.i-case.com/

Ivey (Western Ontario) Case Collection: www.ivey.uwo.ca/IveyPublishing/

Laurier Institute, Wilfrid Laurier University: www.wlu.ca/laurierinstitute

Pearson Custom Publishing—Publisher of Case Research Journal: www.pearsoncustom.com/

Primis Case Database—McGraw-Hill/Irwin Publishing: www.mhhe.com/primis

contents

ETHICS/ENVIRONMENT CASES

INTEGRATING CASES

synopsis of cases

INDIVIDUAL AND INTERPERSONAL-LEVEL CASES

Case 1 A Juggling Act (A-1), (A-2), (B)

Primary focus: Individual behaviour (stress)

Secondary foci: Interpersonal behaviour, human resource policies

Level: Analysis—Introductory; Topic—Intermediate

Synopsis

Case A-1: Anna, a consulting manager, has been a top performer at Global Consulting (GC) for more than five years, enjoying the fast pace and long hours while catching up with personal life on the weekends. For the past year, since having a child, she has been attempting a part-time consulting role and is facing some significant lifestyle choices. Although she enjoys the mix of work and time with her daughter, she is overwhelmed by the various stresses in her life and feels like she is not living up to expectations at work, at home, or with other personal commitments. She knows she needs to re-evaluate and make some changes.

Case A-2 (in Instructor's Manual): Chris, a new consultant, is experiencing constant trade-offs between his commitments at home (and desire to spend time with his wife Anna and daughter Kristin) and his need/desire to make it to the next level at work. While he is trying to share the workload at home and maintain the right balance of life, he feels that he needs to give additional time and effort to work in the short-term to jump to the management level. He wonders how he can effectively do this and whether it's appropriate to give up family time temporarily. He also knows Anna has some big decisions to make regarding her career in order to regain her happiness and reduce her stress; he knows these decisions have to be made jointly within the parameters of their mutual values and principles.

Case B (in Instructor's Manual): Anna re-evaluates her values and priorities, and outlines some of the options that might help her find a balance that will keep her motivated and content. She needs to determine some next steps to help her reduce her stress level while making some significant decisions.

Case 2 Future Vision Digital Services Inc.

Primary focus: Individual behaviour (management of knowledge workers)

Secondary foci: Organization culture and design, project management, human resource policies, interpersonal relations

Level: Analysis—Intermediate; Topic—Intermediate

Synopsis

Blake Randolph, Vice President of Technology Development for Future Vision Digital Services Inc., is faced with managing Andre Gregoire, a very talented but difficult to manage employee. Randolph is responsible for the team of software developers and systems architects that builds complex server-side functionality for clients' Internet sites. His boss, Jacques Riveaux, who is at a client's place, needs to speak to Andre Gregoire—now. And Andre is nowhere to be found—again. What should Blake do about this pattern of behaviour given the needs of Future Vision?

Case 3 John Hamilton's Work and Eldercare Dilemma

Primary focus: Individual behaviour (stress)

Secondary foci: Organization culture, human resource policies

Level: Analysis—Intermediate; Topic—Senior

Synopsis

John Hamilton is facing increasing conflicts between his work and his responsibility to care for his mother. He has not informed people at work of his mother's illness, and has been leaving work to care for her while giving excuses for being out of the office. He wonders how much longer he can manage the balance of work and eldercare and, more importantly, how much longer he can sustain his strategy of silence.

Case 4 Someday My Prints Will Come

Primary focus: Individual behaviour (motivation)

Secondary focus: Organization control systems (unintended consequences)

Level: Analysis—Introductory; Topic—Intermediate

Synopsis

Dr. Finagle is trying to rush an academic paper to meet a conference deadline and is having trouble getting it printed. These troubles are connected to earlier administrative decisions taken to control costs within the university. Students are given the opportunity to investigate the complexities and motivational consequences of such control systems.

Case 5 Working at Wal-Mart

Primary focus: Individual behaviour (motivation, ethics)

Secondary foci: Job design, leadership, organization culture

Level: Analysis—Introductory; Topic—Introductory

Synopsis

Claude has a problem. His father is celebrating a major birthday this Saturday and Claude is scheduled to work at Wal-Mart from 4:00 to 8:00 p.m. Claude comes from a close-knit family where all family milestones are celebrated together over an extended meal. If Claude works his shift, he will have to miss his father's birthday dinner. If he calls in sick, he will feel like a liar since he is not actually ill; he does not even feel a cold coming on. He is sure that his manager will not give him the time off. When Claude first started this job, he had asked that he not be scheduled to work on his day of Sabbath. His manager simply said that the auto scheduler, a computer program designed to create employee work schedules, could not accommodate this, and then walked away. There was no room for discussion. "How much is this job worth to me, anyway?" Claude asks himself.

Case 6 Countryside Environmental Services

Primary focus: Interpersonal behaviour (perception, conflict)

Secondary foci: Leadership, motivation, role clarification

Level: Analysis—Intermediate; Topic—Intermediate

Synopsis

Vince doesn't know how to handle the conflict with a fellow employee, Gwen. He has discussed the issue with his boss several times to no avail. Her role appears unclear and Vince believes that others are leaving because of this lack of clarity and the conflict. He wonders what to do.

GROUP/TEAM-LEVEL CASES

Case 7 Dividing the Pie at Bennett, Jones and Douglas

Primary focus: Group behaviour

Secondary foci: Motivation and incentives, organization structure and growth, perception

Level: Analysis—Senior; Topic—Senior

Synopsis

Joe Douglas is contemplating the problems facing Bennett, Jones and Douglas. As a founding partner of the law firm, Douglas is concerned with the animosity among the firm's partners. At the centre of the conflict is the firm's system of financial compensation. Within the past year, relations among the partners have deteriorated to the point where the firm is facing dissolution. Douglas is determined to develop a plan to rectify the situation.

Case 8 Jaztec Inc.

Primary focus: Team behaviour (stages of group development, committee leadership)

Secondary foci: Leadership, motivation

Level: Analysis—Introductory; Topic—Senior

Synopsis

Recently, Jaztec, Inc., a small online consulting firm, has developed a strategic alliance with FCC Foundations, a not-for-profit organization whose mandate is public awareness about musculoskeletal disorders arising from extended computer usage. The founders of Jaztec and FCC have formed a strategic alliance committee whose purpose is to develop FCC's presence on Jaztec's website and to develop stronger interorganizational linkages between Jaztec and FCC. Jovianna Gucci, Vice President of Marketing and Public Relations for Jaztec, has been assigned by Jaztec's founder to oversee the activities of the strategic alliance committee. Despite some past success with managing teams, Jovianna has found herself in a situation with a number of intragroup conflicts. Jovianna's power and authority are being undermined by the actions of some of her team members. Specifically, a team member has repeatedly failed to deliver the work promised, and two team members have resisted Jovianna's leadership. The situation with her team has deteriorated to the point where some of the team members have faxed a memo to Jaztec's founder requesting Jovianna's termination as committee head.

Case 9 Let's Get Together

Primary focus: Group behaviour

Secondary foci: Interpersonal conflict, group norms and expectations, group composition

Level: Analysis—Introductory; Topic—Introductory

Synopsis

A group of business students are required to analyze the management style in a company and present their findings to the class. The case documents team meetings and the conflicts that arise from different agendas, needs, and expectations. At a final meeting, the group members face significant conflict and wonder how to complete their task.

Case 10 Self-Managed Work Teams at South Australia Ambulance Service

Primary focus: Self-managed work teams

Secondary foci: Leadership and influence, organization structure, task design

Level: Analysis—Senior; Topic—Advanced

Synopsis

Ray Main is a paramedic seconded to the Empowerment Strategic Task Force. He is developing recommendations regarding the next step to be taken in the move by the South Australia Ambulance Service to an empowerment culture. Ray's task is made complex because of the differences in ambulance service for urban centres (principally Adelaide) and rural areas. Nineteen metro teams in Adelaide, 20 rural teams, and 60–70 volunteer teams are involved.

Case 11 The Case of the Unseen Customers (A)

Primary focus: Group behaviour (socio-technical systems)

Secondary foci: Task design, conflict, leadership, organization structure

Level: Analysis—Introductory; Topic—Introductory

Synopsis

Four managers at the City of Townsville Corporate Services Department are tired of the constant bickering amongst their staff and are deciding what to do. The individuals in the case believe the issue to be interpersonal in nature. However, on closer examination, it is clear that the organization structure, the layout of the office and location of the staff, the phone system, and the lack of awareness of each other's jobs are all underlying causes of the situation. Conflict arises because of the job demands, and such conflict quickly becomes interpersonal in nature.

ORGANIZATION-LEVEL CASES

Case 12 The Case of the Amalgamated Laboratory

Primary focus: Organization

Secondary foci: Task design, conflict, leadership, organization structure, organization change

Level: Analysis—Introductory; Topic—Introductory

Synopsis

This case study describes what happens when a health district merges four laboratories into one unit. Although the intention is to develop one centralized, efficient, and high-volume centre, inattention to the "people issues" and the cultural differences of the work units has resulted in chaos. The recently hired laboratory manager has implemented several stopgap measures intended to address the workload issues resulting from high turnover levels and sick-leave usage. However, these measures have not improved the laboratory's morale and performance problems. Time is running out for this manager as his supervisor gives him an ultimatum to "clean house or else."

Case 13 Family Medical Group of Companies

Primary focus: Organization structure

Secondary foci: Organization change, organization culture

Level: Analysis—Senior; Topic—Intermediate

Synopsis

Nancy Needham is the new Director of Human Resources for Family Medical Group of Companies. She is charged with the responsibility of creating a human resource plan for the company's two divisions: distribution and manufacturing. Continuing problems with morale, turnover, succession planning, and training have made these issues important. Nancy joined the company two weeks ago and has been asked to meet with the company president in two weeks to discuss her proposed plan.

Case 14 Just Another Email

Primary focus: Organization communications

Secondary foci: Leadership, organization structure and control, customer service

Level: Analysis—Introductory; Topic—Introductory

Synopsis

President Richmond of Midville, a medium sized university, has received an email complaint from a student. It contains a forwarded message from a staff member to all political science students about the staff member's willingness to assist students. The tone and content of the message appear inappropriate. The email raises issues of communications and quality of information, performance (of administrative staff and faculty), motivation and morale of students, management of managers, and delegation and decentralization. President Richmond needs to decide on an appropriate response and action.

Case 15 Migisi Tribal Council, Inc.

Primary focus: Voluntary organizations

Secondary foci: Conflict, leadership, organization structure, aboriginal affairs, organization vision and goals

Level: Analysis—Intermediate; Topic—Senior

Synopsis

Andrew Ross, Executive Director of the Migisi Tribal Council, Inc. (MTC), has to deal with the potential withdrawal of four First Nations tribes. The chiefs have informed him that the councils they represent have tentatively decided to take their four First Nations out of MTC and join with four non-affiliated First Nations in a neighbouring area to the southeast, to form a new tribal council. The reasons they have given are that the four non-affiliated First Nations are close neighbours and that they share many cultural and historical bonds with them. One of the chiefs has also stated that he thinks "MTC [is] getting too bureaucratic and too self serving." Andrew knows that if the four First Nations leave MTC, MTC will experience major reductions in financial and human resources. The cutbacks will cripple MTC's ability to serve its remaining six members and thus seriously threatens the continued viability of MTC.

Case 16 Northwell Inc.

Primary focus: Organizational change and renewal

Secondary foci: Organizational structure, culture, conflict, alignment of systems

Level: Analysis—Senior, Topic—Senior

Synopsis

Claudia Vee, CFO at Northwell, represents Northwell in the development of a joint venture with Medichek. This joint venture involves the development and launch of a medical supplies e-business for hospitals and the medical community. As such, it represents an entirely new approach to marketing and distribution for Northwell, a mature firm in a highly competitive environment. The launch of the website has fallen behind schedule and the relationship with Medichek has become frayed; senior officials at Northwell have expressed concern over the health of the venture. Claudia is faced with deciding how to improve things for Northwell.

Case 17—Electronic Data Interchange and the Ontario Dental Association

Primary focus: Organization change

Secondary foci: Organization structure and membership, control systems

Level: Analysis—Senior; Topic—Senior

Synopsis

Dr. Steve Smith, Chair of the Electronic Data Interchange (EDI) Task Force of the Ontario Dental Association (ODA), has been given responsibility for what seems to be a great opportunity for dentistry in Ontario. EDI holds the potential to connect dental offices and insurance companies through computers and telephone lines in order to speed transactions and reduce costs. Unfortunately, the Task Force's proposals have met with a wall of opposition from the dentists in Ontario. Moreover, Smith can not understand the depth of feelings that have been aroused over this issue. The opposition is directed not only at EDI, but also at the Ontario Dental Association itself. Smith wonders how he can resolve the issues surrounding EDI in a manner that will help to heal the rifts within the ODA.

LEADERSHIP CASES

Case 18 Western Prairie: The Greenfield Start-up

Primary focus: Leadership

Secondary foci: Team management, reward systems, organizational decision making

Level: Analysis—Senior; Topic—Intermediate

Synopsis

Brian Boydell, Process Superintendent of the Carsland plant, feels good about the progress of the team. The eight plant operators are back from Holland and Texas and are now writing training manuals. He feels proud of the way the operators are developing as a team. Therefore, he is dismayed and surprised to receive a letter addressed to him and his boss stating that the team is underpaid and wants a raise. In spite of his feelings of betrayal, he needs to decide what to do.

Case 19 Christine Carmichael

Primary focus: Leadership

Secondary foci: Motivation, reward systems

Level: Analysis—Introductory; Topic—Introductory

Synopsis

Tony Dunlop, the new president of Roselawn Manufacturing Ltd., is very concerned. He was hired to "turn the company around" and reverse the declining customer service levels and profitability resulting from the disastrous implementation of new enterprise resource software. He has suspected for some time that employee morale is a major problem. These suspicions were confirmed last week when a group of employees went to the Ontario Human Rights Commission and accused Tony's predecessor, John Morgan, of creating a "poisoned environment" for employees, particularly females. Tony has just finished a long discussion with Christine Carmichael, a recently departed employee, and now is convinced that changes have to be made in the way employees are treated. He decides to review what Christine has told him about how her motivation was destroyed during the year she worked at Roselawn Manufacturing and try to identify specific problems that need to be addressed.

Case 20 Oliver Davis's Entrepreneurial Success Story

Primary focus: Leadership

Secondary foci: Team management, reward systems, organizational decision making

Level: Analysis—Senior; Topic—Intermediate

Synopsis

Oliver Davis wonders how he can build on the success of Green Meadows Lawn Care. He is committed to building the business, but only with a continued focus on excellent customer service and delivery. How will he be able to maintain his personal contact with customers and his excellent employee relations as he expands?

Case 21 Northmar Distributors

Primary focus: Leadership

Secondary foci: Downsizing, organizational politics, ethics

Level: Analysis—Introductory; Topic—Intermediate

Synopsis

George Dubroy, the manager of a subsidiary warehouse operation for the convenience store industry, is faced with both ethical and business dilemmas in determining how to go about closing his entire operation. The case opens just as George learns from corporate that the decision is final and all attempts to forestall closure have been rejected. The setting is in Northern Ontario; George knows that many of his longer-serving employees are not likely to find work again in the region. His divided loyalties to his people and his employer are brought into stark relief as he begins to examine the corporate severance policies and is confronted by a friend on staff who is faced with an important career decision that is negatively affected by the severance policy. In addition, George's own severance package has yet to be negotiated, but he suspects that keeping closing costs low is bound to affect his final number positively.

Case 22 Team Ontario (A)

Primary focus: Leadership

Secondary foci: Team building, reward systems, organizational decision making

Level: Analysis—Senior; Topic—Intermediate

Synopsis

Bill Bowker has just been selected as Head Coach of Ontario's women's hockey team for the upcoming Canada Winter Games. It is a great honour to be named coach, and at the same time represents the biggest challenge of his coaching career. The Games are part of Canada's High Performance Hockey Program and are intended to identify and prepare athletes who could succeed at the international level, such as the forthcoming Salt Lake City Winter Olympics in 2002. Bowker knows that the expectations of him are very high. Ontario lost to Quebec in the gold medal final at the last Winter Games, and it is hoped that this time Ontario will be victorious. The challenge facing him is daunting: He has to select the best players from across Ontario and mould them into a team in a relatively short period of time. He knows that this is the experience of a lifetime for many of these young athletes. As good as they are, perhaps one or two from his team would eventually make it to Canada's National Team. How can they win and make this a great experience for these young women?

ETHICS/ENVIRONMENT CASES

Case 23 Alberta Energy Company and the Ethics of Operation Kabriole

Primary focus: Ethical decision making

Secondary foci: Organizational reward systems, organizational culture

Level: Analysis—Senior; Topic—Senior

Synopsis

It is September 1998. Gwyn Morgan, President and CEO of Alberta Energy Company (AEC), is quietly sitting in his Calgary office staring out the window toward the Rocky Mountains. He has a difficult decision to make that could affect his company immensely. He has been approached by the Alberta RCMP with a proposal that may finally put an end to the period of industrial sabotage that has plagued not only his company, but also the entire oil and gas industry. The terrorism has been costly and has intimidated company staff. The RCMP is proposing that AEC property be bombed to secure cover for an undercover agent. Worse yet, for this operation to work, only a select few individuals will be allowed to know the truth. The sting is to be known as "Operation Kabriole." How will Morgan explain his actions to the company's directors and shareholders after the fact? How will they react? How will the industry react? How will the media respond? How will the nearby residents and communities feel? He wonders how things have gotten to this point.

Case 24 A Midsummer Day's Nightmare

Primary focus: Ethical decision making

Secondary focus: Reward systems

Level: Analysis—Introductory; Topic—Intermediate

Synopsis

The manager of a fast-food outlet has found her freezer unplugged! The outlet received an order worth $5,000 to $6,000 yesterday, and now most of the food has thawed. She needs to have food ready for customers in 15 minutes. Her boss instructs her to use all the meat in the freezer, but to make sure it is cooked properly. The young manager doesn't feel right about carrying out these orders.

Case 25 A Gift from the Web (A)

Primary focus: Ethical decision making

Secondary foci: Group norms and dynamics, motivation

Level: Analysis—Introductory; Topic—Introductory

Synopsis

Brian has just received a group assignment for his third-year finance class at University of Ontario and is concerned about the heavy mid-term workload he is facing. On a whim, he decides to enter the title of the assigned case into an internet search engine, and—to his surprise and pleasure—finds the instructor's key to the identical case. Excited about the time-saver he has found, he immediately calls one of his group members to share the good news. Rima's initial response is one of concern, since this initially appears to be cheating. Rima and Brian decide to call a group meeting to discuss what to do with the "great find" and whether it should be shared with the other groups in the finance class.

Case 26 Whooo's Wise Enough to Save the Owl?

Primary focus: Sustainable development

Secondary foci: Organization strategy, not-for-profit funding, volunteer management

Level: Analysis—Intermediate; Topic—Intermediate

Synopsis

The Manitoba Wildlife Rehabilitation Organization (MWRO) is a registered nonprofit volunteer organization with a mission to help injured and orphaned wildlife. With membership of more than 500 and an active base of volunteers, the MWRO provides direct care to more than 1,000 native birds and mammals every year. Funding for the MWRO is from four main sources: membership fees, private donations, corporate sponsorships, and government. Corporate sponsorships seem to be falling off, and government grants are harder to get. Expenses have been reduced wherever possible but there is still a shortfall. Volunteers are being overworked to make up for the reduction in paid staff. What should the organization do to overcome this crisis?

INTEGRATING CASES

Case 27 Atlantic Health Center

Primary focus: Organization

Secondary foci: Compensation schemes, organization structure, performance management

Level: Analysis—Senior; Topic—Senior

Synopsis

This case describes how an entrepreneur started a health club on a small scale, with five employees, and then expanded the business by offering additional facilities. The additional facilities include a restaurant, a bar, a day spa, and a hair salon. With these new facilities the number of employees has grown from 5 to 40. The employees in some facilities require specific technical education and certification, while others need no particular skill or education. With these differing qualifications, the compensation schemes are different in different facilities. These differences, along with numerous interdependencies among the facilities, have led to conflict, reduced morale, and high turnover.

Case 28 EDS Systemhouse (Revised)

Primary focus: Organization structure

Secondary foci: Organization strategy, control systems

Level: Analysis—Senior; Topic—Advanced

Synopsis

EDS Systemhouse is a newly merged information technology (IT) services company with Canadian revenue of well over $1,000 million. The first stage of the integration between EDS Canada and SHL Systemhouse (SHL) has just been completed, and the framework for the new organization is in place. EDS Systemhouse now needs to create a supporting organizational structure that will incorporate SHL's Canadian operations with EDS.

Case 29 Jessica Casserra's Taskforce: Hospital Integration in the Region of Erie

Primary foci: Merger management, integration

Secondary foci: Power and politics, organization structure, change management

Level: Analysis—Senior; Topic—Advanced

Synopsis

The formal organizational integration of Metropolitan with five smaller hospitals and ancillary services (e.g., laundry, food services) is set to proceed in nine months' time; the Ministry of Health has fixed the timing. Given the political heat they have taken throughout the process, which resulted in the mandated restructuring of regional services, it is extremely unlikely that the Province will back down from the start date. Jessica Casserra knows that they would not want to give integration opponents additional opportunities to mobilize resistance or any hope that decisions might be reversed. Casserra has been appointed to lead the taskforce to accomplish this initiative and now needs to design the process that will overcome resistance.

	Topic						Analysis Level			Topic Level				Primary and Secondary Foci																
	Individual and Interpersonal-Level Cases	Group/Team-Level Cases	Organization-Level Cases	Leadership Cases	Ethics/Environment Cases	Integrating Cases	Introductory	Intermediate	Senior	Introductory	Intermediate	Senior	Advanced	Aboriginal Affairs	Alignment of Systems	Change Management	Compensation Schemes	Conflict	Control Systems	Customer Service	Downsizing	Ethical Decision Making	Ethics	Group Behaviour	Group Behaviour	Group Composition	Group Norms & Dynamics	Group Norms & Expectations	Human Resource Policies	Individual Behaviour (ethics)
Alberta Energy					•				•			•										1								
Atlantic Health Center						•			•			•					2													
The Case of the Amalgamated Laboratory			•				•			•								2												
The Case of the Unseen Customers		•					•			•								2							1					
Christine Carmichael				•			•			•																				
Countryside Environmental	•							•			•																			
Dividing the Pie		•							•			•												1						
EDS Systemhouse						•			•				•																	
Electronic Data Interchange and the Ontario Dental Association			•						•			•							2											
Family Medical			•						•		•																			
Future Vision Digital Services Inc.	•							•			•																		2	
A Gift from the Web (A)					•		•			•												1					2			
Jaztec		•					•					•																		
Jessica Casserra's Taskforce						•			•				•			2														
John Hamilton's Dilemma	•							•				•																	2	
A Juggling Act (A-1)	•						•				•																		2	
Just Another Email (A), Part (B) in IM			•				•			•										2										
Let's Get Together		•					•			•														1		2		2		
A Midsummer Day's Nightmare					•		•				•											1								
Migisi Tribal Council, Inc.			•					•				•		2				2												
Northmar Distributors				•			•			•											2		2							
Northwell Inc.			•						•			•			2			2												
Oliver Davis's Entrepreneurial Success Story				•					•		•																			
Self-Managed Work Teams at South Australia Ambulance Service		•							•				•													2				
Someday My Prints Will Come	•						•				•																			
Team Ontario (A) and (B)				•					•		•																			
Western Prairie				•					•		•																			
Whooo's Wise Enough to Save the Owl?					•			•			•																			
Working at Wal-Mart	•						•			•																				1

Primary and Secondary Foci																													
Individual Behaviour (management of knowledge workers)										1																		
Individual Behaviour (motivation)																								1				1
Individual Behaviour (stress)														1	1													
Influence																							2					
Integration													1															
Interpersonal Behaviour															2													
Interpersonal Behaviour (perception, conflict)					1																							
Interpersonal Conflict																	2											
Interpersonal Relations										2																		
Job Design																												2
Leadership			2	2	1	2						2				2			2	1		1	2		1			2
Merger Management													1															
Motivation/Incentives				2	2	2					2	2																
Not-for-Profit Funding																											2	
Organization		1	1																									
Organization Change & Renewal			2						1	2											1							
Organization Communications																1												
Organization Culture & Design	2									2	2				2						2							2
Organization Decision Making																						2			2	2		
Organization Membership									2																			
Organization Politics																				2								
Organization Strategy & Control								2								2											2	
Organization Structure & Growth		2	2	2			2	1	2	1						2			2		2		2					
Organization Vision & Goals																			2									
Organizational Control Systems								2																2				
Perception							2																					
Performance Management		2																										
Power													2															
Project Management										2																		
Reward Systems	2				2													2				2			2	2		
Role Clarification						2																						
Self-Managed Work Teams																							1					
Sustainable Development																											1	
Task Design			2	2																								
Team Behaviour												1																
Team Building																									2			
Team Management																						2				2		
Voluntary Organizations																			1									
Volunteer Management																											2	

preface

This casebook is the product of organizational behaviour case researchers from across Canada. Support has also come from the Laurier Institute, Wilfrid Laurier University, and, of course, the organizations and managers who welcome researchers in and allow cases to be written that reflect the realities they have grappled with. Without such willingness to expose themselves to scrutiny, our ability to think about and learn from their experiences would be impossible.

The primary motivation for the book comes from our desire to enhance the practise of management in Canada. We hope to give students the opportunity to explore quality Canadian cases that reflect important organizational behaviour issues facing managers as they strive to cultivate a more effective working environment for individuals, work teams, and organizations as a whole. We believe that by sharpening their analytic and action planning skills through real case situations, students will develop their capacity to recognize and deal effectively with organizational issues in the real world and contribute to the development of more successful organizations.

While managers in all organizations deal with similar topic areas (e.g., motivation, communication, leadership, and organization structure), the areas manifest themselves in unique and challenging ways, due to the idiosyncrasies of the organizations, the individuals who inhabit them, and the complex contexts the individuals and organizations exist in. The cases selected for inclusion in the book reflect this diversity, covering for-profit and not-for-profit organizations, small to large organizations in a variety of different sectors, and individual differences through to organizational structure and design issues.

The book contains a total of 29 cases, many of them new. All have been peer reviewed through the Administrative Sciences Association of Canada case review process, the North American Case Research Association review process, or classroom field tests to demonstrate their quality and usefulness. Managers and students have found them engaging and powerful as learning vehicles in the application of theory to real issues.

Comprehensive case teaching notes are available from the text's custom Web site (www.mcgrawhill.ca/college/cawsey) to faculty who adopt the book. These notes contain an overview of each case, questions related to the cases, and recommendations concerning how to structure the use of each case in the classroom. A grid matching organizational behaviour concepts, case difficulty, and the cases themselves will assist faculty in choosing which cases to use for each part of their course. Since the cases have been tested in the classroom, student reactions have made an important contribution to our understanding of how to use the cases to advance educational objectives.

As one can see from the table of contents, the book is organized in a manner consistent with most organizational behaviour texts. It starts with individual behaviour and concludes with cases dealing with ethical issues. This was done to assist faculty in linking cases to textual materials and selecting ones appropriate to the agenda in their course syllabus for particular sessions.

ACKNOWLEDGEMENTS

No book is the product of the efforts of a single individual and this casebook is no exception. We are indebted to contributing case authors at our own and other institutions; the efforts of Joan Leach at the Laurier Institute; plus the advice, energy, and enthusiasm of our editorial advisors (Kim Brewster and Darren Hick at McGraw-Hill Ryerson). Without their initiative, this casebook would not have been developed.

As well, we wish to thank the contributing authors whose excellent cases make this book possible:

Tony Atkinson, *University of Waterloo*

Glenn Brophey, *Nipissing University*

Celeste Brotheridge, *University of Regina*

Lisa Carson, *Independent Case Writer*

Tupper Cawsey, *Wilfrid Laurier University*

Nina Cole, *Ryerson University*

Daniel Coleman, *University of New Brunswick*

Gene Deszca, *Wilfrid Laurier University*

Kevin Doucette, *Independent Case Writer*

Bob Ellis, *Wilfrid Laurier University*

Ken Harling, *Wilfrid Laurier University*

David Hemsworth, *Nipissing University*

Elizabeth Husby, *University of Manitoba*

Michelle Linton, *Independent Case Writer*

M. Lohbihler, *Independent Case Writer*

Rosemary McGowan, *Brescia College, University of Western Ontario*

John Melnyk, *University of Winnipeg*

Gary Mischke, *University of Manitoba*

Don Morrison, *Independent Case Writer*

Shripad Pendse, *Saint Mary's University*

Jazz Samra, *Independent Case Writer*

Lindsay Sawyer, *University of Winnipeg*

Robert Sexty, *Memorial University*

Andrew Templer, *University of Windsor*

James Tolliver, *University of New Brunswick*

Michael Wade, *York University*

Since our understanding of cases is an evolving process, we look forward to your insights, and suggestions for improvement.

—*Tupper Cawsey* and *Gene Deszca*

Case Analysis— A Student's Perspective

What am I to do with this "business story"? How should I handle this undifferentiated mass of details and prepare for class in a meaningful way? Most importantly, how do I ever deal with a case as an exam? As a student I liked cases. Classes were dynamic and interesting and the cases themselves told interesting stories. Learning was involved: a struggle between me and the situation described in the case.

However, it took too long for me to realize that cases demanded a disciplined, systematic approach if the information was to be organized in a meaningful way, the volume of work was to be handled effectively, and I was to maximize my learning.

The purpose of this note is to provide a framework for approaching cases and case exams.

Purpose of case method The case method provides students with the opportunity to deal with actual situations faced by decision-makers. Students learn to analyze these situations and develop action plans in a controlled, non-threatening environment.

What do I learn from case analysis? The case method of study provides the student with three enduring capabilities:

- the ability to handle complex problems and situations
- the ability to make sense out of a wide variety of industries and contexts they would not otherwise be exposed to, and
- the ability to make decisions and plan for their implementation.

Case analysis involves:

1. analyzing, interpreting, discerning, and prioritizing complex information
2. considering alternatives, and
3. making recommendations.

GUIDELINES FOR CASE PREPARATION

How to Approach a Case

First reading A rapid first reading of the case is helpful in getting a general idea of what the case is about. The objective in the first reading is to become familiar with the type of business, the apparent problems, the kinds of information, the people, their roles and responsibilities, and other major factors involved in the case.

Determine perspective Case analysis cannot be approached as an academic problem. You cannot assume the passive role of an observer when you analyze cases. Instead, you must assume an active role by taking the perspective of the decision-maker in the case (usually given). Your approach should be, "What would I do if I were this person?" Remember that it is about "What would I do now, given what has transpired"—it is not about "What should I have done?" Certainly you will need to analyze the past to make sense of the situation, but your goal is NOT to figure out who to blame. Rather, it is about what options should I consider and what should I do now.

Second reading The second reading is conducted slowly and carefully in order to gain a comprehensive grasp of the facts. A thorough second reading facilitates the organization and analysis of the facts and the identification of any inconsistencies in the case.

Application of case analysis elements After the careful second reading, the focus moves to completing the case analysis format outlined below.

Elements of Case Analysis

Identification of problems and issues Problems and issues in the case need to be identified and prioritized. This step is crucial as it will provide the basis of your analysis. When identifying problems and issues it is useful to ask yourself the following questions:

- Have I listed the problems and issues in order of importance and immediacy?
- Have I identified underlying problems or merely symptoms of problems?
- Are the problems I have identified free of judgement and evaluation; that is, have I been objective?

Analysis of the situation In this step, application theory is utilized to determine the causes and implications of the identified problems. The following questions may prove helpful in your analysis:

- What are the facts? (Distinguish between case fact and someone's opinion).
- What inferences can I make from the facts? Do the facts support the inferences I have made?
- What theories or models could I apply to this data in order to better understand what is going on and why?
- Have I made good use of theory?

- Have I examined the apparent consistencies and inconsistencies in the case?
- Are there multiple causes to the identified problems?
- Have I drawn clear implications and conclusions from my analysis?

When developing your analysis, ensure that you are NOT rehashing the case or evaluating what should have been done or who is to blame. Your task in analysis is to understand why things have happened as they have.

Decision criteria Decision criteria provide a means of assessing alternative solutions, as they consist of the factors which must be addressed by any final recommendation. Decision criteria may be qualitative or quantitative; however, they must be specific and clearly stated. An example of decision criteria would be: minimum 15% return on investment with no loss in job satisfaction of organizational members.

Generation of alternatives Viable and relevant alternatives should be considered. (Don't make the mistake of considering highly improbable or worthless alternatives.) They are then evaluated in terms of:

- possible consequences (positive and negative and mixed)
- the realities of the situation or context described in the case
- stated criteria.

When generating alternatives, pros and cons, and consequences, don't settle for only one or two or confine yourself to the obvious; in all cases, a reasonable number and range should be examined. Alternatives should represent the major possible options the decision maker needs to consider and not be a laundry list of possible actions. If there is no real choice amongst alternatives, you probably do not have a good list of alternatives! These more detailed elements of the alternative that is selected can be set out in the recommended action plan.

Decision This step consists of a statement of your decision and a brief rationale for that decision (which alternative or combination of alternatives you recommend and why). Your decision should be consistent with your analysis and with the stated criteria.

Recommendation(s)/action plan An action plan is the means of implementing your decision and consists of a "timed sequence of conditional moves." The action plan specifies who does what, when they do it, and how it is to be accomplished (timed sequence). The plan also anticipates the consequences of particular actions and suggests contingencies (conditional moves) should things not unfold as originally planned. A decision tree is helpful in illustrating contingencies. You can evaluate your decision and action plan by asking yourself:

- Do my recommendations fit my analysis? Am I consistent?
- Have I addressed all the identified problems and issues in my proposed solution?
- Have I identified the implications of my recommendations?

- Have I been specific and clear in my recommendations?
- Would I know what to do to implement my plan if I were reading the analysis for the first time?

In developing your action plan, remember that you are addressing what you should do now—NOT what you should have done.

Individual vs. Group Analysis

Case analysis is enriched if each case is discussed in a small group prior to finalization. The trade-off of time for learning is worthwhile, particularly if group members have diverse backgrounds and opinions. It is not possible to go into full details about all issues in this note; however, the following issues should be considered when using groups:

- individual analysis must be done prior to meeting in small groups
- time must be carefully controlled to maximize learning
- the special skills of group members should be used whenever possible
- rules or norms of conduct must be established for the group, including such things as preparation, meeting scheduling, time management, and interpersonal conduct in the meetings (e.g., understanding the difference between rigorous debate and helpful conflict over ideas versus attacks that are personal and not helpful and/or individuals who tend to dominate meetings in order to get themselves heard)
- thought should be given to disciplining members who do not carry their share of work. Too often slackers are allowed to get away with little or no contribution. In our view, if a person doesn't contribute, they are not part of the group! Thought should also be given to how to respond to individuals who breach other norms of conduct or rules that have been agreed to
- teams should set aside some time on a regular basis to assess how well they are performing as a team, with a view to learning from the experience and figuring out how to become more effective

CASE ANALYSIS IN THE CLASSROOM

Participation

There are two elements to the case method: the first is the case itself—the problem or situation presented for analysis; the second is the group discussion of the case which is conducted in the classroom. Classroom discussion places a heavy responsibility on the participants. Casual preparation and inadequate analysis lead only to shallow discussion; careful preparation and serious thought lead to stimulating discussion and mutual benefit. In the classroom, the onus is on each member of the group to contribute to the best of his/her abilities.

The best discussion requires:

- well prepared individuals
- class members willing to risk participating

- sharing of ideas and perspectives
- an unwillingness to permit sloppy arguments
- individuals who challenge each other's viewpoints
- faculty members who engage the class in ways that promote the above conditions

CHOOSING A ROLE, OR "HOW TO MAKE CLASSROOM CASE ANALYSIS INTERESTING"

Participation in a classroom setting is not easy for everyone, as some people are reluctant to speak in groups while others prefer to listen and absorb. With the case method this type of behaviour is discouraged—participation is vital. Fortunately, there are a number of ways an individual can participate in case analysis discussion:

Lead off/summarize This participation role is ideal for the individual who is intimidated by group discussion. This individual could choose to lead off the discussion—which, in the first part of the class, usually consists of reiteration of case facts or a statement of one's action plan. Or the individual could choose to summarize the group analysis at the end of the class.

Key point This role consists largely of actively listening to the class discussion and speaking up only to offer key points which may redirect the discussion.

Devil's advocate The devil's advocate champions the less accepted or approved causes for the sake of argument. Class discussion is usually lively when someone chooses to take this role.

Enthusiast This individual is very comfortable about expressing his/her viewpoint. However, there are different types of enthusiasts:

Challenger—is interested in pitting his/her position against another's for the sake of arguing and testing each position.

Meanderer—is often prepared but has difficulty in articulating his/her position. This individual usually talks around a position without getting to the point.

Supporter—will back up other participants and clarify and add to arguments already made.

Outside expert This person researches the case company or situation and brings in valuable information to the classroom. This can add real-world richness to the case experience.

Parasite The parasite is the quintessential games person. This individual comes to class unprepared, listens to the class discussion until he/she grasps the major concepts and proceeds to participate on this basis. He/she is easy to spot: he/she speaks in generalizations and buzz-words and fails to get down to specifics. (While it might not be obvious, profs can usually spot these as well!)

CLASS NORMS AND DYNAMICS, OR "BEYOND TALKING IN CLASS"

Being prepared and contributing to class discussion are the most evident forms of participation, but participation can mean more than just talking in the classroom. Other forms of participation include:

- encouraging positive participation from your classmates (challenging faculty assumptions and arguments, allowing others to get involved, motivating quiet classmates to participate).
- discouraging negative participation from your classmates (dissuading parasites, preventing personal attacks).
- making constructive suggestions for class process (role plays, presentations, outside speakers, etc.)
- after the class, reflecting on the experience and asking "what was learned?" and "what can I take from the class?"

IN SUMMARY

Case classes can be a stimulating, challenging learning environment. Active participation means that you will learn more and remember more for longer periods of time. You will learn the skills of debate and persuasion. But preparation for class is essential and involvement is necessary for maximum learning. The class objective should be to foster learning in a challenging environment, not simply getting by.

CASE REPORTS AND CASE EXAMS

General Format for Hand-in Cases

Hand-in format For case hand-ins with no page limit, the case analysis format described above provides an acceptable structure.

Page limits Page limits represent a complication as the student not only must conduct a thorough analysis, but also must decide what to include and what not to include in the write-up. The following format is a condensed version of the case analysis elements discussed earlier; the difference is that many of the elements are explicitly identified below:

- executive summary
- problem statement
- analysis
- solution criteria
- alternatives and their evaluation
- recommended, SPECIFIC plan of action and contingencies

Use of exhibits Exhibits are a useful tool in case analysis reporting, especially when there are page limits, because they can illustrate relationships more easily than prose. For optimum use of exhibits, make reference to the exhibits and include only implications and conclusions in the text. Don't reiterate information available in your exhibits.

Quality of the writing A key ingredient in a written report is the quality of the writing. The reader has a right to expect that the report will be well organized (heading and subheadings will assist) and well written (e.g., no spelling errors, well constructed sentences, logical and easy to follow). References should be cited (if used), and exhibits should be easily interpreted and referenced in the body of the report. To do less than this is to risk losing the reader's interest and attention and/or cause the reader to discount your ideas due to your sloppy presentation.

case 1 A Juggling Act (A–1)

Scrambling to pack up her laptop, Anna, a consulting manager for Global Consulting (GC), felt a pang of tension. It was 4:00 p.m. on Monday, March 19th, 2001, and her husband Chris had just called to tell her that he was unable to pick up their daughter from daycare due to an unexpected "fire" at work. She threw her working papers in her bag wondering when she would ever finish her deliverable. "You're going home already?" commented a co-worker jokingly. Anna rushed past John, the program manager, to tell him she would not be at today's status meeting and ran down to the Toronto Dundas subway station, hoping to make the 4:13 GO train. Several minutes later, feeling somewhat panicky and out of breath, she squeezed through the closing train doors, standing room only.

"Where did the day go?" she wondered. Anna had gotten about 20% of what she expected accomplished at the client site today. The rest of the team would be there until late again tonight in attempt to meet the tight deadlines. Thoughts raced through her pounding head: "When am I going to get this deliverable done? Tomorrow is my day at home with Kristin—maybe I can catch up during her nap. I'll definitely have to work tonight after she goes to bed." Then she remembered that tonight the church leadership team was coming over to plan the Spring Community Blitz, and she had promised to prepare some workplans to lead the discussion. Anna tried to take a deep breath. "I need to relax before I pick up Kristin," she thought. "I haven't seen her all day and need to be able to give her some quality time. What in the world am I going to give her for supper?"

TIMES ARE A CHANGIN'

Anna had grown up in a small town outside of Waterloo and moved to Toronto after university to work for Global Consulting (GC), a large management consulting firm. The first five years of consulting were great—Anna thrived in the fast pace, constant change, long hours, and extensive travelling. She felt very motivated as she learned from the challenges she faced each day and the bright, driven people with whom she worked. She was known as a "star performer" and had been promoted rapidly with significant pay increases. Anna had taken the time to interact and socialize with her colleagues, and had developed some strong relationships at GC over the past few years. She had kept her weekends as work-free as possible in order to spend time with her husband Chris and their friends and for occasional family visits. However, things were much more complicated now that she had an 18-month-old daughter.

For the past ten months, she had been working part-time at GC—now she was beginning to question whether it was really possible to work part-time in the consulting world. Anna had received strong support from the GC partners when she had requested a part-time work arrangement; everyone seemed genuinely committed to trying out this unprecedented flexibility. Anna was being paid 60% of her full-time salary of $110,000, and she knew of few other positions that offered this much for a 3-day workweek. During the first few months of part-time work, Anna worked on an internal office project that had provided a great transition phase for her and her daughter. Within a short time, however, Anna realized she missed the pressure and satisfaction of being on a client site. Since October she was now part of the management team on a large project in downtown Toronto, working for a new client with very tight deadlines and challenging work. The GC client partners had worked with Anna to design a role that would give her management responsibility within her 60% capacity; however, everyone else on the team was working at 120% capacity. Anna felt dissatisfied with her level of contribution compared to the other managers. She missed out on key decisions and project progress made on her days at home and struggled to keep up to date. She felt impatient during social interactions at work and rarely took lunch breaks. When she was home, she constantly felt pressure to respond to her urgent voicemails and emails and to cram as much work as possible into her daughter Kristin's naptime.

Becoming a mother had impacted Anna much more than she had anticipated. She now felt that her maternal instincts controlled her emotions and responses, keeping her daughter's well being, safety, and happiness top of mind. Anna believed strongly in high-attachment style parenting and was committed to providing Kristin with security and affection. Anna gave every effort to make the early morning wake-ups and drop-offs enjoyable, to pick up Kristin from the daycare on time, and to not miss more than one home dinner per week. Anna felt a constant conflict between her desire to surpass client expectations and her commitment to being a good mother.

STRESSED OUT!

As she stood on the crowded GO train, Anna tried to reflect on what was going on. What used to motivate her at work seemed to be stressing her out lately. She felt like a "60% star" at work now but also felt guilty for not providing Kristin with enough dedicated time at home. Trying to be the best mother and a star GC manager seemed impossible. Anna knew that she wanted a mix of work and home; she needed the intellectual challenge and personal interaction provided by work, but her top priority right now was her daughter especially during these first critical years of life.

Anna had the tendency to compare herself to those people around her and felt frustrated as she watched several of her peers race past her towards partnership. She thought about the other parents who worked at GC; most of them worked full-time and hired nannies to manage their children and homes. She thought about the general lifestyle at GC—as people progressed to partnership, the lifestyle seemed to get busier with more hours, more stress, and more travel. "Is this what I want in my life?" she questioned. "I want to be successful in every area of my life—not just my career. Working part-time at GC should work," she thought, "if only I could feel content with my level of contribution. I'm only getting paid 60% of my salary even though I'm working a lot of extra hours, so why do I feel this pressure?" Anna reflected on a few conversations she had held over the past few weeks where she had tried to voice her concerns (see Exhibit A). She felt like she had no one close to her who could really relate to her situation and provide her with the support she needed; and she was reluctant to contact someone she didn't know to obtain this. As "Long Branch Station" was announced, Anna left the train and started to focus her thoughts on Kristin; her pulse quickened and she smiled as she anticipated her daughter's affectionate greeting.

exhibit A Summary of Key Conversations

1. Office conversation with John, GC program manager

John:	"So how are things going?"
Anna:	"To be honest, I'm stressed out."
John:	"Yeah, you don't seem yourself. What's going on?"
Anna:	"I just can't keep up. I feel like I'm constantly letting the team down—I feel like a 60% contributor."
John:	"But you're getting the work done, and the team knows you work part-time. You're performing at 100% within your 60% capacity. That should be your measuring stick."
Anna:	"I guess I'm comparing myself to the rest of the management team. I'm missing out on significant decision-making and issue resolution, and I just don't feel like I'm an integral part of the management team. I'm really starting to question whether it's possible to do consulting part-time."
John:	"Well, frankly, I agree with you just due to the very nature of consulting. Have you considered moving into an internal function temporarily, like HR or Marketing?"
Anna:	"That just really doesn't inspire me."
John:	"Well, we really want to help you make this work out if that's what you want right now. Maybe we should try adjusting your role to something less delivery focused and more advisory so you don't feel as much pressure. I have to run to a meeting but can we chat at the end of the day—maybe around 7 tonight?"
Anna:	"Sorry, I have to leave by 5."
John:	"Oh sorry, I forgot. Well I'll discuss it with Rick and get back to you. In the meantime, don't be so hard on yourself—you're doing fine."
Anna:	"Well, thanks."
John:	"Oh before I go—can you help me out? I need to have this report done by noon and am wondering if you can write a few sections...."

2. On the way to a meeting with Rick, GC client partner

Rick:	"So how's Kristin doing?"
Anna:	"She's amazing. Learning something new every day, trying out new words. It's fascinating watching her develop into a little person. How are your kids?"
Rick:	"Oh fine. I feel bad though—I haven't made it home for dinner for a week now. I don't know what I'd do if Dee weren't home full-time. But I think we've almost reached an agreement with the client, and it's going to put us in a terrific position for the next year. This could reach a potential of $60 million!"
Anna:	"Really? That's great."

continued

exhibit A Summary of Key Conversations (*continued*)

Rick: "So how are things going on the project?"

Anna: "Well not bad. It's a great project and an excellent team. I'm a bit concerned about the amount of over-time people are working. I've overheard some complaints."

Rick: "Well doesn't look like it's going to slow down any time soon! We just have to continue surpassing the client's expectations. How are you doing—is the part-time thing working out?"

Anna: "To be honest, I'm struggling with it, Rick. I feel like I'm 60% of the star I used to be. I'm not sharing my weight in the management team, and I'm putting in a lot of extra hours just to keep up."

Rick: "Yeah, I can understand that it would be hard. Have you considered working four days per week—would that be more manageable? Then at least you'd get paid for the hours you're working too!"

Anna: "I'm really enjoying my two days at home with Kristin and am very reluctant to change that. And if I go up to four days, I'll probably end up working full-time hours!"

Rick: "Have you talked to any of the other part-time women in Toronto?"

Anna: "Well, unfortunately, three of the four I know of have left the firm!"

Rick: "Really? Hey, I know of a couple of women in the U.S. who have worked part-time successfully for years at GC—why don't you get in touch with them for some advice? We really want to see this work out for you, Anna. If there's anything you need, don't hesitate to ask. We can bring in another resource if that's what you need."

Anna: "Let me think about it. Thanks for your support."

Rick: "Hey, by the way, I'd appreciate it if you could spend some time thinking about how to keep the team here motivated. Maybe we need a social outing. Can you help plan something?"

Anna: "Sure, I'll give it some thought."

3. Breakfast with Alison, friend and former colleague

Alison: "So how are things?"

Anna: "Frankly, I'm feeling stressed out. I feel like I have too much on the go right now and just don't feel like I'm meeting any expectations—of others or myself! Life seems so much more complicated now!"

Alison: "What do you mean? Who do you think you're letting down?"

Anna: "Well, you know my work situation. I never feel like I get enough done or that I'm living up to my past performance. I'm spending too much time thinking about work when I'm at home with Kristin. Chris and I have little, if any, time alone much less a social life lately! I'm neglecting my family and most of my friends. I know Jon could really use a lot more of my help on the church leadership team. And I have absolutely no time to myself. Sorry for being so negative, but I really think I need to make some changes in my life."

Alison: "Wow, sounds like you're doing some serious thinking. Why don't you take some time off work to re-evaluate?"

Anna: "Would be a great idea except we're at a critical stage in the project and I don't want to let the team down."

Alison: "I really admire you for sticking it out so long at GC. I really didn't think it was possible. Are you considering doing something other than the GC thing? There are tons of options out there you know, even temporarily while your kids are young. What about independent contract work, or working for a 'real' company, or teaching? Hey, we'd hire you!"

Anna: "Y'know, everything's an option right now. I just need to figure out what will motivate me while giving me the balance that I need right now."

"I'm feeling really overwhelmed lately," Anna told her husband late that night after the church leadership planning meeting. "I feel like I can't keep all the balls in the air right now! I feel like I'm going to burn out if something doesn't change soon." During the meeting that evening, each person had gauged the current levels of their physical, spiritual, and emotional "tanks"; this exercise had confirmed to Anna that she was not in a healthy state (see Exhibit B). Chris had been extremely supportive through this time of change and, although working as a full-time consultant, was a very involved father and shared the responsibilities at home. He knew Anna was struggling with finding the right balance between career and motherhood, and he worried about her stress level, which seemed to be impacting her sleep, eating, patience level, and emotional stability. "If only you didn't have to bounce the balls so darn hard!" he laughed. "Why don't I take Friday off as a 'Kristin day' so you can spend some time alone and do some thinking?" he suggested. "Hey if you're going to stay home, maybe I should try to get some work done!" Anna exclaimed sarcastically.

After some convincing, Anna agreed that it would be worthwhile to spend some alone time to re-evaluate. She wondered what steps she should take on Friday to make it a productive day with some clear, actionable outcomes and a renewed state of mind for the weekend.

exhibit B Health Gauges

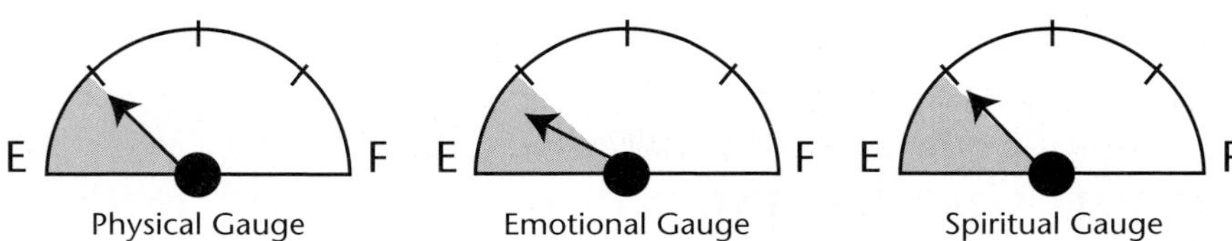

case 2 Future Vision Digital Services Inc.

Blake Randolph[1] glanced at his watch as he put down the phone to consider his options. It was 12:30 p.m. on a Wednesday afternoon. As Vice President of Technology Development for Future Vision Digital Services Inc. (FVDS), Randolph was responsible for the team of software developers and systems architects that built complex server-side functionality for clients' Internet sites. He had just concluded an awkward conversation with Jacques Riveaux, FVDS's Vice President of European Operations. Riveaux, who was currently in Germany working with one of FVDS's largest clients on a new site launch, needed urgently to speak to Andre Gregoire, Randolph's most senior architect on the project. Unfortunately, Gregoire was nowhere to be found.

FUTURE VISION DIGITAL SERVICES INC.

FVDS was a technology consulting and design firm. The company provided a range of services including multi-platform user interface design and marketing, software engineering and technical program management, systems integration, data analysis and customer relationship management. The company's primary line of business, however, was designing, building and managing corporate Web sites. The company had a number of blue chip clients spread over a variety of industry segments.

FVDS was founded in Vancouver in 1996. The company grew quickly, expanding from 30 to 250 employees between 1997 and 2004. By 2004, the company had expanded from its base in Western Canada to open offices in New York, Los Angeles, Amsterdam, Singapore, and Toronto. FVDS had managed to avoid the worst of the dot.com downturn in the early 2000s, and maintained a modest profit on sales ranging from $45 and $90 million per year.

[1]Identifying characteristics have been altered to maintain confidentiality.

BLAKE RANDOLPH

As Vice President of Technology Development, Blake Randolph held one of the most important jobs at FVDS. It was his responsibility to make sure that development projects were of appropriate quality, and were completed in time and on budget. Randolph worked with teams of developers and architects on various projects, and provided an interface between those teams and other senior levels of the firm. Approximately one third of the company's employees reported directly to Randolph.

ANDRE GREGOIRE

Gregoire was an extraordinarily talented software developer. At the age of 27 he had reached the level of Technical Architect at FVDS—the highest technical (non-management) position offered by the company. Attentive and articulate, he was excellent with senior management and clients, presenting a face of deep technical authority and experience. He worked diligently and consistently, especially in the visibility of executives. As a result, his executive sponsorship was very strong.

Gregoire was constantly improving internal processes by implementing new practices and procedures on his own time. He pursued new technical challenges aggressively. Often, he would stay very late working on complex tasks, usually resulting in him arriving late for work the next day—sometimes after lunch.

Gregoire was good at leading technical staff, but was clearly much more interested in doing development work himself than mentoring others. Randolph suspected that Gregoire created his own problems by not delegating work to junior staff, which was why he would regularly end up working after midnight near the end of a project. To make matters worse, his tardiness the next day sometimes made for crises when problems occurred that only Gregoire knew how to fix. During these times, there was typically no way to reach him. Project team members including developers, quality assurance personnel, systems analysts, and others had no choice but to wait for him to arrive. The lost productivity that resulted from this "down time" infuriated the project managers, many of whom refused to accept Gregoire on their projects. They argued that the risk to the success of their projects justified forgoing Gregoire's extraordinary skills.

Recently, for several days, Gregoire had not arrived at work until well after noon, explaining that he had worked past midnight the night before. Although Randolph knew this to be true, it presented serious problems for him. The current project was being managed from Amsterdam, while the production team, including Gregoire and Randolph, was in Toronto. The six hour time difference meant that the only overlap of normal working hours occurred between 9:00 and 11:00 a.m. local time in the Netherlands. With Gregoire arriving after lunch, it effectively cut him off from communications with the team abroad, unless they grudgingly stayed late until he was available. As the technical lead on the project, Gregoire was the point of contact for all technical information and issues. Without his support, any technical change or decision was risky. Randolph had spoken to Gregoire about this problem a few times already. Each time, Gregoire was very agreeable, and promised to change, but eventually slipped back into old patterns.

This morning, Jacques Riveaux had encountered a problem during final testing of the client's 3-tier architecture Web site that required Gregoire's technical opinion, and

Gregoire's unavailability obviously annoyed him. The project was medium-sized by FVDS standards but the client was important. Randolph had calmly assured Riveaux that this was an unusual occurrence—although it was a difficult argument to make—and that Gregoire would be made aware of the problem as soon as he arrived. As he hung up the phone, he knew that he would have to take action soon.

THE ART AND SCIENCE OF SOFTWARE PROJECT MANAGEMENT

There is a profound difference between what many managers perceive software development to be and what it actually is. Some regard the profession as if developers were like construction workers. Once there is an architectural rendering of the system and a project schedule, all that needs to be done is the construction. Programmers are hired who have the proper training in the required skills, and they are set to the task.

The problem with this view is that there are few similarities between bricks and algorithms; bricks are commodities that are put together in predictable ways, while algorithms are products of intellect, each different from the other and requiring a different context in which to operate. Also, construction is a mature field in which novelty is optional, and is achieved via the creative arrangement of accepted and rarely changing standard patterns. In software development, novelty—that is, doing something that has never been done before—is the *raison d'être*. Software developers constantly have to learn new languages, methodologies, paradigms, and interfaces. And although patterns of development are beginning to emerge, there is still—and probably always will be—significant room for variation in implementation approach. In other words, for any piece of software, be it an enterprise system or a small mathematical algorithm, there is an infinite number of ways in which it can be developed. Skill, to a software developer, is a function of the "elegance" of their product, a term that includes factors such as time efficiency, memory efficiency, succinctness, completeness, readability, reusability, and the appropriate allocation of effort to each of these.

Another common misconception about software development is the scope of the work. Often, system requirements are quite simple. The resulting code, however, is typically very lengthy. The source of this inflation effect is the fact that the core task of any system represents only a small proportion (typically between 5 and 10 percent) of the code that is actually written. Significant amounts of code are allocated to performance enhancements, memory management, multi-processing capabilities, or message logging. However, the majority of the code performs exception handling; that is, what to do when things go wrong.

A good example of the inherent complexity of software development is an Internet Web server. Conceptually, the function of a Web server is simple: return files that are found in the server's directories upon request. However, a quick analysis of this requirement reveals that the task is not as straightforward as it seems. Rather than simply responding with success or failure, the HTTP/1.1 specification defines 41 possible response codes that any Web server is required to implement:

- 2 informational responses (1xx)
- 7 success responses (2xx)
- 8 redirection responses (3xx)

- 18 client (i.e. browser) error responses (4xx, including the infamous *404 Not Found*)
- 6 server error responses

Most of these messages are used infrequently, if ever. However, one of the measures of good software is its rigor: any conceivable state is appropriately handled. Sometimes, states that are not appropriately handled result in the well-known Windows "blue screen of death"—which is not considered an indication of good software!

But while implementing all required response codes makes for a compliant Web server product, it does not necessarily make for a high quality product. The industry standard Apache Web server contains highly complex code that makes it the fastest, most memory efficient, and most stable product on the market. The ingenious work of talented software developers, acting not as bricklayers but as creative artists, made the product superior to its competitors. The Apache server was developed using a fraction of the resources of competing products such as Microsoft's IIE server.

As this example shows, any software development project has the potential to be a highly complex endeavour. Some research has estimated that up to 70 percent of all software development projects fail due to time or cost overruns, or the failure of the final product to meet specifications.[2] Many technical managers believe that even if the most sophisticated tools and methodologies are available, the only way to achieve exceptional results, perhaps even acceptable results, is to utilize exceptional developers.

SOFTWARE DEVELOPERS

Some software developers approach their vocation as work. They use whatever approach solves the immediate problem, and then move on to the next problem as an unrelated, independent task. They are competent, but not exceptional developers. Exceptional developers are problem-seekers and puzzle-solvers who look forward to the next challenge. They continuously seek out new ways of producing extraordinary software, reaching for new levels of coding elegance. Part scientist, part artist, each piece of code is considered an original work of art.

The difference between ordinary developers and exceptional developers is profound, not only in approach, but also in productivity. Some researchers have estimated up to a 20 to 1 difference in productivity between developer extremes.[3] This means that what might take a mediocre programmer 4 weeks to complete, an exceptional developer could finish in a single day. Recently, concepts such as development patterns, componentization, and loose coupling have been introduced to make a developer's work simpler and more predictable, and exceptional developers have embraced these ideas and used them to further increase their capabilities.

Exceptional developers have been described as "super-intelligent, curious, passionate, often introverted, talented individuals that can be difficult to work with, yet life-saving employees who can come up with answers when most people don't understand the question."[4] These characteristics bring clear advantages to critical software

[2]"Why Software Projects Fail," (http://www.webreference.com/new/020103.html, January 2002).

[3]Steve McConnell, "Dealing with Problem Programmers," (IEEE Software, 1998).

[4]Dr. John M. Ivancevich and Dr. Thomas N. Duening, "Managing Einsteins, Leading High-Tech Workers in the Digital Age", (McGraw-Hill, September 2001).

development projects: development tasks are done more quickly and with higher quality, resulting in savings of time and money, and increased customer satisfaction. Typically, products are more easily extended as well, resulting in substantial future benefits. Using exceptional developers on project teams means fewer developers are required, reducing the requirement for resources and equipment, and increasing communication effectiveness.

On the other hand, there is a tendency towards building software for software's sake. All developers want to build software that is "cool," even if it has questionable business value. The most talented developers dislike doing anything except writing code, including managing schedules, leading teams, mentoring juniors, or writing documentation. Also, having fewer developers on a team increases the amount of knowledge each one carries, resulting in increased risk to the project should one or more of them become unavailable.

Since senior developers are usually the only people who are capable of designing a proper technical implementation of a software project, the tendency to want to build interesting software quickly leads to "over-engineering"—the design and development of products that go far past the business requirements—with a corresponding increase in time and cost. Sometimes extra sophistication can be justified, especially if it eases maintenance and future development. But more often than not, the result of the extra effort is uneconomical. Confronting a developer with this issue is dangerous, since the manager risks appearing disrespectful or untrusting, which could quickly lead to conflict and feelings of alienation.

Exceptional developers sometimes refer to themselves and each other as rock stars. This analogy may not be too much of an exaggeration with regard to skills and attitude. On the one hand, it is easy for a manager to develop the opinion that the stars on the team are at the core of a project's success, and that without them everything would fall apart. They continuously produce exceptional results at a remarkable pace. Their efforts inspire junior members of the team. And sometimes, their wilful ignorance of the business requirements results in an unforeseen solution that is better than what was initially imagined.

On the other hand, like rock stars, they can be difficult and unpredictable. They tend to want to write their own rules and make decisions for others, including clients. This results in friction within the development team, and between the team and other parts of the firm.

In the worst cases, *Prima Donna* developers can appear who are (or think they are) exceptional, but have a low regard for business requirements, preferring only to write what they consider to be important. They harbour disdain for developers who do not share their genius, and thus may not be popular with team members. Trying to discipline this type of developer often results in them quitting mid-way through a project, sometimes requiring managers to hire them back on contract (at a greatly increased price) to retain their knowledge within the project team. Thankfully, *Prima Donna* developers are rare.

In reality, the skills of developers exist on a continuum; individuals are not either exceptional or ordinary, inspired or bored, manageable or unmanageable. All developers have all of these attributes to some extent. Part of the job of a software development manager is to adapt each project to the traits of the developers. This, of course, comes in addition to managing costs, quality, timelines, client relationships, and so on.

THE MANAGEMENT DILEMMA AT FVDS

Randolph shifted his attention to the problem at hand. FVDS was most of the way through the project and Gregoire had been the Technical Architect since its inception. Riveaux had indicated in no uncertain terms that he was unhappy with the project's progress to date, and that the client was becoming increasingly nervous. He considered some options, none of which was ideal.

First, he could replace Gregoire on the project with someone who was more dependable. Three other competent (although not exceptional) developers had recently completed other projects and either one or all could be made available on short notice. If Randolph were to reassign the project to another developer, the effect on Gregoire's attitude was unpredictable: he might refuse to help in the knowledge transfer, or even leave the company. In any case, Randolph's relationship with Gregoire would be changed.

Second, he could threaten to discipline Gregoire if he didn't shape up. Randolph thought, however, that this would ring hollow. Gregoire had never refused to be helpful; he just continuously slipped back into old habits. In addition, Gregoire knew his executive support in the company would keep Randolph from taking any action that was too drastic.

Third, Randolph could do nothing. The project might still be successful. Randolph even considered trying to cover for Gregoire when he was unavailable. However, Randolph knew that the quantity of knowledge he needed to learn to catch up, and the time commitment needed to keep pace, all while maintaining his current responsibilities, made this option unappealing.

Finally, Randolph wondered if there was another option available that would allow him to maintain good relations with Gregoire while at the same time make sure that the project (and similar projects in the future) proceeded smoothly. Was the problem with Gregoire, Randolph wondered, for being difficult to manage, or was it with him for not being able to manage Gregoire?

case 3 John Hamilton's Work and Eldercare Dilemma: Break the Silence? Sustain the Silence?

It was Tuesday evening at 7:45 p.m. and John Hamilton, senior project head, and his assistant Taylor Roberts were meeting late to review the software revisions prior to Wednesday's 9 a.m. project launch. John's phone rang. It was a call from his mother's Lifeline[1] system. His mother had fallen and needed assistance; John knew that he would have to leave immediately. When he put the receiver down, John looked at Taylor, who sensed that there was some kind of problem. John told Taylor that his home alarm system had been triggered and since his wife was out of town, he had to go home immediately to re-set the system. He told Taylor that he would be back in about 45 minutes and asked if Taylor could stay at the office until his return. He hadn't told anyone at work about his mother's increasing care needs, and more importantly his role as her primary caregiver, and he wasn't about to start now with the project launch date so close. As he quickly prepared to leave his office, he wondered how much longer he could manage the balance of work and eldercare and, more importantly, how much longer he could sustain his strategy of silence.

[1]Lifeline Systems Canada Incorporated provides a 24 hour personal response service. Subscribers are linked to Lifeline through a two-way communication system connected to their personal telephone line. Subscribers wear a small personal communicator fashioned either as a pendant or as a wristband. In case of an emergency, a subscriber presses the emergency button on the communicator. Depressing the button triggers a signal to the Lifeline system. Lifeline then calls back to the subscriber to determine the nature of the emergency. If the subscriber does not answer, or if the subscriber needs immediate assistance, Lifeline calls the emergency contacts on the subscriber's Lifeline contact list. If no one on the contact list is available, 911 is dispatched to the subscriber's home. Additional information on Lifeline Systems Canada Inc. is available through their website: www.lifelinecanada.com.

JOHN HAMILTON'S WORK: ALPHA SOFTWARE

John Hamilton, 46, had been with Alpha Software for almost 25 years. He joined the firm immediately after graduating with a degree in computer science. In his fourth year at the University of Waterloo, one of his professors told John that he was developing a software start-up company and he felt that John's specialized skills would be an excellent fit for the organization. John had been with Alpha Software since graduation. The last ten years of the computer company were marked by exponential growth in product demand and employee numbers. John had no trouble remembering the firm's early days, when "everyone knew everyone" and Christmas parties for the original 20 employees and their partners were held at his boss's home.

Four years ago the firm underwent two major expansions. First, they bought out another local software firm and then eighteen months later Alpha was acquired by a large U.S. software house. The U.S. parent decided to retain the Alpha name for their Canadian operations. The U.S. parent was determined to grow the size of the Canadian operations. In the space of those two hectic years, Alpha went from 65 employees to over 300 employees. Alpha had by and large escaped the high tech meltdown faced by many in the computing industry—in fact, their growth in sales and employees had continued on a positive note. John no longer knew even a small fraction of the employees and, when he looked around the cafeteria, everyone looked so young. In a recent in house human resource newsletter, Alpha offered a demographic profile of the employees. Almost 80% of the employees were under forty. One article titled "Thirty under Thirty" profiled the thirty most recent hires—all, as the title of the article suggested, were in their twenties.

While John really enjoyed working with these young computer graduates, he also felt that their lives were in a very different place. Lunch conversations usually focused on the latest "toys" they purchased—plasma screen televisions, sporty cars, high end mountain bikes, snowboards and snowboard gear. In recent months, he was becoming envious of their ability to work long hours without substantial personal commitments or responsibilities.

John's schedule was pretty typical of those in the software industry—long days (8 a.m. to often 8 p.m. or later), Saturdays and/or Sundays in the office, as well as out of town, out of province and out of country meetings with clients. After dinner, John often retreated to his home office to find thirty or forty e-mail messages in his inbox, most of which needed immediate reply. After almost a quarter century in the industry, John was more than accustomed to the intense work demands. John also knew that in his company if you weren't able, willing or interested in keeping up with the demands, there was always an abundant supply of up and coming software specialists ready to make the commitment. Early in their marriage, John and his wife, Eileen, decided that they wanted to commit themselves to their careers and to travel in their spare time. The decision not to have children had worked out well for them. They had both achieved a fair degree of professional success and had just returned from a trip to New Zealand; the airfare had been managed through their frequent flier points. The busy professional life had been good.

JOHN HAMILTON'S MOM

Eighteen months ago, however, life started to change for John, not because of the dramatic changes in the software industry or his own company's rapid growth, but because his mother's health had started to falter. In the late fall of 2002, John noticed some changes to his Mom's memory. She would repeat herself, forget phone numbers, and misplace her bills and the keys to her house. At first, John didn't pay too much attention to some of these episodes. After all, John's own tendency to misplace his key had become a running joke between himself and Eileen. But then he noticed that even simple, routine activities that his Mom had previously had no problem with were presenting new challenges. For example, grocery shopping was becoming increasingly difficult. His Mom could not remember where items were in the store, a store where she had shopped for almost a decade on a weekly basis. In one of their last shopping trips together, John found his Mom passing her wallet over to the cashier to count out the money owing on the grocery bill. She seemed to have a momentary loss in her ability to calculate change. John felt alarmed and uncomfortable with his Mom's increasing difficulties.

Approximately three months after John had started to notice changes in his Mom's demeanour, John's Mom experienced a fairly dramatic health event that signaled a real change to her and ultimately to John's situation. John had gone over to his Mom's home on one of his regular Friday after work visits. His Mom seemed particularly disoriented. She was trying to prepare dinner for herself but could not remember what she was doing, where the various ingredients were or what she had to do next in the recipe she was trying to make. Worse yet, she gave nonsensical answers to very simple questions. Thinking that perhaps she was just tired, he suggested that he would finish dinner while she went to rest. An hour later, when his Mom arose from her nap, she was still confused and disoriented. John took her to the emergency department of a local hospital. The emergency room physicians diagnosed her as having suffered a minor heart attack and suffering from mild dehydration. His Mom was put on an intravenous drip and kept in hospital for a few days of monitoring and stabilization. That weekend, John spent many hours in the hospital visiting his Mom and helping her with her meals and generally keeping her company. Government cutbacks to nursing services meant that there was minimal assistance available for patients who needed help with eating, getting an additional drink or help getting to the washroom.

When his Mom was in emergency and through her stay in the hospital, John realized that perhaps his neatly segmented life was evolving into something that was new, unfamiliar and somewhat unsettling. Prior to his Mom's discharge from hospital, John and Eileen met with the discharge planning nurse. Through the Community Care Access Centre (CCAC) they arranged for daily visits from the Red Cross Homemaking staff. They also arranged for visits from the occupational and physical therapists. The discharge planning nurse suggested that John, or Eileen, should be present for the first visit by the homecare supervisor and the occupational and physical therapists, so that he could provide information and verify any information given by his Mom. Sheepishly, John asked whether or not those health care professionals made evening or weekend appointments. Not surprised by the answer of "Unfortunately, no," John knew he had to figure out a strategy for being at work and being available for those visits. To get to the hospital for the meeting with the discharge nurse, he just told his assistant that he had a meeting with a client and he left a message on his voice mail that he would be out of the office for the morning meeting with clients and that he would return in the afternoon. For almost all of his working life, John had been able to go to work largely unencumbered by personal or family caregiving concerns. For John, work was more likely to spill over into personal time than vice versa. Now, however, John felt like he was slipping into a situation where the boundaries between work and family during work hours were no longer going to be "neat."

Over the next few months, John found himself spending much more time during the workday assisting his mother than he had ever anticipated. His mother's spotty memory meant that he had to accompany her to every doctor's appointment. Her capacity to manage her bills was diminishing, so John was managing all her financial affairs. John soon realized two things. First, that his mother would not be able to cope on her own much longer and second, that he would not be able to manage his mother's increasing needs. John contacted the CCAC to find out about nursing home placements. He and Eileen visited a few nursing homes in the area to view the facilities and to meet with the personnel. He was impressed with the facilities, particularly those built within the last couple of years. They seemed much less institutional than his grandmother's nursing home that he had visited when he was a teenager.

At the start of April, 2003 he registered his mother's name with a local nursing home. He was told that the wait list for a ward[2] room would be approximately six months to a year. During the spring and summer, his Mom's situation was fairly stable. The homecare worker, who visited twice daily, offloaded much of the day to day responsibility and care for John and Eileen. By late fall, however, his mother was starting to confabulate. She would tell him that there were people wanting to come and live at her home and that people were stealing her things. Of course, none of this was true but it was difficult for his Mom and frustrating to listen to nonetheless. In November, she twice let a pot burn dry on the stove. Shortly thereafter the stove was disconnected and all food was prepared in the microwave by the home maker. His mother could no longer remember how to sequence the buttons on the microwave.

In January, 2004 he called the CCAC again to see where his mother was on the wait list. John was told that there was no movement on the list—there were still two individuals ahead of his mother on the waiting list. Those two individuals had been on the waiting list since 2002. John was concerned because initially he was told that the wait would be approximately six months to a year and now after being on the waiting list for nine months, his mother was no closer to placement than she had been in April of the previous year. At that point he learned that the waiting lists for ward rooms were the longest of the waiting lists. Apparently some people registered for private or semi-private rooms and then once they were residents, they put their names on an internal wait list to move to a ward room.

MULLING OVER OPTIONS

Throughout all of this, John had not mentioned his situation to anyone at work. Part of the reason for the silence while he was at work was that he liked to keep his work and his personal affairs separate. Part of his motivation for silence was that he did not want

[2]Ward rooms were defined as two beds per room with two rooms sharing an adjoining washroom. Semi-private rooms had two beds per room with one washroom for the room. Private rooms accommodated a single resident and had its own washroom.

to seem less than fully committed to work. And, who could he talk to? How could a 23-year-old software/snowboard whiz relate to John's current situation? He had chatted about his situation with a few close friends outside of Alpha Software and the advice on raising the issue of his eldercare with work colleagues or superiors was contradictory. He played their comments back in his mind.

Anne, a friend since university and an IT manager at a competitor, had told him

> There were times where I was, um, not deceptive but I'd have to sneak it in. I didn't always want to own to my employer that I was taking time off to get my Mom to the doctor. The written policy at XXX was that you could take time off in lieu. The cultural policy was that that was not done. So, I would say something like, "Oh, I'm going off, um, I'm going to be at XXXX and then I've got some other running around to do." So, I would make a point of making sure that I went to one of my work-related places. It might just be to drop off an envelope but at least it gave me a legitimate work-related reason to be out of the office.

Karen, another longtime friend suggested to John that

> The prime piece of advice would probably be for the sake of your peace of mind would be for you to figure out how much you could reasonably handle and not try to go beyond that.

Joan, a neighbour and manager at a local financial institution, had herself been a caregiver for her own Mom for the last ten years. Based on her experience, she suggested to John that regardless of what you're coping with, with respect to aging parents, or other personal issues

> You have to maintain a façade, an image of stability, a strength. You can't show people that maybe you're suffering as well.

Vic, a friend who managed an IT department in another local firm, suggested to John that as a manager,

> It is part of your job to sort of shoulder all of the things that are happening in the organization and in turn not pass on any of your own angsts. Talking about any of your concerns about your mom, well, I would consider it unprofessional. Anyone who is a manager should somehow be able to compartmentalize their life. That's what I do when I'm at work. That's my image of how managers should manage competing personal and private demands.

Terry, who had been John's mentor for the past fifteen years, told him simply that

> It's none of their (employee's or employers') business. I don't talk to anyone at work about any of the personal stuff. I believe that managers should be strong, should show strength and should be slightly less human than their subordinates. There is an element of me that expects that if you are a manager, at some level you should swallow a lot of things that are going on and keep going.

Only Francis, a mutual friend of both John and Eileen, offered different advice. She suggested to John that

> I think you should be frank with your boss. Do we really live back in some pre-enlightened era? I don't think that you have to live the kind of lie that I did when I had small children and they were sick. You know calling into the office with the "Oh, I can't come in today because I'm sick," when the reality was that the children were not well and I needed to stay home with them. Please don't tell me that we're now lying about personal responsibilities for our aging parents!!

The advice that John received had almost unanimously leaned in the direction of continuing to soldier on in silence. It was only his wife Eileen who suggested that he talk with the Human Resources (HR) department at Alpha to see what type of programs or policies might be available. John had to admit that contacting the HR department wasn't something that was top of the mind for him. He had little contact with HR, except for the quarterly in house publications that crossed his desk, or monthly statements of earnings or updates to the company's benefits packages. Reviewing the index to the Employee Benefits Package, he noticed a fairly short set of listings for personal leave options such as maternity and paternity benefits and flexible workplace programs for those balancing work and childcare. He knew that an updated Employee Benefits Package was in preparation but did not know if there would be anything relevant to his particular situation. In the meantime, he had just become too busy with current software projects to really follow up with the HR department. It just seemed simpler to take care of things for his Mom first thing in the morning and then come in late for work and make up the missed time by working late, or just weaving his caregiving commitments into his day and masking those commitments by the messages he left with his coworkers on his voice mail.

THE HUMAN RESOURCES DEPARTMENT AT ALPHA SOFTWARE

The HR department at Alpha was less than five years old. For the first few years of Alpha's operations, the company's focus was on software development. A couple of senior managers served double duty overseeing accounting and human resource issues. However, with the growth and organizational changes that occurred over the past four years, Alpha needed an HR department, if only a fairly small one.

Barbara Verdun joined Alpha as the Manager of Human Resources five years ago in 1999. At first, the workload was overwhelming. Human resources programs and policies were needed. Yet, it was an exciting and invigorating challenge for someone who had been a senior HR manager at a large, well-established insurance company. She moved to Alpha because she wanted to work in a less bureaucratic environment and for a company that she perceived to be dynamic and fast-paced. She had looked forward to developing leading edge programs and policies in order to retain employees in a high velocity environment known as much for its volatile stock prices as its employee turnover.

Under her leadership, Alpha formalized its human resource policies and practices. They also brought in a work/family policy. Initially, her senior colleagues questioned the need for work and family policies. After all, they had never had one and there did not seem to be a need. These discussions initially frustrated Barbara. How could an organization where 80% of the staff is under 40 not need work/family policies? She had heard rumours that some of the female software engineers, driven by the demands, competitiveness and rapidly changing nature of the software industry, took less than two weeks off work after giving birth before coming back to work.

Recently, Barbara became increasingly interested in developing programs for the other end of the work/family spectrum—work and eldercare. It was actually the introduction of the Compassionate Care Leave program instituted by the Canadian Federal Government on January 2, 2004 that was her catalyst for thinking more about the needs of those managing work with care for aging parents. She recalled a conversation with a friend in health care who said that the Compassionate Care Leave program was overdue but, in her friend's mind, still inadequate. As a professional in health care, she had seen many individuals burn out trying to balance work and caregiving for aging parents or spouses. Although 80% of the employees at Alpha were under 40, there were still 20% who could be potential caregivers for aging parents. Barbara also realized that just because someone was 37, for instance, did not mean that they did not have caregiving responsibilities.

In reviewing government reports, items in popular business press and health research reports, Barbara had developed a summary of issues relevant to work and eldercare in Canada. Many of the points supported her initial gut feeling about the eldercare issue, but some of the research findings took her by surprise. So, far her list included the following:

Informal Family Caregiving of the Elderly

- Family and friends are frequently the providers of care to aging relatives and friends. Over 2 million (2.1 million) Canadians, or nearly 11% of the population 15 years of age and older, provide informal care to one or more seniors with long-term health problems. More than two-thirds of informal caregivers were between the ages of 30 and 59, with the average age of 46 years for women and 44 years for men (Frederick & Fast, 1999).
- Women tend to be the predominant providers of informal care to aging relatives. The 1996 General Social Survey (GSS) found that 1.3 million women provided eldercare; the 1.3 million represents 61% of those providing eldercare. The GSS survey also found that women employed full-time provided just slightly fewer hours of care per week than did those who worked part-time (4.2 hours versus 4.6 hours). These hours translate to approximately one-half day per week of informal caregiving. By contrast, men who worked full-time reported providing, on average, 2.6 hours of care per week; men who worked part time reported providing, on average, 2.3 hours of care per week (Frederick & Fast, 1999).
- Eighteen percent of men and women expect to provide care within the next five years. Recognizing men in their role as "working sons," not just "working fathers," would factor significantly in balancing the work–family equation in the next decade (Levine, 1997).

Work and Caregiving Interface

- A 1999 Conference Board survey of 1,500 Canadian workers found that a sizable proportion of individuals across all age groups surveyed provided care. While 30% of workers 55 and older provided eldercare assistance, 30% in the 45 to 54 group also provided care; 20% of men and women aged 34 and younger, and a similar percentage in the 35 to 44 age group also reported that they provided eldercare assistance.
- Findings of a regional Canadian study of over 5,000 employees in Southern Ontario reported that 34% of respondents were involved in general eldercare while 12% were involved in providing assistance with personal eldercare. On average, those providing general eldercare were involved in three hours of caregiving per week, while those providing personal eldercare were involved in an average of nine hours of care per week. Twenty-six percent of CARNET's sample reported providing both child care and eldercare (CARNET, 1993).

- A large U.S. national study of caregivers indicated that 31% of all caregivers surveyed were also employed (whether the employment was full-time or part-time was not indicated) (Stone, Caffareta, & Sangl, 1987).
- A survey of over 3,600 employees of a major Southern California employer reported that approximately 23% of respondents provided some level of eldercare (Scharlach and Boyd, 1989).
- One study found that approximately 25% of caregiving employees categorized themselves as management level employees. On median, those caregiving employees had been with their current employer for eight years. The same study found that younger employees were also involved in eldercare. In fact, as many as 23% of employees in their thirties and 11% of employees in their twenties were providing some kind of assistance to an elderly relative (Scharlach and Boyd, 1989).
- Employees are more likely to provide eldercare as their tenure with an organization increases. Hence, eldercare is an activity that tends to present itself later in someone's employment cycle and eldercare coexists with employment for a substantial period of time (Gibeau and Anastas, 1989).

The Caregiving Experience

- Employees seriously underestimate the duration of their involvement with eldercare. Matthews and Rosenthal (1993) reported that 38% of caregivers had been providing care for five to ten years, while 13% had provided care for more than ten years. Wagner et al. (1989) reported that, on average, employees are involved in providing eldercare for five years. As Matthews and Rosenthal (1993) and Wagner et al. (1989) point out, caregiving can potentially affect a significant portion of an employee's working life.

Barbara's concern about the work and eldercare situation facing employers was starting to materialize at her door. In mid-January, one of the department managers came to talk to Barbara about one of his direct reports. The employee had missed a number of days of work since November, 2003; and when she was at work, she frequently returned late to the office from lunch breaks and was on the phone with what, to the manager, did not seem to be work-related calls. Through the company grapevine, he had heard that the employee was trying to manage care for her mother following her mother's hip replacement surgery. The manager was very concerned, yet frustrated. He was genuinely concerned about the health and well-being of his employee but whenever he asked how things were, he always got the same answer: "Fine. No problem. Everything's great." He did not know how to help an employee who seemed so reluctant to talk about her situation. After reviewing the work/family policies, the manager realized that existing policies were not worded in such a way to make it clear that they could apply to an eldercare situation. This was not the first time that Barbara had heard rumours about employees silencing eldercare responsibilities. She was not sure why this was happening but was concerned.

JOHN'S DECISION

Wheeling back into the company parking lot from helping his mother after her fall in her own home, John felt exhausted—exhausted from trying to balance the competing demands for the past few months; exhausted from feeling that he was being deceitful with his boss, his co-workers, his team, and with his company. By his own estimation he was spending anywhere from five to twelve hours a week doing things for his Mom and with the current nursing home situation, there was no end in sight. He had recently read a study suggesting that approximately 35% of employees in the U.S. and Canada are providing some level of care for an aging parent. More startling was the fact that such care usually lasted from five to fifteen years. He wasn't sure if the silence strategy was going to be sustainable much longer.

References

CARNET (Canadian Aging Research Network) (1993). *Work & Family: The Survey* Guelph, ON: The Canadian Aging Research Network.

Frederick, J. A. & Fast, J. E. (1999). *Eldercare in Canada: Who Does How Much?* (Rep. No. 11-008). Ottawa: Statistics Canada.

Gibeau, J. L. & Anastas, J. W. (1989). Breadwinners and caregivers: Interviews with working women. *Journal of Gerontological Social Work*, *14*, 19–40.

Levine, J. A. (1997). *Working Fathers: New Strategies for Balancing Work and Family*. New York: Addison Wesley Longmans.

Matthews, A. M. & Rosenthal, C. J. (1993). Balancing work and family in an aging society: The Canadian experience. In: G.L. Maddox & M. P. Lawton (Eds.), *Annual Review of Gerontology and Geriatrics: Focus on Kinship, Aging and Social Change* (pp. 96–122). New York: Springer Publishing Company.

Scharlach, A. E. & Boyd, S. L. (1988). Caregiving and employment: Results of an employee survey. *The Gerontology*, *29*, 382–387.

Stone, L., Cafferata, G. L., & Sangl, L. (1987). Caregivers of the frail elderly: A national profile. *The Gerontologist*, *27*, 616–626.

Wagner, D. L., Creedon, M. A., Sasala, J. M., & Neal, M. B. (1989). *Employees and Eldercare: Designing Effective Responses for the Workplace.* University of Bridgeport: Centre for the Study of Aging.

case 4 Someday My Prints Will Come

SCENE I: IN THE BEGINNING, SEVERAL YEARS AGO

"We're bleeding to death." The speaker is Ms. Evelyn P. Hotchkiss, Vice President, Financial Affairs, and in the parlance of the day she's "not a happy camper." She's talking with her Administrative Assistant, Jack Jardine, about the current state of the University budget. Let's listen in for a moment.

"Evelyn, the Faculties do need new computer equipment. But that stuff costs a bucket of money and it ages like crazy too, and the software is even worse. We could put it on hold again this year, but you'll be butting heads with the VP Research, as well as the Deans, if faculty productivity drops. They'll say it's due to us and our budget cuts."

"Jack, do they think we're made of money? Every time we turn around some academic type is complaining about the budget. Where do they think it comes from, a money tree planted behind the staff parking lot? We've been forced to raise tuition *twenty percent*, twenty percent, over the last three years. The students are on the President's back and he's on mine. The Government froze our grant at last year's level, the Faculty Association is dunning us for more pay for the professors, and if we go over budget the Board of Governors is going to have my head on a platter. Something has to give."

As you can tell, things are not happy in Ms. Hotchkiss's world. A major battle's brewing over, as the Deans put it, "the purchase of much needed computing equipment." The Deans, it seems, are getting a lot of heat from their faculty members about antiquated equipment; they in turn are lobbying the Vice President, Financial Affairs, and the Vice President, Research ["How can our faculty be productive without the necessary equipment?" which loosely translated means "If we don't get that new equipment you can Kiss Our Research Grants Goodbye"]. So the Vice President, Research, seeing a storm on her personal horizon, is also hammering Hotchkiss.

At this point a little background briefing is in order. This particular game of pin the tail on the academic donkey is rooted in the early rush to computerize the University.

The title of the paper comes from an old joke: Q: What is the photographer's song? A: Someday my prints will come. The joke is known to the authors, but not its source.

Under the banner "We'll Be Wired to the World" [The WWW Programme] the Government dropped a large stack of cash on Ms. Hotchkiss's predecessor and the proverbial race, at least to the local computer stores, was on. Since the Government wanted the University to show "a sense of urgency," "first come first served" became the order of the day. Not only were a number of different vendors used but, as you might expect, since it was the Government's money being spent, a lot of equipment was purchased at significantly inflated prices. And in the rush to be "Wired" every Faculty and, in fact, every faculty member, had a different view concerning the type of equipment to buy. Since there wasn't time to draft a comprehensive purchasing policy for computers, or other equipment like printers and scanners, just about everyone's wish became Purchasing's command.

This all happened before Hotchkiss landed in the VP's job. So awhile back Hotchkiss conducted "a thorough and comprehensive review of our computer situation." Her review revealed a number of interesting things: First the computer support personnel were making a heroic, but unsuccessful, attempt to be familiar with all the different types of equipment on campus, and, since there still wasn't a definitive purchasing policy, a lot of equipment was returned to vendors due to technical incompatibilities. Second some Faculties were subject to what might delicately be called "Computer Envy," replacing equipment well before it was necessary simply to have the "latest" and the "best." Other Faculties, not so attuned to the "Wired World," allowed their computers to become obsolete. As well there was the odd "crisis" which occurred whenever a new round of "Computer Envy" kicked in or when one of the less "Wired" faculties realized they were getting short-changed in the "Wired World." Such a "crisis" inevitably led to more irrational purchases. Finally, the Government, while willing to invest in *starting* the WWW Programme, was less than interested in maintaining it. Simply put there were a lot of political points to be had in starting something but few points to be had maintaining it, so there was very little money to replace aging computer equipment. In short, the audit revealed that the University was not "spending its computing dollars wisely." This led Hotchkiss, in consultation with Computing Support, to develop a purchasing policy emphasizing a small number of reliable vendors and a firm replacement schedule.

Since the policy's implementation, the purchase of new computer equipment has been tightly controlled. A lot of "urgent" requests to upgrade computer equipment are now routinely turned down because they don't precisely follow the policy. Moreover, there's now a definite University-wide schedule to replace worn-out computer equipment but this schedule requires that Faculties "wait their turn," in large part because it seems the Government of the Day has decided that "financial discipline" and "enhanced accountability" is now a good thing for the University, and, as such things go, it falls to the President, and so to Ms. Hotchkiss, to "make it happen." The upshot of all of this is that many faculty members now share computer equipment and most computers are older models which can't handle newer research software.

To complicate the problem a bit more, the pending Computer Wars are only one part of a larger picture. In fact Ms. Hotchkiss now tightly controls most spending across the University, not just spending on computers. It's taken a nasty turf war or two but in the last few years the Deans have learned who rules the financial roost, and everyone is feeling the financial pressure of a number of Hotchkiss's "thorough and comprehensive" reviews. An example, you ask? Well, Deans now give each faculty member an annual "budget" of a few hundred dollars to be used for postage, photocopying course materials and minor computer supplies, rather than routinely approving most minor operating expenses. This small sum is enough for the year, mind you, but extravagance can easily result in an "overdrawn" account with the miscreant having to ask the Dean for additional funds. The faculty member's budget is, of course, tied to his or her Dean's budget and if *that* budget is overdrawn the Dean has to ask Hotchkiss for additional funds, a task that is a notoriously "hard sell." Really, it's a very hard sell, if the truth be known, and after the turf wars it's generally acknowledged across Campus that it doesn't pay to get too well known by Ms. Hotchkiss. As it stands most Deans would rather be caught in a nest of vipers than ask for a top-up of their accounts and risk a trip to Ms. Hotchkiss's office, or "The Woodshed" as it's unofficially known across Campus.

Understandably Hotchkiss has received a lot of praise from the Government of the Day and the Board of Governors for running a "tight ship" but this year's freeze in the Government's grant threatens to push the budget into the red. And even though the Deans lost the turf wars there is still some strength in numbers, so the sniping continues with the yearly budget submission being a time for those under Ms. Hotchkiss's financial thumb to make their collective displeasure known. This year the Deans, however, are collectively adding to Ms. Hotchkiss's woes by contending that the slow implementation of the computer replacement policy resulted in some computers completely failing, and others only marginally operational. But let's return to Ms. Hochkiss's office....

"Boss, there might be a way around the problem."

"What's that, Jack?"

"I've been talking to Grant Cypher, you know the President of 'Speed O' Light' Computers."

"Yeh?"

"Well, the pitch he made to me is that he'd like exclusive distribution rights on Campus. Now we could tell him that we'd agree; the Campus Bookstore would handle only his computers and that everyplace on Campus would have his equipment and software too, if he funds the initial change over. He'd give us a start with new equipment, enough to replace the stuff we have to replace, and we'd get a discount on future updates. We'd get a deal on the equipment and software for the students, too. It's a classic "win-win": We get reliable, compatible, equipment at discounted prices; he gets a guaranteed future market, his equipment gets known by the students, and he gets bragging rights that the University uses his stuff exclusively. What do you think?"

"Jack, that just might fly, get him on the phone and see if he could meet us for lunch next week. And it's even better since we own the Bookstore, so some of our money will come back to us. This is so simple we can't lose."

And so, lunch happened. Hotchkiss agreed in principle, but told Cypher that the contract would have to be tendered, which it was. Not surprisingly, being the originator of the idea (or call it insider information), Speed O' Light Computers won the contract.

Shortly thereafter, "Purchasing Policy #1946: Computer Equipment and Software" came from Ms. Hotchkiss's office. There was the obligatory ribbon cutting ceremony in the Computer Section of the Bookstore, the Picture of the Ceremony in the "Alumni Times" and a nice article "Alumnus donates Computers" on page 3 of the "Our Town" section of the local paper. And the University continued on its way, until one winter's day, about two years later.

SCENE II: A DARK AND SNOWY DAY, IN THE PRESENT

A comma here, an exclamation point there; hmmm ... should that word be underlined or in italics? Better make it italics to drive the point home.

Dr. Finagle is putting the finishing touches on his paper for the Down South Management and Teaching Conference ["Motivated Students: Are their grades always a Bimodal Distribution?" By I. Finagle and A. Dromedary]. It's a good paper, Finagle thought. He'd done the conceptual work while Dromedary did the statistical analysis. It was sure to be accepted at the annual Down South Conference, the high point of the academic conference season. Five glorious days of academic presentation, the cut and thrust of questions and answers, the Plenary Session [Does Money Motivate: A Final Answer!] and the palm trees. Ah, yes, the palm trees and the tropical sunsets by the Conference hotel pool.

The annual Down South Management and Teaching Conference is always held someplace tropical in the middle of the winter semester, and while there might be some question in the collective mind of the Organization Committee if money motivates or not, it's clear to one and all that an opportunity to spend a few days in one tropical location or another is highly motivating, especially to those who, by mid-February, feel the call of palm trees, warm breezes, and the hibiscus-lined walks of the Conference hotel. So Finagle is hard at work on the Conference paper—his ticket, literally—to sunnier climes.

There has been a significant upturn in research, at least on Finagle's part, from the day the University deemed that airfare, hotel charges and meal costs could only be reimbursed at the prescribed rate if "the traveller presents a paper" at the Conference. So no paper, no freedom from ice, a bitter wind and a week's teaching. But in fairness to Finagle, he did have a good idea occasionally, usually about Conference time, and with Dromedary's statistical help he was assured of a large helping of sun, sand, and hibiscus. And let's not forget the sunset cocktail hour around the pool; he'd gotten quite fond of those tropical fruit drinks—by now he could almost imagine the taste of his first "Missionary's Downfall" in a year as he clicked the "print" button on his computer screen.

Yes, just print his paper, photocopy it, then send four copies by courier to the Chairperson of the Conference. The courier service would pick up the paper in the next hour, plenty of time to copy the original, put the whole thing in the envelope and leisurely walk it down a flight of stairs to the Faculty's main office where courier packages were picked up and delivered. Finagle was sleepily contemplating that Missionary's Downfall when he first heard it: a musical "ding," like a small doorbell on a very good home. Finagle sat straight up and stared at the computer screen. A casual observer would reach the conclusion that Pavlov was right. Finagle was now tilting his head to one side, as if trying to comprehend the message "PRINTER NOT RESPONDING" that floated on the screen in Arial Black font. He leaned forward, as if to strangle the monitor, as the message reached those cognitive centres the chime had effectively bypassed.

The message was from the "faculty printer" located some two corridors away and one floor below Finagle's office. Now something you should know about the "faculty" printer. While a good one when it was installed about two years ago the poor thing was shared by some sixty faculty members, assorted graduate students, research assistants, and secretaries. Nor was its printing restricted to strictly academic works: e-mail, memoranda of all types, pressing personal correspondence, and the occasional recipe was grist for its mill. In short it was over-worked and, because it was one of the few printers in the Faculty, it was under-maintained since there was, understandably, a collective howl whenever it was taken off-line.

In the last three months it had started to express its mechanical displeasure at this state of affairs by simply stopping. During such strikes it informed all and sundry by the "PRINTER NOT RESPONDING" message—which was the cause of Finagle's slightly glazed look—and then sat in the Faculty work-room humming softly to itself. This condition would sometimes last an hour, sometimes a day, and occasionally longer if the Faculty's technical specialist couldn't bring it around. And bringing it around was becoming an ever more difficult task; Finagle remembered a time when it had to be "sent away" for maintenance and was off line for a week. All this was in Finagle's mind as he went down the corridor that led to the stairs, that led to the corridor that led to the ex–broom closet that was occupied by an abused photocopy machine, storage cabinets with extra paper, a small work table and the currently "on-strike" printer. Jim, the Faculty's computer support expert, was already there, having fielded about ten phone calls saying, in rather colourful language, "the printer's not working again" in the time it had taken Finagle to launch himself in the general direction of the workroom.

"Jim," said Finagle, a bit of desperation in his voice, "will you have it running in the next hour?"

Jim explained to Finagle what was wrong with the printer, why it couldn't be fixed within a week let alone an hour, and why the printer would have to "go away" again. Jim's explanation was accurate, detailed, and technical. Unfortunately, Finagle was not well versed in the language of computers. He was more of a "type, save and print" guy; that is he was a type, save and print guy when the damn printer would print, so after the first thirty seconds of Jim's explanation Finagle felt like a collie in obedience class—generally understanding only every eighth word or so which happened to be words like "not," "no," and "bad." It slowly dawned on Finagle that the printer was going away and, unless fate intervened, he wasn't.

"Jim, why don't you just order a new printer?!?"

"Actually, I did," replied Jim, "but Financial Services is sitting on the purchase order. They say this printer is not due for replacement until the next budget year."

"But it's broken *now*," Finagle concluded. Jim nodded in quiet agreement.

Back to his office tramped Finagle; thank God e-mail still worked, he might salvage the situation yet. Off went an e-mail to the Organizers of the Conference begging for an exception to their deadline for paper submissions. An hour comes and goes, and the courier with it, when Finagle receives a reprieve of sorts. It seems the Conference Organizers, in their Wisdom, knowing the Difficulties in meeting Deadlines, would grant, on a one time basis, Dispensation and Permission to submit the paper Late as long as it was in Their Hands by Friday Next. That gave Finagle another two days, and a bit. Those palm trees were still within his grasp.

But this left the problem of getting the paper printed. The obvious, but unsavoury, solution was now rather straightforward. Finagle would simply have to buy his own printer and not be dependent on the Faculty's aging, over-worked machine. This move had some precedent in the Faculty. About two or so years ago when the last shared Faculty printer was giving up the ghost, one or two faculty members had used their Professional Accessories and Development account, that small one usually used for postage, photocopies, and minor computer supplies, to buy a printer. This strategy could result in a very unpleasant meeting with the Dean if the account was overdrawn, but it was still an option since the purchase effectively meant not relying on the Faculty printer and, not incidentally, forgoing the walk from office to workroom and back. This had all occurred to Finagle on his subsequent tramp back to his office, and, after the response from the Committee, his mind was made up—desperate times call for desperate measures, he would use some of the money from his P.A.D. account and buy a printer from the local computer store. The only detail was to secure a purchase order and, for good or ill, the deed was done.

Now, purchase orders are agreements from the University to local suppliers to pay, up to a limit indicated on the purchase order, for equipment or supplies. The printer Finagle had in mind was a small and not entirely sturdy printer, but then Finagle would be the only user. The good news was that it would cost about $200, something he hoped he could afford and still avoid a "full and frank" discussion with his Dean.

Securing a purchase order was, in theory, quite straightforward. It required filling out a P.A.D. Memorandum of Exchange [Form 63.2a] and taking it to Accounting who would issue the purchase order to a local supplier. The usual terminology was "for an amount not exceeding $200.00." The local computer store would give Finagle the printer, submit a bill to the University for the exact amount of the sale, and this amount would be taken from Finagle's P.A.D. account. It was as simple as could be—with the paper in the hands of the Organizing Committee by Friday. So Finagle fills out the P.A.D. M.E. and picks his way through the snow-drifts and ice covered walks to Accounting. Fifteen minutes later Finagle stands, slowly dripping, at Accounting's reception counter as snow melts from his coat, boots, and eyebrows. He whistles tunelessly to himself as he waits to be recognized.

"Yes?" This from Henrietta Spencer, Assistant Accounting Clerk.

"Ms. ah, Spencer," said Finagle, quickly checking the nameplate on her desk, "could you be good enough to make out a purchase order to 'Bits and Stuff' for two hundred dollars? I'm off to get myself a printer, really need it for research, think I have enough money to cover it." This last more in the tone of a prayer than an assertion; Finagle was babbling, in part from the bone-chilling cold he endured walking to Accounting, in part from a desperate desire to get the printer. Snow slowly dripped from his coat collar onto the back of his neck as Spencer typed numbers and his name into her computer.

After a three second pause: "Nope, can't do it," Henrietta said, with some obvious delight.

"Why?" asked Finagle, in desperation after counting to ten, slowly, twice.

"Well, Professor, seems we've got an agreement with 'Speed O' Light' computers. In exchange for good prices and their gifts to the University we've agreed not to use any computer equipment but theirs. Only the University Bookstore handles their stuff; so you'll have to get it from there, not 'Bits and Stuff.' "

"But Ms. Spencer, I think others may have used 'Bits and Stuff' in the past."

"Nope, sorry Doc; that was before the implementation of 'Purchasing Policy #1946: Computer Equipment and Software.' All purchases now have to go through our Bookstore."

"Oh, well, ah, I didn't know." Finagle was thinking that one printer if it just *worked* would be as good as any other. "Could you make out the purchase order to the University Bookstore?"

"Yeah, but it won't do you any good."

Finagle felt the walls closing in. "Why might that be?"

"Well, Millicent from our office was just there ordering her new printer. Seems that with the demand from the students for printers they're sold out. Next shipment in about a week or so, they say."

Finagle started to count again, slowly, to himself.

"So Henrietta, let me see if I understand. I need a printer today. There are lots in the shops, but we can only buy from one supplier who we've struck a deal with. They in turn struck a deal with the Bookstore where this is the only place their equipment is sold. But the Bookstore is out of printers for at least a week, since everyone on campus now buys their equipment from them, so I can't get one today."

"You got it."

Trapped, thought Finagle—while thoughts of palm trees started to fade. Perhaps he could use another Faculty's printer; perhaps someone in his Faculty would be good enough to set his or her work aside, perhaps.... It has been said that necessity is the mother of invention, and Finagle was in need of a loophole, so, in an act of desperation, he asked—"Henrietta, what are the regulations concerning renting a printer?"

"I'm not sure," she replied. "Let me check. Hmmm. Looks like there's no policy. I suppose that you can rent any printer you want."

"Come again?"

"Simple, Dr. Finagle, just fill out your P.A.D. M.E., you know, tell us the type of equipment, the place and the price and I can have you a Purchase Order in five minutes. Seems like you've got the money in your account. We've got an agreement about *buying* equipment from 'Speed O' Light' but nothing about *renting* it."

So that was how Dr. Finagle found himself standing at the "Bits and Stuff" service counter about thirty minutes later. The conversation with the clerk went something like this:

"I'd like to rent that printer, the one that costs about two hundred dollars."

"Well, I don't know, we don't usually rent them."

"I really do need that printer, what would you say to a rental of $190.00 for the year?"

"Why would you want to do that? You could buy it for $10.00 more."

"Yes, I know, but University regulations, and all that."

"Well, if that's what you want it's up to you; just sign this lease agreement."

So Finagle signed, and happily carried the printer out to his car and eventually to his office.

Jim, accommodating as ever, had it up and running in about ten minutes. And in due course Finagle's paper was printed and on its way. So was Finagle, I might add. Now this tale closes with a happy ending except for one small detail. Finagle had rented the printer for a year; and next year the rent would be due again. That would mean that Finagle would have to come up with another $200.00, but perhaps his students didn't really need all those handouts, and he did need that printer—and after all, that's what the money was there for, wasn't it?

case 5 Working at Wal-Mart

Claude had a problem. His father was celebrating a major birthday this Saturday and Claude was scheduled to work from 4:00 to 8:00 p.m. Claude came from a close-knit family where all family milestones were celebrated together over an extended meal. If Claude worked his shift, he would have to miss his father's birthday dinner. If he called in sick, he would feel like a liar since he was not actually ill; he did not even feel a cold coming on. He was sure that his manager would not give him the time off. When Claude first started this job, he had asked that he not be scheduled to work on his day of Sabbath. His manager simply said that the auto scheduler, a computer program designed to create employee work schedules, could not accommodate this, and then walked away. There was no room for discussion. "How much is this job worth to me, anyway?" Claude asked himself.

Claude was a 22-year-old fourth year Engineering student living at home. Wanting to avoid student loans, Claude applied to work at Wal-Mart as an associate in the photo lab processing film. Since the store was new, all the associates had to undergo orientation before the store could be opened. Groups of 30 to 40 associates met in the basement meeting room of a hotel. Each associate received a copy of the Wal-Mart associate handbook. The store manager reviewed portions of the handbook related to codes of conduct and told the associates, "At Wal-Mart, you should never hear the phrase 'it's not my job,' since associates are empowered by Wal-Mart." He explained the profit sharing program and the stock ownership plan along with the benefits. The associates then watched a video entitled "You've Picked a Great Place to Work" that described Wal-Mart's success as a business and how it had grown from a single store that Sam Walton had opened to become the world's largest retailer. Various quotations from Sam Walton such as, "If you want a successful business, your people must feel that you are working for them—not that they are working for you" were sprinkled liberally throughout the videos. The manager also outlined Sam Walton's guiding principles:[1]

1. Be committed to your work. Your passion will be contagious to those around you.
2. Treat associates as partners and be a servant leader.
3. Make your work exciting and motivational by setting high goals, using job rotation, and encouraging competition.

---

4. Communicate as much information as you can to associates. Associates with information feel empowered and care about the organization.
5. Demonstrate appreciation on a regular basis. Praise is priceless.
6. Have fun at work, show enthusiasm, and celebrate successes.
7. Listen to your associates. They know what the customers are thinking and they have ideas about how to improve operations.
8. Go beyond meeting your customers' expectations.
9. Pay careful attention to expenses and keep them to a minimum.
10. Be open to trying things that haven't been tried before. Take risks.

The manager then taught the associates the infamous Wal-Mart cheer:

Manager: "Give me a W"

Associates: "W"

Manager: "Give me an A"

Associates: "A"

Manager: "Give me an L"

Associates: "L"

Manager: "Give me a squiggly"

Associates: "Squiggly" (while doing something that resembles the twist)

Manager: "Give me an M"

Associates: "M"

Manager: "Give me an A"

Associates: "A"

Manager: "Give me an R"

Associates: "R"

Manager: "Give me a T"

Associates: "T"

Manager: "What's that spell?"

Associates: "Wal-Mart!"

Manager: "Who's number one?"

Associates: "The customer always"

Manager: "What store is number one?"

Associates: "[Store number] 999 customer service all the time"

The associates were required to sing this song at every morning meeting and after the store had closed for the evening. At these meetings, the associates would also be informed of how the store was doing in terms of sales levels. The orientation ended with a presentation in which each associate's name was called and the associate was presented a nametag that doubled as a swipe card to be used for the time clock. Claude left the orientation session feeling excited about being part of the Wal-Mart team. It was his first real job and he was impressed with the "family" approach that the managers talked about during the orientation. The managers had encouraged employees to become passionate about Wal-Mart, to share in Sam's vision, and to put Wal-Mart's needs first.

A few days after the orientation session, Claude began working in the photo lab. During his four-hour shift, he placed the film in one end of the developing machine and out the other end came the negatives. Next, he placed the negatives in a scanner, made adjustments for color, and ordered prints. He then placed these prints and negatives in an envelope and started the process over again with another film. Although Claude sometimes enjoyed looking at the prints, Claude found his job to be rather routine. He looked forward to troubleshooting when a machine would break down. He tried to process the film as quickly and perfectly as possible so that the customers would be happy with the service that Wal-Mart provided. As did other employees, he learned his job within a few days. There were very few skills to master and the procedures were clearly laid out. Claude realized that employees could be easily replaced (and were) but having the right attitude, one of commitment and a sense of duty, seemed to be particularly important.

At first, having the right attitude was not a problem for Claude. Claude believed that it was better to light one candle than to curse the darkness.[2] Because he always thought the best of others and let any problems slide off like jello nailed to a wall, he had simply dismissed any doubts that he had about his work as unimportant. After a few weeks, however, Claude began to notice that his coworkers were complaining about many things such as shifts, management, procedures, and, especially, the song that they were taught as part of their orientation. Ever since his manager criticized him for suggesting some new procedures (or "complaining" as his manager called it), Claude thought that it was best to keep quiet. When he had an idea, he thought of a line from a poem that he had read in high school, *The Charge of the Light Brigade*: "Theirs not to make reply, Theirs not to reason why, Theirs but to do and die." Whereas Claude used to "go the extra mile," now he did only as much as he needed to keep his job. He would tell himself that Wal-Mart was a means to an end, just like he was a means for Wal-Mart. He was glad that he was getting an education so that he wouldn't have to be a Wal-Mart "lifer." He almost felt bad for the lifers. In a year or two, he'd be a professional engineer, a prestigious occupation paying more than they could ever dream about. More importantly, he had choices; they did not.

Within a year, most of the people that had started at the same time as Claude had left. There seemed to be an increased focus on following rules. For example, although they brought water into the photo lab for the equipment, associates were not permitted to bring in water or other beverages for themselves. Also, although the photo lab employees were able to develop a workable holiday schedule for themselves, the manager refused to accept this schedule because the auto scheduler "would not permit it." Exceptions, negotiation, and relaxation of the rules were not possible.

There were four additional incidents along the same theme that stood out for Claude. After doing an inventory count for several hours, an associate named Roger stepped outside the store for his coffee break. Once back on the job, he noticed that he had left his electronic inventory scanner outside. So, Roger went outside and found his scanner where he left it. However, when he went back into the store, his manager confronted him, indicating that it was inappropriate for an associate to take two coffee breaks and that this formal warning would be placed on Roger's personnel record. Roger quit his job that afternoon. On her last day of work, another associate, Judy, came into the store wearing a pair of khaki shorts. Her manager rushed toward Judy, stopped her within a few feet from the door, used his badge to measure her shorts, and told her to go home and change her clothes because her shorts were more than the length of a badge above her knees. Judy did go home but did not return to work.

Similarly, Colette, a cashier, had joined the army reserves and then informed Wal-Mart that she would require every third weekend off. Colette thought that this minor unavailability could be inputted into the auto scheduler and that all would be fine. Even during weeks in which she could not work weekends, she was available for 30 hours of work. However, as with Roger, Colette was informed by her manager that he would not be able to schedule her for the minimum 12 hours per week and that she would have to make a choice between the army and Wal-Mart. Colette then requested a leave of absence that was also denied by her manager. Although she was only one of a handful of employees to receive the four-star cashier award for excellent work and customer service, Colette was subsequently dismissed.

Claude thought about another incident in which Michel, a high-school student, requested holidays during the first week of August so that he could participate in an annual family camping trip. Although Michel had submitted his request four months in advance, his manager waited until the middle of July to inform him that he could not find anyone to cover for Michel and, that, as a result, he would have to either work those days or lose his job. Michel decided to miss his family holiday. He didn't want to work at McDonald's or some other place that paid new employees about two dollars less per hour than Wal-Mart did.

On this day at work, Claude was especially apprehensive. Besides having to make a decision regarding his father's birthday dinner, Claude was also concerned about some material that he had come across while surfing the net. Several websites reported that Wal-Mart is sued, on average, two to five times per day by customers, employees and other parties.[3] The case that really stood out for Claude dealt with the issue of religious discrimination.[4] A store manager who was displeased with the unwillingness of a Seventh Day Adventist to work during her Sabbath made disparaging comments about the plaintiff's religion and provided an inaccurate account of the activities of the plaintiff and another employee who had both accessed the company's computer system using a management password. Although he fired the plaintiff, he did not fire the other employee who did not practice the plaintiff's religion.

Even though most of these sources contained actual court documents, Claude was sceptical. After all, it is reasonable to expect that any organization would experience these sorts of issues, especially one as visible and as large as Wal-Mart with its $244.5 billion in sales in the 2002–2003 fiscal year, more than 1.3 million associates worldwide, over 3,200 facilities in the United States and 1,100 units in other countries, and more than 100 million customers per week.[5] In fact, it may well be that Wal-Mart is the target of even fewer lawsuits than other companies its size. And, after all, Claude thought to himself, Wal-Mart has earned the title of top Corporate Citizen by the 2000 Cone/Roper Report of philanthropy and the third most admired company in America by *Fortune* Magazine in 2001.[6] However, after reflecting on what was happening in his own workplace, Claude did not know what to think.

As he walked into the store, Claude felt as though hundreds of eyes were watching him from every direction. He ducked into the rest room but this only reminded him of a case[7] in which a Wal-Mart manager had secretly set up a camera in a unisex washroom in an attempt to catch potential shoplifters in the act. Two employees, however, found this to be invasive and the courts agreed. Although the camera did not actually record anything, the jury considered this irrelevant. "Rightly so," Claude thought, "The rest room is the last sanctuary of mankind." After glancing at the ceiling, Claude slipped into the employee lunchroom.

The walls of the lunchroom were plastered with posters containing slogans such as "Our people make the difference" and "Associates are partners." On the table was an open can of cashews. Although Claude and the other associates normally enjoyed eating whatever food was on the lunch room table, on this occasion, Claude muttered, "I'd have to be nuts to eat any of those!" He was reminded of another case[8] in which Wal-Mart was ordered to pay 20 million dollars in damages to four employees for defamation, eavesdropping and outrageous conduct. A manager who was concerned about theft in the store set up a video camera in the employee break room and placed several open packages of nuts and candy on the table as bait. After the manager viewed the tape, he fired four employees without notice. During the resulting trial, another Wal-Mart manager testified that opened packages of nuts and candy were regularly donated to charity or given to employees.

Claude normally has a friendly chat with Monique, a visible minority woman who worked in electronics, but "Not today," he thought, "Why take chances?" Claude was referring to a case[9] in which Wal-Mart was fined $40,000 for secretly recording employee conversations. Claude waved at Monique as he proceeded to the photo lab. He also thought about a case[10] in which a manager fired a white female employee, telling her that she "would never move up with the company being associated with a black man." Wal-Mart was subsequently ordered to pay her $94,000 in damages. "What's the deal here?" Claude thought, "Wal-Mart seems to concern itself with associates' choice of marital partners, elimination of bodily fluids, and religion. If this is how the world's largest retailer treats its employees, what do I have to look forward to in the rest of my career? Maybe, I'm expecting too much. After all, this is just a job."

Having reached the photo lab, Claude started loading film into the processor, something he would do for his entire shift. He tried to block out all the questions that he had about his workplace. One question that he was unable to stop thinking about, however, was what he should do about his father's birthday dinner. "Should I not go to dad's birthday party at all, should I try to ask my manager for time off (and, if so, how), should I pretend to have a cough and ask to go home early on Saturday?" Claude was contemplating his options when another possibility entered his mind, "Or ... should I just leave for 20 minutes or so and get my coworkers to cover for me?"

Reflection Questions

1. What are Claude's alternatives regarding attending his father's birthday party? What should he do? Why?
2. What are Claude's alternatives regarding his general employment situation? What should he do? Why?
3. How representative is Claude's job of jobs that you have held or the kind of work in which youth normally engage? What may be the longer-term implications of this?
4. What other organizational behaviour concepts are illustrated in this case? How?

Debating the Issues

Your instructor may assign you to one of the following groups:

Group 1: Argue in favour of the employment practices described in the case.

Group 2: Argue against the employment practices described in the case.

End Notes

[1]Walton, Sam (1992). *Made in America: My story*. New York: Doubleday.

[2]Christopher Leadership Course.

[3]Laska, L., *99 verdicts against Wal-Mart*. Retrieved from www.wal-martlitigation.com/99verdic.htm on November 8, 2001.

[4]Tincher v. Wal-Mart. 155 F3d 1317 in Laska, 2001.

[5]Retrieved from www.walmartstores.com/wmstore/wmstores/Mainnews.jsp?BV on November 10, 2003.

[6]Retrieved from www.walmartstores.com/wmstores/Mainnews.jsp?BV on November 8, 2001.

[7]Pierce, L., & Appell, B., *Jury fed-up with employer*. Retrieved from www.silver-freedman.com/library/mar_99_br5.html on November 8, 2001.

[8]Stringer v. Wal-Mart. Wayne Co. (KY) Circuit Court, in Laska, 2001.

[9]Desilets v. Wal-Mart. 171 F.3d711, 1st Cir. 1999 in Laska, 2001.

[10]Deffenbaugh-Williams v. Wal-Mart. 156 F.3d 581 in Laska, 2001.

case 6 Countryside Environmental Services

John straightened his tie as he walked down the hallway to the conference room. Vincent paced eagerly at his side. "You've told Andy and Gwen exactly what my role in this project is, haven't you?" Vincent muttered nervously to John. He was quite sure he knew the answer, but wanted to be sure he was going into this meeting in tune with John. Vincent had met with John on many occasions during the preceding month to negotiate his joining Countryside Environmental Services (CES). Once the contract had been negotiated, John had provided Vincent with a general orientation and overview of the company's operations. Now, Vincent was to meet the rest of the team.

"Oh don't worry, I'll make it clear in this meeting this morning" replied John. "As we've already discussed you're to be the guiding authority in this project. I'll be overseeing your progress, however you will be responsible for the team's success or failure. We both know that you are more familiar than I with the procedures and politics involved in getting a landfill approved. We can benefit tremendously from your input. Yes, there's no doubting it, you'll be the key player, Vincent." John hurried through this last sentence as they reached the meeting room and pushed open the door. He was pleased that Andy and Gwen were already seated and awaiting his arrival.

"We've been given the green light with the new name, so Countryside Environmental Services it is," John said with pride as he entered the small meeting room. This was an exciting moment in the history of Countryside Construction. It was the beginning of another venture for John and his company. Currently, Countryside employs eighty-five people and grosses more than $15 million. John attributed much of the company's success to his own management philosophy of diversity and perseverance.

John Hopkins established Countryside Construction some thirty years ago. The company started business as a small aggregate producer, excavating and selling sand and gravel from a local gravel pit. Today the company supplies aggregate to most of the region's sand blasting and construction businesses. Countryside also has a dominant presence in the local waste management industry. It ventured into waste management a decade ago after being awarded the City of Blensford's contract for the curb side pickup of household waste.

In response to this success, John created a new division of the company to handle waste management. It had been a successful venture for Countryside and John remained close to the action, personally managing the division. During the past five years the division acquired two additional contracts for the operation and management of two other County landfills.

Countryside Environmental Services (CES) had just been established as a spin off company from Countryside Construction to develop a new landfill on a parcel of land centered around one of the company's old gravel pits.

John had visualized owning his own landfill ever since Countryside first became involved in waste management. He believed that the owners of the landfills (in most cases the Government) pocketed all the profits. John was aware of the crippling environmental problems of the existing waste management system and knew that current landfill capacity was rapidly diminishing. He believed the economic potential for opening a new large scale landfill was promising.

Vincent Woodman had just been hired as the environmental consultant and manager of Countryside Environmental Services. Recently Vincent had vacated his seat on County Council, where he had been the County Warden and Reeve of the Town of Innsport for nine years. In this role, he had chaired the County Waste Management Committee and had represented the County on the Provincial Waste Management Steering Committee.

John was very pleased to have recruited Vincent. Vincent had developed an impressive reputation for effective input into waste management planning during his terms in County politics. He eventually became frustrated with the lack of vision with which the County approached its worsening waste management problems. Vincent, like John, could see that the increasing public outcry for environmentally safe landfills combined with a strong push towards the three R's (Reduce, Recycle and Re-use) was an opportunity for private enterprise. The best way to handle the County's waste was for the County to enter into a joint venture with the private sector. The County simply did not have the necessary funds and pressure was mounting both from the public and provincial government officials for change. Vincent knew this better than anyone.

Once Andy and Gwen had joined Vincent and John in the boardroom, John pulled a few papers from his briefcase and shuffled them on the table. "Well I know you've met Andy and Gwen prior to today albeit for a brief moment. I've talked to Andy and Gwen about you joining CES and I am sure they are as enthusiastic as I am. However I should perhaps fill you in on my aspirations for this team and what I would like to see happen. As you know, Andy has been with us now for nearly three years in the capacity of Projects Engineer. Gwen is the Office Manager and joined us about six months prior to Andy." John was speaking quickly, his excitement evident. "Gwen is responsible for the day to day running of the office. She has been involved with the bookkeeping of some of our accounts. However I know that you are well acquainted with accounting Vincent. Andy will be in charge of all the technical/engineering work and Vincent, you will handle the political end of the plans as well as managing the project. I believe we have the basis for a solid and valuable group and I look forward to seeing progress. Vincent has briefed me on what we will need to concentrate on and he will be directing us through the environmental approval process. He has a wealth of knowledge and experience to share with us, so let's work together, be productive and have some fun at the same time. Perhaps now is a good time, Vincent, for you to brief us on what you consider our plan of attack should be." John leaned back in his chair keen to listen to Vincent's remarks to this newly established team.

"Thank you John. I feel you have provided us with a very exciting opportunity here and I am honoured to be a part of this team. I believe we all have very valuable and relevant skills to utilize in this project and I can't stress enough the importance of working as a team. I truly believe we can make this vision of yours a reality."

"Just as I thought. A long winded politician," Gwen muttered for Andy's benefit. He heard her comment but decided to ignore it.

Vincent continued. "John, you have provided me with an overview of the situation here at Countryside. I would appreciate a day or so to settle in and become familiar with the environment. Then we could get together and go over some specific task assignments. For now you could all help me by answering a few questions. First of all have any business cards or letterhead been printed yet?" Vincent turned and faced Gwen.

"No, I haven't!" Gwen was quick to respond. "I thought we should wait until we can come up with a company logo, perhaps a tree or a dove or something like that would be fitting. I'll organize that tomorrow."

"I think it is important to get that taken care of quickly. I have a meeting next week with the County Waste Management Committee and I would like to have some cards to hand out. Andy, it might be worthwhile for you to come along to the meeting." Vincent paused to consider his next remark.

Gwen interjected. "John, I think I should be a part of that County meeting as well. We know that County is cash strapped at the moment. I think I should give them some figures regarding the cost savings they could benefit from if they adopt our landfill proposal."

Vincent looked to John, a little startled by the authority in Gwen's voice. John turned and looked out the window. Vincent continued. "I don't think that will be necessary for this meeting, Gwen. They are not really interested in the costs right now, they just want a brief as to what approach we will be taking. It is encouraging to hear that you have already collected some cost data, perhaps you should pass it on to me. I'll combine it with the work I have already done. John had not informed me that any costings had been tabled yet. What figures have you put together?" Vincent enquired.

"Well I ummm..." Gwen stammered. "Well you know it's just preliminary figures. However I could get up and talk about costs just as well as anyone else here and it sure would be a darn sight cheaper to have me there than you, Vincent."

Vincent again turned to John, hoping he would offer some comment to ease the situation. John continued to stare out the window. Vincent was concerned that he had not been forewarned of this conflict. He sat back carefully considering his next remarks, still hopeful that John would break the silence. "Gwen, I have been placed in charge of this project and I will not be requiring your presence at this meeting. I know the people on the Waste Management Committee well and I know what they are wanting to hear at this early stage. I respect your eager attitude, however must insist that I go alone or with Andy." Vincent paused, feeling satisfied that he had handled the situation well. He continued. "With John's approval I have drafted up a structural layout for the team, defining each individual's tasks and whom they are responsible to. I shall bring you all a copy in the next day or so. If you have any comments or suggestions regarding the content then please feel free to come and see me." Vincent thought hard about this last comment, perhaps he would have to revise Gwen's task description. "Well I feel that is all we need to cover today, so perhaps we could meet again in a couple of days. Does anyone have anything else which they feel needs to be discussed?" Vincent searched for somebody to take the conversation away from him.

Andy cleared his throat and addressed Vincent. "Perhaps we could sit down together after you have settled in and go over the current status of our landfill application in detail. We really have just touched the surface of what is required, but nonetheless there are several key site-specific facts that I can brief you on." Andy was a no-nonsense, hard working individual who had been involved in a wide variety of projects in his time with the company. He looked forward to the work ahead of him. Vincent turned to face Andy, acknowledging the value of his suggestions with a smile.

John considered it was time to put an end to the meeting. "O.K. then. I think you have given us all a taste of what lies ahead. Perhaps next Tuesday we could meet again. Is that suitable?" John glanced around the room, noting everyone's agreement. "Let's wrap it up for now. Thank you all for your time. Gwen, could you stay behind for a minute? I want to go over a few things with you."

Vincent packed his suitcase and quickly left the room. "Wait up, Andy," Vincent called to the young engineer as he closed the meeting room door and hurried down the hallway after him.

John gazed out the window, watching the passing traffic and waited till he could no longer hear Vincent and Andy as they continued down to the hallway, locked in serious conversation. "Well, what in the hell was that all about? Do you realize the position you're putting me in here?" John turned to face Gwen, and waited for her response. "Well?"

"I'm sorry, but I just can't understand why Vincent has to exclude me. Why does he have to get paid so much? It's a joke. How could you pay him so much more than me? I tell you now, I am not going to sit around here and have him tell me what to do. As office manager, I assume I'm in charge of everyone in the office and that includes Vincent. O.K.!!" Gwen exclaimed. "Please understand me, John. We've worked hard to build this company and I've played a key role in building client relationships and been at the table in the earlier deals we've developed. I want us all to be happy here but that isn't going to happen if we let this guy come in and start calling the shots."

"Listen Gwen, there is no doubting that you're an efficient and dependable worker. Everyone here recognizes and appreciates that, but I have to warn you, don't push it this time. Vincent seems to be a very nice and reasonable fellow and by all accounts he can add a great deal to this team. I don't believe your attack on him was necessary."

"Well John, you know I have been on edge with all that I am going through at home and perhaps I am overreacting somewhat, but I would like you to talk to Vincent and get him to include me in this waste management meeting at the County. I think it is very important that I attend. For what it's worth I could even take Andy's place, I know a little about the engineering of a landfill. I just think you need to have me there to keep an eye on things." Gwen was unrelenting.

John knew of the turmoil in Gwen's family life and felt a real sense of pain every time he thought about it. Gwen seemed to take every opportunity to fill John in on the current traumas with her husband. John had been divorced less than two years ago, he knew of the pain and the sense of rejection. He could not bring himself to look at Gwen, he just quietly said, "Just leave it with me, I'll have a word to Vincent about it, O.K.? Don't worry, we'll work something out."

Gwen smiled and got to her feet, feeling like she had salvaged some grace from this morning's meeting. She liked John. She patted him on the shoulder and walked out the door.

John remained in the meeting room by himself for some time, contemplating the morning's events. He felt hopeful.

Vincent returned to his office after a lengthy conversation with Andy, who had filled him in on the internal workings of the company. Andy warned Vincent to tread lightly if he was going to confront John about Gwen's behaviour. He told him that it was a well-circulated rumour (and one that he did not believe) that John and Gwen were having an affair and that Gwen had been experiencing difficulties with her husband. Even though it was Vincent's first full day with the company, it was not a surprise when Andy mentioned that John was very supportive of Gwen and was allowing her tremendous flexibility at work. Gwen's behaviour of late apparently had many other people in the company on edge. Andy reported that two secretaries had just resigned and that he knew of another staff member who was currently looking for a new job. It was, according to Andy, no coincidence that this was occurring just as Gwen was becoming more difficult. John was not offering any assistance or advice to anyone apart from Gwen.

Vincent was interested to hear that John had asked for Andy's input in the selection of a secretary for Countryside Environmental. John, however, had made it clear at the time that he wanted Gwen to be transferred. Andy knew his objections would be in vain and so decided that he would have to learn to deal with the situation as best he could. Andy did however think highly of Gwen's work, but had pointed out that over the past six months her performance had suffered and her attitude to fellow employees had changed for the worse. He had lost a great deal of respect for her and now felt that working with her would be a very testing experience.

Vincent was surprised by and appreciative of Andy's openness. He considered Andy to be believable and knew that John saw Andy as talented and credible. Vincent was all too familiar with situations like this and considered that the time to act was now, before the situation was allowed to get out of hand. He sat down at his desk and picked up the documents he had prepared for Gwen, defining her tasks and position. It was only now that he remembered that John had studied Gwen's job definition very closely and had made Vincent make several changes before approving it. Each alteration tended to make her job description vague and her position somewhat unclear. He decided that it was imperative to define exactly what she would and would not be required to do and who she would be accountable to. Vincent read through the documents again, making note of any changes he would like to make. In the light of the morning's events he knew he would have to discuss this further with John.

Vincent felt unsettled about the conflict that existed at Countryside and remembered all the petty squabbles, power struggles and internal politics he had to deal with in his term as County Warden. He was disgusted at the lack of maturity exhibited by some of his former colleagues and certainly did not want to be put in the same situation again. Vincent pushed his papers aside and reclined in his chair trying to relax. He considered the possibility that he was overreacting, but quickly dismissed this thought. He found himself wondering why he had chosen to accept John's offer to work for Countryside. Everything had seemed so promising and full of hope when he had met with John. One particular comment that John had made stuck in his mind: "If you have any troubles, then feel free to come and see me, my door is always open. I don't imagine however that you will encounter any major problems, the waste management division has been very successful in the past. I am excited to have you with us, Vincent." Vincent had been very impressed with John; he had seemed very warm and sincere and had been a key factor in Vincent's final decision to accept the position. "...My door is always open." Vincent pondered over this comment for a minute before rising to his feet and heading down to John's office. He knocked lightly on the door and walked in. "Yes Vincent, what can I do for you?" John looked tired and worn out.

"I want to discuss with you Gwen's performance in the meeting this morning. I fail to see a need for the comments she made regarding her ability to outperform me at the County meeting. I'd appreciate it if you could provide me with some insight here." Vincent's statement was just what John had feared.

"Well you see, Vincent, Gwen has always been an excellent performer here. She is just having a tough time with her personal life at the moment. I don't think there is any cause for alarm, she'll get over her problems soon and I know that she will bounce back to her former cheerful self. I ask you not to be overly critical of Gwen for now and that you give me a little time to work things out. We can't be too tough on her." John glanced up at Vincent, hoping he would understand.

"I would rather deal early with anything I see as potentially harmful to our progress, and this concerns me. If you consider that we should go easy, then I will respect your judgment. I just want you to know where I am coming from. Perhaps it would be advisable for one of us to sit down with her and go over just where she fits in here."

"No I don't think that is necessary. Don't let it get you down, it will clear itself up in time. Oh by the way, I was pleased with the way you handled the meeting this morning." John turned back to his desk and began sorting through some papers. Vincent took the hint and decided to hold off discussing the issue further. He returned to his office to concentrate his efforts on becoming familiar with company protocol and making his office a more workable environment.

The next Monday morning, Vincent approached Andy and handed him a copy of his job description, which included an itemization of both individual and group goals. Andy quickly glanced through the listed points but offered no immediate objections. Vincent suggested he take his time and thoroughly study the papers and come to him with any other comments.

Vincent looked around the cluttered office noting how claustrophobic it felt. Andy's desk was in one corner of the square room, desks belonging to secretaries were in two of the other corners and at the far end was Gwen's desk. Vincent was glad he had his own office. Since Gwen was away from her desk. Vincent pulled out her job description and scribbled on it:

"INTER-OFFICE MEMO

To: Gwen

From: Vincent

Subject: Job Description"

He placed the document on her desk and returned to his office.

About a minute after Gwen returned to her desk, Vincent heard her march boisterously past his office down the hallway in the direction of John's office. He suspected what the commotion was about and expected that he would soon be summoned into John's office. Much to his surprise he was not. Half an hour later John's office door was opened and Vincent heard John say "just leave it with me, I'll have a word with Vincent and straighten this out." Gwen glared at Vincent as she walked past him back to her own desk. John left the office and Vincent did not see him again at all that day. Neither John nor Gwen approached him regarding the job description report.

One morning, a week later, Vincent was the first to arrive at work. He noticed that a package had arrived overnight addressed to Countryside Environmental Services. It was from Hasty Print. He opened up the package and discovered that the company letterhead and business cards had arrived. He retrieved his own cards, and as he lifted them out of the box he uncovered Gwen's. He was shocked to see the title that appeared on them: "MANAGER—FINANCE AND ACCOUNTS." His eyes nearly popped out of their sockets. He now understood why he had not heard the slightest mention of letterhead or business cards since their first meeting.

Vincent felt very frustrated and believed the team was going nowhere. Any efforts he made were being thwarted by Gwen. He considered that the time for letting things settle out had well passed and as soon as John arrived in his office, he cornered him.

"Can I have a word with you, John?" John swiveled in his chair to see Vincent standing at his office door. Vincent's concern was noticeable both in his appearance and the serious tone of his voice.

"Sure, come on in," John replied.

Vincent closed the door behind him. "I am of the understanding that Gwen is the office manager. Is that correct?" Vincent paused and waited for John's response.

"Yes that is right," John said with some hesitation.

Vincent's voice increased in volume. "I have just this morning received our business cards. Are you aware of the title she has put down for herself?"

"Yes, she actually came to me last week to complain about the job description document you had given her. She was in quite a rage when she came storming in here. She figured she would be in charge of managing the finances of this project. You see she has just started going to night school for her Certified General Accountant's certificate and I think she's pretty keen to practice what she is learning. I explained to her that you were responsible for deciding who did what and suggested that she sit down and discuss the matter with you. I figured that if she wanted to call herself the financial manager or anything else then so be it. You and I both know where she is at." John's face turned a pale shade of red. He could not bring himself to look up at Vincent. "Vincent I firmly believe that we should not intervene here. We need to give her some room and a bit more time to sort out her problems."

"Well John I'm no more for hitting someone when they're down than you are, but can you not see that she is the sole cause of the terrible atmosphere in this place? I'm not the only one that is affected here. I think we're in danger of losing some valuable players if you allow this kind of behaviour to continue. I have already been approached by a couple of the staff in this office who have voiced their objections. They believe she has changed dramatically over the past six months although certain individuals commented that she has always been somewhat bossy and power hungry. I gather my presence here has caused an escalation of the problem. I don't believe this is something we can just turn away from and hope that it will go away. It needs to be dealt with. When I first met with you I shared some concerns about the small size of this office and the necessity for a close knit team effort. I feel I can't perform effectively if this is allowed to continue." Vincent waited for John to respond to his comments, but was not surprised to receive nothing but silence. John slowly got up from his chair and left the room. Vincent could see that he was very troubled. He desperately hoped that John could see the ramifications of his action.

A couple of days following Vincent's discussions with John, Gwen was away sick for two days. She returned to work one morning and began quizzing Andy as to what Vincent had been working on while she had been away. "Well I believe he was reading through the Environmental Assessment Act and making some notes. Perhaps you should ask him when he comes in." Andy was young and had become somewhat intimidated by her, a fact that she was well aware of.

"I thought you had already made some notes from the Act. You did, didn't you?" Gwen continued, determined to create a scene.

Andy reluctantly replied, "Well yes I did look at part of it, but that was some time ago."

Just as Andy finished these last comments, John walked into the office. Gwen was quick off the mark. "John, I think we need to do something about Vincent. Andy says Vincent has been duplicating work. That's a waste of time and with the money we pay him it's something we cannot afford."

"Well you're right, we don't need anyone to duplicate another person's work. I'll have to have a word to Vincent about that." John reached the coffee machine and filled his cup. He wanted to change the subject, but Gwen continued before he had a chance.

"And another thing," Gwen was winding up, "How is it that he can just come and go as he pleases, he is never in here before 8:30 a.m. Who gave him special rights?"

John ignored this last question and walked into his own office, hoping to escape the outburst. Andy had followed him and startled John when he spoke. "John I feel I should clarify what Gwen was referring to in there about Vincent duplicating my work. I think that was a very unfair comment to make. She is taking what I said completely out of context. You see Vincent and I can read the same article, looking for different facts. That is exactly what happened here. I was looking for the engineering data, while Vincent was looking at the same papers with a political slant, extracting different material. I do not appreciate someone taking something I say out of context and blowing it up, especially in front of you. I ask you to consider this before you approach Vincent." Andy was rarely one to speak his mind, but felt a great sense of satisfaction with his remarks.

"Don't get your dander up Andy, I wasn't even going to mention it to Vincent. I was pretty sure that Vincent would not duplicate any work. Thanks for your comments though." John picked up his coffee and nervously smiled at Andy before taking a sip. Andy turned and left John's office, almost knocking over Gwen who was standing just around the corner, apparently listening in on what had been said.

Two months passed by. Vincent had been working for Countryside Environmental Services now for nearly three months. He was still feeling the frustrations of working with Gwen. Her behaviour continued to be erratic and her performance as a team member left a great deal to be desired. Vincent had approached John many times and on three specific occasions asked him to resolve the problems. Each time John had expressed his concern but asked Vincent to put up with the situation for a little longer. Vincent's personal secretary had resigned, stating that she required more time with her family. Vincent was well aware that the true reasons for her departure were not aired. In addition to this, Andy had confided with Vincent that he had been given a temporary offer of employment with a large mining company in the north of the province and would probably be accepting the offer when it is finalized. Vincent was very disturbed and troubled as to what he should do.

case 7 Dividing the Pie at Bennett, Jones and Douglas

Joe Douglas contemplated the problems facing Bennett, Jones and Douglas. As a founding partner of the law firm, Douglas was concerned with the animosity among the firm's partners. At the centre of the conflict was the firm's system of financial compensation. Within the past year, relations among the partners had deteriorated to the point where the firm was facing dissolution. Douglas was determined to develop a plan to rectify the situation.

BACKGROUND

The Company

Bennett, Jones and Douglas, a medium-sized, full-service law firm, provides legal counsel to corporate and non-corporate clients in matters ranging from real estate and matrimonial law to corporate law. The full-service aspect of the firm's operations results from the fact that the firm houses both barristers and solicitors. The firm's barristers specialize in courtroom and litigation work. The solicitors, on the other hand, are referred to as the "office lawyers," counselling clients in matters involving real estate, property, matrimony, corporate law and wills. As is common practice in Ontario, the distinction between the domains of the barristers and solicitors is "fuzzy," with some of the firm's solicitors representing clients in court.

The firm operates as a partnership with senior and junior partners. Each partner has his/her area of specialty and is well-experienced within the firm, having been with the firm for at least 5 years before being considered for partnership. In addition, there are non-partnered associate lawyers, law clerks and administrative staff. The firm's success lies in its reputation for providing quality legal counsel to a full range of clients.

The firm was founded 14 years ago by George Bennett to handle the needs of non-corporate clients in the area. Bert Russell and Don Richardson joined George and, one year later, they formed the law firm, Bennett, Richardson and Russell.

Recognizing the need to expand their services in non-corporate areas, Bennett, Richardson and Russell approached Jack Jones, Bennett's brother-in-law, to join the firm. The addition of Jack to the firm increased the company's annual billings by 20% and increased the firm's contacts within the community.

Eight months later, Joe Douglas, a high-profile barrister with 8 years of legal experience, joined the firm. Douglas was well-known locally for his wealthy client base. The firm then became known as Bennett, Jones and Douglas and was informally organized into two "divisions." One division concentrated on corporate clients and the other on non-corporate clients.

Bennett, Jones and Douglas's full-service concept has proven successful. The firm's growth in the last three years has been estimated at 40% per year. Currently, there are thirteen partners: seven barristers, five solicitors, and one administrative/management partner (Dave Wise). The company represents a growing force among law firms, with a reputation for quality service and an ability to penetrate the business community for new business. The team approach has worked well for the company in that once one division has dealt with a client and established some credibility and trust, the groundwork has been laid for the other areas to service the same client.

The company's primary objective is growth through new clientele, expanded penetration of existing clients' needs and the development of new specialties.

INDIVIDUALS IN THE FIRM

The firm is comprised of highly competent individuals who are specialists in their respective areas. They were attracted by the reputation of the firm, its stress on the "full service" concept, and its proven success. All are high achievers and at the top of their fields. They see themselves as ambitious and competitive (profiles of the partners are provided in Exhibit I).

Competition among the partners has developed in many ways. Lifestyle, cars, manner of dress and appearance all play a role in the competitive "game" in the firm. The focus of competition, however, is maintaining one's "numbers"—meeting billings objectives set at the beginning of the year. New lawyers were expected to double their billings within four years of entering the firm. The "numbers" were published monthly, creating a lot of discussion and rivalry.

The partners recognize that in many respects the firm is an incredible winner for them as individuals. However, there is some controversy as to whether this success can all be attributed to the full-service concept. To a great extent, it is believed that the firm's success is due to the concentration of a young, aggressive and very capable group of individuals who would be successful either inside or outside the firm.

DIVISIONS

The Barristers

Seven of the partners are barristers who specialize in litigation, both in the courtroom and in administrative tribunals (e.g., the Workers' Compensation Board, Liquor Licensing Board). Much of the barristers' work is in corporate/commercial law. Corporate/commercial work is viewed as "good quality work" because it generates

exhibit I Individuals in the Firm

Senior Partners

Name	Area	Age	Years with Firm	Background	Goals
George Bennett	Solicitor	47	14	–5 years at major law firm –founded firm 14 years ago –merged with Jones 10 years ago	–emphasis on billings and diversifying firm's areas of specialization
Jack Jones	Solicitor	45	10	–solicitor for 7 years at major law firm –merged with Bennett 10 years ago –one of the largest non-corporate client bases in city	–wants financial independence –interested in growth opportunities to expand firm's worth
Joe Douglas	Barrister	42	9	–strong reputation for courtroom representation –chose Bennett et al. over 3 other firms offering attractive incentives	–financial security –build personal reputation
Bert Russell	Barrister	54	13	–14 years as legal counsel of head office of major steel manufacturer –with George Bennett 13 years	–looking forward to retirement
Don Richardson	Solicitor	43	13	–associate lawyer for 4 years with mid-sized firm –along with Russell, one of Bennett's original partners	–wants to achieve billings comparable to most productive partner –wants to build firm's billings by 10% per year

Junior Partners

Name	Area	Age	Years with Firm	Background	Goals
Barry Johnson	Barrister	37	9	–only partner with a Masters in law	–to become a senior partner
John Jacobs	Barrister	35	8	–recruited by Joe Douglas –extensive courtroom experience	–increase his billings by 20% in next 18 months –to become a senior partner
Larry Anderson	Barrister	34	7	–3 years experience with a major Toronto firm	–enjoys challenge of representing clients in court/wants challenging litigation cases
Dick Howard	Barrister	31	7	–joined firm after law school –articled with Bennett	–wants to catch up in terms of income
Bob Gates	Solicitor	46	6	–with 2 other firms before joining Bennett –frustrated with company politics	–working to change basis of remuneration
Bill Wilson	Barrister	33	6	–increasingly becoming involved in litigation	–expand areas of specialty –increase billings and salary
Glen Woods	Solicitor	30	5	–newest partner in firm –does considerable courtroom work	–increase billings and position within firm
Dave Wise	Administrator	35	7	–increased focus on management responsibilities	–wants to be a valued partner –develop firm's internal systems and procedures

high and consistent revenues for the firm. Receipt of payment from clients is almost always guaranteed and the ongoing nature of corporate legal work ensures a steady source of billings and revenue. In addition, the barristers provide a valuable source of referrals for the solicitors. Also, the barristers provide a high profile for the firm, particularly when representing major corporate clients.

The Solicitors

The five solicitors primarily counsel private individuals in matters involving mortgages, estates, wills, divorce and personal injury claims. Although much of the work in this area is fairly straightforward, it can be more time consuming and with less financial reward than the corporate work. Most of the firm's overdue accounts are matrimonial accounts. In addition, solicitors occasionally take legal aid cases which bring limited revenues to the firm. Much of the work is strongly affected by external economic conditions. For instance, an active real estate market increases billings for real estate transactions dramatically.

PARTNER REMUNERATION

Bennett, Jones and Douglas's system of remuneration for partners is based on billings, seniority and the percentage share owned by each partner (or "points" as it is called). Each partner receives a monthly draw and, at the end of the year, a share of the profits. The monthly draw reflects a partner's contribution to the firm which is primarily based on billings and seniority. A partner's share of the profits is based on his/her point holdings within the firm which, like the monthly draw, is tied to billings and seniority.

Billings are the most visible measure of an individual's contribution to the firm. Billings, the charges to the client, are apportioned among the lawyers working on a particular case. Billing allocations are an area of conflict because they do not necessarily reflect an individual's efforts in a case. A senior lawyer may spend half the time of a junior lawyer on a case, but claim 60% of the billings. Weighting is given to the senior lawyer's experience and reputation. In addition, senior partners are often credited with a portion of the billings from a client that they originally brought into the firm, even if they did not provide any counsel with respect to the current service. Billing allocations are usually decided by the partner in charge of the case or service.

Points represent the "share" a partner owns of the firm. The firm's "100" points are distributed among the partners. The number of points owned by a partner is a function of seniority and billings. When a new partner is added to the firm, each partner relinquishes a share of their points to the new partner. Insofar that senior partners generally have a greater number of points than junior partners, they contribute more points to the pool for the new partner. New partners "buy" points in the firm often incurring heavy personal debt in the process. These funds are sometimes provided by the firm and are then repaid through deduction from that partner's share of the profits.

As Bennett, Jones and Douglas grew it became evident that the contributions some individuals made represented a greater proportion of total revenues than was reflected in their proportion of points. Relatively junior partners (and thus with fewer points) felt severely disadvantaged. Their billings were high but their remuneration reflected their low seniority and low points total. The issues around points are further confused by substantial billing differences characteristic of the different areas of law. A barrister, for instance, may bill a corporate client for $50,000, while a solicitor's fee for a real estate transaction may only be $2,000. As a result, some partners were putting in considerably more effort than others but their level of billings was considerably less. Since billings impact on "points" and subsequently profit sharing, feelings of inequity existed between the two groups.

Lawyers involved in real estate law and similar areas often complained of their workload. They felt that they were continually under pressure to produce more work. During boom times, they were swamped. During slack periods they were scrambling to find work. They also felt that the corporate lawyers' work was "cushy," marked by long lunches in the executive suite. Finally, they felt disadvantaged because a corporate lawyer could generally be guaranteed a significant amount of work each year through the ongoing needs of their clients. Real estate work, on the other hand, demanded a fresh start every year.

Another point of contention involved remuneration for administrative work. For example, Wise and Bennett's remunerations were adjusted upwards because of their managerial workload, although their billings had dropped considerably.

Finally, some partners were upset over the inattention of some of the founding partners. Bennett and Jones had diverse community interests which they pursued during business hours. It was not always clear how these activities benefitted the firm.

The Management Committee

Bennett, Jones and Douglas's operations are overseen by a four-member management committee consisting of George Bennett, Jack Jones, Joe Douglas and Dave Wise. The committee's responsibilities include the day-to-day management and administration of the firm on behalf of the partners. The committee is also responsible for decisions on annual salaries. Consultation and agreement among partners are sought for many issues. However, with the increasing need for timely decisions, the committee assumed the role of decision maker leaving the responsibility for developing clients and completing the legal work to the remaining partners.

Membership on the committee had evolved over time. George Bennett and Jack Jones were the principal founders of the original firms and were viewed "naturally" as senior partners and committee members. Joe Douglas's position on the committee evolved from his role in the development of the firm's non-corporate client base. Dave Wise was added in order to help implement many of the decisions made by the committee.

To instill a feeling of equality and participation by all partners, there had been some discussion of rotating membership on the committee. It had been tentatively agreed that John Jacobs, another barrister, would replace Joe Douglas at year end.

The Decision Making Process

Two key factors influence the decision making process within the firm. One factor is the "weighted-vote" given the founding partners in the firm, and the other is the power used by the management committee.

The partnership agreement includes a clause giving senior partners a "weighted vote." The weighted vote means that no major decisions concerning expenditures or new partners could be made without the vote of at least one of the senior partners. Even if a majority of the partners had decided on an issue, the change was not adopted unless one of those who voted was a senior partner. Twice in the past year, conflicts arose because of the bargaining power of the senior partners. In one particularly acrimonious incident, an associate lawyer was denied partnership because a group of junior partners could not obtain the weighted vote of a senior partner. Three months later, a less experienced associate lawyer with the backing of two senior partners was offered a partnership.

The rapid growth of the firm also impacted on the decision-making processes within the firm. Rapid growth meant that the partners no longer knew each other well. In addition, the increasing number of partners makes it difficult to get everyone together at one time in order to maintain communications. The formation of the management committee was an attempt to accommodate some of the efficiency demands. Over the past year, the committee assumed a greater decision-making role leaving the remaining partners torn between conflicting levels of involvement. On the one hand, partners desire to influence corporate decisions by participating in the management of the firm. On the other hand, this desire is offset by the inclination to minimize administrative involvement. Consequently, there is confusion over what roles should be played by the management committee and the rest of the partners.

Adding to this dilemma was concern that the management committee, like the senior partners, did not always respond as the partners wished. For example, recently the partners decided to terminate the firm's involvement in a particular investment venture. This decision was never carried out by the management committee and the investment remained.

These issues led to significant frustration within the partnership. One group felt left out while the other felt untrusted.

The partners had varied opinions of the decision process:

> The decision process is impulsive. We have a tendency to act that way: quick moving and quick decisions. That was OK when we were smaller but now we need a new process. The size of the decision is much larger than it was five years ago and the financial commitment is that much larger. Because of our historical success our impulsiveness is reinforced. (Glen Woods)

> Decisions are often made on the immediate cash flow produced rather than the long term. Sometimes I feel we are risking the relationships with some corporate clients. (Glen Woods)

> There needs to be some mechanism by which the management committee can make decisions and the partners can be involved in what they need to be involved in and no more. There has also been a tendency to sometimes let the management committee make decisions because it is too painful for the group of partners as a whole to make those decisions. The animosity has grown too much. (George Bennett)

> The company is in a crisis because some individuals feel that they can make divergent decisions after there has been an agreement not to do so. (John Jacobs)

> We don't take the time to analyse issues before we act on them. We make a decision and then it gets changed outside the partners' meetings without anyone knowing except George or the management committee. Presumably we were participating in decisions but George and Jack seem to feel often that they can do what they want. (John Jacobs)

> I don't want to be on the management committee but I want better communications and consistency. (Larry Anderson)

> This notion of giving the impression of having input, and then making changes after the decision, is a real problem. The partners should be involved in anything long term that affects the direction of the firm. (Larry Anderson)

COMPENSATION PROBLEMS

As mentioned, the compensation system remunerates partners on the bases of salary (or draw) and profit-sharing. Disputes over compensation arise because of differing perceptions of effort, contribution and billings produced. It seemed to both the solicitors and the junior partners that they were committing the energy and time needed to produce but were not receiving the financial awards commensurate with their efforts.

Meanwhile, the barristers and those specializing in corporate law charged that they were subsidizing the non-corporate division and that solicitors did not contribute to the company profits to the same degree as barristers.

Those on the management committee were concerned that the cohesion of the firm was in jeopardy as a result of the combination of perceived imbalances between the contributions of individual partners and the disaffection with the management committee. It was evident to all partners that something needed to be done.

A NEW REMUNERATION SYSTEM

A task force, headed by Joe Douglas, was established to study the compensation conflict and to recommend a new remuneration system. The task force's objectives were as follows:

1. To ensure that the proposed system is consistent with corporate goals and objectives and, in particular, reflects the team approach.
2. To ensure that the proposed system is fair to each participant, taking into account the inherent differences among the various activities.
3. To ensure that the proposed system permits due recognition of total input by individuals. This included the volume of production as well as indirect efforts such as participation in corporate management, new service development, visibility through service club membership, etc.

After three months of study, the task force reported back to the partners. Excerpts from its report are provided in Exhibit II. Essentially, the task force recommended a three-component compensation system which took into account a partner's investment in the firm, a partner's billings and a partner's qualitative contribution.

Since the qualitative contribution was deemed too difficult to measure, the task force set out operating guidelines for partners to follow. It was also concluded that client referrals were an ordinary part of the firm's operations and therefore should not require separate remuneration. Thus, the attempt to compensate producers for referrals was dropped.

The equity component consisted of two elements: salary and profit sharing. Salary related directly to the level of an individual's billings and years of experience in the firm, while profit sharing reflected point holdings.

Compensation for output or performance attempted to consider the differing nature of business in each area by adjusting the earnings rates. Allowance for time spent on management responsibilities was also built into the new system. Of the three proposed components, the billings component was the most heavily weighted.

The task force planned to implement the new system by the previous March 1 for an initial period of ten months.

exhibit II

BENNETT, JONES AND DOUGLAS
PARTNER REMUNERATION
FIRST PROPOSAL

Components of the Remuneration System

It was concluded that the remuneration system should have three components. Firstly, a portion of current compensation should reflect the investment of each partner in the company. Secondly and most significantly, remuneration should be a function of billings, since this is the primary role of each partner. Thirdly through some form of peer review, qualitative contributions to the firm should be reflected in compensation.

Peer Review Component

In the early stages of the study, it was felt that contributions to the firm outside of billings would best be assessed by each partner's peers. It was concluded that these contributions would be very difficult to measure, and any resulting assessment would be relatively subjective. Therefore, in the absence of a formula or otherwise objective measuring tool, peer evaluation would be a very sensitive component of remuneration. Consequently, this component at best would have to have a minimum weighting in overall compensation. It was concluded that, at least for the early stages of operation under the new system, this component should not be specifically formulated into compensation. At a later stage, with greater experience with the system, this component may be added especially if some form of compensation for these very important contributions is necessary to motivate the partners.

The following operating guidelines are the basic expectations of each partner:

- each partner has a responsibility to devote a reasonable amount of time to the job—bearing in mind that production and the impact on the production component of remuneration is largely a function of time.
- each partner has a responsibility to keep current in terms of education and current developments in his particular area of practice.
- each partner should have some degree of community involvement, necessary for the development of new business.
- each partner should maintain some degree of industry involvement, and contact with the clients with whom we deal, to maintain success in placing business and developing new opportunities.

Referral of Clientele

The problem of tracking referrals which leads indirectly to the generation of commissions is very tedious. Referring business is appropriately an operating guideline as opposed to a factor in the production component of remuneration. In the course of his practice, each partner should be sensitive to opportunities for expanded service to clientele. When this falls within the activities of another individual, the partner should refer the client to the appropriate individual, whose expertise and other qualities will best serve the client's needs.

Equity Component

The equity component of the proposed remuneration system is a combination of salary and profit sharing. Salary levels are established annually by the management committee. Salary is primarily based on the number of years of experience, billings with some recognition given to additional degrees or courses.

The second component of the remuneration system is profit sharing which is a function of point-holdings. This component of remuneration is the most significant, consistent with the fact that billings are central to the firm's operations.

Consideration for point increments within the firm will be based on the following schedule. This schedule indicates the minimum billings level required for consideration of point increments. This schedule takes into account the differing revenue potential of barristers and solicitors:

continued

exhibit II (continued)

Minimum Billings Volume for Consideration of Point Increase

Solicitors	– no court work	$200,000
	– 25% or less court work	225,000
Barristers	– less than 50% court work	250,000
	– more than 50% court work	300,000

In future, it is contemplated that compensation levels for the current year will be an average of the two previous years' actual billings. In this way, swings in billings will have less impact on level of compensation. This will protect the partner in the event of a significant drop in production, and affords better control for management in anticipating remuneration levels for budget purposes.

In addition to the assumed billing levels for year one of the new remuneration system, other adjustments to the base production level are necessary. The most significant of these modifications relates to management time. Particular partners serving a management function should be credited with a compensating amount of production volume since management responsibility reduces time which otherwise would be devoted to production.

Implementation

It is proposed that the new system of remuneration be implemented commencing March 1 to be applied prospectively, for an initial period of ten months to December 31. Review of the system will occur in December and any proposed modifications would then be implemented commencing the following January.

PARTNER REACTION

Individual partners were quick to react to the new system. Many were visibly upset by the proposals and clearly voiced their anger to the committee members. In a progress report to the task force in mid-April the following criticisms of the new compensation plan were forwarded by the partners:

- system is too heavily based on billings
- system does not provide sufficient support to the solicitors
- system yields differentials in income levels which are too great
- system lacks enforcement of "operating guidelines" described and, in particular, does not provide tangible rewards for referrals
- proposed levels of compensation for management time were viewed as excessive
- proposed two year rolling average for billings component should instead be an average of last year's actual and this year's budgeted billings
- partners should only be compensated for billings in their primary stream of activity

After careful reflection, the task force modified the rates of compensation as shown in Exhibit III. Otherwise, the recommendations of the original proposal remained largely unchanged. However, the task force did commit to refine the system after the year's billings.

exhibit III

BENNETT, JONES AND DOUGLAS
PARTNER REMUNERATION
NEW PROPOSAL

The billings component of compensation is to be modified. Originally we recommended the following rates of compensation:

Minimum Billings Volume for Consideration of Point Increase

Solicitors	– no court work	$200,000
	– 25% or less court work	225,000
Barristers	– less than 50% court work	250,000
	– more than 50% court work	300,000

Our proposed changes are summarized as follows:

Minimum Billings Volume for Consideration of Point Increase

Solicitors	– no court work	$180,000
	– 25% or less court work	200,000
Barristers	– less than 50% court work	225,000
	– more than 50% court work	275,000

With the exception of the barristers who do more than 50% court work, the new minimum billings requirements are approximately 10% lower than previously outlined. The lower dollar requirements for solicitors who do no court work recognizes the relatively more difficult task facing solicitors in achieving yearly billings levels, as explained in our original report.

THE CURRENT SITUATION

Six months after the new remuneration system went into effect, the following comments were indicative of divergent attitudes with respect to the compensation system:

The Solicitors' Perspective

> There's a lot of heat on the solicitors. We are reminded all the time of our low billings. There is a lot of polarization between the two divisions. Unhealthy. We feel like we're weak sisters. (Glen Woods)

> There is a major issue of workload. Some people are not making the time commitment and I see that as a lack of consideration of others. Golfing 42 times per year is too much regardless of the amount of billings produced. (Jack Jones)

> There is an inherent inequity in the demands placed on the non-corporate side of the firm. Non-corporate legal work is exceedingly tough. Our contribution is not recognized by others. I'm not sure if we are going to be able to continually add more and more dollars per person—there are only so many hours in the day and I'm over 40 years old now. (Don Richardson)

> There is extreme resentment at the amount of time put into the business by certain partners. Though they may say their production is okay, the reality is that they work in easier areas of the business. Why should special treatment be accorded simply because one is positioned in an easier role overall? All should contribute equal effort. (Don Richardson)

The Barristers' Perspective

> I had rose coloured glasses on. Eight months after I joined the firm it was evident that I made wrong decisions over the method of compensation. People producing less were making more money and that's unfair. I can accept that we have to subsidize the solicitors' side. I can accept a $50K or $75K difference in production but if it's $100K then I'm not sure. I think I should get more at that point. (John Jacobs)

> I'm not one of the winners under the compensation system. I have no problem with subsidizing the solicitors' side but there gets to a point where the billings growth is not equal to the contribution. (Larry Anderson)

> I have real questions as to whether or not it makes sense to have as active a solicitor group as is presently constituted. Several of the solicitors seem to be in real trouble with respect to their planned billings. While the corporate division produces both profits and equity for the business, non-corporate doesn't seem to be as profitable. I'm concerned that the solicitors are winning more than their fair share in light of their productivity. (Barry Johnson)

Douglas wondered where to go from here. How could he satisfy all of the individual partners' concerns and still adhere to the firm's overall objectives of the compensation system? Furthermore, he wondered what the implications on the firm as a whole would be if he could not find an acceptable remuneration system. Finally, he was concerned over the growing conflict among partners. Partner meetings often degenerated into shouting matches. Animosity between some individuals was high and growing.

case 8 Jaztec Inc.

As the remaining employees of Jaztec Inc. drifted in from their lunch break, Jovianna Gucci, Vice-President of Marketing and Public Relations for Jaztec Inc., breathed a sigh of despair. She was unable to focus and was fully aware that her demeanor likely revealed her concerns. "Can I get everyone's attention for a minute?" Although only 12 of the 17 Jaztec employees were actually in the office, it took some shuffling and a few minutes for everyone to stop what they were doing and focus on Jovianna. "I think that we can all agree that we have seen this place more than our own homes for this past week. Everyone finish up what you are doing and head home to your families for a long weekend." Jovianna could feel the atmosphere lighten as her co-workers prepared to leave for the weekend. "Go on get out of here!" It was only Thursday, but everyone had put in a lot of overtime this last month working on the marketing and promotions plan for the strategic alliance between Jaztec Inc. and FCC Foundations.

As the room emptied, Jovianna forced a smile through her troubled mind and wished everyone a happy weekend. She dragged herself back to her desk where she sat and stared at the three memos that were the source of her concern. One was a copy of an e-mail from Miguel Cameron, Jaztec Inc.'s Web Designer. It arrived in Jovianna's inbox at 11:30 a.m. that morning. In the e-mail he indicated why no one could get a hold of him; he had taken the overnight flight to Spain and would return in one week. The second memo was an e-mail from Tate Andrews, a Director for FCC Foundations' 2002–2003 Board of Directors. In her e-mail, Tate expressed her concerns about Miguel's lack of performance on the team (Exhibit A). The third memo was a fax to Jaztec Inc.'s CEO and Founder Jerome Blaze, which outlined a list of requests from two of FCC Foundations' staff members: Rachelle Ricardo, Executive Director of Marketing and Communications, and Kareena Gonsalves, Executive Director of Logistics and Planning. Rachelle and Kareena had sent this memo directly to Jovianna's boss Jerome, without Jovianna's knowledge (Exhibit B). Tomorrow afternoon Jerome was returning from Italy and had scheduled a meeting with Jovianna to discuss these three memos. Jovianna did not look forward to the meeting. She would not get much sleep tonight.

---

exhibit A E-mail from Tate Andrews to Jovianna Gucci

From: tateandrews@FCC.com
Sent: November 16, 2003
To: joviannagucci@jaztec.com
Subject: Miguel

Hello Jovianna, I am writing this email about Miguel's performance or lack of performance on our team. It is very obvious that he does not care about how his actions affect the rest of this team. I have been approached by many other FCC Foundation Directors who have been inquiring about this special project and I continue to say that it is going well. This is when they want to see progress and the only visual indicator of our progress at this point is the website. But, I am always hesitant to direct anyone to the site, because I do not know its condition.

I do not want to put another one of my team members down for he has confided in me about his personal affairs, but he is always late for meetings, that is if he decides to show up at all. I feel disappointed and discouraged because none of the other group members would ever think to be late or miss a meeting without a justifiable cause. We all take our commitment to this project very seriously and that is why he is letting us down.

If I were Miguel, I would want someone to approach me and tell me that my behaviour was unacceptable and clearly a violation of our established covenant. I feel very frustrated. I signed the same covenant as all the other team members—including Miguel—and I try to ensure that my behaviour follows each guideline.

I think that he needs to be held accountable for his actions and the covenant. There is no question that he is talented but his behaviour is not appropriate. I think that you need to address this issue before it really gets out of hand.

Best Regards,
Tate Andrews
Director, Board of Directors 2002–2003
FCC Foundations

JAZTEC INC. BACKGROUND

Jaztec Inc. is a small online firm that specializes in ergonomic consulting for small to medium sized organizations. Jaztec provides on-site and online workstation assessments. Their goal is to reduce serious computer related injuries in the workplace. Jaztec investigates employee computer workstations, as well as employee posture and positioning while at their workstations. They provide quick tips on how to avoid injury and strain to your arms, wrists, eyes, neck, back and shoulders and they also suggest correct positioning for monitors, keyboards, and surrounding office equipment. Through their equipment suppliers, they offer the latest ergonomically designed computer equipment products on their website. The majority of their clients were organizations looking to enhance productivity by reducing workplace injury through ergonomically designed equipment. Other clients were simply looking at ways of improving the effectiveness of their current equipment and used Jaztec's consulting services. In operation for less than three years Jaztec Inc. enjoyed profits of $2.1 million in their last fiscal year.

exhibit B Fax to Jerome Blaze

FCC Foundations

To:	Jerome Blaze	**Fax:**	
From:	Rachelle Ricardo, Executive Director of Communications and Marketing, FCC Foundations Kareena Gonsalves, Executive Director of Logistics and Planning, FCC Foundations	**Date:**	19/11/02
Re:	Strategic Alliance Committee	**Pages:**	1
CC:			

X Urgent ☐ For Review ☐ Please Comment ☐ Please Reply ☐ Please Recycle

Notes: Enclosed in this fax you will find a list of our needs from both Jovianna and the Strategic Alliance Committee. Implementing these changes is pivotal for the productive functioning of this team and for FCC to remain a part of this strategic alliance.

- Meeting agendas one week in advance to the hour of the scheduled start time of the meeting
- Agenda minutes to follow within eight hours of every meeting
- Weekly progress reports from each member of the team in order to quantitatively measure our success
- Daily website reports
- Miguel to be reprimanded and or removed from this team for his inadequate behaviour and disregard for other team members
- A more comfortable tone at the team meetings
- A tone where we are permitted to share our thoughts and are not criticized for doing so
- A leader that uses motivational techniques to stimulate the team
- A leader that appreciates our time and efforts for this project
- A leader that does not unnecessarily involve others into the team meetings
- A leader that does not take everything as a personal attack, and learns to separate herself from her position or steps down as the Team Leader
- Detailed reports of Jovianna's meetings with you about this project

THE INITIATIVE

About three months ago Jerome had proposed that Jaztec Inc. form a strategic alliance with FCC Foundations, a nonprofit organization that raises money and awareness about repetitive strain injury. Jerome thought that this initiative could benefit both organizations. Jerome thought that by revamping Jaztec's website, they could benefit both organizations. Currently, Jaztec's website allowed Jaztec's clients to purchase enhanced ergonomically designed computer equipment online and/or access Jaztec's consulting services. The new website would allow Jaztec's regular clients or unique web visitors to donate money to FCC Foundations, thereby supporting the Foundation's mission. The website would also expose Jaztec's services to FCC's client base.

After in-depth discussions with Nathan Gerron, founder of FCC Foundations, Jerome had assigned Jovianna to coordinate the strategic alliance and to ensure that the needs of both organizations were met. Jovianna was also responsible for drafting the marketing plan and aligning the operative goals and mission statements of both organizations. Jovianna rose to the occasion; she thought that it was a great idea. Not only would she be able to enhance her marketing skills, but she would also be able to develop her leadership skills as Team Leader of the strategic alliance committee. She was very excited; she could almost feel her career advancing as Jerome spoke to her about the project.

FCC FOUNDATIONS

FCC Foundations' mandate was to share information about musculoskeletal disorders (MSD) arising from extended computer usage. Nathan Gerron founded FCC Foundations seven years earlier at age 30. Nathan himself suffered from Thoracic Outlet Syndrome, a severe Cumulative Trauma Disorder (CTD), and was unable to continue with his computer engineering career. Specifically he suffered from repetitive motion disorder, a disorder of the musculoskeletal and nervous system caused and exacerbated by repetitive motions, awkward postures and positioning of the arms, wrist, neck, back and shoulders for extended periods of time.

FCC Foundations grew from a handful of employees in the late 1990s to its current size of over 40 employees in its central Canadian location. It also had small satellite offices in Baltimore and Dublin. Currently, Nathan was on the verge of expanding promotions to European markets. Nathan was a huge fan of Jaztec Inc. He avidly supported the alliance. He recognized the current trends of e-business and the importance of an online presence. FCC Foundations currently had no website. This alliance would create their online presence, and realize Nathan's ambition to increase awareness and ultimately eliminate computer related MSD worldwide. Although a full advocate of the strategic alliance, Nathan was preoccupied with strategizing his own global vision for FCC Foundations. Therefore, he entrusted Rachelle to make all final decisions.

THE STRATEGIC ALLIANCE COMMITTEE

Three staff members from FCC Foundations and two from Jaztec Inc. including Jovianna composed the Strategic Alliance Committee. The committee was responsible for the development of all marketing and promotions activities for the strategic alliance. However, Jerome would be in regular contact with Jovianna to ensure that his interests were protected and Jerome would finalize all decisions.

The team members included:

Jovianna Gucci—Team Leader, VP Marketing and PR, Jaztec Inc.

Miguel Cameron—Web Designer, Jaztec Inc.

Rachelle Ricardo—Executive Director of Communications and Marketing, FCC Foundations

Kareena Gonsalves—Executive Director of Logistics and Planning, FCC Foundations

Tate Andrews—Director, 2002–2003 Board of Directors FCC Foundations

Jovianna thought that a flexible leadership style, which had served her well in the past, would work well with this team. She knew that sometimes she would need to be participative and involve her team members in the decisions but she reserved the right to sometimes be more autocratic in her approach. Jovianna did not foresee many problems in this leadership style because she had been a member of many teams and as a result she understood that each group functioned differently according to the group dynamics. Based on her previous experiences, she felt strongly that she had a good idea of which types of leaders were effective and vice versa. She had also spent a lot of her time volunteering, so she understood the fundamental nature of a nonprofit organization. She knew even though these members were staff, their hearts were not a part of FCC Foundations because of their salary. It was most likely because of their desire to help others and for a cause that they felt passionate about. Jovianna was excited to work with this team because she thought that these team members would have a strong commitment to make the project succeed. She thought they would be agreeable and easy to work with.

THE FIRST TEAM MEETING

Jovianna spent the afternoon reading about FCC Foundations and tried to find information on each of her new team members. To her surprise she recognized two names from her university studies—Rachelle and Kareena. This was going to be great! Jovianna recalled that they were hard workers in university and strong members of a marketing group for an undergraduate marketing course. Since they had already built a working rapport, the transition from University peers to a corporate strategic planning team should be smooth and the team's productivity would increase with time. Jovianna arranged for the first meeting in the following week. To her surprise all members of the team were willing and able to meet with only one week's notice.

The following week Jovianna was anxious to meet her new team. She wanted to do a great job in order to prove to Jerome that she was capable of carrying out this project. As well it was a great experience for her career and would definitely help her advance at Jaztec Inc. Jovianna knew how valuable everyone's time was these days; no one ever seemed to have the patience to wait for anything. She wanted to set a serious and professional tone.

The meeting began right as scheduled at 10:30 a.m. She planned a small icebreaker, which included an introduction of each team member. The next agenda item was a brainstorming session for the affiliation of the two organizations.

The morning went well, however as the time drew closer to noon, Jovianna saw a slight split in the group. Both Kareena and Rachelle, the ones that she was most familiar with, interrupted the pace of the meeting on occasion to give voice to their extreme points of view. At one point Jovianna briefly mentioned restructuring Jaztec's mission statement as well as their organizational goals and objectives to include FCC Foundations. Jovianna had not even finished speaking when Rachelle boldly stated, "I don't think that is why we are here. FCC Foundations will not support us spending time brainstorming for the advancement of Jaztec!" Jovianna was caught off guard with this statement. Rachelle was obviously very comfortable speaking to her with such an aggressive tone.

Now Jovianna found herself defending Jaztec rather than making an effort to be patient and trying to understand these comments. "We are here to align our two organizations, and Jerome would like us to restructure Jaztec's mission statement to include FCC Foundations and clarify the new direction of Jaztec. This by no means implies that your organization is obligated to do the same. Or that we have to do it at this very moment. But it is important for everyone to understand the nature of this alliance."

A moment of brief silence filled the room following Jovianna's words until Kareena spoke. "I have to agree with Rachelle, we need to keep our focus on the project and not how to improve Jaztec." Jovianna was stunned. She needed to take a break from this situation and adjourned the team for lunch.

Jovianna was glad that she could stop to just breathe. She was heading towards the washroom when she overheard Tate speaking to Miguel.

"So how long did it take for Rachelle, Kareena and Jovianna to prepare for this meeting and the project?" Tate was inquiring about Rachelle, Kareena and Jovianna's professional past. Miguel was uncertain for this was his first time working with Jovianna.

"To my knowledge Jovianna has been working on this alone and today was the first time everyone met. This is the first time I have worked with Jovianna." Tate reacted with slight surprise.

"Wow, really? Then I am surprised that Jovianna is letting them speak to her that way. I would not let someone else lead my team. But on the other hand, I have never seen Rachelle and Kareena act like that before."

Jovianna quickly slipped into the washroom. Great! She thought. It was only the first meeting and she had already lost her credibility with Tate. Tate probably viewed her as a weak leader and a pushover. And she could not avoid the strange feeling that was developing in her stomach. She could not understand why Rachelle and Kareena had made such absurd and inappropriate comments throughout the morning. She was confused and upset because things were not going well. She knew this behaviour was not what would normally be expected for an initial group meeting. Usually everyone was more introverted and humble while they got to know each other, exhibiting behaviour similar to Tate's throughout the meeting, who only spoke when she had a good point to add to the discussion.

They reconvened shortly after lunch and to Jovianna's surprise, Rachelle and Kareena still continued to display their resistance towards her authority through both their body language and through their facial expressions. At times they even made comments under their breath while Jovianna was in mid sentence.

Since she was unable to focus her thoughts, Jovianna thought there was a possibility that she might be overanalyzing the situation so she brushed away her concerns and carried on with the meeting. The next agenda item was setting the goals of the team and developing the team's covenant (Exhibit C). Immediately Rachelle had a pained look on her face. Jovianna had a tough time trying to understand what was bothering her and wondered if there were some underlying issues. Again thinking that it was probably just because the first meeting had gone sour, Jovianna brushed aside her thoughts and proposed a meeting in the following week, to which Rachelle boldly responded, "What! I have a million things to do. Just because I agreed to this project doesn't mean that I am going to let it take over my life."

exhibit C Committee Covenant

We Value:

- Each other's opinions and ideas
- Each other's time and efforts
- Each other's unique personality and diverse skills
- Each other's decisions and bear no hard feelings for decisions made by the team
- Our responsibility and role on the team
- This opportunity to learn and grow as a person
- The dynamics of the team
- Our commitment and trust for one another
- Meetings that start on time and follow an agenda
- Open brainstorming sessions
- Timely feedback
- Up to date information and technology for the website
- A right to ask a member to resign from the team if they do not meet the established expectations

We will not tolerate:

- Meetings without agendas
- Team members that arrive late to meetings
- Disrespectful comments made to attack any member of the team
- Discussion killers
- Decisions made without consensus from the team
- Severe negative feedback or overly critical comments
- Inadequate performance
- Unethical behaviour that clearly contradicts the purpose of both organizations
- A leader who does not encourage and appreciate their team members
- Team members that withhold their personal concerns

Name: ______________________________

Signature: ______________________________

Title: ______________________________

Organization: ______________________________ Date: ______________

Jovianna was stunned; Rachelle's statement did not bode well for the group and immediately challenged Jovianna's Team Leader position. "Well, we all have to make some sacrifices to get this project done. Besides we don't have a lot of time." Jovianna then asked each person individually if they could meet the following week and everyone but Rachelle was willing to meet. Then all of a sudden Kareena was inflexible as well. However, since they would have quorum to make any necessary decisions, they decided to meet next week without the two, who reluctantly said they would try to stop by if possible.

FEEDBACK SESSION WITH JEROME

Jovianna sat outside Jerome's office mulling over her thoughts of her first team meeting. She was searching for the right words to explain her situation to Jerome. She wanted to sound capable of handling the team, but at the same time wanted to inform him of her uncooperative team members. Perhaps she needed Jerome to get involved and speak to the two ladies to make it clear to them that they needed to respect Jovianna's authority.

"Come on in Jovianna," Jerome's voice called from within his office. "So tell me all! How is the team coming along?"

Jovianna hesitated, knowing that Jerome would immediately know that something was bothering her. Jerome walked towards the back of his office to close the door.

"Jerome, I don't want you to think that I cannot handle this, but these two women, my university colleagues, are really making it hard for me to build a rapport with the rest of the team members." Jovianna avoided direct eye contact with Jerome. This sentence had sounded more professional when she rehearsed her comments in her head outside his office. She continued to fill him in, stating that they had brought the team to a standstill by mid morning. She continued to explain that the tone of the meeting had turned sour because of the attitudes of the two women and ultimately she was concerned that she would lose her credibility as the Team Leader.

"Oh come on Jovianna! This is childish!! I am sure that if you can handle large corporate clients you can handle this team. Fix the problem, and show me a marketing campaign!"

Jovianna left Jerome's office in a worse condition than when she had entered. She could not believe that she had even thought of asking Jerome to get involved. She was very glad that she had not mentioned it in their meeting. She was frustrated and could foresee a personal conflict developing between herself and Rachelle, and maybe even with Kareena. The source of the conflict still baffled her. Nothing catastrophic had happened in the two years since her university graduation and the formation of this team. She could not help but wonder if Rachelle was influencing Kareena to rebel against her authority. But why?

THE WEEKS TO FOLLOW

Jovianna's prediction was accurate; Rachelle and Kareena prevented a comfortable team setting from developing. Jovianna did not know what to do. She tried to run the team with a flexible leadership style—but it backfired; nobody took her seriously. She tried every approach she could but was always stymied. Last week she had finally resorted to involving Jerome. He came into one of the team meetings and spoke of his expectations for this project. He stressed his support of Jovianna as team leader and asked that each member show respect to Jovianna. He left saying that if anyone had any concerns or problems with this they could speak to him about it.

Jovianna thought the meeting with Jerome went well, but now Rachelle and Kareena would not even speak at team meetings. To make matters worse, an additional problem began to arise with Miguel. He clearly was not pulling his weight for the team. It was blatantly obvious that he was not showing up on time, that he did not really care to be at team meetings and his work was lacking in consistency to say the least. Jovianna would only be fooling herself if she thought that the rest of the team did not notice. Miguel told Jovianna about a personal situation that was interfering with his work and Jovianna tried to be as understanding as she could but at this point it was getting out of hand. She had approached him on several occasions to discuss his progress on the website. He would evade the questions and yet produce magnificent templates for the Web Pages when he felt he needed to. This was a great challenge for Jovianna. She knew that he loved his work, but did not care about the team's work ethic; it was his style to do his own work on his own time and on his own terms, which was not fair to the rest of the team or to the established team covenant. Jovianna's last resort was to change her approach and get to know Miguel as a person and not simply as a teammate. She knew that the others thought that he was a slacker because they did not see the templates that he created and at what frequency they were created.

Her evaluation of the situation was interrupted by a phone call from Rachelle who was asking if Jovianna had time to meet with herself and Kareena. This meeting needed to take place as soon as possible to discuss an important issue. Jovianna recognized the urgency and scheduled a meeting with the two in mid-week at 11:30 a.m. Rachelle's tone did not indicate a problem, yet Jovianna was still rather apprehensive. She knew that these two could not have decided to become active and cooperative team members overnight, especially after the rough weeks they had already put her through. However, to be courteous Jovianna asked if there was anything she could do to prepare for the meeting, to which Rachelle stated that there was not. She was told all she could do was bring herself. This served to calm Jovianna's nerves only slightly. She was a bit more relaxed; she suspected it was about Miguel's lack of commitment on the team.

THE MEETING

While on her way to meet her two team members, the numerous things on her "to do list" for the day ran through Jovianna's mind. She had finally set up an appointment with a very important European client with whom she needed to meet in less than two hours. This meeting was pivotal for Jaztec Inc., as it would set the pace for Jaztec's entry into the European and UK markets. She needed to meet with Rachelle and Kareena quickly in order to finalize her presentation for the afternoon's meeting.

Jovianna was not worried; she had already prepared a response in regards to Miguel's attitude towards the team. She knew exactly what to say to assure the two that she was aware of Miguel's performance and they were working together to improve his current situation. All she had to do was explain that she had sat down with Miguel on several occasions, that he had promised that he would make more of an effort to work with the team and within the covenant and maintain that she trusted all her team members. She realized that they did not know how much time and effort she was putting in with Miguel. Everything would be fine if it all went according to her schedule.

Jovianna entered a meeting room at FCC Foundations.

"Well, ladies, what can I help you with?" Before she could even sit down the two began with their concerns.

"I hate working with your organization...."

"I am not motivated to do anything ... you need to motivate me...."

"You are causing the failure of this alliance...."

"Your meetings are unstructured and useless; we feel they are a waste of our time...."

"We have tried and cannot conform to your leadership style...."

"We have studied motivational theory and this is not the correct leadership style to motivate a team...."

Jovianna grit her teeth. She was angry! She could not even tell from whom the words were coming. But in essence it didn't matter.

"Basically Jovianna, we are trying to be proactive and we will not allow you to screw up this alliance, our names are attached to it too. That is what we foresee if this operation continues under your direction."

Jovianna took a deep breath. "Ok...."

She was speechless. Their forceful manner made her feel extremely defensive. Their tone of voice and language was extremely tactless. She did not know what to think. What was she doing wrong? How much of this was true? Was it really that unbearable? Did the other two really feel the same way? Or were these ladies simply pulling them into the discussion to defeat her and magnify their own feelings? Was this their way of getting attention? Was Rachelle pulling Kareena along?

"Well, you know my philosophy, don't come to me with a problem, come to me with a solution. Help me to see what you are seeing." It was hard for Jovianna to be this positive and separate herself from her position, when somehow she knew it was a personal attack on her.

"Well first of all you are so unorganized Jovianna.... You are not motivating us, and we hate this project because of you. We want a more relaxed tone at the meetings. We didn't appreciate that you invited Jerome to our meeting to yell at us. You should be proud of your team and boast about their accomplishments, and not tell your boss to put them down. We give you all of our time and you take us for granted. We feel like we are prevented from speaking our minds, like we are robots."

Jovianna wanted to sink into her chair. She still could not believe that these words belonged to these highly successful women.

By this time it was quite late in the morning. Her time to finalize her afternoon presentation was now really limited.

"That is enough!" Jovianna screamed. "I don't want to hear another word of this rubbish! I have an important meeting to attend for which I have no time to prepare! I cannot waste any more of my time here!" Jovianna quickly gathered her belongings and rushed out the door.

JOVIANNA'S REFLECTIONS

That same Wednesday evening, Jovianna called her assistant Amelia.

"Who do they think they are? They are not in my position! They do not know how hard it is to manage people. Proactive?! How dare they say that this project is going down the tubes! I have worked my butt off for the last three years to get Jaztec where we are. I have been with this organization since it was a sketch on the back of a napkin! Jaztec's clients have more than doubled in the last year alone under my promotions and marketing plans. Besides we have been working on this alliance for a short while. Who are they to judge me? And our promotions committee is doing a fabulous job in increasing awareness; everyone has complemented me on the fantastic job the team has done this far. Any other Team Leader would never have this problem. No one would dare say these things to him or her. They would respect him or her and would never approach the situation in such a tasteless manner. It is clearly a personal attack against me. Just because they could joke around with me in university does not give them the right to treat me this way in the business world. How dare they!! I cannot believe they even spoke to me with such mean-spirited words. I would never approach Jerome in that manner! I know they are wrong!"

"Jovianna I don't know what to tell you, it is always challenging to establish yourself as a leader within a peer group and with individuals with whom you had previously been friends. But you know there are times to be autocratic and times to be more flexible."

The more Jovianna spoke of her situation the more she was convinced that Rachelle was dragging Kareena along to give her a hard time. She was probably slandering Jovianna behind her back and encouraging others to feel the same. She wished that she could just remove Rachelle from the team. But she knew that was not a viable option. It was already extremely personal between her and Rachelle. And it would just appear as if Jovianna was acting unprofessionally. Everyone knew that they were old friends and it would not do any good in terms of her image with the rest of her team. Jovianna was ready to quit this project. Where would she find the time to balance her efforts between Miguel, these two ladies and most importantly her job? She still felt that she had done the best that she could in this situation.

"What I need is a little respect around here. I am about to hand in my resignation. I don't need recognition, just a bit of respect. When I make a decision to cancel or call a meeting, my team should be willing to compromise, just conform! When I say that it is not feasible they should try to understand rather than continue to tell me I am wrong. When I am flexible everyone takes me for granted, when I toughen up I am too mean. What do they want from me?"

Jovianna sensed that a problem was brewing from the first meeting. She knew that there was something in the air between her and Rachelle but she didn't think that it would get this out of hand and even in hindsight she could not think of any way that she could have prevented it. Did everyone feel this way? There was no real way of knowing. And on top of everything one could not forget Miguel, who had flown to Spain without telling anyone.

THE PREDICAMENT

The next morning, Jovianna received a call from Amelia.

"I hope you are feeling better than last night, Jovianna. I am not sure if you want to hear this right now, but Kareena and Rachelle left an urgent message for Jerome last night. They have informed him that they met with you and said that you were unwilling to listen to any of their concerns or solutions. They said that they were appalled with your lack of professionalism in your meeting when you were rude to them and had insulted them. They were not sure if FCC Foundations wanted to be associated with such an unprofessional organization and they were on the verge of telling Nathan to pull out of the agreement. They were irate when you did not even consider their requests and are shocked at your style of leadership.

"Tate is also trying to get a hold of you. She left a couple of messages for you to check your e-mail. She really wants to talk to you about Miguel."

Jovianna had no more energy left. She felt that she knew more about Miguel's personal situation than her own life. She had met with him on many occasions to discuss his progress and even just to chat about his life. Jovianna had been both a professional and personal acquaintance with Miguel. But how could she and why must she prove it to the rest of the team? They did not see her spend endless hours with Miguel. And to make it worse he had always promised that he would make a conscious effort to be a part of the team and she had trusted him. He just never came through with his promise to commit to the team. How could he simply go to Spain after she defended him endlessly and gave him numerous opportunities to improve his working relationship within the team? How could he possibly justify leaving without telling anyone? Jovianna had bent over backwards trying to accommodate and motivate this team member, but regardless of her efforts she was still left with an unreliable team member. Had she been foolish in thinking that he would change his work behaviour?

JEROME'S WISHES

Jerome was faxing over the list of requests from Rachelle and Kareena. He insisted on an immediate meeting on Friday afternoon to address these issues, for which he would fly in from Florence, Italy. He explained to Jovianna that Rachelle and Kareena had insisted that their demands be met otherwise they were asking for Jovianna's resignation as the Team Leader.

Jovianna was horrified. How could they be asking her to resign? They were the uncooperative and difficult team members. She wasn't surprised when she received the fax that many of these requests had never arisen in their meeting. Was it because Jovianna had ended the meeting so abruptly? To make matters worse Jerome had also requested the latest revisions to Jaztec's website and was unaware that Miguel had left for Spain under her supervision.

case 9 Let's Get Together: A Student Group Assignment

In many management classes, students are required to work together on group assignments. This case describes four meetings of such a group. Readers may find themselves identifying with the experiences of the individuals described.

The first time that Dan, Lisa, Michelle, Paula, and Stavros met was at the conclusion of their second Management Systems class. They had been assigned together by their instructor to perform a critical analysis of the management philosophies at a local company with a view to providing recommendations for improvement. Their analysis was to be based largely on data from a case and their results were to be presented to the class. Their instructor suggested that some form of example or illustration of the problem as well as class discussion would help bring them a good grade. Furthermore, they were told that the presentation would be graded on an individual basis.

They had not known each other previously, so their first task was to introduce themselves. Following the introductions, Dan initiated a discussion about the requirements of their presentation, which was scheduled for four weeks later. He informed the other members of the group that his uncle had worked for the organization that they were studying, and would therefore be able to give him all the information they needed about its management practices. A few minutes into the discussion, Stavros scribbled his phone number on some paper and announced that he didn't have time to talk things over at the moment. After Stavros's abrupt exit, Michelle attempted to refocus the others' attention by reminding them that their instructor had urged them to start working on their project right away. Paula added that she felt they could all benefit from reading their textbook chapter on management philosophies, and offered to research the background of the company at the local library and through the internet. Lisa volunteered to go to the library with Paula, noting that it would be more fun to work as a team. This first meeting concluded with a tentative agreement to meet again the following week at the same time.

A week later, all of the group members except Dan met again at the student centre. The meeting started out with a spirited exchange on the previous night's hockey game between the Montreal Canadiens and the Edmonton Oilers. After a few minutes of hockey, Paula initiated a discussion about the presentation. Paula said that Dan had told her that his uncle probably couldn't help them after all because he had left the organisation under something of a cloud. Eventually the conversation drifted to the subject of presentation styles and a debate developed about the style the group should use. Stavros felt that the group should present a formal, serious, professional image to impress the instructor. Paula agreed that they should have a professional image, but also felt that some humour and lightheartedness would make the presentation more interesting to the class. Lisa said that she would go along with whatever the other group members decided while Michelle tried to prevent the others from getting into a heated argument. The discussion finally ended with Michelle saying that she would speak to their instructor and ask which presentation style was recommended. Paula then went on to show the others the information she and Lisa had researched at the library over the weekend. Lisa invited the group to meet at her house the following Saturday afternoon, offering to make popcorn and order a pizza. The others agreed, and so the second meeting was concluded.

All the group members were able to meet at Lisa's house the following Saturday. All, except Dan, had done the background reading and the group proceeded to discuss the content of the presentation. Michelle reported that the instructor had encouraged them to make the presentation interesting, adding that humour was fine as long as they didn't stray too far from the topic they were covering. She suggested that a short skit demonstrating some management philosophies in action might be a good way to conclude their presentation. Responding to Michelle, Dan suggested that they should actively involve the class with a participative exercise that he could introduce at the beginning of the presentation. Dan also pointed out that, with the presentation date only two weeks away, the group needed to give the go-ahead on his exercise as soon as possible.

After some discussion it was decided that Michelle would write up a short script for a skit, while Dan would prepare a class participation exercise. Paula and Lisa would write up the bulk of the information which needed to be relayed to the class, while Stavros would use his computer to make any handouts which were needed as well as a banner to hang at the front of the classroom. Conflicting points of view arose regarding the number of people who would be involved in the skits. However, this disagreement was quickly settled when Michelle pointed out that they were each being marked separately for their part in the presentation and the more each person did, the more material the instructor would have upon which to assess each of them. After settling a few more details, the group members agreed to meet again the following week to tie everything together.

At the fourth meeting, Stavros explained to the others that he had not been able to prepare any handouts because he had lost the folder that contained his rough notes. As he began collecting information from Lisa and Paula, Michelle distributed copies of the skit. After they read through it as a group, Dan described his participation exercise. A difficulty became apparent when they practised the exercise and realised that it would take close to 20 minutes to complete. Paula told Dan that, with the amount of information they were going to cover, there was no way they could devote half of their time to a class exercise. Dan argued that he had based the exercise on a past work situation and that he could not shorten it without taking away from its meaning and effect on the class. Lisa tried to help by suggesting that the class be divided into groups so they could work through different parts of the exercise simultaneously. Dan continued to react strongly, emphasising that he had spent a great deal of time preparing this part of the presentation and could not believe that all the others could do was criticise him. Michelle calmly tried to explain that, since they were each being marked separately, it was only fair that they all had approximately equal amounts of time to present. At this point, Dan told them that if they didn't want his help he wouldn't give it to them. With that, he stormed out of the student centre.

The others were silent for a few moments, somewhat shocked by Dan's performance. Eventually Michelle brought the group back to focus by saying that Dan would realise how self-centred he was being after he had had a chance to cool off. She suggested that it would be best if they continued to work out the details for the remainder of the presentation. The group wondered whether they would be able to work things out with Dan before their presentation day and they began to contemplate what they should do next and how they could resolve the situation.

WHAT NEXT?

Teamwork is an integral part of the working world and as such it is a skill that must be developed as soon as possible. Schools, and in particular business schools, often aim to develop these skills in their students, often in the manner illustrated in the above case. Readers may find that the problems experienced by Dan, Lisa, Michelle, Paula, and Stavros are all too familiar to ones that they have experienced. What can we learn from this?

In groups:

1. Imagine you are one of the other group members (but not Dan). What is your assessment of what has led to the current situation?
2. What should your group do now, given that Dan has stormed out? For example, should you: present as you are (without Dan), speak to the Professor and complain, or try to reason with Dan? What is the likelihood that you can put the group back together before presentation day?
3. How would your group resolve the situation? What specific action steps would you take?
4. What can we learn from the analysis of this type of group process?
5. How common and applicable is this example to the world of work? Have you had any similar experiences and how were they resolved?

case 10 Self-Managed Work Teams at South Australia Ambulance Service

Ray Main pondered the box of questionnaires received from the Ambulance Officers (AO's). Normally a 45% response rate would be a good response to a survey. But in 35 out of the 60 stations less than half of the AO's in the team responded. Without the input of more than half of their team members, he didn't feel he could provide representative feedback to the station teams.

Next Wednesday, the Empowerment Strategic Task Force was meeting to hear his report on the survey. He knew they would want recommendations regarding the next step in moving South Australian Ambulance Service (SAAS) to an empowerment culture.

SOUTH AUSTRALIAN AMBULANCE SERVICE

SAAS provides emergency paramedic and advanced life support services as well as routine ambulance transfers throughout the state of South Australia on a self-funding basis. The service is provided by 600 full and part-time staff and some 1100 volunteers in areas difficult to service. Emergency calls go to one of 4 communications centres who pass the message to one of 19 metro teams in Adelaide, to one of the 20 rural teams or to one of the 60–70 volunteer teams.

Until the late 1980's, SAAS was an integral part of St. John Ambulance Service (under the St. John Priory) and was staffed by both full time AO's and volunteers. Full time employees worked Mon–Fri from 9 a.m. to 5 p.m. Volunteers handled all evening and weekend work.

One manager described the old culture in strong terms:

> SAAS was a traditional, hierarchical organization with 9 managerial levels for approximately 650 employees and 1500 volunteers. We were very inward looking in our approach. It was lots of "jobs for the boys" and as long as you were obedient and followed orders you were ok.

A senior executive described SAAS as a "militaristic" organization with "an extreme number of levels: regional superintendent, assistant regional superintendent, regional director, assistant regional director, station officer, assistant station officer." Most decisions were made by 3 managers at the top of the organization who then had difficulty getting things implemented because of the powerful middle managers and station officers.

In 1989, a strike by the full time employees led to the professionalization of the service and the beginning of its separation from the St. John Ambulance Service. After the strike, the use of volunteers was minimized and full time employees operated the service 24 hours per day, seven days per week.[1] This change required an influx of several hundred new AO's and an increase in their professionalism and training. All full time AO's were now required to complete a three year program leading to a diploma through the TAFE college system.[2]

In 1992, a new CEO, Ian Pickering was appointed to re-organize the service and complete the separation of SAAS from the St. John Priory. His mandate was to improve the clinical expertise in SAAS and to make it the best ambulance service in Australia. Shifting the organization from the old military model to an empowerment one was a key part of his strategy to achieve excellence.

The South Australian Government passed legislation on 16 March 1993 changing the nature of SAAS. On 17 March 1993, Pickering restructured SAAS. Nine levels of management were reduced to 4. All middle and lower level managers were invited to apply for the new positions that were created but there were no job guarantees. Retirement packages were offered and many managers took them. The day lives in organizational memory as "the St. Patrick's Day Massacre."

At the same time, all employees were organized into the teams mentioned earlier, 19 metro AO teams, 20 rural AO teams, 20 support staff teams and 60-plus volunteer teams. (See Exhibit 1 for a partial organization chart.) The team leader positions often went to younger, better qualified and newer employees,[3] since many older employees needed to retrain in order to be qualified for team leader positions.

In 1993 a strategic plan was developed. As one manager put it, "It was the first time we asked ourselves, 'What was our mission? Why are we here?' Never before had we defined patient service (as opposed to patient care)."

This strategic plan was reworked in 1995 (see Exhibit 2 for a summary of the vision, mission, key objectives and major strategies). The plan included a commitment to "an empowered and accountable workforce." Seven cross-functional project teams were established to help implement the strategic plan: theWorkforce Empowerment Team, the Workforce Development Team, the Information Technology Team, the Commercial Team, the Structure Team, the Volunteer Team and the Business Development Team. Chris Lemmer, Regional Director (Metro) headed the Workforce Empowerment Team with Ray Main seconded full time as project coordinator.

By 1997, SAAS had changed significantly. Paramedic courses had been run for the first time and 35 AO's had received this higher level qualification. An Advanced

[1] Full time employees provided ambulance services except for difficult to serve rural areas. South Australia has vast areas of outback with few people. Providing service to these areas is costly.

[2] TAFE is a community college system.

[3] One senior manager speculated that the really good AO's did not apply for the team leader position initially because they wanted to become paramedics first.

Life Support qualification had been developed as an intermediate step between basic AO training and paramedic training and many AO's had completed this qualification. Clinical performance improved dramatically. Survival statistics for ventricular fibrillation arrest, for example, improved from 4.1% in 1994 to 26% in 1997. Performance measures can be found in Exhibit 3.

The 1995–96 Annual Report stated that "a restricted patient transport licence was granted to another patient transport service" for non-emergency ambulance transfers, introducing a competitive threat to SAAS. The St. John Priory continued to withdraw its links with SAAS. And a new amalgamation with the SA Metropolitan Fire Service was under way.

THE JOB OF THE AMBULANCE OFFICER

Two ambulance officers were assigned to each vehicle. In the Metro area, most stations had two emergency vehicles plus one or two routine transfer vehicles. Each station had kitchen facilities, a lounge, sleeping areas for night shifts and exercise rooms. When an AO began his/her shift, assuming the previous crew was in the station, they would ensure that the vehicle was ready for a call. A lengthy, detailed list of supplies had to be checked. Materials used had to be replaced.

A typical Metro morning shift is described in Table 1.

Getting to a call was considered urgent and was carried out at speeds up to 100 kph. On arrival, AO's unloaded the emergency equipment (in the cases above,

table 1 A Typical Morning Shift for a Metro AO Team

0800	Arrival
0800–0830	Checking and restocking vehicle
0830–0840	Relaxation
0840	Communications moves the vehicle to a central location in the service area
0840–0900	Wait at location
0900 (approx)	"Shortness of breath" call
0900–1030	Travel at high speed to call, attend patient, take patient to hospital
1030–1100	Travel to SAAS workshop to have air conditioning switch replaced
1100–1215	Assist a second AO team in a pick up
1215–1245	Return to station, quick lunch
1245	"Fainting patient" call
1245–1400	Travel at high speed to call, attend patient, take patient to hospital
1400.....	Continue

oxygen and an electro-cardiograph and stretcher) and entered the house. One AO took the lead in each case, making decisions on the immediate response demanded by the patient's condition (e.g. if blood pressure was down, should a saline drip be attached?).

AO's prided themselves in their clinical skills. They had developed sophisticated medical protocols to assist in the diagnosis and were skilled in asking relevant questions about the individual's medical history. Paramedics had 8 or 9 drugs at their disposal to help deal with cardiac patients where speed was essential. As one paramedic described, "we can do everything an emergency room can, only we do it sooner. If we can't help the patient, they won't survive."

While AO's were trained to present themselves as confident professionals to reassure anxious patients and relatives, they were also able to listen closely to the patient and any others present to understand the circumstances of the patient's difficulty in order to improve their diagnosis. Often, prior to any treatment, the AO would carefully explain what they were going to do and its consequences. For example, if an AO was attaching a saline drip she would state why she was doing this ("With your blood pressure a little low, you need some fluids and we are just going to give you some"). She would describe what to expect and the consequences of her actions ("I need to inject this needle. It will hurt but only for a moment. By giving you fluids, it will help your blood pressure and you won't feel so dizzy").

Friday evenings and holiday weekends were often the most stressful times to be an AO. Major car accidents occurred and some family disputes became violent. AO's then dealt with people with severe injuries. In car crashes, extraction of the injured could be a problem. In family disputes, violence could continue during their intervention. SAAS had counsellors available to help AO's deal with the trauma they faced.

AO's had complained for years that they dealt with emergency situations, made life saving decisions and could commandeer thousands of dollars of equipment (including helicopters) in an emergency, but couldn't order a shirt for themselves if one was ripped. Someone "in authority" had to authorize it.

By 1997, SAAS had evolved a customer service orientation. Its definition of success went beyond the survival rate of its patient to include thoughtful treatment of relatives, effective relations with hospital medical staff, and considerate patient care. In terms of emergency services, the aim was to have "a patient ready for ongoing treatment delivered in the best possible condition with accurate information about the patient's health." Exhibit 4 shows the cause and effect chart leading to having a patient ready for ongoing treatment.

Key performance indicators were developed with success measures for each of the indicators as shown in Table 2.

THE EVOLUTION OF TEAM MANAGEMENT

A key component of the strategy articulated for SAAS was an empowered workforce. Pickering changed the structure of the organization as one of his first and one of his most dramatic moves. The transition to team management was sudden and the organization was not fully prepared. As one manager put it, "the catchword was empowerment. We didn't know what it meant but we told everyone."

Ian Pickering articulated the reasons for team management in an address to a community group. One enthusiastic supporter stated, "Team is the only way I will

table 2 Key Performance Indicators and Success Measures

Key Performance Indicator	Measurement	Method of Measurement
Patient Ready for Ongoing Treatment	Patient condition on delivery Accuracy of information to hospital	Monthly sample of cases by peer audit and hospital feedback Monthly sample of cases by peer audit and hospital feedback
Timeliness	Time from emergency call to arrival at hospital Delay in meeting Ambulance Transport Service commitments	Response time + scene time + transport time for each trip Contracted time minus actual time for each trip
Communication with Patients	Communication with Patients	Sample of cases by patient and hospital feedback on interpersonal skills, etc.
Cost	Cost Relative to Best Practice	Monthly figures from each department
Revenue	Revenue	Monthly revenue
Preparedness for Disasters	Preparedness for Disasters	Rolling 3 monthly survey to rate staff knowledge of roles and availability of equipment and supplies
Community Awareness	Community Confidence Rating	Annual community survey
Staff satisfaction	Employee Satisfaction	Rating Annual survey of staff and volunteers

survive. One peer of mine is looking so old. He does things I just won't. For example, he drove hundreds of miles just to discipline a person, to tell them off. My aim is to be an invisible manager, to influence, and to be a facilitator and let the teams do their own thing. It seems to be working as I spend most of my time educating, encouraging and modeling."

In the Metro area, teams had 10–13 members, organized by stations. Some larger stations had two teams of 10–13 members each. The rationale for this was that it took that many people to operate two ambulance teams 24 hours per day, seven days per week, including as well, time off for vacation, illness, training and other absences. Because of the shift schedule it was very difficult for Metro teams to meet. As one AO put it, "We suffer from a tyranny of roster that prevents us from really forming and acting as a team." (See Exhibit 5 for an example roster rotation.)

Country AO's on the other hand had considerable time together. Calls were not as frequent. As one manager described it, "if someone wants to study and learn, then they should come to the country as there is lots of time if you use it. I got books and a laptop and began to improve myself."

Several teams "raced ahead" in acting as empowered teams and then became frustrated when they couldn't operate as they felt appropriate. For example, one team immediately decided to assign team members all the responsibilities previously held by the station officer. The team met and made decisions and individual team members carried them out. Unfortunately, SAAS organizational systems were not prepared for this and team members were refused service or stores because they did not have the correct authorizing signature.

Another team decided to do away with the team leader (TL). As one would expect, leaders emerged anyway. Interpersonal issues arose that the team couldn't resolve. Factions developed and the team couldn't handle these resulting conflicts. As well, health and safety regulations require an individual with formal responsibility for these areas—assigning the responsibility to the "team" was illegal.

Other teams decided to choose their team leaders by voting. It became a popularity contest. One team dismissed their team leader because "they didn't like him." In this case, the union played a significant role in reconciliation. They asked the team how they would feel if management dismissed one of them because they didn't like that person. In this case, the TL did resign—he felt he could not be effective without the support of the team. But the union intervention was critical in increasing the employees' understanding of the responsibilities that went with empowerment.

Bernie Morellini, the Staff Development Officer, held workshops on the concepts of empowerment and quality management. In these two-day workshops, teams developed vision and mission statements and began identifying key objectives for their team. (See Exhibit 6 for an example team vision-mission-values statement.) While these seminars were greeted with enthusiasm, AO's often left them uncertain about exactly how to translate these ideas into their operations. Who had what authority remained unclear.

Nevertheless, SAAS developed increasing confidence in itself with the introduction of paramedics. It had taken considerable skill on Pickering's part to convince the Medical Advisory Committee to accept the need for and usefulness of paramedics.

A major marketing campaign was created to announce the change in SAAS. The launch was at the Adelaide Festival Theatre with major television coverage. Uniforms were redone, ambulance vehicles repainted, all to symbolize the change to more professional empowered services. Unfortunately, changes at the political level prevented the complete implementation of the plans. This failure encouraged the cynics who "had seen change attempts before and nothing really would happen."

Teams improved their clinical practices with the introduction of a case card audit.[4] The case review process protected AO's from individual liability. It was assumed that the AO's did the best that was possible under the circumstances.

PROGRESS TOWARD SELF MANAGEMENT ACROSS SAAS TEAMS

The progress toward self-management varied considerably across teams. Summaries of interviews with three teams are given below.

---

[4]A case card audit is a review of the write up (the card) of each case dealt with by the Service. That is, after each call, a case card describing the situation and what was done is produced. The audit is a team review of these cards in order to learn and improve.

Team Hodgson[5]

Team Hodgson declared that "the team is us."

In the first year our team had some personnel problems. The Team Leader was a nice guy but he didn't seem to be working for the team. He expected us to come up with concepts and when we did he would say "that's a silly idea." Or when we brainstormed, he would say "That's not going to work!" There were some personal issues as well. He kept an "I'm all right, Jack" attitude when it wasn't. For example he would do all the administrative work without help. He would be in here until all hours of the night working. And even then, the paperwork didn't get done on time. He would ask our opinion and then change things. He and one of the other team members started annoying each other and this put this team member under a lot of pressure. Finally, this team member couldn't handle being questioned and he would start yelling at other team members and demanding details of any calls. We weren't sure what was going on until after the TL had left. We were too close to the situation.

Once the TL had left, there was a bit of a vacuum. We decided to take a step "back" and we had 3 team meetings. During them we were spending too much time on "in house" activities and not enough on developing the team. We spent a lot of time on maintenance activities—who is going to clean up the station; sheets aren't being signed like they are supposed to.

The person who was in a dispute with the TL has been much better since the TL left.

Finally, we got rid of the station running stuff and moved on to learning and improving. But there were no measures for each thing we were doing so we drew up our practices manual and focussed on three areas: human factors, customer service and cost. We have to revamp this now as only a few of us were here when the original planning was done.

The process started when we had a day session with Bernie. This got us going but we needed another day to really put together some plans. We realized that if we want something we have to cost it and put a proposal together. If we want a training day per month, we have to show how it helps and how to get it done. If a member wants time off, we decide. Soon we will have the training plan for next year finalized. We will have it finished by the end of the year.

We wrote our station work practice manual so it contained a statement of team focus, a vision, mission statement, guiding principles and values and key objectives in the three critical areas. (See Exhibit 7 for the set of clinical care objectives.)

Team Boulder

The idea and concept is good but getting there could have been better. Two years ago they started the team concept. We thought it was "about time" as we had hinted long ago we shouldn't have a boss. We were all sort of lost when teams started. We were told to document what we did, make up the rules. So, we said "ok" and began meeting once each week. Perhaps we needed more education to make the transition easier.

There was some attempt to educate us. Each centre sent 1 person to a course. But by the time he got back, the message was confused. Most AO's had been here a long time and were confused by what was taught.

---

[5]All team names are fictitious.

We are starting with our own mission and vision and standard operating practices. We are starting to make our own rules. It used to be a computer would arrive and we would wonder "why and when." Now we talk about what we need and put it in a budget. Before, the attitude was we don't care where money went as long as I get paid. Now we are accountable for budgets. So if we put a hole in the wall we have to pay for fixing it. We are allowed to talk to DM's as humans and get respect.

We meet monthly or every 6 weeks or so. We put the holiday list up and get input. This year we got joint input on the budget. Next year individuals will do sub budgets.

Next year we will really have a clear picture of the team concept and fully understand it and be comfortable operating as a self directed team. Sometimes we lacked confidence and expected to get a "no." Instead, we were asked "what took you so long to ask?"

We worry about vehicle maintenance as a team. The usage of the station is our responsibility and we get others to use it. We have set our vision and mission and now we are just working on how to specify objectives and how to achieve them.

I'm sure that we can become pace setters.

Team Crossover

We always ran as a team. The old Station Officer (SO) discussed things with us and we had input. When the SO went away, one of the team got to see the administrative work he did. Now we all see some of it and get a bigger picture. Now there is more input.

At our team meetings, we solve problems. For example we had a communications problem in the region and decided the best solution was a satellite phone (which wasn't budgeted for). So at the team meeting we figured out how to get support and raised $3000 of the $4200 cost.

We work on documenting our procedures. This gives us a benchmark against which we can improve our practice. We create graphs and track our performance. Work practices have been developed for 32 of our procedures. Other teams have asked for copies but we have refused. If they just took ours, they wouldn't own them. You can see on the wall our system for duty roster. We organize it by week with a list of responsibilities for each job which have to be done and the person checks them off when they are done.

We are concerned as we have just had two new members added to our team and we need to figure out how to include them in the team. We aren't certain how comfortable the new members are with the team concept. We sure hope that we get along as well as previously. We need to make certain that we don't assume too much. We have planned a team building day where we will get to know one another and then we can discuss how we want to operate. Only after all this will we look at the 32 work practices to see if changes should be made.

We think we can handle most things. We did have to get help with a team dispute that got out of hand—but we did try our procedures first. We do most things. We develop and implement our own training program. Our budget is zero based and we spend a lot of time figuring out what we need and how that should be budgeted for. For example, we figure out how much to budget for tires based on the condition of the tires—head office could never figure that out.

Team Carleton

> We are not sure what we are supposed to do with this team management stuff. We think we do a good job as AO's—our clinical performance is excellent, we think. And that's what our job is.
>
> We are on the road most of the time responding to calls. That keeps us busy. I don't know what they expect us to do—come in on our days off to build a team with people I never see from one week to the next? Most of the guys don't want to do that. And how will the Ambulance Transport Service AO's fit in? They don't even do the same job that we do.
>
> We are out there dealing with people who need our help. I find that by the time I am finished my shift—particularly if it is a Friday night, I just want to leave this place and escape. Some of the things we have to deal with are pretty gruesome and I want to get out of here. The last thing I need is to spend time talking about something that isn't important.
>
> If it will affect our clinical practice then we should be trained properly. If it isn't part of our clinical practice, why are we doing it?
>
> They tell us to manage our own budget but there's nothing in there that helps pay for overtime so we can meet. If we wanted to get together as a full team, we would have to ask for money for it and it's not worth it.

THE ROLE OF THE TEAM LEADER

As was mentioned earlier, many team leaders were uncertain of their role. Some team leaders became adept at talking team and empowerment language but not doing it. AO's were used to making decisions on the spot and continued doing so as team leader. Old autocratic habits died hard, particularly when a station officer switched roles and became a team leader. In one team, the station officer had been particularly dominant. That person continues that behaviour. The team continues to look at him and ask, "Is this ok?" even though there was encouragement for the team to take responsibility.

One station officer who became team leader completely reversed his style. He wouldn't do anything without team input. This slowed all decisions and frustrated the AO's. He believed that everyone had to be "nice" to each other and agreeable. It took a while before he realized that teams and team leadership didn't mean being nice, rather it meant using teams and team skills to improve service.

Another team leader saw his role as being a facilitator and providing guidance when a team needed it. If the team has a problem, the team leader helps them to solve it rather than solve it for them. He describes his role as follows: "Often, I present the team with new and different alternatives to broaden their thinking. Or I ask some questions to get them to consider aspects of an issue that I think they haven't covered. Much of my role is ensuring I learn and then pass that on to the team. So I have been taking courses and have taught them about Pareto charts, fishbone analysis and PDCA (plan, do, check, act). This gives them the tools to improve their own performance.

A more typical response was simple confusion over the team leader role. One team leader commented, "I had little experience and education about working in a team. And there doesn't seem to be any support for me when I need help. I know the vision and what we were trying to do, but I don't feel I have the tools to get there. I think some team leaders have no idea whether they are doing well or not—they have nothing to refer to."

One team leader questioned how he was to operate. "I can't get my team together because of the shifts we are on. How can I get team decisions? My guys want to do good AO work and they aren't certain how this empowerment stuff fits in. Finally, I just rented a hall and had everyone come to a session where we talked about team issues. I just sent them (management) the bill and said, 'pay it.' "

One team leader went to a team referred to as "Jurassic Park" because the AO's had been there so long. Many of the misfits had gravitated to this team and most managers predicted this individual would not be able to make things work at that location. However, he listened and got stuff done. He convinced the team to be patient for changes and always explained why he was doing things.

This team leader was frustrated enough to summarize his feelings in a memo to AO's in March 1996:

> The honeymoon is over!! Team members feel that the Team Concept is failing—dismally. Team members believe that the new Clinical Team Leaders are Station Officers with a new title. The team does not believe they are empowered to make any Team based decisions.... Empowerment implies ownership. Ownership implies responsibility. Responsibility implies that there is no one else to blame. If the Team accepts empowerment, they also accept the responsibility.
>
> How does my Team become empowered?
>
> Team meetings will be held with the District Manager and Clinical Team Leader. The purpose of these meetings is to establish what Station activities the Teams are willing to take responsibility for. Once these areas are identified the Team and Team members are locked into a commitment to ensure that those tasks are undertaken.... It should be noted that Teams will not be forced to accept responsibility if they so desire.... As stated previously, having items such as time sheets and leave approvals signed by the Clinical Team Leader is somewhat questionable. Under the Team Empowerment concept these and many other tasks would become the responsibility of the Team. This would allow the Clinical team Leader to perform the function that they were employed to do—that is, facilitate the training requirements as identified by the Teams and to provide clinical support.

THE WORK-FORCE EMPOWERMENT IMPLEMENTATION TEAM

This cross-functional team headed by Chris Lemmer, Metro Regional Director, was created as a result of the strategic planning sessions in 1995. Members had been chosen because of their expertise and their interest in the project. Nine people were on the team, representatives from all key areas of the organization (2 team leaders from operations, 2 district managers, a rep from the training college, from the communications team, from the workshop and from administration). Initially, the team met bi-weekly. Now with the survey being tabulated, it had been about 2 months since the last meeting. At each strategic planning review, each task force team has to report on its progress.

The Work-force Empowerment Implementation Team stated its mission as: "We are committed to the development of systems, processes and resources to enable work-teams to become self-managed."

The task force believed that the first stage in moving to an empowered culture was the structure change that had occurred. The second stage entailed teaching the work-force about "empowerment." In order to develop a "base line" for the change, the workforce survey was developed. Exhibit 8 shows a sample feedback sheet that could be made available to the teams.

The Implementation Team believed that an education program for team leaders and then teams was necessary. The workforce survey would provide information to assist the design of an education package and would enable a "re-measurement" after training in order to judge the progress toward self managed teams.

Ray Main, as mentioned earlier, had been seconded to the Team as Project Coordinator for two years. His responsibilities included developing and implementing the programme of education mentioned above, in concert with the Implementation Team. A preliminary allocation of $165,000 for the 1997 year had been set up to support the Implementation Team's activities.

RAY MAIN'S DILEMMA

As a previous team leader, Ray had been frustrated by the apparent lack of systems and support for the move to an empowered culture. Now he was in a position to create that support. But where to begin? Should he work with the teams that want to evolve as a team and help them develop plans? What should be done about the teams who have ineffective team leaders? Should that be the district manager's or the regional manager's responsibility? How can the Metro teams be helped when they can't even meet?

As he sat there, he pulled the pile of surveys over and wondered how these could be best used.

List of Exhibits

1. Partial Organization Chart SAAS
2. Strategic Plan Summary 1996–2000
3. Performance Measures for SAAS
4. Cause–Effect Chart for "Patient Ready for Ongoing Treatment"
5. Example Shift Rotation Roster for a Metro Team
6. Example Vision-Mission-Goals for a Team
7. Team A Clinical Care Objectives
8. Sample Feedback Sheet for Team on 13 Dimensions Compared to SAAS

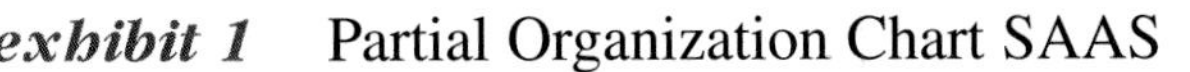

exhibit 1 Partial Organization Chart SAAS

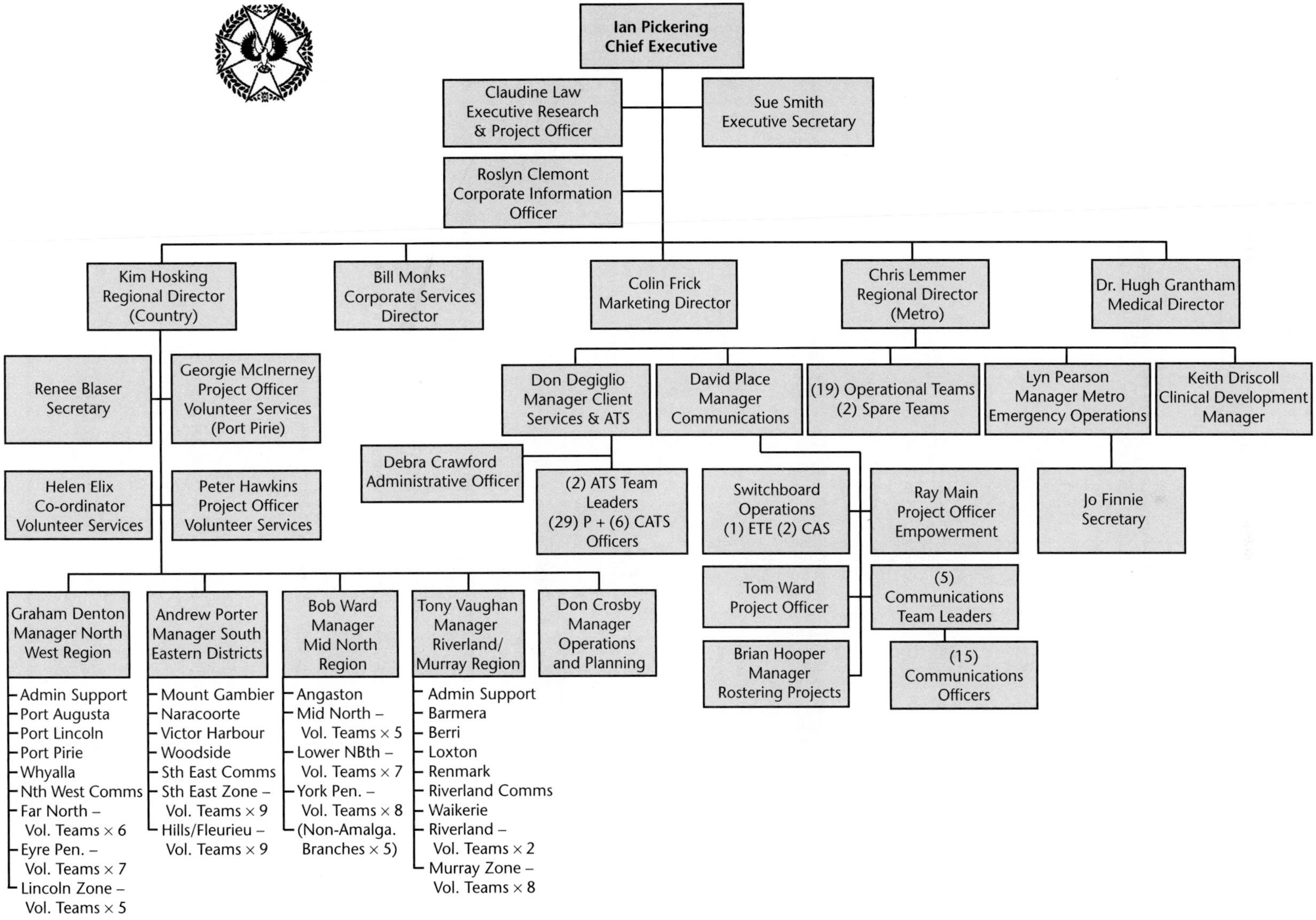

Ian Pickering
Chief Executive

Claudine Law
Executive Research
& Project Officer

Sue Smith
Executive Secretary

Roslyn Clemont
Corporate Information
Officer

Kim Hosking
Regional Director
(Country)

Bill Monks
Corporate Services
Director

Colin Frick
Marketing Director

Chris Lemmer
Regional Director
(Metro)

Dr. Hugh Grantham
Medical Director

Renee Blaser
Secretary

Georgie McInerney
Project Officer
Volunteer Services
(Port Pirie)

Helen Elix
Co-ordinator
Volunteer Services

Peter Hawkins
Project Officer
Volunteer Services

Graham Denton
Manager North
West Region
- Admin Support
- Port Augusta
- Port Lincoln
- Port Pirie
- Whyalla
- Nth West Comms
- Far North – Vol. Teams × 6
- Eyre Pen. – Vol. Teams × 7
- Lincoln Zone – Vol. Teams × 5

Andrew Porter
Manager South
Eastern Districts
- Mount Gambier
- Naracoorte
- Victor Harbour
- Woodside
- Sth East Comms
- Sth East Zone – Vol. Teams × 9
- Hills/Fleurieu – Vol. Teams × 9

Bob Ward
Manager
Mid North
Region
- Angaston
- Mid North – Vol. Teams × 5
- Lower NBth – Vol. Teams × 7
- York Pen. – Vol. Teams × 8
- (Non-Amalga. Branches × 5)

Tony Vaughan
Manager
Riverland/
Murray Region
- Admin Support
- Barmera
- Berri
- Loxton
- Renmark
- Riverland Comms
- Waikerie
- Riverland – Vol. Teams × 2
- Murray Zone – Vol. Teams × 8

Don Crosby
Manager
Operations
and Planning

Don Degiglio
Manager Client
Services & ATS

Debra Crawford
Administrative Officer

(2) ATS Team
Leaders
(29) P + (6) CATS
Officers

David Place
Manager
Communications

Switchboard
Operations
(1) ETE (2) CAS

Tom Ward
Project Officer

Brian Hooper
Manager
Rostering Projects

Ray Main
Project Officer
Empowerment

(5)
Communications
Team Leaders

(15)
Communications
Officers

(19) Operational Teams
(2) Spare Teams

Lyn Pearson
Manager Metro
Emergency Operations

Jo Finnie
Secretary

Keith Driscoll
Clinical Development
Manager

exhibit 2 SA Ambulance Service—Strategic Plan Summary 1996 to 2000

Vision

Our aim is to provide the best Ambulance Service in the Asia Pacific region and maintain this position into the 21st century.

Mission

The SA Ambulance Service is committed to the provision of total quality clinical care and transportation of patients.

Guiding Principles and Values

We will be focussed and responsive to the needs of our patients and customers in both clinical and commercial terms.

In all things we do will maintain our leadership and expert status on all pre-hospital patient care matters and be recognised as the best by both our peers and the community.

We will be innovative in our approach to business and strive to add value to the services we provide to our patients and clients.

Implementation

The implementation of our plan depends on all of us. Implementation is being carried forward by seven project teams.

Workforce
Structure
Volunteers
Diversification
Information Technology
Commercial
Structured Communications

The teams are implementing our Strategic Plan, using Continuous Quality Improvement principles, bringing together the results of our detailed organisational assessment.

Key Objectives

We will have an empowered and accountable workforce (that is committed to achieving the vision).

We will ensure our selection, placement, competencies and personal development of staff matches the challenges facing the organisation.

We will support our volunteer ambulance services in all aspects of the business.

We will investigate issues associated with the withdrawal of St. John Priory and amalgamation with the Metropolitan Fire Service.

We will implement structural changes associated with amalgamation with the Metropolitan Fire Service being cognisant of cultural issues.

We will have IT systems to support our new structure and processes.

We will have a cost effective service.

We will effectively manage our assets – replace, maintain, upgrade.

We will have a well informed public and staff.

We will retain and expand existing revenue generation.

We will establish a Trust for securing funding of development initiatives.

We will diversify our business.

continued

exhibit 2 SA Ambulance Service—Strategic Plan Summary 1996 to 2000 (*continued*)

Major Strategies

Creating an understanding and commitment to the team concept which will include processes for staff awareness and staff development. Identifying and implementing the most appropriate structure to support and enable teams and to define relevant roles and responsibilities.

Identifying the competencies and/or educational requirements of all positions within the structure identified in the empowerment review.

In cooperation with teams, overcome obstacles that restrict the development of team performance.

Reviewing selection and promotion procedures.

Creating an awareness of the state-side Ambulance Service which incorporates career and volunteer staff.

Creating an awareness of the value of volunteers to the organisation.

Linking the Country Volunteer structure to the empowerment goal as part of our workforce objective.

Ensuring that all strategic objectives apply to country volunteer systems.

Researching and developing an understanding of relevant legislation including the Ambulance and South Australian Metropolitan Fire Service Acts.

Define and recommend to the Minister for Emergency Services and Ambulance Board our future status.

Developing an understanding of each other's culture.

Preserving our identity and promoting our culture.

Including amalgamation in Enterprise Bargaining negotiations.

Developing, understanding, actively lobbying and promoting the service needs and timetables for Whole of Government initiatives.

Resourcing and supporting the IT plan.

Ensuring the IT plan is updated to meet any new objectives.

Developing business units to perform within a commercial environment.

Training leaders in business issues.

Developing an asset management policy (cognisant of the SA Government Strategic Asset Management Plan).

Recommending to Government, asset strategies that support the best interest of the Service.

Optimising the location of our assets.

Reviewing and improving our internal communication systems.

Obtaining commitment from the Executive and the Ambulance Board to continue to fund commercially justifiable marketing initiatives.

Developing product specific marketing.

Obtaining government funding commitment for 5 years.

Identifying specific areas in SAAS for the responsible allocation of cost savings in a timely manner.

Advising the Minister for Emergency Services and Ambulance Board of the most commercially viable fee rates.

continued

exhibit 2 SA. Ambulance Service—Strategic Plan 1996 to 2000 (*continued*)

By setting up a Trust structure.
Developing guidelines for funding of development initiatives.

Financing a Research and Development Study of market opportunities.
Developing an action plan based on outcomes of study.
Implementing a business development plan.

exhibit 3 SA Ambulance Service—Performance Measures

Ambulance Response to Patients by Priority

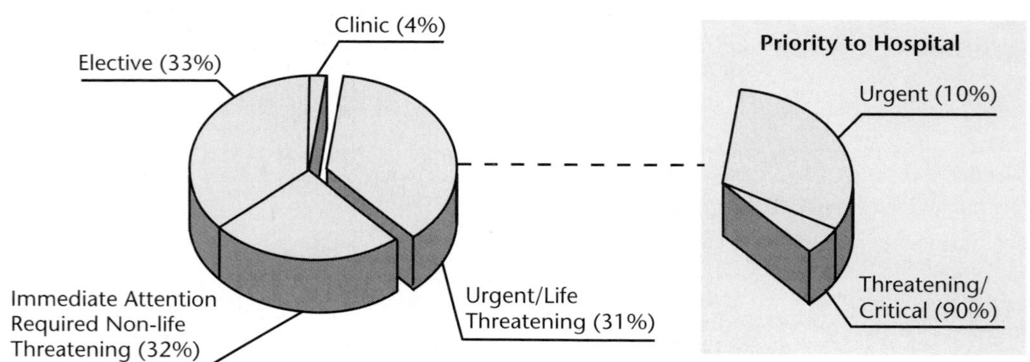

Number of Staff Employed

Ambulance Operations (72.5%)
Communications (6%)
Operational Administration (4.2%)
Directors (1%)
Logistics (4%)
Administration and Clerical (12.3%)

Career Staff (Executive)

Number	Gender	Basis
6	M	4-contract 2-permanent

Ambulance Cover Members

Year	Number
1995	147 735
1996	161 590

exhibit 3 SA Ambulance Service—Performance Measures (*continued*)

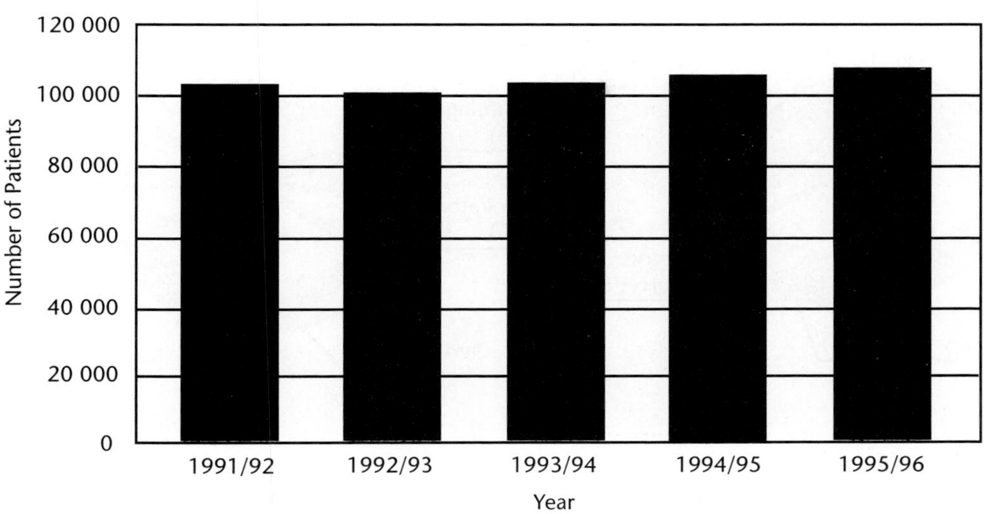

Priority One Response Times

Criteria

Metropolitan:
- 50% responded to within 7 minutes
- 95% responded to within 14 minutes

Country:
- 50% responded to within 8 minutes
- 95% responded to within 18 minutes

Performance

SA Ambulance Service's performance is as follows:

Metropolitan:
- 50% of cases are responded to within 7.62 minutes
- 95% of cases are responded to within 13.88 minutes

Country:
- 50% of cases are responded to within 5.45 minutes
- 95% of cases are responded to within 22 minutes*

* Country performance figures are influenced by a few very long distance transports

exhibit 3 SA Ambulance Service—Performance Measures (*continued*)

Patients Transported by Region

Metropolitan (78%)
Country Volunteer (7%)
Country Paid (15%)

Emergency Casetypes

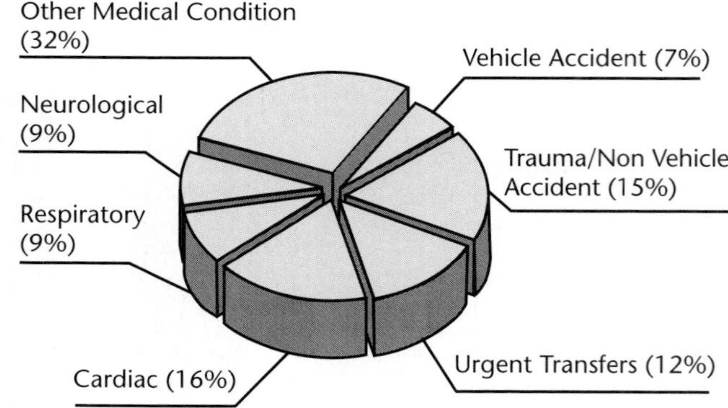

Revenue 1995-96

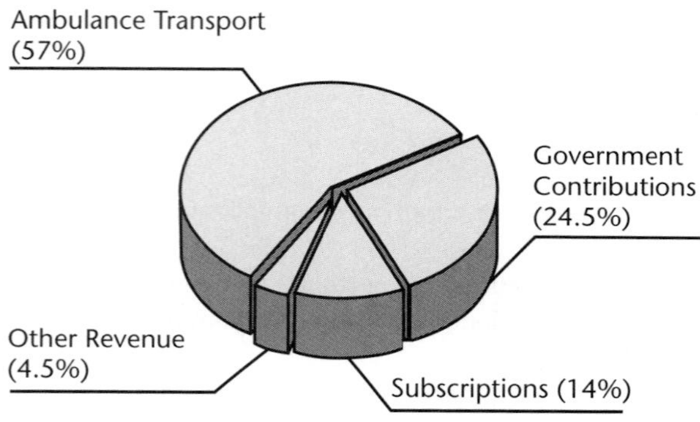

Expenses 1995-96

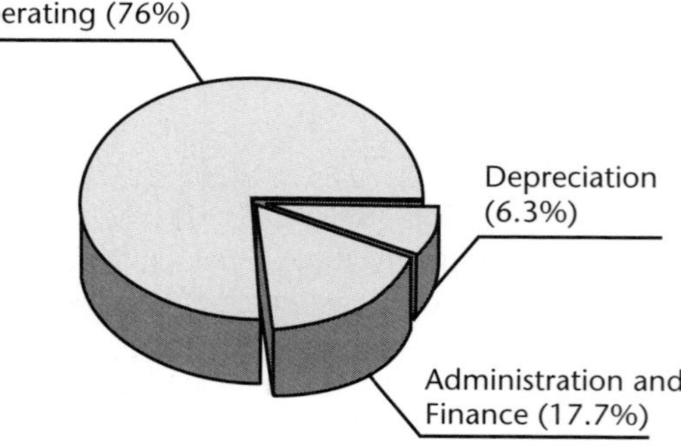

exhibit 4 Cause–Effect Chart for Patient Ready for Ongoing Treatment

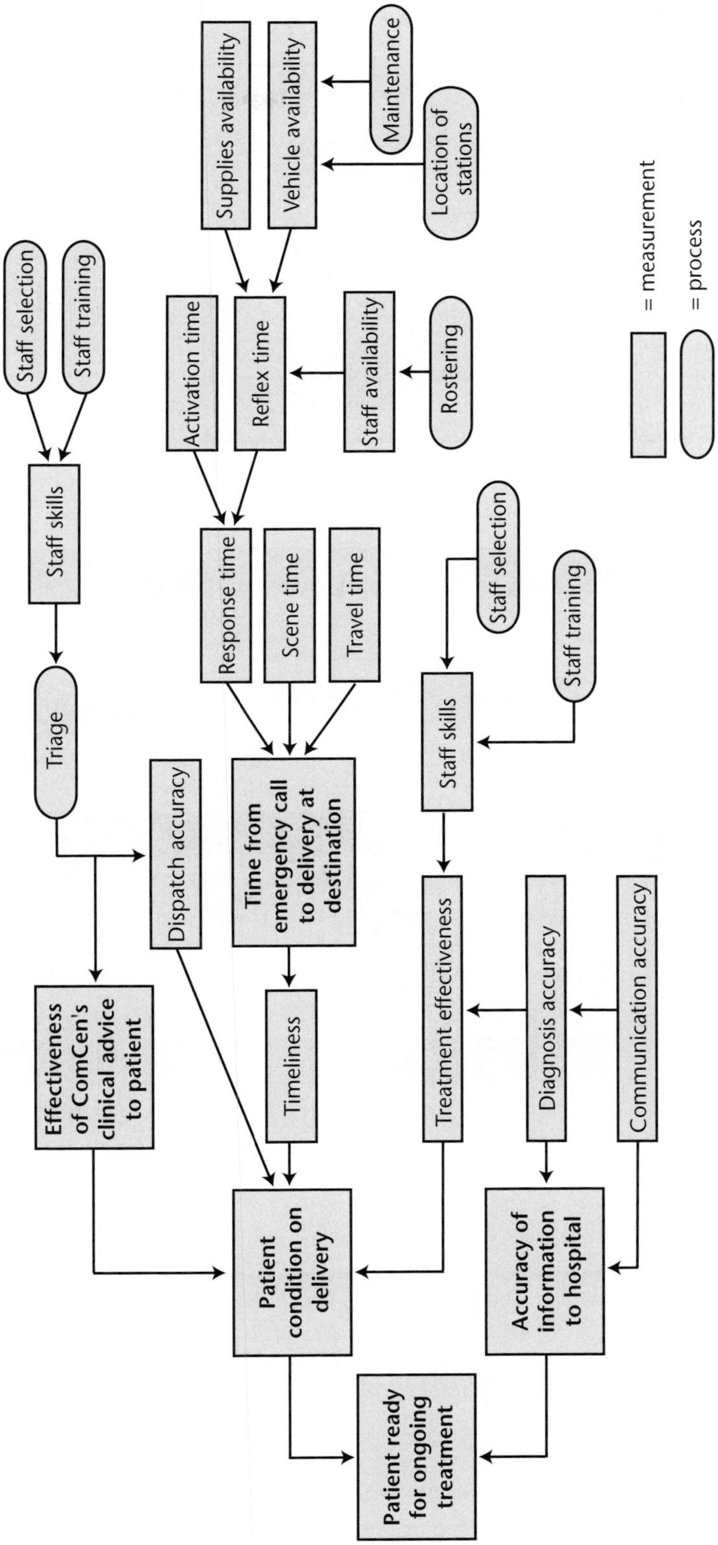

exhibit 5 Rotating Roster for Metro Region

This roster assumes 4 groups, each with 4 days on and 4 days off.

9 members are needed to operate the team. One person would be on annual holidays, one person would be on other duties and one or two persons are spare, ill or have other responsibilities.

Team A	Day	Day	Night	Night	Off	Off	Off	Off
Team B	Off	Off	Day	Day	Night	Night	Off	Off
Team C	Off	Off	Off	Off	Day	Day	Night	Night
Team D	Night	Night	Off	Off	Off	Off	Day	Day

Examining this chart shows the amount of interaction between members and the difficulty in getting together as a team of 11–13.

exhibit 6 Ambulance Team—Example Vision-Mission-Goals

VISION

The aim of the Waikerie Ambulance Team is to be the best team within the SA Ambulance Service and to maintain this position into the 21st century.

MISSION

The Waikerie Ambulance Team is committed to the provision of clinical care, customer and community service.

GUIDING PRINCIPLES AND VALUES

1. We will be focused and responsive to the needs of our patients and community.
2. In all things we do we will maintain our knowledge, skills and attitude to ensure a professional relationship with our peers and our community.
3. We will strive to lead, compete for, and deliver a service that is innovative and value adding to our patients and our community.

IMPLEMENTATION

The implementation of our plan depends on all of us. We are implementing our Strategic Plan using the principles of Continuous Quality Improvement

exhibit 7 Clinical Care Objectives

We will ensure that our knowledge, skill base and attitudes are being continuously developed to provide total quality clinical care to our patients.

ALS

- We will all be fully ALS qualified by the completion of 1998.
- If appropriate or required, the cost of training will be incorporated into the next financial year.
- Knowledge and skill maintenance will be incorporated into the station based study plan and skill practice plan.

continued

exhibit 7 Clinical Care Objectives (*continued*)

PARAMEDIC

- We will have at least one team member Paramedic qualified by the end of the year 2000.
- As part of the station study plan we will incorporate knowledge which will guide us toward Paramedic status.
- The cost of Paramedic training will be budgeted into the appropriate fiscal year.

TOOLS

- We will maintain and upgrade our existing station library.
- We will subscribe to associated periodicals.
- We will subscribe to the Internet.
- We will build a Medical associated CD library.
- We will develop an "Adopt-a-Doc" program.
- We will ensure the maintenance and availability of training equipment. This may be co-ordinated through the CTL.
- We will utilize the resources of the Ambulance Service Education Unit.
- We will involve the District Manager and CTL appropriately.
- We will have an annual review of the acceptability and relevance of current tools.

CONTINUED EDUCATION PROGRAM

- We will develop a program for each module to meet the needs of the CEP in consultation with the CTL.
- This program must meet the individual needs of each team member.
- At the end of each module we will review the effectiveness of the program.

STUDY PLAN

- We will develop a yearly plan, based on our teams' aims and objectives for the coming year.
- The plan will consist of monthly and weekly topics. These topics will be value adding to our knowledge.
- The plan will incorporate a series of short and long written questions. The appropriateness of these questions will be determined by the Team.
- The effectiveness of the plan will be reviewed bimonthly at team planning days.
- This plan may be reinforced by the CTL through station visitations.
- We will develop a review program which incorporates:
  1. Identifying Key Performance Indicators
  2. Conducting monthly case reviews
  3. Conducting continuous case card audits
  4. Recognition of measurable results
  5. Six-monthly review of station based and associated clinical training
  6. Ensuring the CTL is programmed into our station based program to provide regular useful feedback.

SKILLS PRACTICE

- We will develop a monthly review program which incorporates skills not included in the current CEP. This will be done in consultation with the CTL.
- We will develop a program which fosters integration and skills review with our volunteer sub-branches.
- We will develop a program which encourages skill sharing with allied health professionals, e.g. doctors, nurses, District Nurses, CAFHS nurses.
- We will initiate a clinical placement program with the Health Services.
- We will maintain a skill log book recording protocols as they are performed in the field and in practice.

exhibit 8 Sample Feedback Sheet

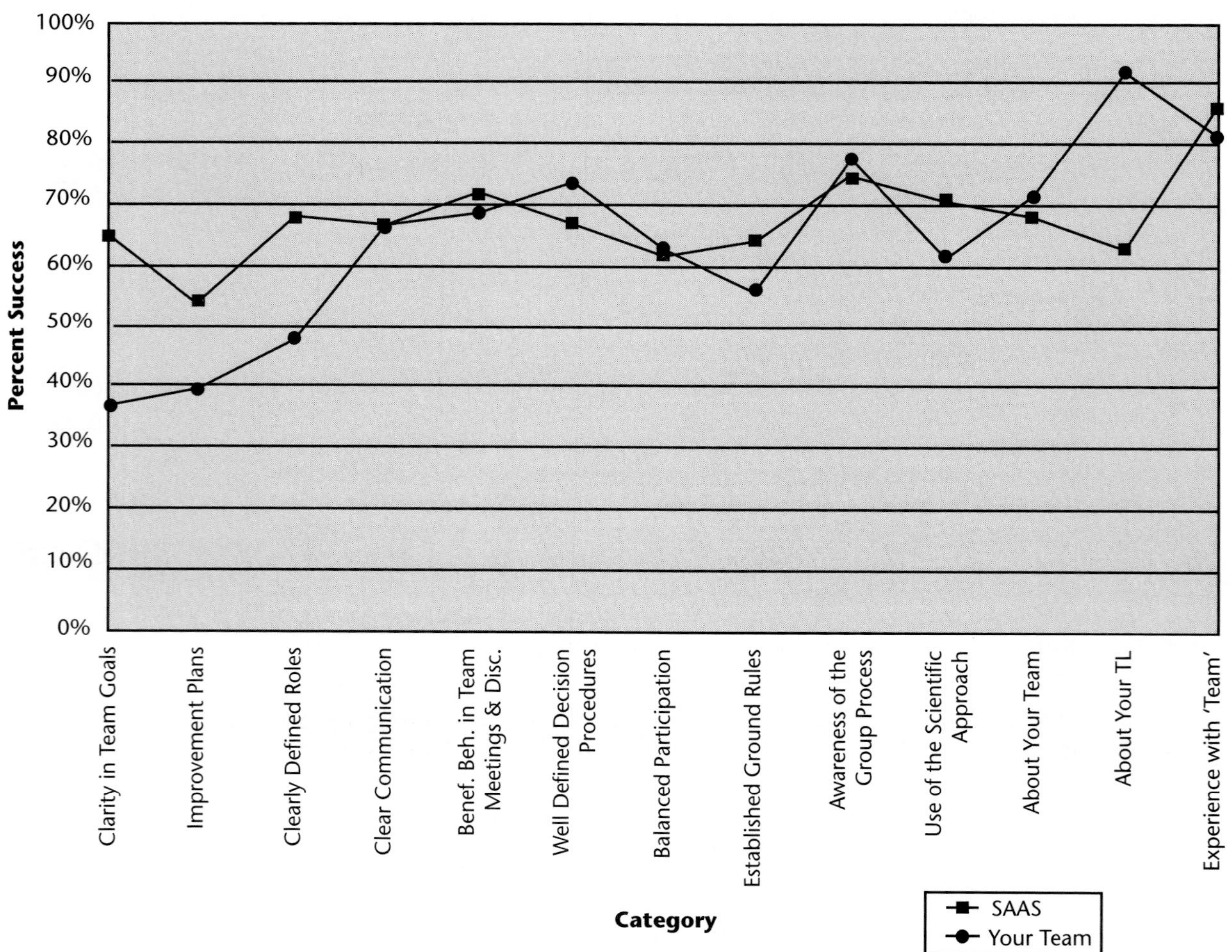

case 11 The Case of the Unseen Customers (A)

"I've had it!" exclaimed Chris to the other managers as she closed the boardroom door.

Chris was Committee Secretary and one of four supervisors of the Licensing and City Clerk Sections of the City of Townsville. Yet again, one of the younger clerks had complained to her that, although she felt like she was doing more work than anyone else, she was being continually picked on by one of the more experienced clerks, or "mother" as she vocally referred to her. The two clerks constantly bickered with each other, even in front of customers. All the arguments were essentially the same: "I end up dealing with customers when they need licensing service and I don't get help." Or "When someone finally does help me, they do so reluctantly." Or "I always have to answer the phone even though it is seldom for me—I can't get my committee minutes done as a result."

Mark and Rob, Assistant City Clerks, agreed that they too were getting fed up with the constant complaining. "Our Deputy always used the principle 'If I don't hear about it, I don't care.' We have certainly heard about it now. I'm not getting my own work done!" said Mark. "I've tried asking some of the other clerks what the issue is, but they never seem to give me any direct feedback," stated Rob.

"Well," said Chris, "Something has to be done. This has finally reached a point where I need to do something about it. I know we managers don't usually work together, but maybe this time we need to. I think this last emotional outburst has pushed all of us over the edge. So what should we do?"

CITY OF TOWNSVILLE

Townsville was a city of 167,500 people or 62,780 households located in the Region of Binhampton in the heart of Southwestern Ontario, less than one hour's drive from Toronto. Townsville was a vibrant, confident and cosmopolitan community that had a strong industrial and business base. Its industrial base and growth rate it an attractive community to live in.

The City was the local, municipal governing body of Townsville and employed approximately 1,000 people. City Council was chaired by the Mayor and consisted of a local councilor for each of the nine wards within Townsville. The Chief Administrative

Officer was the senior administrator of the City and was responsible to City Council for the effective and efficient operation of the City. All City Departments reported to Council through the Chief Administrator who served as Chairman of the Senior Management Committee. The Corporate Services and Clerks Division included both the Licensing Section and the City Clerk Section, the location of the conflict. (See Exhibit 1 for a partial organization chart.)

Just prior to the events of the case, the employees of the City of Townsville had moved to a new, modernly designed building located in the downtown. The building was designed in a U-shape, around a large atrium that reached from ground to the roof and was used for various community exhibits and activities throughout the year. Winding stairs and a bank of elevators led to the second floor offices; some of the parking entrances also entered onto the second floor. On the North side of the second floor were the Mayor's Office and the City Council Chamber. On the South side, there were the Chief Administrative Officer's Office and the City Clerk and Licensing Sections.

exhibit 1 Partial Organization Chart: Corporate Services and Clerks Division

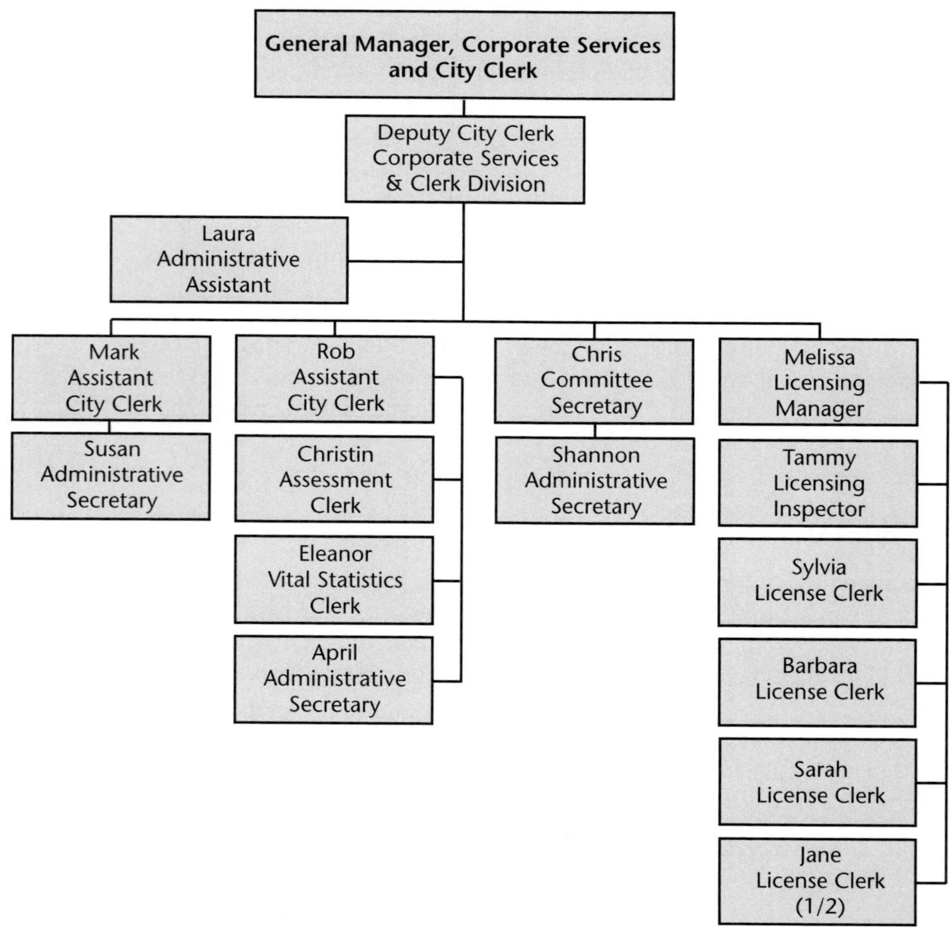

THE CITY CLERK AND LICENSING SECTIONS

The elevators and stairs on the second floor led immediately into a wide hallway leading to the office space that housed the City Clerk Section and Licensing Sections. This wide, narrow room was dominated by a 60-foot counter where a resident could get service. While these two sections were in the same Division, they had distinct operational responsibilities. They shared the same office space and had joint responsibility to serve the public at the front counter. The four managers within these sections also had distinct responsibilities and operated relatively independently. (See Exhibit 2 for a physical layout of the office.)

exhibit 2 Physical Layout of the Operation

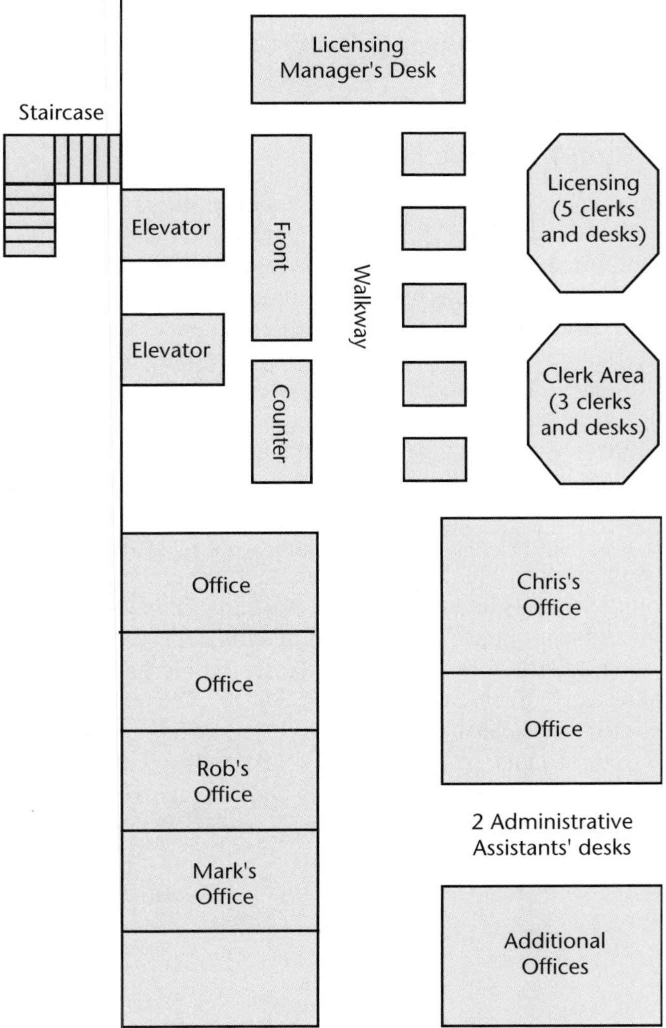

Licensing Section

The Licensing Section was responsible for issuing City of Townsville business, marriage and lottery licenses (in accordance with provincial requirements), auditing lottery activities, and producing related reports.

Melissa, the Licensing Manager, was overall supervisor. Tammy as the License Inspector spent much of her time on-the-road checking for licenses and auditing bingo groups, bazaars, Monte Carlos, and raffles. Sylvia, Barbara and Sarah were License Clerks. Jane worked as a half time License Clerk. They issued licenses, handled customers who came into the office, dealt with customer phone requests and inquiries, and conducted computer-based administration activities. They also performed other administrative duties: photocopying, sorting and filing. Although the workload was fairly evenly distributed throughout the year, it did become hectic every two months when bingo licenses had to be renewed. All License Clerks plus Tammy, when she was in, were expected to respond to customers at the front counter when needed. As well, each person's phone rang when a call came in to the department. Clerks who were free were expected to pick up the calls.

Most of the Licensing Clerks had been in their jobs for several years. Their salary grades were between 9 and 16.

Clerk Section

The Clerk Section ensured that the responsibilities of the City Clerk were carried out in accordance with the statutes of Ontario and City by-laws. It provided assistance for municipal elections, issued marriage licenses and burial permits and registered births. The section also had the responsibility for providing corporate support services to City Council. It was also responsible for taking and managing council/committee minutes and agendas, managing corporate records, and handling unanswered calls to the Chief Administrative Officer's office, Mayor's office, Licensing Section, and Records Centre.

Rob, an Assistant City Clerk, managed the clerks' activities and had three clerks reporting directly to him. Christin was the Assessment Clerk who handled property ownership questions and lot rezoning, severing and adjustments. Eleanor was the Vital Statistics Clerk who handled birth and death registration and marriage licenses. April operated primarily as Rob's administrative secretary and occasionally assisted with customer requests and counter traffic when others were busy. Another clerk/administrative assistant, Susan, was an administrative secretary for Mark, the other Assistant City Clerk. Chris was Committee Secretary and had Shannon reporting to her as an Administrative Secretary.

Similar to Licensing Clerks, City Clerks were to respond to customers when they came to the counter. As well, phone calls to the Clerk's Section and unanswered calls to the Chief Administrative Officer's Office rang to all five clerks' phones. Clerk positions had job grades ranging between 7 and 10. The section was typically seen as providing entry positions for employment with the City; despite recent vacancies in the Clerk's Section, few employees within the City of Townsville had applied for these positions.

THE PHYSICAL LAYOUT

Upon entering the office, either from the stairs or the elevators, customers were faced with a 60-foot-long front counter. A five foot walkway was directly behind the counter. (See Exhibit 2 for Physical Layout of Operation.) On the left side of the counter was the Licensing Section where Melissa and the five licensing employees' desks were located. On the right side of the counter was the City Clerk Section, which was occupied by the three front-line clerks and their desks. The walkway led to a long hallway where other managers' offices (including Mark's and Rob's offices) were located. April's and Susan's desks were located directly outside of Mark's and Rob's offices.

THE NATURE OF COMPLAINTS FROM THE CITY CLERK SECTION

As they wondered what to do, each of the managers reflected on what they had recently heard from their staff.

"One of the most common complaints that I remember," said Rob, is " 'You're not pulling your weight, dear; you didn't answer the phone enough today.' And answered by, 'Yes, mother!' That ends up coming to us as a complaint, 'Why does she always pick on me? I'm working as hard as anyone else here!' "

"That's where the key issue is located," Chris reflected. "I always hear 'My desk is right at the front counter, so I'm the first person the customers see. I'm getting tired of always being the one who has to stop work to help a customer! It means that I am late with my own work.' And then there is the 'Why can't she help out? She never goes to the counter or answers phones! And she was so miserable today, I can guarantee that she'll call in sick tomorrow.' If only there was no truth in what was said. And then, if confronted the other clerk just says, 'I'm sorry! I didn't see that there was a customer waiting! I sit behind this pillar, and it makes it difficult to see.' "

As they talked the three managers were surprised at the volume of complaints they could recall, including:

- "I'm the only one answering phones here! No one else is helping out!"
- "Why don't Mark and Rob's Assistants have to help out at the front counter or with the phones! They're being paid the same as the rest of us clerks but they sure seem to get preferential treatment!"
- "When a customer calls, all our phones ring—but Mark and Rob's Assistants never pick up the phone."

It was also apparent that the interpersonal and workload issues were being aggravated by the overlap in assigned duties between the Licensing Section and the Clerk Section. As Rob recalled, one person had commented, "Licensing is not helping out enough! Why can't they pick up our phones like we do for them? And why do they get paid more than me, just because they are in Licensing? What do the License clerks do anyway that makes them so great?"

Mark, Rob and Chris knew that everyone was busy with their own work. Doing "joint work" was an issue. As one clerk had reported, "I knew that customer was here for Licensing—why should I get up? Customers see one counter and assume anyone can help them. I was busy with my work and they clearly were not here to see me.

Yesterday, Licensing ignored this customer so I got up and, of course, I just had to send them to the other end of the counter."

Other issues resulted from the location of the office. As one clerk stated, "I feel like we're the reception for the full City! It seems like half of the customers who come here are just looking for directions!"

The phone system had created other issues. Chris talked about how one customer was on hold, while the clerk ran around finding the right person. Not only did this block a line, it took up the clerk's time as well. Other clerks handled things differently. As one had said, "If I can't answer the customer's question on the phone, I just take a message; I don't get involved in what others do."

"You know," said Rob, "when we have tried to do something, perhaps we haven't followed through as we should have. I overheard two people griping: 'How can management not notice her poor performance? That's just unacceptable!' Maybe we should be thinking more about performance management?"

Other comments were more general but related to the overall performance of the Section:

- "Why should I talk to management—they don't listen to what I have to say anyway!"
- "I'm getting tired of having to walk to the other end of hall to drop off photocopying and mail."
- "All anyone thinks I can do is type! I can handle harder work than that!"
- "We still need new dictaphones! These are really wearing out."
- "I still haven't received training on WordPerfect."
- "I feel bad asking for help from Susan and April during lunch; I feel like I'm imposing on them or disturbing their work."

THE NATURE OF COMPLAINTS FROM THE LICENSING SECTION

Later on that day, Chris asked Melissa how things were going in the Licensing Section.

Melissa sighed. "I'm getting really tired of hearing their constant complaining and arguing—I have to sit right in the middle of it all day long! But quite frankly, I have no idea what I should do with these types of issues! 'How am I supposed to get my work done if I have to constantly answer the phone?'; 'I don't understand what the Clerks are so busy with! Why does it take so long for them to answer the phones?'; 'I knew that customer was the funeral director and thus not my client; why should I get up?'; 'I was busy concentrating on my computer work when suddenly a customer showed up beside me out of nowhere! He had walked right past the counter to my desk!'; 'Why does management constantly interfere? I'll ask for help if I need it!'; 'Management doesn't give a rip one way or the other! They never do anything if we raise issues anyway! I've given up trying to give them ideas.' The complaints seem endless. 'I can't believe we still don't have a legal-sized tray for the front computer! And what about those new fonts we asked for?' 'I'm really tired of always having to wait for the photocopier!' 'How are we supposed to issue all of these licenses with three people? There's just too much work.'

"And to add one of my own complaints," continued Melissa, "I have a clear view of the full counter from where I sit, but I really don't need to! Lately I end up waiting on the customer when really I should be back up to back up! The clerks don't seem to understand that I have too much to do...."

THE DECISION

At the end of the day, Rob dropped by Chris's office. "Well, we all know what the Deputy's response to this would be!" said Rob. "He'd say, 'This is just how it is given the nature of the people and the nature of the task. Don't worry about it; just get people to do their jobs. If they are not doing their jobs then begin discipline proceedings. In other words, we're paying them for their job, so just get them to do it!' "

"Which is exactly what we've all been doing so far!" exclaimed Chris. "What concerns me most is that this has gotten severe enough to start affecting our level of service. To date, we managers have been operating independently and minding our own business. We probably all have different perspectives on what's going on here and on how we should handle this situation, but we are all responsible for maintaining an acceptable level of service to the Deputy. Where do we go from here?"

case 12 The Case of the Amalgamated Laboratory

Claude quickly walked into his office and locked the door behind him. He closed the blinds, lunged into his chair, put his head in his hands, and started shaking uncontrollably. He had just met with his supervisor, who ordered him to "get the situation in the lab under control by the end of the year 'or else.' " Claude was expected to improve productivity two-fold, stop the hemorrhaging of employee resignations, and bring a "calm, friendly disposition" to his work unit within six months—all without any increase in budget allocation. "I feel betrayed," Claude thought to himself as he cried in despair. He has been the manager of the Amalgamated Laboratory for only four months. Prior to this assignment, Claude had been the successful manager of a similar operation in another city. He has 20 years of experience working in a laboratory, moving his way up the career ladder from being a laboratory technologist, a supervisor, and, finally a lab manager for the past 5 years. During the employment interviews, Claude's supervisor described his prospective work situation as "an exciting and challenging opportunity to work with a team of motivated professionals in building a world class laboratory in a progressive health district." "It's challenging all right," Claude muttered to himself, "But it's also a war zone with heavy casualties, and I'm going to be the next casualty if I don't figure out what to do."

BACKGROUND

One year prior to Claude's arrival at the Amalgamated Laboratory, the medical laboratories of three acute care hospitals, one rehabilitation centre, and numerous private facilities were amalgamated into a single laboratory. This centralization effort was one of several initiatives undertaken by an urban health district as a means of reducing health care costs and in direct response to decreased provincial and federal funding to the district. The implementation of the amalgamated laboratory was phased in over a three-year period. The centralized laboratory was designed as a multi-site laboratory and was situated primarily at two of the acute care facilities due to the shortage of space at any one site and the lack of funding to develop a separate site. The centralized laboratory was expected to provide an efficient, high volume centre for the entire health district, meeting both its day-to-day and specialized laboratory requirements.

This restructuring was planned by the health district's senior management team in a series of planning meetings. They frequently dispatched representatives to "talk to the staff" as a means of providing the laboratory staff with a certain level of involvement. During these staff meetings, the management representative would describe management's plan and then solicit comments and ideas from the staff. Although the staff members were pleased with the opportunity to voice their concerns and opinions, when the final restructuring plan was announced, it became evident that their input was discarded.

THE PLAN

It was determined that the multi-site laboratory would consist of a high volume core-lab and small stat labs at two acute care facilities. These latter facilities required stat labs in order to respond to urgent requests for lab work. Also, 13 collection centres with minimal testing capability would be provided to the community (as a replacement for privately operated laboratories). The laboratory at the rehabilitation centre which had previously provided a "full-service menu" to the centre would be providing only collection services and, therefore, would result in the lay-off of one full-time medical laboratory technologist. Of the three acute care facilities, one was slated for closure one and one-half years following the completion of the project. Because this facility provides trauma care which requires laboratory service, a stat lab was to be maintained until the trauma service is relocated to another centre.

The Amalgamated Laboratory required the development of three new specialities: (1) the laboratory information system (LIS); (2) the accessioning, or order entry area; and (3) the call centre which would handle inquiries. Within each section of a laboratory were supervisory personnel who acted independently under the general guidance of the institution's laboratory manager. Prior to the amalgamation, there were four laboratory managers, each of whom was allocated a position as an assistant manager in the new centralized laboratory, with one to be selected as the overall laboratory manager. In addition to supervisors, each lab section also had two other levels of medical laboratory technologists. In the amalgamated laboratory, nineteen separate sections were to be combined to form seven sections. However, during the restructuring, these seven sections were further combined to form four units. Thus, the 19 supervisory positions were replaced by 4 Unit Manager positions. Unit Managers were responsible for all of the existing supervisory duties and also for the unit budget. Only two of the four Unit Managers who were hired were past supervisors. The other two Unit Managers were a biochemist whose job had been discontinued and a Level I Laboratory Technologist (the lowest level of the medical laboratory technologist job classification). Another biochemist whose job was discontinued became the LIS manager. See Appendix A for organization charts of the laboratories in the three acute care facilities prior to the restructuring and the organizational chart for the centralized lab (the Amalgamated Laboratory).

The supervisors who were not hired into the new Unit Manager positions became "working level senior technologists"—a step down in the hierarchy. These staff members were "grandfathered"—retained at their current salary rate. Many had excellent performance records and had continuously improved their educational level. In addition to performing routine bench work, these senior technologists were given responsibilities associated with the Laboratory Information System for their areas. They were also required to perform relief supervisory functions, in the event of unit manager absence. Former Level Two Technologists became Level One Technologists (grandfathered at their current wage rate) and were no longer required to perform any supervisory activities, but were expected to work all the shifts that were previously level one duties.

All laboratory staff belong to different locals of the same union, and union permission is required in order to shuffle staff to various facilities throughout the district. Negotiations with the union are currently under way which would see the laboratory staff become members of a single local. Staff employed at the acute care centre scheduled to close would not lose their jobs, but will be retained by seniority. However, the junior staff members at the remaining facilities were threatened with the possibility of being "bumped" from their jobs. Management assured the staff that the overall number of staff would not be reduced to any great extent past the normal level of attrition for the laboratory, including normal and early staff retirement. The total number of technical, office and support staff within the hospital laboratories prior to the amalgamation was 237 and would be reduced to 195. The majority of the job loss would be at the privately owned labs which would be reduced to collection centres only (i.e., no testing performed). The development of the new areas would result in fewer medical laboratory technologist positions and more "non-medical" staff in the overall projected numbers for staffing the new centralized laboratory.

THE IMPLEMENTATION

Each unit met to standardize procedures, and formulate plans for their implementation. Training for the implementation of the LIS, and for movement of staff between sections was initiated. The amalgamation was to proceed in steps over a three-year period, with sections moved as soon as the renovation of their area was complete. However, in some cases, some sections were moved "just to test the waters" even though their area was fully renovated. Some sections were shuffled before the LIS was in place and operational, but the bulk of the movement of staff occurred when the LIS became functional. Within two years, the new sections were implemented and the core lab came into existence. As planned, the laboratories at the other two acute care centres became stat labs. One entire "unit" was located at the acute care facility which would not be closed, and the remaining "three" units were centered at the facility with the "high-volume" core lab. The staff worked hard and within a few months were ready to take on the increased workload from the community.

ONE-YEAR POST AMALGAMATION

When Claude arrived at the laboratory, the amalgamation had already been in place for a year. He found that, although the restructuring appeared to be successful "on the surface," many troubles were brewing within the laboratories. Staff morale was exceedingly low. The technical staff (the laboratory technologists) within the units were accusing the other units of having too many staff members, having staff who do nothing or don't do what they were hired to do, not working shift work, or, more generally, having better working conditions. Intra- and inter-unit conflict within the laboratory erupted on a continual basis.

This conflict was fuelled by the existence of distinct cultures in the laboratories prior to the restructuring. The laboratory at Institution 1 was the only CAP accredited facility. CAP is a prestigious designation which certifies that a laboratory adheres to extremely high standards of quality. In order to qualify for and maintain this certification, the staff were required to put in many extra hours of work to write and adhere to stringent procedures of quality assurance. In contrast, the laboratory at Institution 3 maintained a very relaxed and casual atmosphere. This congenial atmosphere facilitated the development of a very close working relationship with the other specialties within the institution and served to ease a potentially highly stressful work situation. The culture at Institution 2 fell somewhere between that of Institution 1 and 3.

In one particular unit, the antagonism between members who were previously employed by two different laboratories undermined the well-being of the unit. The unit existed as three cultures within one. Each sub-culture retained its own methodology and techniques and each refused to cooperate with the other or adopt the "standardized procedures." The sub-cultures used different specimen logging (numbering) practices and refused to "cover" for each other at break time. Also, one sub-culture would discard another's reagents and stains because "they were not labelled correctly." As a result of this year of ongoing discord, the frustrated and berated unit manager resigned.

Claude also had to contend with the issue of annual and sick leave benefit usage. Employees were making full use of their sick leave benefits to the extent that, on any given day, every unit had one or more staff members away on sick leave. Also, the laboratory staff were some of the most senior staff within the health district and had accumulated four to six weeks of annual leave. Many had carried over their annual leave in the previous year as a means of boosting staffing levels during the amalgamation process. Now that the restructuring was completed, many employees began applying for annual leave.

A higher than normal level of attrition has occurred throughout the laboratory as staff have chosen to move into other jobs within the district, or into positions in different organizations. Unfortunately, those individuals who have departed from the laboratory are among its most talented and qualified. Although staffing shortages are being experienced throughout the Amalgamated Laboratory, staffing levels in one particular unit have plunged to a critically low level.

In response to this urgent problem and as a means of ensuring that minimal staffing levels were maintained, Claude reallocated staff from other sections and hired casual staff as needed. These measures, however, required that existing staff (who are already burdened by an excessive workload) train and closely supervise the new, inexperienced, and generally under-qualified staff members. In addressing the issue of the heavy workload, Claude decided to streamline the frequency and availability of testing services. Whereas in the past some tests were performed on several samples, they were now limited to being performed on only one sample. Also, testing now became available "at regular hours only" rather than at all times as needed by other specialties within the healthcare system. Unfortunately, this measure seems to have backfired. Staff seem to have a reduced level of pride in their work and the service provided to clients. Also, the removal of some laboratory services from several institutions has made it difficult for the medical and nursing staff from these institutions to obtain information on testing and specimen collection from laboratory staff. This situation stands in stark contrast to previous service levels where laboratory staff provided services in person and with pride, so that overall quality of patient care was improved. Laboratory staff no longer view themselves as a member of a team working towards improving the health of a patient. Rather, they feel like they are part of a bureaucracy, just trying to get as much work done as possible.

Since his arrival four months ago, Claude has been attempting to familiarize himself with his new work situation and has been responding to situations and incidents on a continual basis. He has met with staff members as a group and individually (where possible) to discuss options for improving the performance and the morale of the laboratory. These meetings seem futile, however. They consist of a great deal of talk, blaming, and demands for higher staffing levels. The staff appear to be drowning in a sea of confusion—unable to look beyond their more immediate needs. But another important issue looms on the horizon. In the next two months, an acute care facility will close and its laboratory staff will need to be absorbed within the Amalgamated Laboratory. Claude was determined to resolve the problems of the Amalgamated Laboratory. "After all," he thought to himself as he adjusted his tie in the mirror, "I'm a winner and winners never quit."

appendix A Institution #1—Technical and Aide Organizational Chart

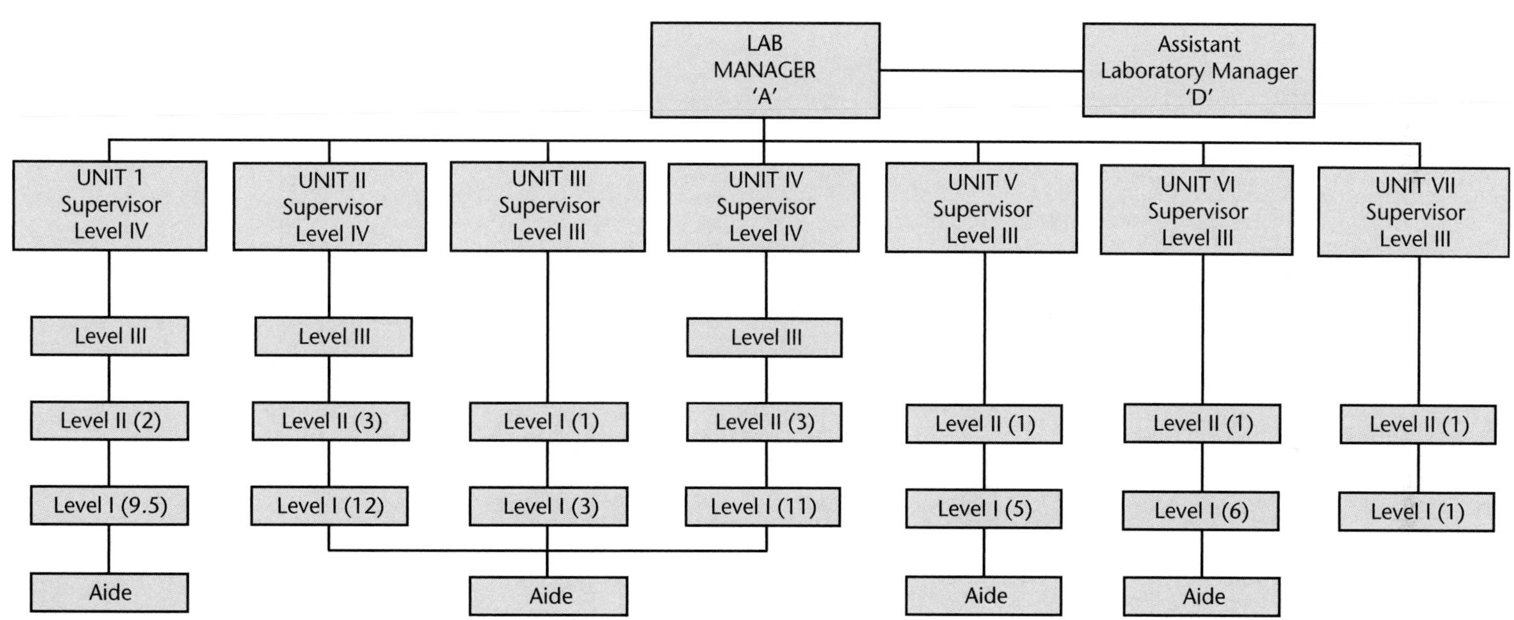

Number in brackets = (FTE>1)

appendix A Institution #2—Technical and Aide Organizational Chart

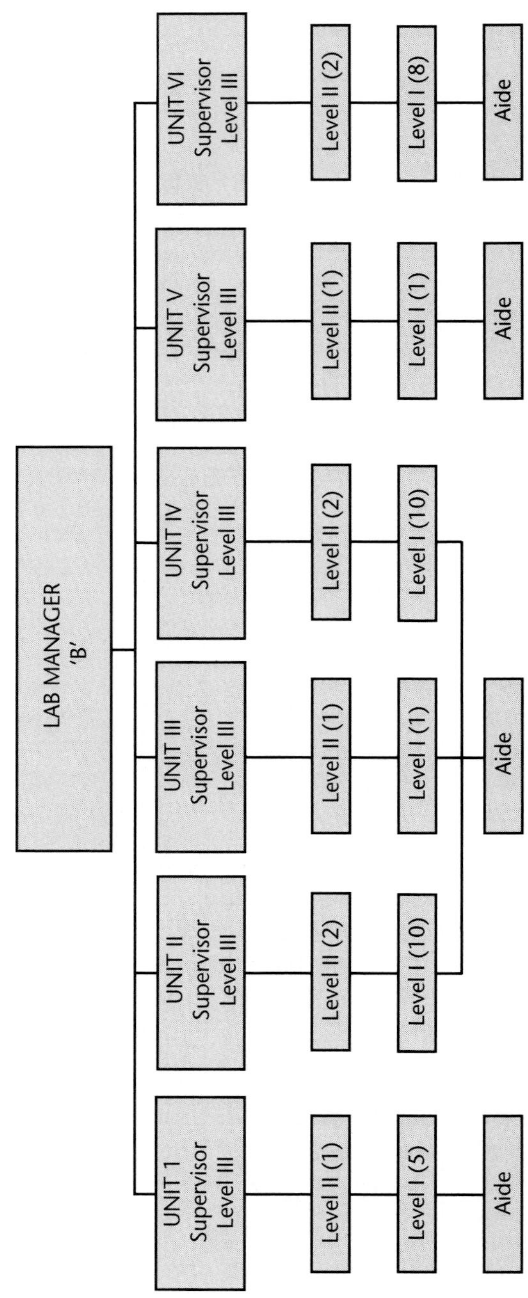

Number in brackets = (FTE>1)

appendix A Institution #3—Technical and Aide Organizational Chart

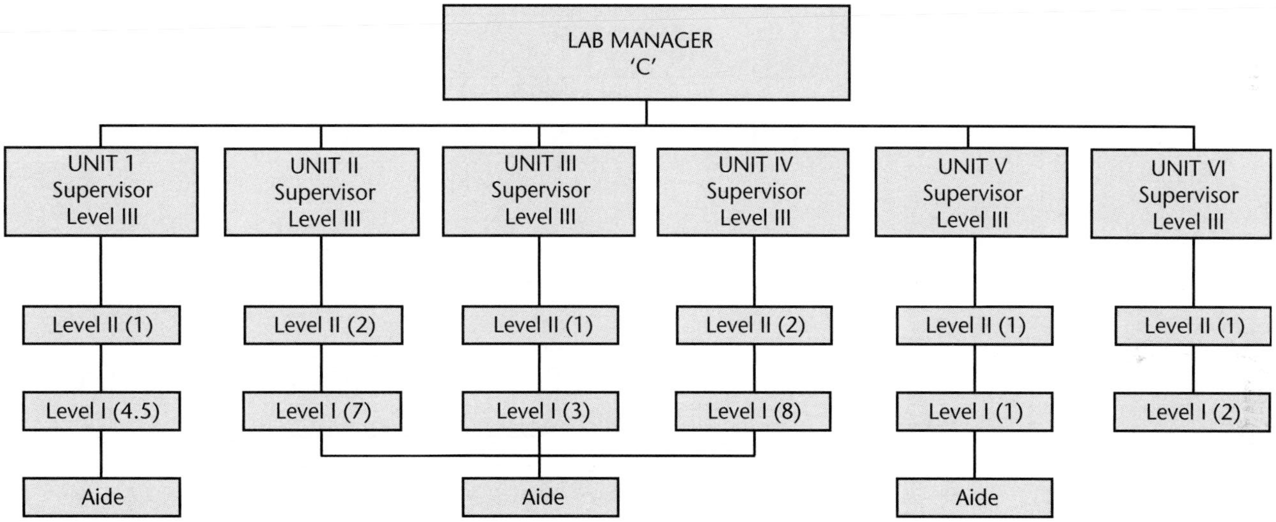

LAB MANAGER
'C'

UNIT 1
Supervisor
Level III
Level II (1)
Level I (4.5)
Aide

UNIT II
Supervisor
Level III
Level II (2)
Level I (7)

UNIT III
Supervisor
Level III
Level II (1)
Level I (3)
Aide

UNIT IV
Supervisor
Level III
Level II (2)
Level I (8)

UNIT V
Supervisor
Level III
Level II (1)
Level I (1)
Aide

UNIT VI
Supervisor
Level III
Level II (1)
Level I (2)

appendix A Centralized Lab—Technical and Aide Organizational Chart

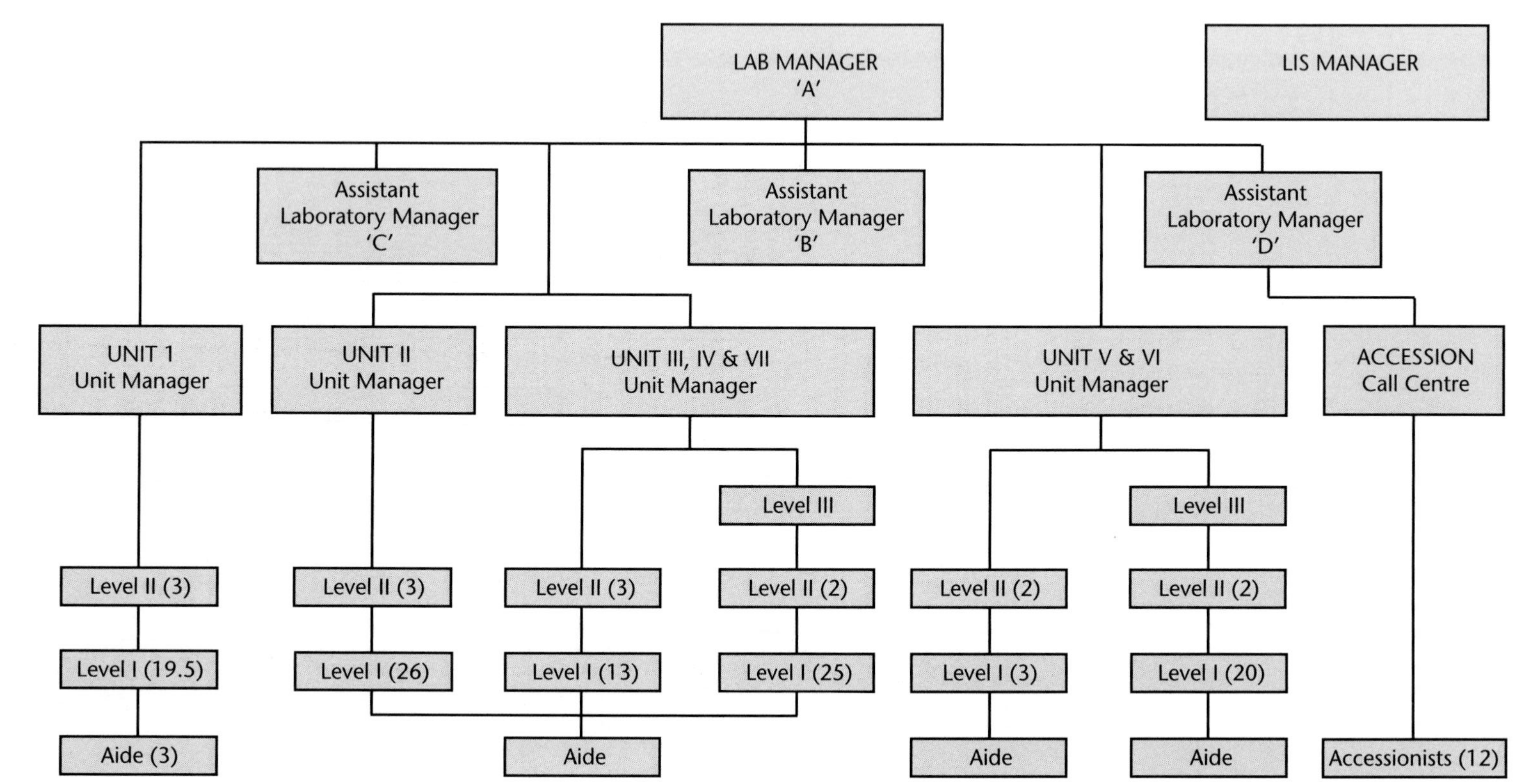

Number in brackets = (FTE>1)

case 13 Family Medical Group of Companies

It's a bright April morning and Bill Maron smiles towards the sun shining into his office. "Finally," he thinks to himself. "The missing piece to the puzzle that's going to let us move forward." But before Bill has long to dwell in this moment of satisfaction, the phone rings and it's his secretary, Monica. "Nancy Meyers has arrived for your 9 a.m. meeting," Monica chants. After lingering for a brief moment, Bill turns his attention back to the issue at hand. "Thanks Monica. Show her in."

Nancy is Bill's newest employee at the corporate head office of Family Medical. She was hired less than two weeks ago to become the Director of Human Resources. Nancy has several years of Human Resources experience and particular expertise in human resource planning. Nancy has worked for major companies in the transportation industry throughout Canada and has gained a reputation for her energy and practical attitude. Bill needs Nancy to develop a comprehensive human resource plan for his two divisions (distribution and manufacturing). Continuing problems with morale, turnover, succession planning and training have kept Bill from concentrating on his next endeavour: a new division that would provide home-nursing services.

Bill had just finished his daydreaming when Monica brought Nancy into the office. "Good morning, Nancy," Bill offers cheerfully with a firm handshake. "Have a seat" as he motions to the leathery chairs in front of him. "I understand you are just the person to solve our HR problems."

Although Nancy was given selected information about the company and the challenges during her interviews, there was key information that Bill wanted to share with her before she plunged into her new responsibilities. Nancy would also need to speak to the Vice Presidents of each company. But, nevertheless, the appropriate place to start off was at the beginning. Bill began by giving Nancy a brief history of the company.

FAMILY MEDICAL DISTRIBUTION

The original company, Family Medical Distribution, had been created by the grandfather of Bill's wife Helen. The company began operations in 1924 selling medical supplies, such as syringes and bandages, to local hospitals in the Kingston region. For 45 years, the company maintained its quiet, but consistent, presence in the local medical community. Over this time, the company had built a solid reputation for quality products and reliable service which the owner credited to his dedicated employees. Probably as a result of the company's small size, employees often felt like family members and stayed with the company until retirement.

Customer service was largely responsible for the company's early direction. The owner's philosophy was to satisfy the needs of the customer—regardless of what it might entail. Bill can't help but smile to himself when he recalls one of his favourite stories. Helen's grandfather, Mr. Halton, spent considerable time and energy to find and import a number of special religious articles from Europe as a favour to the nuns at St. Joseph's Hospital. It was these extraordinary business decisions that convinced Bill that Mr. Halton was as interested in being a socially useful organization as in making a reasonable income—evidenced by the modest bottom line each year on the income statements.

Bill shakes his head now when he thinks back to 1969 and how he came to purchase Family Medical Distribution. At the time, Bill was thirty years old and had a promising career as a Chartered Accountant with Ernst & Young. He worked long hours and enjoyed the challenges and perks of public accounting. Bill thought he'd be an accountant for life. Looking back now though, Bill is thankful for the bullish style of his father-in-law. When Mr. Halton became ill and passed away suddenly in 1968, it had been Helen's father who convinced him to take the risk and purchase the business. Helen's father was convinced that Bill had the youthful energy and determination to take control of the foundering company.

BILL'S EARLY YEARS

In the first few years Bill had no choice but to learn about his company by rolling up his sleeves and getting involved. With only eight employees, Bill's role was far from glamorous (Appendix A—Organizational Chart). Bill would often take customer orders, speak to vendors and hunt for product in the warehouse—all within the same hour. Bill also spent countless hours on the road talking to customers and suppliers.

Bill's new surroundings had also been a bit of a let-down. The plush, modern facilities of Ernst & Young were out of reach for Family Medical. In fact, Family Medical Distribution consisted of an 18,000-square-foot warehouse and a single open-concept office for all staff to work—including Bill. The office space was full of assorted old furniture that needed to be shunted around to allow staff enough room to maneuver from the coffee station back to the warehouse.

Despite the humble initial stages of ownership, Bill was driven to make his investment a success. Bill spent countless hours at Family Medical Distribution. He was determined to grow the company beyond the boundaries of the Kingston region.

Thankfully, the efforts began to pay off. In the fifteen years since 1969, Bill had begun to realize measured success. Family Medical Distribution had grown out of its original facilities when the company expanded into the rest of Ontario (especially Toronto) and later into the rest of the country through strategic acquisitions. By 1984, the company had become a true "national entity" with a distribution network that stretched from coast to coast. Branch offices in Vancouver, Winnipeg, Montreal, Fredericton and St. John's were now supplying hundreds of Canada's leading hospitals with quality medical products and systems (Appendix B—Timeline). Family Medical Distribution's reputation for service and quality had also grown nationally.

NEED FOR CHANGE

But Bill wasn't satisfied. By 1984, he craved a new entrepreneurial challenge. He had grown passionate about the medical business and the new technologies that were making significant improvements to medical treatments. Among the many changes, surgeries were becoming less invasive and hospital stays shorter. Bill's fervour for new technologies was not a secret. Family Medical Distribution had become a known supporter of leading-edge technology.

A few years earlier, Bill received a frantic call from the Emergency Room Supervisor at Toronto Hospital. Although it was quite late in the day, Bill, as usual, was found in the office. A young accident victim was being transferred to Toronto Hospital and was in desperate need of a specialty non-invasive ventilator. Although considered new technology, the equipment was the young girl's best chance for a full recovery. Bill immediately ran back to the warehouse to gather the required equipment and accessories and headed to Toronto. Bill recalls the night vividly. It was 7:20 p.m. The sky was black with snow clouds and Bill was determined to get to Toronto and make a difference.

That special trip to Toronto had a lasting effect on Bill and his desire to make a difference to the medical community. As a distributor, Family Medical was limited in its ability to significantly advance technology. That trip to Toronto had given Bill the vision and desire to create a new division of Family Medical: a company responsible for developing and manufacturing innovative, new medical products.

ADDITION OF FAMILY MEDICAL MANUFACTURING

Over the years, Bill had been approached by physicians several times to consider partnering in the manufacture and distribution of a particular invention. Bill was always careful to balance his interest and excitement against the potential risks. Such ventures typically require a substantial capital investment and particular expertise that was, at the time, not available in Family Medical Distribution.

Nearly two years after Bill's memorable trip to Toronto, an invention had caught his attention—and the timing was right. Family Medical Distribution was operating smoothly and generating a reasonable income. Bill was presented with an idea that would help asthmatic patients deliver their medication through puffers more effectively. Like many great inventions, the principle behind the product actually appeared rather simple; a plastic holding chamber attached to the patient's puffer. The chamber would hold the medication until the patient was ready to inhale. Bill immediately funded the additional research necessary to perfect the prototypes and further analyze the market opportunities. After two years of laboratory research, the simple little product had become quite a complex, but none-the-less successful innovation. In 1986, the AeroTube product was launched and the new business division formalized under the name Family Medical Manufacturing.

NEED FOR HELP

By 1996, Bill was exhausted. The drastic funding cuts to the healthcare community by both the federal and provincial governments in the 1990's had been squeezing the profits out of Family Medical Distribution. The company reacted to the industry chaos and drastic sales slump by reorganizing internal operations and refocusing the overall corporate direction. The company needed to make some drastic changes in order to reverse the negative sales trends (Appendix C).

Meanwhile, Family Medical Manufacturing continued to grow at an almost uncontrollable rate. The sales and marketing departments were aggressively promoting the AeroTube product internationally. Within the past six years, the AeroTube product had expanded its sales network to over 50 countries. New product-line extensions had been developed but the resources were not available to begin producing and promoting the products. Although profits were significantly ahead of projections, the growing pains within the company were becoming increasingly more obvious (Appendix C).

The demands of both companies were taking their toll on Bill. The pace was relentless and despite working 7 days a week, he could no longer keep up with the responsibilities of each company. After careful consideration, Bill decided he had no choice but to hire a Vice President for each company. Bill needed to relieve himself from more of the day-to-day tasks of each company to allow him time to manage the enterprise's overall direction.

NEW VICE PRESIDENTS

Early in 1997, Sam Collins was promoted to Vice President of Family Medical Distribution. Sam had joined the company 15 years earlier and had successfully risen through the ranks. Sam was first hired as a Sales Representative for the province of New Brunswick and was a natural at building rapport with his customers. Sam had an easy-going personality and a sharp wit that customers loved. After 8 years in the field, and some coaxing, Sam agreed to join head office in Kingston to become a Marketing Manager. Although leaving his roots in Maritime Canada was difficult, Sam made a successful transition into his new position. After this initial move, Sam continued to progress through the company accepting opportunities as Senior Marketing Manager, District Sales Manager and Director of Marketing. Sam has always been considered a trusted and loyal employee. When Bill needed to create the Vice President's role in Family Medical Distribution, Sam was his obvious choice.

A few months later, Bill hired Mark Olsen to become the Vice President of Family Medical Manufacturing. Finding the right person for this position had been a bit more of a challenge. Bill needed to find someone with the experience and vision to continue expanding the markets for the AeroTube product line, yet also possess the technical ability to manage both the production and R&D departments. Mark's previous employer was a related manufacturing company in the Kingston area. Mark had been quite successful as their Director of the Manufacturing and Engineering Operations. Although Mark is a relatively young Vice President at 45 years of age, his charm and approach to business have earned him respect. Mark had also studied engineering while at university, which has been helpful in overseeing the activities of the R&D division. Bill counted on Mark to grow the AeroTube line and expand the markets for new products.

"This is where I need your help, Nancy" offers Bill. "Family Medical Distribution is starting to make a financial turn-around but really needs some HR help to deal with the change process and the resulting fall-out of staff. As well, Family Medical Manufacturing really needs your help to develop an appropriate structure to cope with the growth. Both companies have made some strategic mistakes recently which have resulted in the loss of some key staff to the competition. The environmental changes and our lack of organization have been very stressful for staff. I think some staff have simply grown tired of waiting while top management worked out the problems. I really think addressing our human resource issues will help each of the companies gain control. I want to feel confident that both companies are on solid ground before we enter the home-nursing market."

Bill stopped for just a moment before proceeding. "Before I get ahead of myself, I really should give you some background on our Human Resources department."

NEED FOR HUMAN RESOURCES EXPERTISE

"In addition to hiring Sam and Mark in 1997, I also realized the need to formally establish a Human Resources Department. The human resource issues in each of the companies had become increasingly more time consuming and complex. It had become obvious that the needs for human resources management had grown beyond an amateur's role and required a professional" (Appendix A—New Organizational Chart).

Bill stopped for a moment and Nancy could see a cloud come over his eyes. Bill shook his head. "Unfortunately, the HR department has been a bit of a disaster. The HR Manager we hired has been on leave for the past 13 months. The Human Resources Associate, Claire Jackson, has done a wonderful job and taken charge of the department but the issues the department needs to address are just too much for her. In the past year, Claire has been spending almost all her time interviewing for vacant positions and handling the orientation and paperwork of the new employees. At any given time, she has a minimum of ten vacancies that she is working to fill. The growth in the manufacturing division has kept a steady pressure on Claire to find quality staff, FAST. Although Claire has a clerk to help with the day-to-day paperwork, she really has not been able to deal with all the issues in the department. The training and development programs have really suffered. As well, we have not done any strategic planning or forecasting for either of the companies.

"You can now understand how delighted I was when you accepted the challenge and joined Family Medical. We certainly need your expertise in developing a human resource plan for the companies. We promoted Claire recently to the Manager's position so that she would be ready to help you. I know you will find her a tremendous asset. The bottom line is, Nancy, the department is in desperate need of your leadership and the company is in desperate need of your expertise. We need a solid human resource plan in order to move forward. I need the current problems addressed before I can create the home-nursing division.

"I'd like to give you a chance to prepare some preliminary information for the human resource plan before we meet again. I also know that you need to meet with Mark and Sam to gather their perspectives on things. Would it be okay to meet in two weeks to discuss the plan?"

NANCY'S INITIAL ACTIONS

Bill had been very clear; he wanted Nancy to develop a human resource plan to encompass both the manufacturing and distribution divisions. Nancy had to get moving—she just did not have the luxury of time to painstakingly review her every option. Bill wanted to meet with her in two weeks. She decided that the obvious place to begin was by finding out what her Human Resource Manager and the two Vice Presidents thought. Nancy asked Claire to write a brief memo to her outlining the pertinent issues in the human resource department (Appendix D) and kept notes of the extensive interviews she had with Sam and Mark (Appendixes E & F).

With less than 10 days to go until her meeting with the President, Nancy closed her office door, turned off her phone and began work on her strategy for the Family Medical Group of Companies.

appendix A

Family Medical Distribution
December 31, 1967

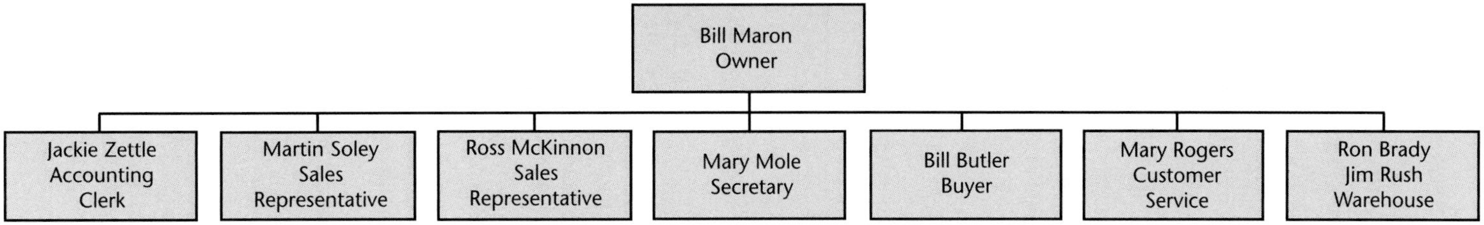

- Bill Maron, Owner
  - Jackie Zettle, Accounting Clerk
  - Martin Soley, Sales Representative
  - Ross McKinnon, Sales Representative
  - Mary Mole, Secretary
  - Bill Butler, Buyer
  - Mary Rogers, Customer Service
  - Ron Brady, Jim Rush, Warehouse

Family Medical Group of Companies
April 30, 1999

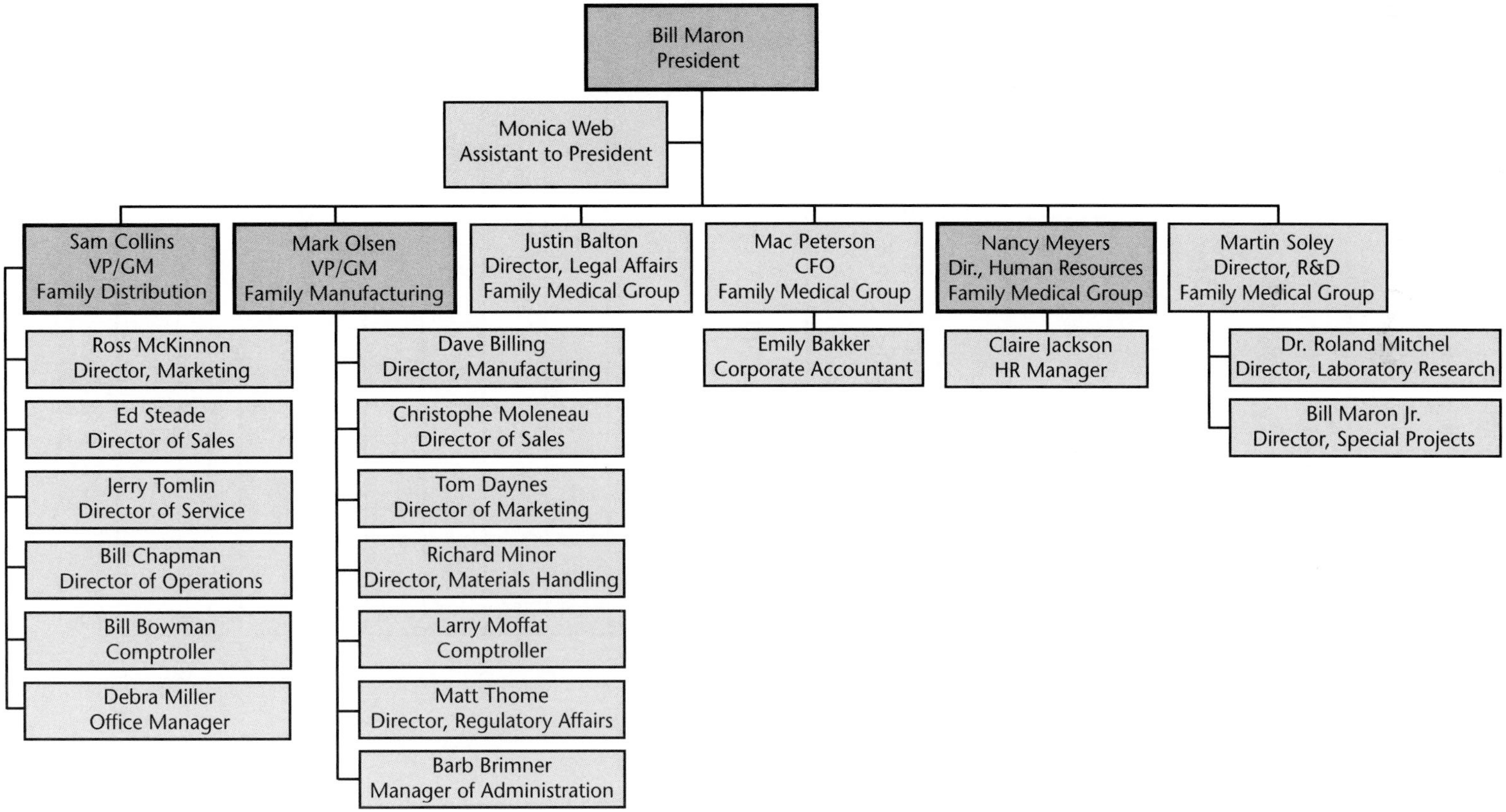

- Bill Maron, President
  - Monica Web, Assistant to President
  - Sam Collins, VP/GM, Family Distribution
    - Ross McKinnon, Director, Marketing
    - Ed Steade, Director of Sales
    - Jerry Tomlin, Director of Service
    - Bill Chapman, Director of Operations
    - Bill Bowman, Comptroller
    - Debra Miller, Office Manager
  - Mark Olsen, VP/GM, Family Manufacturing
    - Dave Billing, Director, Manufacturing
    - Christophe Moleneau, Director of Sales
    - Tom Daynes, Director of Marketing
    - Richard Minor, Director, Materials Handling
    - Larry Moffat, Comptroller
    - Matt Thome, Director, Regulatory Affairs
    - Barb Brimner, Manager of Administration
  - Justin Balton, Director, Legal Affairs, Family Medical Group
  - Mac Peterson, CFO, Family Medical Group
    - Emily Bakker, Corporate Accountant
  - Nancy Meyers, Dir., Human Resources, Family Medical Group
    - Claire Jackson, HR Manager
  - Martin Soley, Director, R&D, Family Medical Group
    - Dr. Roland Mitchel, Director, Laboratory Research
    - Bill Maron Jr., Director, Special Projects

appendix B Timeline—Family Medical Distribution

1924	Family Medical Distribution created by Herbert Halton, a former stock keeper for the Kingston General Hospital
1968	Herbert Halton dies after a brief illness at the age of 70
1969	Bill Maron purchases the company with a bank loan and the family house as collateral
1971	Family Medical successfully expands the Ontario market with key customers in Toronto, Ottawa, London and Windsor
1975	Family Medical Distribution purchases a local distribution business in Montreal, Quebec. Under the purchase agreement, the 12 staff members in Montreal become the newest employees of Family Medical.
1977	Kirkland Medical is purchased in Vancouver, BC. The business and staff become the Western Branch for Family Medical Distribution.
1978	A small operation in Winnipeg, Manitoba is converted to Family Medical. Few customers are gained through the acquisition but Family Medical Distribution is now able to comfortably supply all the Western provinces.
1982	McArthur Medical Supplies is purchased. Both branches (Fredericton, NB and St. John's, NF) are converted to Family Medical Distribution.
1986	Family Medical Manufacturing created. Family Medical Group of Companies name established to represent the corporate company.

appendix C Family Medical Group of Companies

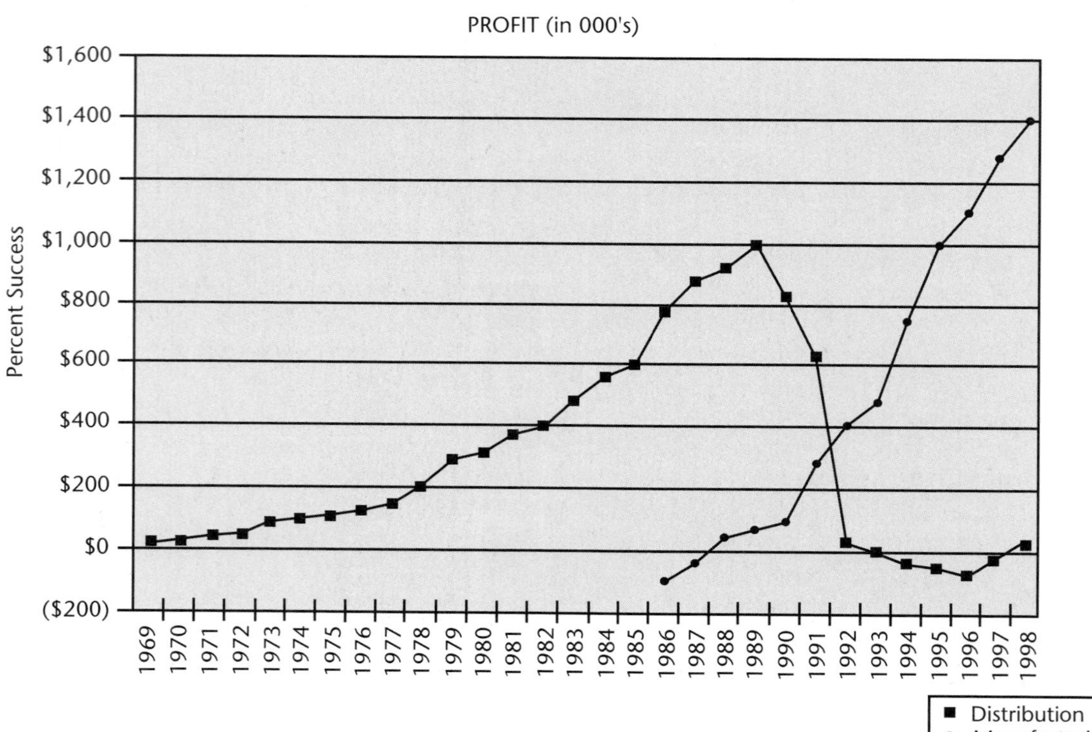

appendix D Notes to File

DATE: April 28, 1999
BCC: Bill Maron
RE: Interview with Sam Collins (Family Medical Distribution)

- Company has now grown to about 145 employees with most working in the sales, marketing and operations departments. Many of the employees hired during Bill's early years continue to enjoy successful careers with the distribution business.
- Family Medical Distribution still has a solid reputation in the medical community but has been faltering in past five years due to government cutbacks in the medical industry. The restructuring has meant that hundreds of hospitals across the country have closed while others have been forced to significantly reduce their number of beds.
- Sam feels the company has lacked a strategic focus and become "lazy" in the years leading up to the budget cuts.
- Sam is committed to returning Family Distribution to its former profitability. Sam feels personally responsible to deliver the bottom-line to Bill.
- Family Medical Distribution has had to reposition itself as a specialty distributor of high-end medical products and systems in order to survive. The goal is to represent only key suppliers in Canada in the key areas of Critical Care, Anaesthesia, Respiratory and Surgery.
- As a result of these industry stresses, there has been a significant change in the company's corporate culture. The new atmosphere is one of cost restraint and continuous change. The company has had to reduce its inventory and improve its processes to remain competitive in the increasingly smaller market.
- Sam has spent considerable effort evaluating the operations, sales and marketing departments. He feels these areas will be the keys to turning the company around. He thinks staff needs to work "smarter" and not "harder."
- Up until recently, the company had operated for many years with relatively few changes. Many of the employees had a considerable amount of seniority, had risen through the ranks and had hoped to retire from Family Medical. In the past two years, however, the external forces have created a need for change in the organizational mix and structure of the company. About 5 or 6 long term employees have been terminated. Some of the vacancies have been filled from within the company but staff is still generally feeling nervous and uncertain. Sam has been pushing hard to focus the company and turn the company around.
- Sam is a bit hesitant about the role and value of a HR department. His past two years have been very disappointing with problems around hiring methods, confidentiality, knowledge/expertise and lack of support for the new company Vision.
- Sam is willing to consider a HRP for Family Distribution but is more concerned with making the company profitable again.

appendix E Notes to File

DATE: April 27, 1999
BCC: Bill Maron
RE: Interview with Mark Olsen (Family Medical Manufacturing)

- The pace has been hectic since Mark joined Family Medical Manufacturing two years ago. The company is very successful having continuously exceeded its growth and profit projections each year.
- The AeroTube product is currently marketed in over 50 countries and secures about 47% of the market for valved holding chambers worldwide. The lab has also completed successful prototypes for two new products to be launched in the next year. One product will allow intubated patients in a hospital to receive their medications orally through puffers. The company is close to receiving their approval from Canada's Health Protection Branch. The other product is a much larger version of the AeroTube product and will soon be launched to veterinarians for use on animals with breathing problems.
- Bill still remains fairly involved in the day-to-day operations of Family Medical Manufacturing. This is the company that has brought him international recognition. Bill still approves all research projects that take place in our laboratory.
- The company has just moved into its "state-of-the-art" manufacturing facility in the past year. The building has been a showcase for other such companies in the region and boasts all the modern amenities including a programmable pass-card entry system, contemporary cafeteria with home cooked meals and a Research & Development lab worth over $3 million.
- The company now employs approximately 180 people (55% on the production line who work one of two shifts per day). The company also employs over 12 engineers and 6 laboratory technicians.
- Mark believes that staff is generally happy and that the company is positioned for yet another "better-than-expected" year.

appendix F Notes to File

INTEROFFICEMEMO

DATE: APRIL 23, 1999

TO: NANCY MEYERS

FROM: CLAIRE JACKSON

RE: HUMAN RESOURCE ISSUES

CONFIDENTIAL

The following list is a summary of the urgent/priority Human Resources issues that I have been working on in the past two months:

Family Medical Group (Corporate)

- Our request for a part-time HR Assistant has been declined once again and the purchase requisition for the HRIS has been put on hold until Mr. Maron gives further authorization.

Family Distribution

- The staff at Family Distribution seems to be unsettled. Several staff members have left the company through terminations and voluntary resignations within the past two years. Most recently, Dorothy Haffrey was terminated after sixteen years of service. Dorothy has had several formal complaints in her permanent record over the years for inappropriate behaviour and language. Despite several warnings her behaviour has not changed. Three weeks ago she swore at the Director of Marketing in the presence of a supplier. Although staff does not generally condone Dorothy's behaviour, I believe they are genuinely concerned about their own futures.
- Staff at Family Distribution has also been applying aggressively to posted openings at Family Manufacturing.

Family Manufacturing

- Four formal complaints have been submitted about the hiring practices at Family Manufacturing. These employees feel that they have been overlooked for key openings despite being able to fulfil the education and skills required for the positions. In all cases, the positions were filled by former employees of King Manufacturing (Mark Olsen's former employer). I completed the entire first round interviews and have reviewed the files carefully. The positions have all been filled with incumbents who can "hit the ground running." Mark felt Family Manufacturing did not have the time or luxury of training an internal employee.
- Laura Davies, Senior Administrator, has tendered her resignation effective June 11th after not being successful in her application for the new Office Manager position. She has been a strong contributor to the overall administration of the company and has steadily been accepting increasing responsibility. During an informal meeting Laura shared the source of her unhappiness. Barb Brimner, the new Manager of Administration, inadvertently mentioned that Mark had promised her the position before the opening was posted. Laura has obviously perceived the hiring process to be unjust.

case 14 Just Another Email

PART A

In his early morning email sweep, one item caught Bill Richmond's attention. It was a brief note of concern from Janice Sharma, a student at Midville College, where Bill had been President for the past five years. The student had provided a copy of a message from an administrative assistant in the Applied Studies department. (See Exhibit 1 for a copy of her email communiqué.)

Bill Richmond was used to working with a very busy meeting schedule and a daily avalanche of issues and concerns. Through his tenure in this role, Richmond had presided over significant growth in his institution's enrollment base, from 6000 to over 8000 students in arts, science and several professional programs. (See Exhibit 2 for Midville College's partial organization chart.) Over these years Midville continued to position itself in the marketplace as a small, quality-teaching oriented College. Student satisfaction ratings and reputation surveys were important marketing targets for the College.

President Richmond read the message from Janice Sharma thoughtfully, and considered how he should respond.

exhibit 1 Email Message Dated February 12, 2003

To: William Richmond, President, Midville College
From: Janice Sharma

Dear Sir,

Below you will find an email I received from a fellow MC student.
I was saddened to read it as I feel this is not how students should be
treated.

I look forward to hearing from you soon in regards to this matter at
your earliest convenience.

Thank you for taking the time to listen to a concerned student,

Janice Sharma

>Hello, students. Some important points for your consideration...

>1) If a class is cancelled I may or may not send a message to this
>email group. If I find out in time, and enrolment in the class is high (I
>won't send 300+ people a message to advise 6 students in a seminar that class
>is cancelled), and I happen to be at my desk and not in a meeting or
>elsewhere on campus, I MIGHT send a message as a courtesy—this is not a
>requirement! If you happen to show up for a class that has been cancelled, it's not
>the end of the world, people!
>
>2) I do not live in the Applied Studies Office. I start work at 8:30 a.m. and leave at
>4:30 p.m., so if an early morning class is cancelled I won't know until I get here myself.
>
>3) Pre-registration: Late forms will NOT be accepted under any
>circumstances (except the "I was in a coma" excuse). Anyway, by the
>time the deadlines come and go, you all will have received sufficient notice
>and warning that there will be no need for anyone to be late, right?
>
>To those of you who do choose to ignore these warnings and the
>deadlines ... please don't even bother to come in; that only makes things
>awkward and difficult for both of us. You can choose your courses in
>May, on your Intent to Register form or in September.
>
>Thank you for your understanding! Now, everybody go and have a nice day.
>
>S.
>—
>Susan Charmaine
>Administrative Assistant / Undergraduate Advisor
>Department of Applied Studies
>Midville College

exhibit 2 Midville College, Partial Organization Chart

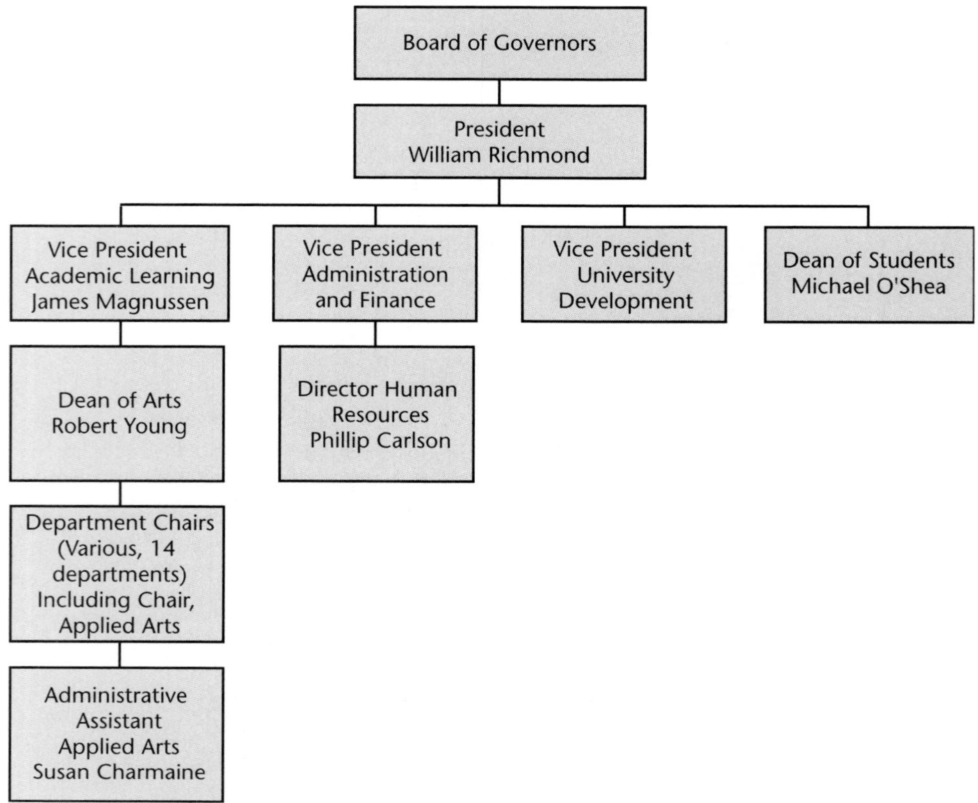

case 15 Migisi Tribal Council, Inc.

Andrew Ross, Executive Director of the Migisi[1] Tribal Council, Inc. (MTC), eased the prow of his fishing boat toward the early evening sun. The lake was quiet, except for the rumble of his outboard motor. Swallows skimmed the water surface for mosquitoes and occasionally the glassy surface of the quiet lake was broken by a hungry fish after its share of the plentiful water insects. Andrew hoped that he could catch a walleye or two in the three hours until the June Canadian sunset. He loved to fish, not so much for the sport of it, but rather for the isolation it gave him to think.

Andrew had a lot to think about this evening. He had met most of the day with the ten First Nations Chiefs that make up the Board of Governors of the MTC. After the closing prayer, four of the Chiefs had asked to see him privately. They informed him that the Councils they represented had tentatively decided to take their four First Nations out of MTC and join with four non-affiliated First Nations in a neighbouring area to the southeast, to form a new tribal council. While there were still loose ends to be considered, they told Ross that the decision to form a new tribal council was highly likely. The Chiefs had told Ross in April that the new tribal council was being considered. Now the decision was much closer to being closed. The reasons they gave were that the four non-affiliated First Nations were close neighbours and that they shared many cultural and historical bonds with them. One of the Chiefs also stated that he thought that "MTC was getting too bureaucratic and too self serving." Andrew knew that if the four First Nations left MTC, MTC would experience major reductions in financial and human resources. The cutbacks would cripple MTC's ability to serve its remaining six members and thus seriously threaten the continued viability of MTC.[2]

This case was prepared by Gary A. Mischke, University of Manitoba, and Donald C. Morrison for the sole purpose of providing material for class discussion. It is not intended to illustrate either effective or ineffective handling of a managerial situation. The situation, data, and characters in this case are real; however, the names of the Tribal Council, First Nations, and managers and some of their characteristics have been disguised at their request. Any reproduction, in any form, of the material in this case is prohibited except with the written consent of the authors.

---

[1]Pronounced Mi-giz'-ee; "eagle" in the Ojibway language.

[2]Tribal councils require a minimum of five First Nation members to qualify for federal funding.

Andrew knew that if these First Nations decided to leave, there was little he could do to stop them. He needed to develop a plan that would convince them to stay. Member First Nations are required to give MTC a one year notice of their intent to leave. The Chiefs felt that they had given MTC fair notice of the four bands' intentions at the April Board of Governors meeting, hence they planned to leave MTC on April 1, 1998. Andrew had less than nine months in which to convince the four to stay or to develop and implement an alternative plan to deal with their leaving.

Late this afternoon, when he met briefly with the four MTC senior managers to debrief the Board of Governors meeting, he found his managers strangely ambivalent about the potential loss of the four members. The staff had seen these threats before. They believed in time the Chiefs and Councils would lose interest and the threat would blow over, so there was little to worry about. This time Andrew wasn't so sure....

ABORIGINAL SELF-GOVERNMENT

For many years the Aboriginal peoples of Canada have sought to control the future of their communities and to preserve their distinctive cultures through the exercise of self-government. The Government of Canada recognizes the rights of Aboriginal peoples to such self determination in section 35 of the *Constitution Act, 1982*. Since 1982, the Government of Canada has conducted lengthy negotiations with Aboriginal people regarding the definition of self government and how it should be implemented.

Aboriginal people believe that self government should include the determination of an economic base so that native people have control over an economic, as well as a political, entity. The Royal Commission on Aboriginal People (RCAP), initiated in 1991 and concluded in 1996, recommended a new partnership within Canada between Aboriginal and non-Aboriginal people. The recommendation is based on the following principles:

- Recognition that Aboriginal people are the original inhabitants and caretakers of the land,
- non-Aboriginal people now also have strong ties to the land,
- respect of each other's culture, heritage, structures and laws,
- an equitable sharing of land and resources, and
- mutual accountability.[3]

The partnership envisioned by the RCAP would be formalized through new and renewed treaties. The RCAP recommends that Aboriginal governments be entitled to share in the sovereignty of Canada.[4]

The RCAP contains recommendations that will require major changes in the way First Nation organizations operate. To exercise the right of self-government, individual First Nations will have to reconstruct themselves as the nations they once were, design constitutions and structures, train personnel in law and decision making, and negotiate new relationships with other governments in Canada.[5] The RCAP acknowledges the

[3]"People to People, Nation to Nation: Highlights from the Report of the Royal Commission on Aboriginal Peoples," Minister of Supply and Services Canada, Ottawa, Ontario, Canada, 1996, pp. 20–21.

[4]Ibid. p. 25

[5]Ibid. p. 26

need for extensive training and development of Aboriginal people to take on the roles of self-government.[6]

When First Nations secure an equitable share of lands and resources, it is expected that First Nation governments will become self-financing.[7] First Nation organizations will be required to develop additional skills in fiscal policy and financial management. Additional lands and resources will allow First Nation members to follow traditional pursuits and will promote economic self-reliance.[8] New economic opportunities will increase the need for business development skills among First Nations.

The time frame identified in the RCAP to complete the full transformation of the relationship between Aboriginal and non-Aboriginal people is twenty years. The RCAP recommends an immediate infusion of resources to stimulate First Nation economic development, significantly upgrade community infrastructure, promote social healing and develop human resources. The time line anticipates completing several land claim and self government agreements by year five. By year ten, most First Nations should be economically self reliant. By the end of the twenty year implementation period, the RCAP anticipates that the financial benefits of self-government will overtake its costs.[9]

The Canadian government has neither formally accepted nor rejected the recommendations put forth in the RCAP. Instead, the Federal Government has advanced its own proposals for self government, proposals which fall well short of the recommendations in the RCAP in the eyes of most Aboriginal people. The Federal proposal offers municipal-style government to First Nations, not sovereignty. The Federal proposal lacks the development of an economic base for First Nations that could lead to economic independence from the government of Canada. Rather, the municipal-style government proposal would leave First Nations dependent on the Federal government for economic security, community infrastructure, health, social and human services.

The Federal Policy Guide on Aboriginal Self Government, issued by the Liberal government of Jean Chrétien from the Office of the Minister of Indian Affairs and Northern Development, Ronald A. Irwin, outlines the Federal Government's position on the parameters of Aboriginal self-government and establishes the requirements the Federal government believes must be met to grant self-government status to First Nation and other Aboriginal communities. The Government's position on the scope of self-government is presented in Appendix 1.

In addition to defining the scope of self-government, the Federal Government has also established guidelines for the transition from current laws and governments to Aboriginal self-government. These guidelines address jurisdiction or authority over non-Aboriginal people, changes in fiduciary obligations of the Canadian Government, recommendations to ensure political and financial accountability in the Aboriginal governments, financial arrangements including funding and cost-sharing, and future access to Federal and Provincial Government programs.[10] The ongoing negotiations

---

[6]Ibid. p. 44

[7]Ibid. p. 31

[8]Ibid. p. 36

[9]Ibid. p. 142

[10]Federal Policy Guide—Aboriginal Self-Government, "The Government of Canada's Approach to Implementation of the Inherent Right and Negotiation of Aboriginal Self-Government." Department of Indian and Northern Affairs Canada, Room 1415, Les Terrasses de la Chaudiére, 10 Wellington Street, Hull, Quebec, K1A 0H4, Canada, pp. 11–16.

between First Nations and the Federal Government over their differing view of what self government should be, and the transition guidelines to create Aboriginal governing entities have created a vibrant market for consulting, management and advisory services among First Nation Communities.

MIGISI TRIBAL COUNCIL, INC.

Migisi Tribal Council is a non-profit organization created to provide advisory and management services to its ten member First Nations in northwestern Ontario. The First Nations have a collective membership of about 3000 people living on First Nations' land in the area around the Lake of the Woods.

Each First Nation is governed by a Chief and First Nation Council, elected by the First Nation membership. The ten Chiefs form the Board of Governors for MTC. The Board of Governors meets quarterly to review MTC performance and set general direction. In addition, each First Nation Council appoints a Director to provide more direct governance of MTC. Directors meet monthly to review MTC programs and make recommendations to improve performance. They also oversee the implementation of any changes in MTC programs. Andrew Ross, the Executive Director, reports to the Board of Directors, and to the Board of Governors. He presents activity reports prepared by staff members, monthly financial statements, and issues of importance at the Board meetings. The Board of Governors and Directors are the primary communications links between MTC and the First Nation's staff and citizens.

At MTC, senior advisors report to Andrew Ross. In practice, MTC's programs operate as autonomous units. Ross reviews and approves all major program initiatives and expenditures. He is responsible for settling any difficulties that arise between the First Nations and his staff. An organization chart for MTC is shown in Exhibit 1.

Exhibit 3 shows the location of the 10 current First Nations that comprise the MTC. They can be grouped roughly as 6 western First Nations located south and southwest of Kenora, and 4 eastern First Nations located near Dryden. In addition, the locations of 4 unaffiliated southern First Nations in the Fort Frances area and 4 unaffiliated northern First Nations north of Kenora are shown. The new tribal council proposes serving the 4 unaffiliated southern First Nations and the 4 southernmost MTC affiliated First Nations.

In 1994, the four eastern area First Nations indicated that they wanted to leave MTC and form their own tribal council. The effort failed when they were unable to attract an additional member so that they would have the necessary five members to qualify for federal funding. In 1996, the six western area members considered aligning themselves with the four northern non-affiliated First Nations, but the effort eventually dissipated.

Ross believed the current effort to join the eight southern First Nations was being driven by external consultants who had developed considerable trust among the eight potential members. The consultants had identified \$166,000 of MTC's accumulated \$370,000 surplus that they argued should transfer to the new council. Gaining control of a share of the MTC surplus was an incentive for the four southern affiliated First Nations to leave MTC. In addition, the members of the new tribal council had made it known to MTC employees that some of them would be offered jobs in the new council on a selective basis. The consultants stand to benefit monetarily from consulting arrangements with the new council.

SERVICE DELIVERY AND COMPETITION

Tribal councils, such as MTC, are primarily service delivery organizations, created to achieve economies of scale by delivering services to multiple First Nation members. The services are broadly categorized as advisory services and management services, with the difference being whether or not the tribal council employee assigned as a consultant takes control of program delivery and/or finances. The services may also be categorized into four general program areas: Government Advisory Services, Financial Management, Technical Services and Education. Exhibit 5 provides descriptions of each of these program areas.

The Advisory Role of MTC

MTC grew out of an agreement among the founding First Nation members to join forces in their efforts to improve their communities. The founders developed MTC's mandate, presented in Exhibit 4. This mandate is reflected in the informal goals established by MTC and the four program areas. In practice, MTC advisors see their roles and responsibilities as encompassing two broad goal sets, related to 1) First Nations development, and 2) internal or external problem solving. First, external government program transfers and initiatives fall within MTC's goals to promote First Nation self determination, development, and authority transfer. With respect to such initiatives, advisors fulfill facilitation, proposal development, and negotiation roles. Second, MTC staff responds to problems that the First Nations are having internally and with outside agencies. Advisors act as mediators and put policies and processes in place that mitigate the difficulties that the First Nation is experiencing.

From a cultural perspective, most advisors take "ownership" of First Nation aspirations. There is a strong sense of finding creative approaches and solutions to fulfill these aspirations. MTC personnel recognize that their actions must be consistent with First Nation political processes. Ignoring political processes could jeopardize an individual's future with MTC. This political sensitivity has created a risk-averse culture at MTC.

MTC strives to increase the scope of services offered, but in a controlled manner dictated by funding limitations. Expansion opportunities are analyzed to ensure financial viability and consistency with MTC's mandate. In each program, MTC competes with professional firms and consultants to provide services. While tribal council advisory services are essentially free to member First Nations (their costs being covered by federal grants to the tribal council), fee-for-service consulting still makes inroads in providing advisory services. The two most often cited reasons First Nations members pay for these services are that: 1) the tribal council lacks sufficient resources to provide the service in a timely manner, or 2) the tribal council lacks competent personnel to deliver the service. Both factors are exacerbated by recruiting among tribal council personnel by consulting firms. As tribal council personnel expand their knowledge and skills, entering the consulting industry becomes very attractive. The structured, risk averse, sometimes bureaucratic nature of the tribal councils does not appeal to aggressive, entrepreneurial individuals. Tribal councils usually cannot offer high caliber professionals the same financial rewards as professional firms or private consulting.

First Nation advisory services utilization varies widely among First Nation members in MTC (Exhibit 6). Although service use is indicative of First Nation requirements, other factors exist that cause variation. Some First Nations feel that the caliber of services available through MTC is inferior to the services available from other sources. This perception has resulted from:

- inconsistent service received from MTC in the past,
- the lack of some service delivery skills since most MTC advisors are generalists and have in-depth skills in limited areas,[11] and
- past success using external sources.

Most of the First Nation members of MTC are not aware of the full range of services available through MTC. Existing communication channels, primarily through the Chiefs and Directors, cannot keep up with the development of skills available through MTC. Many of the projects completed by MTC for the First Nations are in response to external government initiatives. Often, this work is directly transferable to other First Nations. For example, a proposal that generates additional funding for one First Nation can be used as a template for other proposals. Many projects of this nature executed by MTC do not get communicated to all member First Nations.

Many First Nations keep their organizational issues to themselves. This occurs for political reasons and because of pride. It is inconsistent for a First Nation with strong beliefs in self-government and self sufficiency to ask for external help. Further, communities are reluctant to discuss their internal problems with other communities or outside agencies.

Management Service Contracts

Most management services contracts are imposed by funding agencies on the First Nation. The funding agency, in most cases the Department of Indian Affairs and Northern Development (DIAND), will withhold funds from the First Nation until an external manager is in place. The First Nation frequently disagrees that an external manager is necessary. First Nation clients are often apprehensive about giving control to a non-First Nation business entity, however control outside the First Nation is usually mandated. Management services contracts usually arise from perceived or real financial mismanagement, or the simple lack of skills and knowledge within a small First Nation to successfully manage the program. Management services contracts usually grant the external manager full or joint signing authority on the First Nation's bank account(s). The external manager may assume additional responsibilities including:

- financial accounting, budgeting, and reporting,
- capital project management,
- administrative and financial training,
- conflict resolution, and
- organizational restructuring.

While skill transfer to First Nation personnel and long-term financial stability are stipulated as long term objectives of management services contracts, those objectives are often not realized.

The MTC's competitors for management services contracts have been local and national accounting firms. Other competitors such as national consulting firms will

---

[11]See Exhibit 2, biographies of Migisi Tribal Council senior managers, for areas of expertise and experience.

likely enter this lucrative and growing market. While the accounting firms have the expertise to implement effective financial accounting and control mechanisms, most contracts also involve program delivery requirements in areas involving capital, operations and maintenance, health and social services, and education. Accounting firms do not have the expertise in these areas and must either contract out program delivery or rely on the First Nation to execute these program delivery requirements themselves. When tribal councils win management services contracts, they usually have both the professional skills to execute financial controls and the program delivery skills to manage program delivery.

Management services contracts are paid for by the First Nation, the funding agency, or are cost shared by both parties. Contracts are awarded through bids, usually to the low bidder. A tribal council can often absorb some of the costs and most of the overheads in existing, government-funded operations and can thus under-bid other competitors. As a result, professional services companies competing for management services contracts face a cost disadvantage.

Within MTC, there has been significant disagreement about how management services should be executed, or if they should be executed at all by MTC. Some Directors feel that management services contracts stray too far away from MTC's mandate to provide advice (Exhibit 5) and place MTC in conflicting roles. For example, MTC is accountable to First Nation leadership, yet, a management services contract stipulates that First Nation activities must be authorized by the assigned MTC manager. While the Board of Governors has authorized MTC managers to hold management service manager positions (for which they may be compensated), several of the Chiefs are concerned that MTC managers who take on such positions might be distracted from fulfilling their advisory services responsibilities. Since 1992, MTC has entered into six management services contracts (Exhibit 7). Three of those contracts are still in force.

MTC STAFFING AND CULTURE

Andrew Ross and MTC senior program managers are well qualified and experienced in their respective program areas. Most MTC staffers hold university degrees in their area of specialization (Exhibit 2). Because MTC is a small organization, senior program managers are active in the delivery of services to the First Nations. As program delivery demands by member First Nations have increased, MTC's senior managers have spent less time on managerial activities at MTC, like establishing program goals, directing resources, and coordinating programs.

MTC has successfully attracted, retained, and developed highly competent staff. The specialized nature of job requirements requires low staff turnover to deliver a successful program. Most staff members at MTC have long tenure with the organization. Most are themselves Aboriginal people. Staff members spend a significant amount of time in gaining the trust of First Nation staffs and management. First Nations are often wary of organizations or individuals offering assistance. Staff members consider the long-term impacts of their recommendations to the First Nations and avoid "quick fix" solutions since they expect to retain their relationship with their First Nation clients over the years.

Within the ten member First Nations, MTC is not specifically market-focused. Requests are rarely refused for reasons other than time constraints. This lack of focus is embedded in the organization's culture. Advisors are expected to address any concern that the First Nations have within the broad descriptions of their program areas (Exhibit 5). There is no specific concentration on high value-added activities.

Cultural beliefs and the expectations of First Nation clients have led to some conflict within the MTC organization over the degree of autonomy programs should have. Some Directors feel that programs should operate based on policies and pre-established goals and objectives established by the member First Nation Councils. Most MTC senior managers feel that since they are MTC's front-line workers involved daily with government and agencies, they are in a better position to monitor the environment and should be allowed significant latitude in program design and execution.

Although stringent policies and guidelines exist, there are very few formal controls enforced within MTC. Andrew Ross gives his staff significant autonomy. Mutual trust is high. Senior staff are expected to use their professional judgment and do whatever it takes to get the job done. Individual program planning by the staff is encouraged. Staff are encouraged to maintain strong linkages to their First Nation clients. MTC places a high value on staff training. Staff are not seriously reprimanded for making mistakes or for minor policy violations. Performance deficiencies are not harshly addressed, but are used instead as learning or training opportunities.

Every staff member is expected to be a leader. Staff are to take responsibility for errors and remain modest about accomplishments. MTC personnel are encouraged to be role models for First Nation Councils, their staff members and citizens, by exhibiting a high degree of professionalism in their work habits and personal lives.

FUNDING AND FINANCIAL CAPABILITIES

MTC is a non-profit organization. The majority of MTC's funding is from the Department of Indian Affairs and Northern Development (DIAND). Financial statements for MTC are shown in Exhibits 8 & 9. An operating projection based on business as usual at MTC for 1997/98 is shown in Exhibit 10.

Funding levels projected in Exhibit 10 are determined by two methods 1) formula-based funding and 2) program funding. Formula-based funding is driven by the number of First Nations members served. For example, the *Core* funding formula considers the number of affiliated communities and First Nation remoteness and population. Formula based funding is employed in DIAND core and instructional services funding (but *not* including ancillary, special education and tuition since they are considered specific management services programs to some area schools). Second, *program* funding is proposal driven. Funding for membership, enhanced technical services and economic development is program based. Fewer members would result in fewer opportunities to write program proposals in these areas. In addition, the education transportation program is administered on behalf of one of the departing First Nations and would no longer be administered by MTC should the First Nation leave MTC.

MTC, as a non-profit organization, retains surpluses or must absorb deficits. Given these funding methodologies, it would be expected that MTC's funding would tend to equal its expenditures over time. This has not been the case, however, and as shown on the Balance Sheet in Exhibit 8, MTC has accumulated a surplus of about $370,000. The surplus resulted for the following reasons:

- The Federal government operates on a cash basis and is inclined to prepay future obligations to MTC as the Federal fiscal year-end approaches, if a surplus is anticipated.

- Many programs operate on a retroactive basis due to delays in funding negotiations and decisions. If MTC reaches agreement on a new program or a program enhancement say in February, funding may be based on a full fiscal-year beginning the previous April to compensate for bureaucratic delays.
- MTC generates significant interest revenue from short-term deposits on funds not immediately dispersed.

THE FUTURE OF MTC

As Andrew Ross cast for walleyes in the long Canadian evening, he identified three options that he would place before his staff when he returned to the office the next morning. One option was to try to convince the four Chiefs and First Nation Councils to stay with MTC. That would require that MTC eliminate a backlog of requests for management services contracts and enhance service provisioning on current contracts. MTC would need to become more "customer driven" by responding more quickly to First Nation demands and by being more sensitive to the cultural and political needs of the Chiefs and First Nation Councils.

Better service would not come without costs. Ross knew that he lacked sufficient staff and in some areas sufficient skills to deliver more management services without affecting the advisory services his busy staff was mandated to deliver. Andrew believed he needed to hire at least one additional staff advisor to catch up and to enroll certain of his staff in specific training programs. As he matched the service needs he was currently unable to fill due to lack of specialized knowledge with the staff members who should be assigned to deliver those services, he could easily see 26 person weeks of additional training needs in the staff. Additional services would also encounter additional delivery costs. Travel costs and *per diem* rates were reimbursed to staff at industry rates. Further he would need to be sure that his efforts did not go unnoticed by the Chiefs and the Councils. It wouldn't do much good for staff members to upgrade their skills and for MTC to increase its services provision capabilities if those services were only used to clear the backlog, and not made available to other members.

Ross also considered a plan to replace the departing members with some of the unaffiliated First Nations in the area north of Kenora. He believed that he might be able to attract two or three of those four, unaffiliated First Nations to the MTC. It would take quite a selling effort, since these First Nations had been approached on other occasions to join MTC. The efforts had been casual because MTC had all the work its staff could handle with member First Nations. Nonetheless, three of the four had expressed interest in joining MTC. These new member initiatives had died for lack of strong support at MTC. MTC would need to mount a concerted effort to recruit the new members. News of the loss of the four current members would put MTC in the vulnerable position of needing the new members to survive. That would mean that the new members would likely drive a hard bargain to gain concessions from MTC. Further, MTC's remaining existing members would want the same terms as new members if terms were changed. Andrew wasn't sure what he would have to negotiate in terms of free services or reduced contract costs to attract the new members, but he believed that recruiting expenses for travel and conferences would cost at least $5000 per First Nation. The concessions and recruiting efforts would also create more work for his already busy staff.

The loss of four First Nations would mean the loss of the current management contracts MTC had with them and the programs that were underway. New members would only add new management contracts and programs as their needs required them. As a result, the loss of existing members would require an adjustment in the numbers of MTC staff managers since the current staff levels could not be supported indefinitely without the management contract and program revenues. Ross believed that some combination of middle level managers (salaried at about $57,500 per year) and lower level managers (salaried at about $33,000 per year) would need to be laid off until MTC secured sufficient new revenues to replace those lost with the departing four First Nation members.

A third option was to change the mandate of MTC and to restructure the organization into a management services company. Ross believed that several of his current managers had skills and education that were competitive with those of managers in the consulting and professional companies that were bidding for First Nation management services business. MTC had the added advantage of a strong First Nation culture, staffing by Aboriginal people and close ties with some of its member First Nations. Perhaps MTC should reposition itself as a management services consulting company, specializing in the management of First Nation programs. The existing organization could be split into an advisory services organization that would continue to provide advice to the remaining member First Nations, and a management services organization that would take over the remaining existing management services contracts. The new division could aggressively compete with consulting and professional service firms for new management services contracts among member and non-affiliated First Nations in Ontario and Manitoba.

Whichever course Ross and his staff elected for MTC, Ross believed that the solution must provide financial stability and long term viability for MTC. He also wanted to retain the competent staff he had worked so hard over the years to assemble. MTC was a small, close knit organization, and many of the staff had become his personal friends. Andrew knew their families. He was committed to treating the staff equitably in any changes made to MTC. The solution would need to fit MTC's culture and the values of its managers, as well as continue to meet the service needs and cultural preferences of the First Nations MTC served. Finally, the solution must support Aboriginal self-government efforts, and not jeopardize program funding for First Nation people during the changes.

Andrew Ross eased the prow of his fishing boat into the dock in the setting Ontario sun. Despite the fact that the walleyes weren't biting and he had come home empty handed, it had been a good outing. He had some ideas to try out on his staff in the morning. It would take some study to decide which to pursue, and a lot of work to put their decision into action, but for the first time since he first heard about the four Chiefs' plans in April, he felt that MTC had some good options for survival.

appendix 1 Scope of Aboriginal Self-Government[12]

Scope of Negotiations

Under the federal approach, the central objective of negotiations will be to reach agreements on self-government as opposed to legal definitions of the inherent right. The Government realizes that Aboriginal governments and institutions will require the jurisdiction or authority to act in a number of areas in order to give practical effect to the inherent right of self-government. Broadly stated, the Government views the scope of Aboriginal jurisdiction or authority as likely extending to matters that are internal to the group, integral to its distinct Aboriginal culture, and essential to its operation as a government or institution. Under this approach, the range of matters that the federal government would see as subjects for negotiation could include all, some, or parts of the following:

- establishment of government structures, internal constitutions, elections, leadership selection processes
- membership
- marriage
- adoption and child welfare
- Aboriginal language, culture and religion
- education
- health
- social services
- administrative/enforcement of Aboriginal laws, including the establishment of Aboriginal courts or tribunals and the creation of offences of the type normally created by local or regional governments for the contravention of their laws
- policing
- property rights, including succession and estates
- land management, including: zoning; service fees; land tenure and access; and expropriation of Aboriginal land by Aboriginal governments for their own public purposes
- natural resources management
- agriculture
- hunting, fishing and trapping on Aboriginal lands
- taxation in respect to direct taxes and property taxes of members
- transfer and management of monies and group assets
- management of public works and infrastructure
- housing
- local transportation
- licensing, regulation and operation of businesses located on Aboriginal lands

In some of these areas, detailed arrangements will be required to ensure harmonization of laws, while in others, a more general recognition of Aboriginal jurisdiction or authority may be sufficient.

There are a number of other areas that may go beyond matters that are integral to Aboriginal culture or that are strictly internal to an Aboriginal group. To the extent that the federal government has jurisdiction in these areas, it is prepared to negotiate some measure of Aboriginal jurisdiction or authority. In these areas, laws and regulations tend to have impacts that go beyond individual communities. Therefore, primary law-making authority would remain with the federal or provincial governments, as the case may be, and their laws will prevail in the event of a conflict with Aboriginal laws. Subject matters in this category would include:

- divorce
- labour/training
- administrative justice issues, including matters related to the administration and enforcement of laws of other jurisdictions which might include certain criminal laws

[12]Federal Policy Guide—Aboriginal Self-Government, "The Government of Canada's Approach to Implementation of the Inherent Right and Negotiation of Aboriginal Self-Government." Department of Indian and Northern Affairs Canada, Room 1415, Les Terrasses de la Chaudiére, 10 Wellington Street, Hull, Quebec, K1A 0H4, Canada, pp. 5–8.

continued

appendix 1 Scope of Aboriginal Self-Government (*continued*)

- penitentiaries and parole
- environmental protection, assessment and pollution prevention
- fisheries co-management
- migratory birds co-management
- gaming
- emergency preparedness

There are a number of subject matters where there are no compelling reasons for Aboriginal governments or institutions to exercise law-making authority. These subject matters cannot be characterized as either integral to Aboriginal cultures, or internal to Aboriginal groups. They can be grouped under two headings: (i) powers related to Canadian sovereignty, defence and external relations; and (ii) other national interest powers. In these areas, it is essential that the federal government retain its law-making authority. Subject matters in this category include:

(i) Powers Related to Canadian Sovereignty, Defence and External Relations

- international/domestic relations and foreign policy
- national defence and security
- security of national borders
- international treaty-making
- immigration, naturalization and aliens
- international trade, including tariffs and import/export controls

(ii) Other National Interest Powers

- management and regulation of the national economy, including:
  - regulation of the national business framework, fiscal and monetary policy
  - a central bank and banking system
  - bankruptcy and insolvency
  - trade and competition policy
  - intellectual property
  - incorporation of federal corporations
  - currency
- maintenance of national law and order and substantive criminal law, including
  - offences and penalties under the Criminal Code and other criminal laws
  - emergencies and the "peace, order and good government" power
- protection of the health and safety of all Canadians
- federal undertakings and other powers, including:
  - broadcasting and telecommunications
  - aeronautics
  - navigation and shipping
  - maintenance of national transportation systems
  - postal service
  - census and statistics

While law-making power in these areas will not be the subject of negotiations, the Government is prepared to consider administrative arrangements where it might be feasible and appropriate.

exhibit 1 Migisi Tribal Council Structure

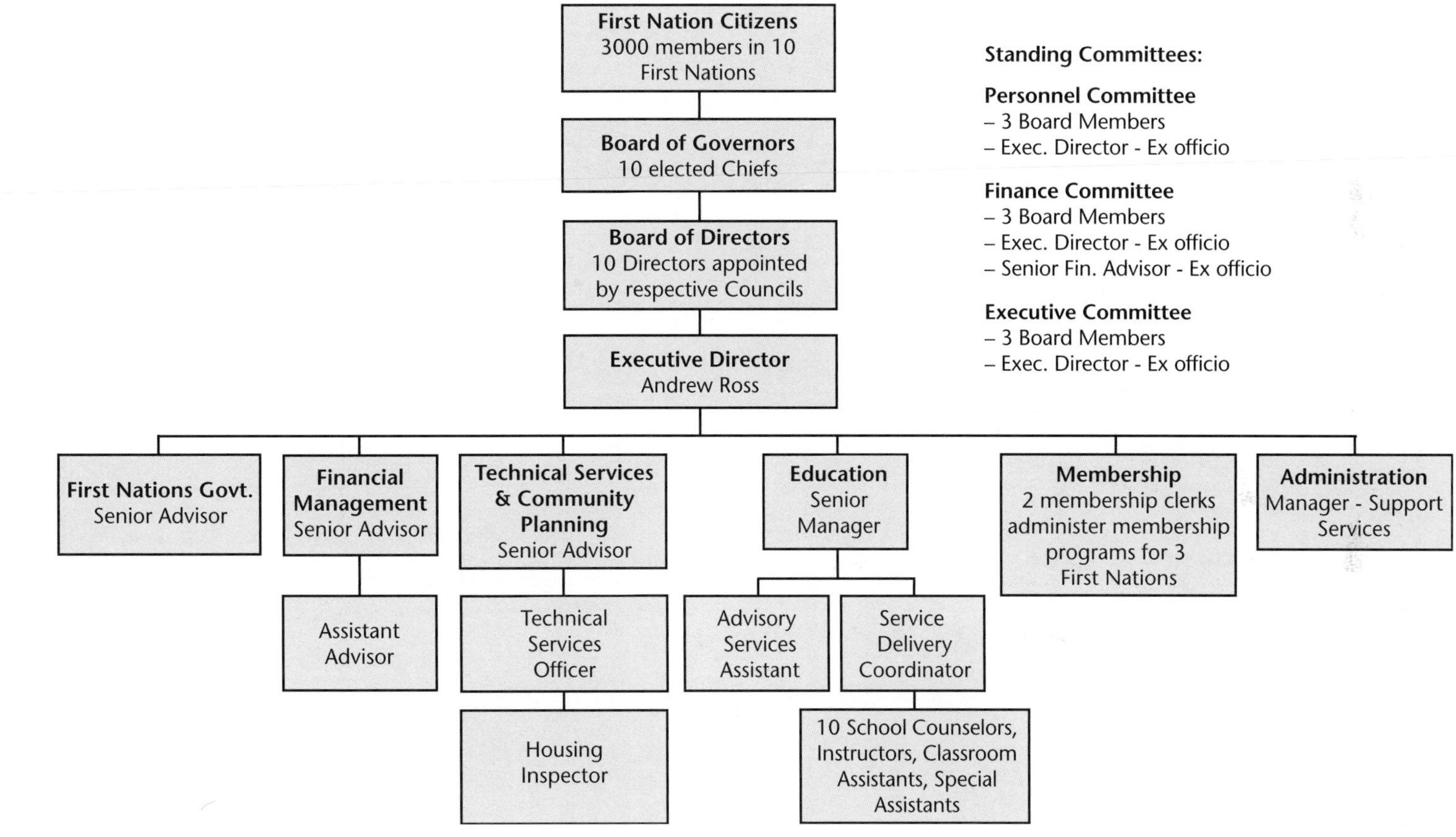

exhibit 2 Management of MTC

Andrew Ross—Executive Director
Age 43. MBA—University of Manitoba
Previous experience:

- 1975–1981 Served as Councilor of a Manitoba First Nation
- 1974–1981 First Nation Administrator
- 1981–1985 Served as Chief of a Manitoba First Nation
- 1986–1987 Assistant Director of a Saskatchewan Tribal Council
- 1987–Present Executive Director of Migisi Tribal Council

Ruth Petquan—Senior Advisor—First Nations Government
Age 54. BA—Political Science—Lakehead University
Previous experience:

- 1967–1975 Policy Analyst, Department of Indian and Northern Affairs Canada, Hull, Quebec
- 1975–1982 Funding Manager, Department of Indian and Northern Affairs Canada
- 1983–1990 Project Manager, Big Sand Ojibway Nation
- 1990–1991 Private Consulting
- 1991–Present Senior Advisor—Migisi Tribal Council

David Fobister—Senior Advisor—Financial Management
Age 38. MBA—University of Manitoba
Previous experience:

- 1983–1984 Financial clerk—Dunwoody Chartered Accountants
- 1984–1987 Assistant Financial Advisor—Thunder Bay Area Tribal Council
- 1988–1991 Assistant Financial Advisor—Migisi Tribal Council
- 1991–Present Senior Advisor—Migisi Tribal Council

Emil Keejick—Senior Advisor—Technical Services
Age 46. BS—Civil Engineering, University of Manitoba
Licensed Professional Engineer
Previous experience:

- 1974–1979 Capital Projects Analyst—Department of Public Works, Winnipeg, Manitoba
- 1979–1986 Capital Projects Manager—Department of Public Works, Winnipeg, Manitoba
- 1987–Present Senior Advisor—Migisi Tribal Council

Nicole Kinew—Senior Manager—Education
Age 36. M.Ed.—University of Saskatchewan
Previous experience:

- 1986–1988 Teacher—Grade 5 and 6—Sioux Falls First Nation School
- 1988–1990 Substitute Teacher, Saskatoon Public Schools, Saskatoon, Saskatchewan
- 1990–1992 Education Director—Sioux Falls First Nation
- 1992–1995 Education Services Coordinator, Grand Council Treaty #3[13]
- 1995–Present Senior Manager—Education, Migisi Tribal Council

Deloris White—Manager—Support Services
Age 31. Associate Degree—Red River Community College
Previous experience:

- 1990–1993 Receptionist and Secretary—Lake of the Woods Realty Co.
- 1994–Present Manager—Support Services

[13]A First Nations political organization

exhibit 3 Location of First Nations Served by Migisi Tribal Council

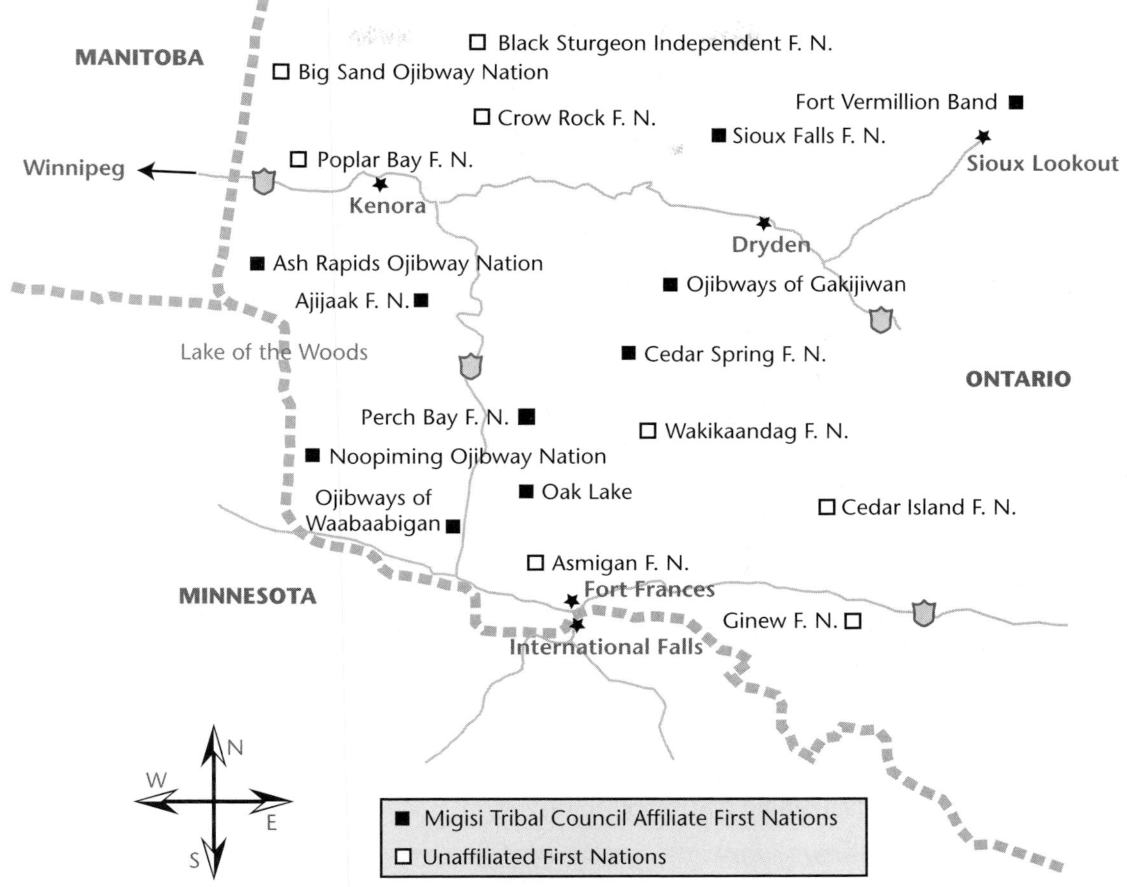

exhibit 4 Migisi Tribal Council's Mandate

The original founding First Nations developed an appropriate leadership structure which would ensure that community requirements would be addressed.

The Board of Directors and the Secretariat were then entrusted with some specific tasks which included:

- establishing policies and strategies which would effectively meet the work requirements as stated by the communities,
- promoting self-government and self determination,
- facilitating First Nation development through whatever appropriate mechanisms have been deemed most acceptable by the individual leaderships,
- assessing the transfer of authority, responsibility, and accountability to the identified First Nation entity, and
- provide a centralized vehicle to the communities whereby they can readily access needed resources to work on issues of regional concern.

exhibit 5 Description of Program Areas

I. Government Advisory Services

This program supports a broad range of services which cater to the diverse needs identified by the communities. The primary focus is to assist the communities in upgrading the quality of services that they provide to their membership.

This activity range includes self-government activities, transfer of programs, development of community institutions, and assisting in the development of the administrative unit.

II. Financial Management

This program is responsible for assisting communities in establishing and maintaining effective and efficient financial systems. These systems must accommodate the needs of the communities as they relate to planning, budgeting, controlling and reporting.

Skill transfer activities are emphasized in the delivery of these services and the service incorporates a range of activities to fulfill this role.

III. Technical Services

This program assists First Nations in matters related to the management of community infrastructure, housing and utilities, the operation and maintenance of capital assets, and community and capital planning.

This program assists with meeting different building standards and codes, providing professional engineering advice where needed, participating in major facility construction, assisting in accessing funds, assisting in negotiation processes, and developing necessary training programs.

IV. Education

This is a relatively new program area. Staff concentrate on assisting communities with their educational initiatives. The program encompasses activities such as counseling students, assisting in tuition agreement negotiations, curriculum development, and ongoing advice to First Nation Education Authorities.

exhibit 6 First Nation Advisory Services Utilization

I. Eastern Area First Nations

1. **Sioux Falls First Nation**
   A. First Nation Government—Use these services regularly for policy development and meeting facilitation.
   B. Financial Management—Heavy users of these services for financial accounting/planning and proposal development/negotiation.
   C. Technical Services—Heavy users of these services for inspections and proposal development/negotiation.
   D. Education—Occasional users of these services for general information.
2. **Fort Vermillion Band**
   A. First Nation Government—Not utilized.
   B. Financial Management—Not utilized.
   C. Technical Services—Occasional users of these services for land surveys.
   D. Education—Not utilized.
3. **Ojibways of Gakijiwan**
   A. First Nation Government—Not utilized.
   B. Financial Management—Not utilized.
   C. Technical Services—Heavy users of these services for inspections, proposal development/negotiation, and hands-on technical/construction assistance.
   D. Education—Occasional users of these services for meetings with external agencies and general information.

continued

exhibit 6 First Nation Advisory Services Utilization (*continued*)

4. Cedar Spring First Nation

A. First Nation Government—Use these services regularly for policy development.

B. Financial Management—Heavy users of these services for financial accounting/planning and policy development.

C. Technical Services—Use these services regularly for inspections and hands-on technical/construction assistance.

D. Education—Occasional users of these services for meetings with external agencies and general information.

II. Western Area First Nations

1. Ajijaak First Nation

A. First Nation Government—Not utilized.

B. Financial Management—Occasional users of these services for financial accounting/planning and general advice.

C. Technical Services—Use these services regularly for inspections and proposal development/negotiation.

D. Education—Occasional users of these services for meetings with external agencies and general information.

2. Ash Rapids Ojibway Nation

A. First Nation Government—Not utilized.

B. Financial Management—Regular users of these services for financial accounting/planning and general advice.

C. Technical Services—Occasional users of these services for inspections and planning.

D. Education—Occasional users of these services for general information.

3. Perch Bay First Nation

A. First Nation Government—Occasional users of these services for elections.

B. Financial Management—Occasional users of these services for financial accounting/planning.

C. Technical Services—Occasional users of these services for inspections and planning.

D. Education—Not utilized.

4. Noopiming Ojibway Nation

A. First Nation Government—Use these services regularly for policy development and meeting facilitation.

B. Financial Management—Heavy users of these services for financial accounting/planning and proposal development/negotiation.

C. Technical Services—Heavy users of these services for inspections and proposal development/negotiation.

D. Education—Occasional users of these services for general information.

5. Ojibways of Waabaabigan

A. First Nation Government—Occasional users of these services for elections.

B. Financial Management—Occasional users of these services for financial accounting/planning and general advice.

C. Technical Services—Occasional users of these services for inspections and planning.

D. Education—Not utilized.

6. Oak Lake First Nation

A. First Nation Government—Not utilized.

B. Financial Management—Occasional users of these services for financial planning and proposal development.

C. Technical Services—Regular users of these services for inspections and proposal development/negotiation.

D. Education—Not utilized.

exhibit 7 Current and Closed Management Services Contracts

1. **1992–Current: Ojibways of Waabaabigan Education Authority Capital Projects**
   This contract involved co-managing approximately $483,000 in education capital funds (major schools repairs, landscaping etc.). A major component of this project is still outstanding pending further direction from the First Nation.
2. **1994: Oak Lake First Nation C.M.H.C. Housing Construction**
   This contract involved co-managing approximately $389,000 in C.M.H.C. housing funds.
3. **1994–1997: Ojibways of Waabaabigan Health and Welfare Transportation**
   This contract involved assuming full management responsibility for approximately $167,000 per year. This contract expired March 31, 1997.
4. **1995–1996: Ojibways of Waabaabigan Capital Projects**
   This contract involved co-managing $1,000,000 in capital projects as part of a land claim settlement.
5. **1996–Current: Cedar Spring First Nation Third Party Management**
   This two-year contract involves assuming full management responsibility for all of the First Nation's funds received from the Department of Indian and Northern Affairs Canada (approximately $750,000 per year). First Nation program areas include education, housing, operation and maintenance, and administration.
6. **1997–Current: Cedar Spring First Nation Co-management**
   This contract involves co-managing all of the First Nation's funds until March 31, 1998.

exhibit 8 Migisi Tribal Council Adjusted Balance Sheet ($)

	1995–96	1994–95	1993–94	1992–93	1991–92
ASSETS					
Current Assets					
Cash	513,055	298,133	334,531	344,137	291,133
Accounts Receivable	279,617	205,630	26,682	171,094	241,559
Due from Affiliated Company		5,000	5,000	5,000	
Due from Third Party Management			102,056		
Prepaid Expenses		8,861	3,019	2,219	1,875
Total Current Assets	792,672	517,624	471,288	522,450	534,567
Capital Fund					
Office Furniture and Equipment	123,870	108,973	85,310	63,040	63,546
LIABILITIES AND EQUITY:					
Current Liabilities					
Accounts Payable and Accruals	359,433	48,409	57,141	27,542	22,499
Employees Deductions Payable	9,954	13,139	8,579	7,946	3,700
Due to Affiliated Company	12,300	12,261	5,000		58,432
Deferred Revenues*	38,683	28,395	41,878	97,664	104,029
Total Current Liabilities	420,370	102,204	112,598	133,152	188,660
Equity					
Surplus (Deficit)	372,302	415,420	358,690	389,298	345,907
Total Liabilities and Equity	792,672	517,624	471,288	522,450	534,567
Capital Fund					
Investment in Capital Assets	123,870	108,973	85,310	63,040	63,546
***Adjusted Deferred Revenues**					
Maintenance Training				11,998	
Homemakers					1,406
Workshop			4,548	24,660	24,689
Economic Development Group		5,000	5,000	5,000	
Ojibways of Waabaabigan			32,330	56,006	27,934
Co-Managership					
Health and Welfare	38,683	23,395			
Maintenance					50,000
Total	38,683	28,395	41,878	97,664	104,029

exhibit 9 Migisi Tribal Council Adjusted Statement Revenues & Expenditures ($)

	1995–96			1994–95		
Program	**Revenue**	**Expenditure**	**Surplus**	**Revenue**	**Expenditure**	**Surplus**
Core	942,618	908,752	33,866	920,393	881,912	38,481
Membership	6,715	6,254	461	16,808	19,577	(2,769)
Education	1,782,374	1,755,413	26,961	697,912	631,029	66,883
Workshops			0	4,548	4,548	0
Health Study	34,236	34,236	0			0
Council Program	42,158	20,937	21,221	21,523	20,059	1,464
Technical Services	188,950	287,960	(99,010)	107,000	162,914	(55,914)
Health & Welfare Transport	166,730	147,682	19,048	28,507	19,922	8,585
Economic Development	121,600	121,600	0	121,561	121,561	0
Total	3,285,381	3,282,834		1,918,252	1,861,522	
Surplus (Deficit)			2,547			56,730

	1993–94			1992–93		
Program	**Revenue**	**Expenditure**	**Surplus**	**Revenue**	**Expenditure**	**Surplus**
Core	697,316	756,118	(58,802)	716,418	732,002	(15,584)
Membership	16,256	21,353	(5,097)	15,673	13,333	2,340
Education	260,000	263,680	(3,680)	80,001	103,783	(23,782)
Workshops	20,112	20,112	0	45,029	45,029	0
Waabaabigan Co-Managership	23,676	23,676	0	62,034	62,034	0
Council Program	19,497	22,310	(2,813)	33,211	17,035	16,176
Maintenance Training			0	38,002	38,002	0
Technical Services	136,775	96,991	39,784	140,222	75,981	64,241
Economic Development	145,325	145,325	0	264,000	264,000	0
Total	1,318,957	1,349,565		1,394,590	1,351,199	
Surplus (Deficit)			(30,608)			43,391

	1991–92		
Program	**Revenue**	**Expenditure**	**Surplus**
Core	647,468	531,198	116,270
Membership	14,126	8,509	5,617
Workshops	10,869	10,869	0
Council Program	12,916	10,281	2,635
Technical Services	134,962	29,683	105,279
Economic Development	250,513	250,513	0
Education	70,000	0	70,000
Homemakers	59,405	59,405	0
Total	1,200,259	900,45	
Surplus (Deficit)			299,801

exhibit 10 1997/98 Projected Revenues and Expenses ($)

Program	Core	Member-ship	Education	Council Program	Technical Services	Economic Develop.	Total
REVENUE							
Indian and Northern Affairs Canada							
Core	688,000						688,000
Instructional Services			145,000				145,000
Membership		6,700					6,700
Ancillary			315,400				315,400
Special Education			263,600				263,600
Transportation			145,800				145,800
Tuition			650,000				650,000
Enhanced					188,950		188,950
Economic Development						121,600	121,600
Sundry				40,000			40,000
Administration Fees	54,000						54,000
Total Revenue	742,000	6,700	1,519,800	40,000	188,950	121,600	2,619,050
EXPENSES							
Advertising	500						500
Asset Condition Reporting					5,000		5,000
Audit and Accounting	10,500		5,000				15,500
Administration			35,000		19,000		54,000
Bank Charges	100						100
Board Honoraria and Travel	120,000		21,000		4,000		145,000
Conference			11,000				11,000
Consultation	5,000						5,000
Employees Benefits	27,000		56,500		13,500		97,000
Equipment Leases	600						600
Equipment Purchases	5,500		9,000		3,000		17,500
Goods and Services Tax	1,400						1,400
Group Insurance	14,000				5,600		19,600
Insurance	3,000						3,000
Legal	2,000						2,000
Miscellaneous			3,000	21,000			24,000
Office and Postage	24,000		3,800		1,700		29,500
Ontario Health Tax	1,200				1,200		2,400
Rent and Parking	42,100		15,400		2,400		59,900
Salaries	380,000	6,000	540,000		120,000		1,046,000
Staff Training	16,000		11,000		8,000		35,000
Staff Travel	97,000	300	33,000		25,000		155,300
Telephone	11,400						11,400
Transfer to First Nations						121,600	121,600
Transportation			96,000				96,000
Tuition			650,000				650,000
Workshops	12,000				15,000		27,000
Goods and Services Tax Recovery	(20,000)						(20,000)
Total Expenses	753,300	6,300	1,489,700	21,000	223,400	121,600	2,615,300
Excess of Revenues over Expenses	(11,300)	400	30,100	19,000	(34,450)	0	3,750

case 16 Northwell Inc.

When Northwell's Senior Management and Board first gave Claudia the leadership role in the development of a virtual medical product and service mall with Medichek, a year and a half ago, she was delighted. She and Nathan Daniels (V-P Marketing) had uncovered the opportunity, Medichek was an excellent organization, and it had been clear that this was a venture well worth embracing. Claudia Leung, CFO of Northwell, had an excellent working relationship with senior management at Medichek. Since Northwell's major contribution in the shorter term would be cash ($7.5 million as of now), she was the ideal candidate for the assignment. The development of this initiative would increase her entrepreneurial skill set and profile and looked to be a manageable addition to her portfolio of responsibilities.

Claudia was beginning to wonder if this dream assignment was about to become a nightmare. The project had run into technical problems, was 4 to 5 months behind schedule, and the Board and Senior Management at Northwell were frustrated and putting pressure on Claudia to get things moving. Executives at Medichek were pushing back, in response to their own frustration, stating that Claudia's interventions were hindering progress. In addition, she'd been hearing growing rumblings of concern and unhappiness in the sales and marketing areas, evidenced in the recent resignation of three staff members and the loss of a good distributor from the mid-west U.S.

Northwell's Senior Management and Board Chair had asked Claudia to recommend a course of action that would rectify problems with this undertaking. They were expecting this advice to be tabled within the next two weeks.

HISTORY OF THE FIRM

Northwell Medical was founded 25 years ago, as the result of a merger between a Canadian and a U.S. firm. Northern Medical, the Canadian partner, had specialized in durable hospital/medical products, while Wellness Medical had focused on consumable hospital products. Both had distributed their products in Canada and the U.S. for a decade prior to the merger, and had shared marketing and distribution services for five years.

The actual merger announcement was anticipated and welcomed by most shareholders and managers. There were some initial difficulties as structures, systems, processes, roles, and reporting relationships were sorted out during the first year. By year three the merger was viewed by both insiders and outsiders as a success. Market penetration and sales accelerated while average costs declined (after accounting for one-time restructuring costs). Growth rates averaged 20% (discounting for inflation) throughout the first 15 years in what was a fairly mature market. Northwell made aggressive investments in technology and product development during this period. Profitability grew at rates 10% above industry norms, with the return on equity averaging 18% during this period. This growth was partially stimulated by the addition of new and/or improved products, but it was largely due to Northwell's spreading reputation for value, service and support. They won market share from competitors, even though their price structure was typically 2% to 10% higher.

As consolidation occurred in the hospital and nursing care delivery systems, it was clear that Northwell was well positioned to solidify its position as a preferred supplier amongst purchasing agents, administrators and hospital user groups. In U.S. industry surveys of hospital suppliers, Northwell regularly placed in the top 5 for quality, service, support, and overall customer satisfaction during the two decades that followed.

Northwell Medical produced a wide range of medical products for institutional usage. Products ranged from consumable patient supplies such as wound dressings, bandages, and disposable surgical supplies to more durable products (e.g., IV units, walkers, canes). In addition to the products it produced, Northwell used its sales network to distribute high quality, higher margin products, sourced largely from European and smaller North American specialty manufacturers. Ten years ago these accounted for 10% of the products listed, 15% of sales and 6% of the profits, and by the most recent year end they represented 10% of products listed, 15% of sales and 25% of profits. These products included hospital beds, wheel chairs, and orthopedic supports (braces for limbs and neck). The intent was to provide purchasing agents and their therapeutic committees with one stop shopping for their medical product needs in particular product categories.

Northwell's production facilities were located in the U.S., Canada, and Mexico. The Canadian plant specialized in products that involve metal fabrication (approximately 20% of total manufactured products, 25% of sales and 30% of profits in the most recent year end), while the two U.S. plants manufactured both plastic and fabric related product (40% of manufactured products, 30% of sales, and 15% of profits). The Mexican plant also produced plastic and fabric related products (20% of manufactured products listed, 15% of sales, and 10% of profits). In addition, Northwell sourced manufacturing services for some of its products in the Asia-Pacific area (10% of manufactured products listed, 10% of sales, 15% of profits).

In North America, Northwell marketed and sold its products primarily through its own sales force. In addition, a number of medical product distribution companies carried some or all of the Northwell line. They were prequalified by Northwell and tended to service smaller hospitals and nursing homes, medical and dental offices, and regional medical product retail supply outlets. The prequalification checks included financial stability, reputation, and service quality. Those selected committed to agreed-to minimum sales volumes. Distributors were not given exclusive territories, but over the years they had sorted themselves out in ways that meant that most American markets were well serviced. These independent distributors accounted for 25% of sales and approximately 30% of the profits. Wholesale prices allowed for dealer margins that varied from 15% to 30%, depending upon the type of product and the complexity involved in selling and servicing the product (e.g., in-service hospital staff training in product use).

Over the years certain managers and board members had expressed interest in extending their activities into foreign markets (Europe and Japan were the ones most frequently mentioned). However, Northwell had shied away from these opportunities, due to concerns over their ability to compete and the belief that there were more profitable growth opportunities available in North America. Throughout the years, at the request of specific European firms they trusted, Northwell had engaged in the export of a limited range of relatively unique products. For the most recent year end, these accounted for approximately 5% of sales and 5% of the profits.

Growth and profitability slowed at Northwell nine years ago and flattened thereafter. A year ago, sales growth was 4%, profitability had fallen to 6% of sales and the return on equity was 6.5%. Their reputation as a benchmark to be emulated in the medical products sector was now a memory.

Two notable new product failures about a decade ago had resulted in staff changes and a new Director of New Product Development. Since Sales and Marketing were seen as the primary clients of New Product Development, funding responsibility for R&D shifted to Sales and Marketing eight years ago. The changes succeeded in reducing costs in this area by 33% through more careful screening and approval processes and tighter budget controls. However, within two years of the change, most of the output from New Product Development was in the form of incremental product improvements, and there was limited work underway in the area of significant product innovations. In an effort to increase their productivity, New Product Development personnel restricted their direct field involvement with sales personnel and clients. The problem/opportunity finding role was delegated to marketing and sales personnel, who were expected to forward project and product suggestions to the Product Development Approval Team. The Director of New Product Development chaired this committee, with representation from Sales, Marketing, and Finance/Accounting.

The percentage of sales coming from products introduced in the previous four years declined from 25% a decade ago to 8% a year ago. Finger pointing had become the order of the day, as frustration surfaced over the slow pace of innovation. New Product Development staff complained about a lack of resources, equipment, and bureaucracy, while Sales and Marketing personnel grumbled that Northwell's reputation as a problem solver and innovator was being eroded due to the inability of R&D to deliver the right products at the right time and price.

Profitability was negatively affected during the past eight years by competitive pressures on price and customer servicing costs. Northwell was still a preferred supplier, but the emergence of health care cost containment pressures and powerful buying groups had reduced Northwell's capacity to command a price premium. More importantly, key competitors caught up with Northwell in the areas of sales, support, and solutions, but were able to do so in innovative ways that reduced their sales costs (e.g., call centers, logistical streamlining, and electronically distributed training support). Sales and servicing costs at Northwell were now approximately 15% higher than their key competitors. However, customers did not perceive significant differences in the levels of support and responsiveness.

Exhibit 1 summarizes the financial results and performance over the last 4 years.

THE MEDICHEK OPPORTUNITY

Two years ago Northwell's Senior Management Team received clear feedback that stockholders were very dissatisfied with cost containment and market expansion activities.

exhibit 1 Northwell Medical

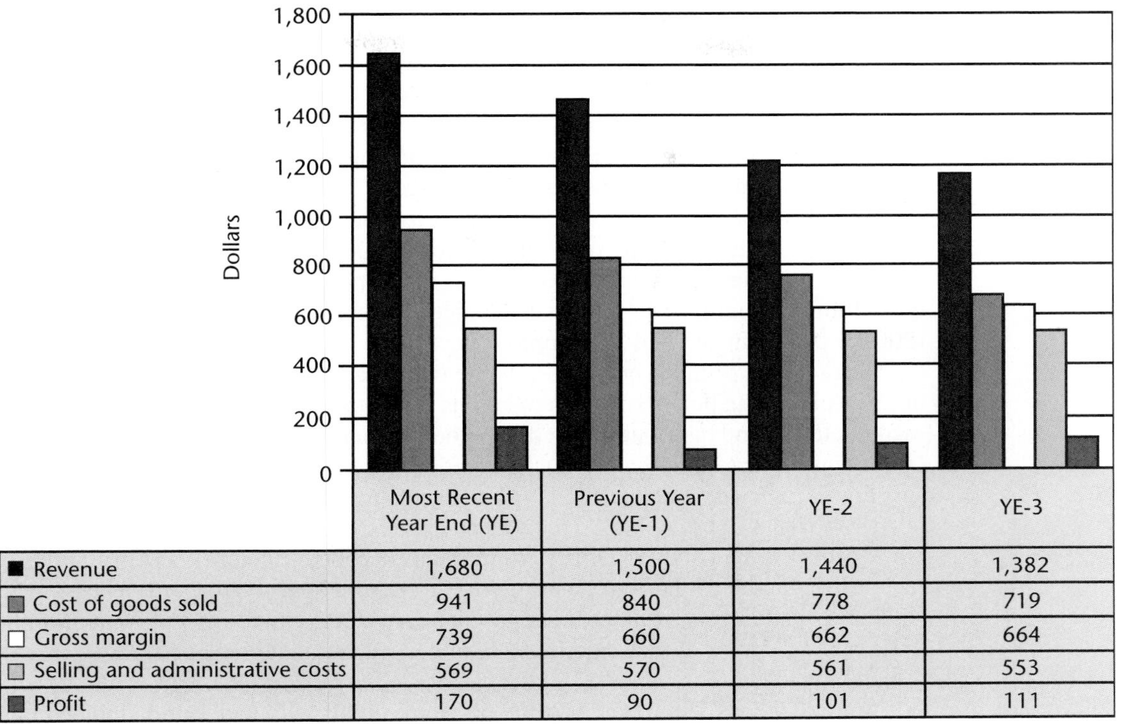

	Most Recent Year End (YE)	Previous Year (YE-1)	YE-2	YE-3
■ Revenue	1,680	1,500	1,440	1,382
■ Cost of goods sold	941	840	778	719
□ Gross margin	739	660	662	664
□ Selling and administrative costs	569	570	561	553
■ Profit	170	90	101	111

At that time, the Board replaced the Vice Presidents of Sales and Manufacturing (the President had been replaced a year earlier). All 3 appointments were from outside the organization—something unheard of in the past. In addition, the Board instituted performance contracts with members of the Senior Management Team. These performance contracts required the following improvements to be achieved within a four year period: sales growth of 30% over levels in the most recent year; a return on equity of 18%; a return to gross profitability levels that exceeded industry averages by 10%; 15% of sales coming from products introduced in the previous 4 years; and a return of customer satisfaction levels to those achieved a decade earlier.

Nathan Daniels, the V-P Marketing and Claudia Leung, the CFO, had grown up in Northwell and both had the trust and respect of the new CEO and the Board Chair. Both were appointed to their senior roles three years ago, following the early retirement of their predecessors. Approximately 2 years ago the CEO gave them joint responsibility for identifying growth opportunities. Nathan and Claudia had bumped heads in the past over the value of marketing expenditures, but they recognized the assignment's importance and decided to set aside past difficulties. Both possessed a strong interest in emerging information technologies and this quickly led them to investigate Web-based marketing, distribution, and E-commerce opportunities for Northwell.

Research conducted three years ago told Northwell that their primary customers were either currently able to order and receive information over the Internet or soon would be Internet-enabled. Sales personnel reported that an increasing amount of their customer communications was being conducted over the Internet and that Northwell's capacities in this area were lagging behind their key competitors, as they were in other areas of technologically enabled customer support. Further, many of these primary customers seemed quite interested in exploiting this technology to enhance efficiency, speed, communications, and the efficacy of training and development. These interests seemed to fit well with the ideas that Nathan and Claudia were pursuing.

Shortly after being assigned responsibility for identifying growth opportunities, Nathan and Claudia decided to meet with the senior management of Medichek. Medichek was an emerging net-based U.S. firm, specializing in health care. They had been founded eight years ago, were located in Dallas, were growing very quickly (200+% per year) and had 275 employees.

Medichek's primary business was the design and management of Web sites for a number of leading health care organizations (hospitals, nursing homes, pharmaceutical manufacturers and distributors, medical product manufacturers), including Northwell's (as of approximately 2 years ago). In addition, three years ago, Medichek launched a subscription service that provided on-line access to medical information to health care professionals and researchers. This was an expensive service to develop and maintain, but subscriber growth over the first 18 months exceeded Medichek's expectations by a factor of 2. Medichek had a reputation for innovation, honesty, responsiveness, quality, candidness, and trustworthiness. They were very selective in terms of whom they chose to do business with. It was said that Medichek picked its clients and those who were selected were the lucky ones.

Medichek was 75% owned by the five individuals who had founded the company (all were in their 30's and directly involved in the business). They had resisted takeover and IPO opportunities, preferring to develop and control their own organization. Nathan first met Medichek's owners 3 years ago, when he was looking for a Web-site designer for Northwell. True to form, it was Medichek who, after careful deliberation, selected Northwell as a client. While initially "put off" by Medichek's approach, Nathan and Claudia quickly became fans, and this enthusiasm extended to other members of senior management. Their work was fairly priced by industry standards, but more importantly, their strategic approach to site design and management resulted in customer accolades and industry awards in recent years. Sales and marketing personnel responded favorably to Northwell's new Web site when it went live, reporting positive customer reactions to its layout, content, and functionality. Though they still felt that technology-enabled customer support was lagging (e.g., electronic access to technical training support materials), they viewed this as an important step in the right direction.

Medichek's owners and employees often commented about how comfortable they felt working with Northwell. They particularly appreciated Northwell's commitment to dealing with its clients in ways that emphasized customer knowledge, value, and informed decision-making. Medichek officials complained that Northwell's decision-making sometimes took too long, that Northwell over-attended to cost rather than value, and that Northwell had difficulty keeping its "fingers out of the pot" once decisions were made. However, they discounted these frustrations, chalking them up to Northwell's concern for quality and competitiveness.

During the development of Northwell's website, it became apparent to Claudia and Nathan that there might be good reason to get closer to Medichek concerning another venture they were pursuing. Medichek had been exploring the development of a virtual health service mall, for use by the health care industry. The idea was that professional end users (hospitals, nursing homes, physicians, pharmacists) could access this site in order to electronically shop for the products they needed. Products and services supplying firms would be carefully screened to ensure that they met quality, value and customer service standards. Quotes could be solicited, orders placed, and payments received electronically. Further, the mall would serve as a primary source of product information, product warnings and recalls, educational on-line health care forums, health care news, and distributed web-based training in health care matters (e.g., product use education).

From the initial meeting on the virtual mall approximately two years ago, Medichek was clear that it wanted to partner with Northwell in the development of this undertaking. They proposed that the mall be established as an independent business unit and that Northwell and Medichek own it equally. Northwell would commit to becoming a prime occupant in the mall and would supply the needed development funds (estimated at $5 to $10 million). Medichek would develop the necessary technology platforms, structure the services and pricing arrangements with mall occupants, structure the entry criteria, and market the mall service. Medichek's reputation would prove very helpful here. They estimated that it would take a year to make this project a reality.

Nathan and Claudia were excited by this opportunity. It had the potential to significantly reduce costs for both customers and suppliers and provide Northwell with opportunity to dramatically extend its reach into foreign markets. Though quality competitor products would also be listed at the mall, these were already readily available in the marketplace. More importantly, the mall would be selective concerning who was allowed to be listed and exhibit. When combined with the quality of the information, news and other services available, it was anticipated that there would be a very positive halo cast on firms allowed to market their goods and services at the site.

When Nathan and Claudia talked to Northwell's IT group and the CEO about this opportunity, interest and excitement spread. Sales and marketing personnel also expressed interest, but were concerned with the implications on existing channels of distribution and customer contact. This was a company that had built its reputation on its personal relationships with its distributors and customers (i.e., responsiveness and support), and they were concerned with how things would be affected by this new venture. Nathan and Claudia asked them to relax and give the new venture time to develop. They told staff that the new venture would increase the exposure and reach of Northwell, thereby opening up new opportunities. Channels would not change overnight, and staff was advised that Northwell would monitor things closely and help employees adapt and transition into new roles, as needed. They were told that this was new territory for everyone, so the keys were to be patient and open-minded, communicating information, questions, and concerns in a timely fashion.

Claudia worked with Medichek's CFO to develop the business plan, projections and a Letter of Understanding during April a year ago. Northwell's Board was first informed of the possible opportunity in January a year ago. In May, Northwell's senior management team recommended the partnership (as set out in the Letter of Understanding) to its Board. Medichek and Northwell jointly signed the Letter of Understanding in June a year ago, with the first $2 million installment of development support issued in June. Northwell's managers were shocked (pleasantly) by the speed of the approval process. Primary responsibility for managing the relationship with Medichek was assigned to Claudia.

During the latter half of the previous year Medichek hired additional staff and proceeded with the development work. By February of the current year Northwell had advanced $4.5 million in development support. During this period Northwell had focused on shoring up its internal operations and improving its profitability. By December of the previous year, products introduced within the past 4 years had grown to 9% of sales, and growth had increased 12% over the previous year. Profitability had improved to 10% of sales and an 8% return on equity, and customer satisfaction results had improved marginally. Both the Board and the Senior Management Team were pleased to see progress, but felt there was still a long way to go. Discussion amongst these groups clearly indicated that they saw the virtual mall as the initiative with the greatest potential, as well as the greatest risks.

Personnel in sales and marketing expressed increasing concern over how their functions and roles would be affected by the new venture and what would be the impact on their customers. Nathan continued to tell them to relax while they were waiting to see how roles and functions would need to adapt in the wake of the virtual mall. Though he couldn't guarantee there would be no job losses, he truly believed this new venture would open up significant new opportunities and more meaningful customer relationships for many. In spite of these words of reassurance, the number of voluntary resignations in these areas rose by 15% and there were rumours that others were looking as well. Many of these resignations involved individuals viewed as high performers. In addition, some distributors were also expressing concern and looking for alternative lines of business to represent, in the event that they became redundant to Northwell.

Human resources advised the executive to slow its recruiting initiatives for departing personnel until the effects of the new venture were better understood. Nathan and other senior managers in sales and marketing saw the wisdom in this advice, but they were also concerned about sending the wrong message to staff, customers and distributors. As a result, recruitment was slowed, positions were left unfilled for longer than in the past (150 days on average vs 60), and contract employees were brought in to help, where needed. The consideration of a new call center was also put on the back burner until the ramifications for Northwell of the virtual mall were better understood.

By April the Senior Management Team was placing increasing pressure on Claudia to get the mall up and running. Marketing of the mall was going extremely well. Product and service suppliers had been solicited and screened and a critical mass of these organizations was signed and ready to go (i.e., their initial product information, visual material, and related systems and supports were developed). The news and related information services and site features had been developed, staffed and beta tested by those who would be using the mall. Primary customers were anxiously awaiting access to the new service. However, Medichek reported that the development of the technological platform and related supports (in particular, the E-commerce and security components) were proving more difficult than originally anticipated and that the complete Mall's formal launch was about 4 months behind schedule.

Claudia began to spend more time monitoring the pace of developments at Medichek. Monthly visits became weekly. In May she requested bi-weekly reports on progress achieved, funds expended, and the time allocations of the various project teams. These were very similar to the reporting Northwell required from its own operations.

Relations with Medichek chilled in response to the increased frequency of site visits and the request for more detailed reporting. At first they resisted complying with the reporting request, but after a month of mounting pressure they acquiesced. Medichek's senior management wrote that such information would be furnished under duress, because it would serve no useful purpose, be expensive and time consuming to develop, and divert attention from where it was most needed.

The resignation of three more capable staff members from the sales and marketing area and the loss of a valued distributor from the mid-west U.S. in the late spring elevated Nathan's anxiety over progress and he wanted to know just how much longer it would be before "Virtual Northwell" would be fully operational. Nathan continued to believe that it would be unwise to make major changes in sales and marketing until they really knew how customers would react to the new channel. He felt that it was difficult to predict, with any degree of certainty, what the ideal approach to sales and marketing should be, and he preferred to adopt an approach that reacted to what evolved as a result of the new channel. However, he was also aware of the need to address employee and distributor uncertainty as quickly as possible, recognizing that the "be patient until we have a better understanding" strategy was not working well. Since Claudia was in charge of the new venture and since there would be organizational design, budget and control implications, he wanted Claudia's advice on how best to handle the matter.

When Medichek reported continuing development problems in July, Senior Management at Northwell voiced increasing dissatisfaction with the progress to date and asked Claudia to recommend a course of action that would rectify matters.

QUESTIONS FOR CLASS DISCUSSION

1. What are the management and strategic issues that Northwell faces?
2. What are the opportunities, costs, benefits, and strategic implications of developing the Internet site?
3. What decision would you make here and how would you implement your choice?

case 17 Electronic Data Interchange and the Ontario Dental Association

Steve Smith began the long drive back home from the Board of Governors' meeting in Toronto, in May 1997. The meeting had unleashed a barrage of criticism and most of it had been directed his way. For someone who had spent much of his career working to help his fellow dentists, the criticism was particularly painful. The drive home would give him time to collect his thoughts and try to figure out why things had gone so wrong.

As Chair of the Electronic Data Interchange (EDI) Task Force of the Ontario Dental Association (ODA), Dr. Smith had been given responsibility for what seemed to be a great opportunity for dentistry in Ontario. EDI held the potential to connect dental offices and insurance companies through computers and telephone lines in order to speed transactions and reduce costs. Unfortunately, the proposals of the Task Force had met with a wall of opposition from the dentists in Ontario. Moreover, he could not understand the depth of feelings that had been aroused over this issue. The opposition was directed not only at EDI, but also at the Ontario Dental Association itself. Steve Smith wondered how he could resolve the issues surrounding EDI in a manner that would help to heal the rifts within the ODA.

THE ONTARIO DENTAL ASSOCIATION

Organized dentistry had a long history in Canada; indeed, it was as old as Canada itself. The Ontario Dental Association was founded on July 2, 1867 and celebrated its 130th anniversary in 1997. The Mission of the ODA was to represent and serve the dental profession in Ontario:

> The Ontario Dental Association is the voluntary professional organization that represents the dentists of Ontario, supports them in the provision of exemplary oral health services and promotes the attainment of optimal health for the people of Ontario.

The ODA represented approximately 5,500 (80%) dentists in Ontario, although that number was declining. With a staff of over 50 professionals, the ODA was active on three fronts. First, it addressed current challenges confronting dentistry, from policies on patient recall and mercury amalgam fillings, to managed care and the fee guide. Second, it lobbied government on behalf of the dental profession on issues such as the proposed taxation of employee dental benefits. Third, it supported members by setting standards of patient care, providing opportunities for continuing education, and promoting the public image of dentistry. Taken together, the Ontario Dental Association saw its role as a leader in lobbying, protecting, advancing, and communicating the interests of dentists and their patients in Ontario.[1] There were comparable dental associations in each of the provinces, as well as a national organization, the Canadian Dental Association.

GOVERNANCE OF THE ONTARIO DENTAL ASSOCIATION

As shown in Exhibit 1, the ODA used a representative structure to govern the affairs of the Association. The ODA was organized into local dental societies across the vast Province of Ontario. Each society elected representatives to the Board of Governors, which met twice a year to set policies, amend bylaws, and set fees. The Governors elected an Executive Council from among its members to act on their behalf between meetings. The Executive Council was composed of 7 Governors and the 4 Officers of the ODA: the Vice-President, the President-Elect, the President, and the Past-President.[2] The role of the Board of Governors was to *set ODA policies* for the year, whereas the Executive Council was to *implement those policies* through its standing committees and special task forces, with the assistance of the staff of the ODA. A Management Committee composed of the four Officers dealt with day-to-day issues that arose between meetings of the Executive Council, and worked closely with the staff of the ODA. The purpose of this structure was to encourage initiatives from local dental societies and to vest power for important decisions with their representatives on the Board of Governors. In practice, however, many decisions were made by the Executive Council itself.

The Executive Council assigned work to committees and co-coordinated their operations. Council members also sat on various committees as an Executive Liaison, to communicate Board policy to the committees and, in turn, to communicate from the committees back to the Executive Council. As well, Council members had responsibility for communicating with local dental societies. These linkages were designed to promote effective communication with the Executive Council. In practice much of this intended communication was *not occurring*, likely because of the heavy responsibilities placed on Council members.

---

[1]The body that regulated the profession of dentistry is the Royal College of Dental Surgeons of Ontario, founded in 1868. The College had several key responsibilities under the *Act Respecting Dentistry*, namely, to control the education of dental students, to licence who can practice dentistry, and to enforce professional standards of practice and conduct.

[2]Once a Governor was elected to be Vice-President, he or she progressed automatically through the other three positions, without the need for a further election. This policy was designed to ensure continuity and stability at the executive level of the ODA. It also meant that the same individuals worked together for years and exerted considerable influence over the direction of the ODA.

exhibit 1 Governance of the Ontario Dental Association

Entity	Membership	Meetings	Role
Dental Societies	Local dentists	8 times a year	To examine local and provincial issues
Board of Governors	90 members elected by dental societies	May and November	To set ODA policies, amend bylaws and set fees
Executive Council	11 members elected from the Board of Governors	6 or 7 times a year	To implement ODA policies
Management Committee of Executive Council	The 4 Officers of the ODA: Vice-President, President-Elect, President, and Past-President	Frequently, in person or by telephone	To deal with the day-to-day issues that arose between meetings of the Executive Council

The various committees of the ODA examined issues facing dentistry in Ontario, and recommended policies to resolve those issues. The Board of Governors elected standing committees, such as the Dental Practices Advisory Committee, and had their responsibilities defined through its Bylaws. As well, the Board of Governors formed special committees or task forces to deal with important issues confronting the ODA. On occasion, ad hoc committees were formed as required by the Executive Council to deal with issues that fell outside the mandates of the existing committees. The Electronic Data Interchange Task Force was created in this manner. The authority and responsibility of the Task Force were not clearly defined at the time, but its general purpose was to explore EDI on behalf of the ODA.

ELECTRONIC DATA INTERCHANGE

Although the profession of dentistry continued to make great advances in patient care, dental office procedures had remained largely unchanged over the past fifty years. During a patient visit to the dentist, office staff typed information on the Standard Dental Claim Form of the ODA and gave it to the patient, who then paid for the treatment received. The patient, in turn, submitted the Claim Form to an insurance company for payment (the majority of Ontario residents are covered by employer or union sponsored dental insurance plans). Upon receipt of the claim, the insurance company would enter the information into its computer files and issue a cheque to the patient. As may be apparent, such a system is slow, labour-intensive, and prone to errors.

Staff at the ODA first became aware of the opportunities inherent in electronic data interchange (EDI) between dental offices and insurance companies in 1994. Some pharmacies in Ontario had begun to use computer systems to expedite payment to customers on pharmaceutical plans, by sending claims electronically to insurers. Insurance companies had also started to explore the possibilities of using EDI to process dental claims faster, and especially to reduce processing costs. The ODA felt immense pressure to become involved in EDI. The ODA sought out the Canadian Dental Association (CDA) as a partner on the EDI project.

While the ODA saw opportunities in electronic data interchange, it was aware of some clear dangers as well. What had transpired in the United States was a very unappealing prospect for the dentists of Canada. In the U.S., insurance companies and entrepreneurs controlled EDI, and the dentist had to *pay* for each EDI transaction for a patient on a dental plan. Further, the dentist was paid by the insurer for dental treatments rather than directly by the patient. The concept of *assignment* of insured dental benefits from the patient to the dentist was strongly opposed by the majority of Ontario dentists and by the ODA itself. The basis for this opposition was the belief that if dentists were paid by insurance companies rather than by their patients, the big insurance companies would begin to use this power to regulate patient care practices and ultimately to reduce dental payments. Dentists' distaste for assignment went beyond a fear that insurance companies would use their power to lower incomes. Dentists were independent professionals who managed their own dental practices and who prescribed dental treatment for patients based on their professional judgement. If insurance companies paid dentists, many dentists feared losing their independence and becoming de facto employees of those companies. Further, insurers could downgrade standards of patient care and impose their own judgements of appropriate treatment on professional dentistry.

Interviews with several individuals who held key vantage points on the events leading up to the May 1997 Board of Governors' Meeting revealed sharply divergent interpretations of how the ODA handled the issues surrounding EDI.

Steve Smith, Chair of the EDI Task Force

"I first got involved in the ODA by helping to form our own local dental society. Then I got elected to the Board of Governors, but it was quite disappointing, as we would rubber-stamp things that had happened in the past, rather than looking forward. Later I got elected to Executive Council and that was much more stimulating. We studied a broader range of issues, in greater depth. I was Executive Liaison to a number of committees. I also helped to turn the Annual Spring Meeting of the ODA from just a social event to one that had a strong focus on continuing education. I'm proud that I worked on the Dentists at Risk Program to help my colleagues who were encountering problems. On Executive Council, we also had 5 or 6 local dental society assignments and we were supposed to be communicating with them. This was reactive rather than proactive; if they call you, you go. Otherwise, you didn't go to the local society. How are you going to run around the country with your practice, Executive Council, and all your committee assignments?"

Prior Issues at the ODA

"There was an interesting issue at the ODA prior to EDI. The ODA fought the insurance companies on capitation and won. In this scheme, the insurance carrier would pay the dentist a flat fee for each patient, regardless of the level of service. This would have given the insurance companies control over our incomes. The only thing they forgot was that they had to get dentists to sign up for this. We created a slogan, 'No dentists, no capitation!' In the end, only 3 or 4 dentists in Ontario signed on. Capitation was dead. There is a deep mistrust of insurance companies among dentists."

Creation of the EDI Task Force

"The ODA employs people who are expert in areas important to dentistry and they're looking to the future. We knew what was going on in the insurance industry and through gossip we heard that the insurance carriers were thinking of implementing

EDI. We were astute enough to think they weren't going to control it. We had to act fast. Insurance companies' getting together was unheard of, so we got ourselves invited to the game.

"While I was on the Executive Council as Past-President, I was asked by the President of the ODA to Chair the EDI Task Force. There were things happening daily. The meetings were fast and furious. My problem is, here I am doing this and I'm trying to run a practice. I couldn't communicate the changes fast enough. By the time I got to write down the changes, there had been another meeting. I was reporting to the Management Committee; we met at least once a month, with many conference calls. I also reported directly to Executive Council."

Discussions with the Board of Governors

"By the time you got back to the Board of Governors, virtually everything was new because the issues were changing so fast. The membership did not understand or care to understand. People were afraid that if all my claims are in the computer, they'd be able to *profile* me.[3]

"EDI got turned back three times by the Board of Governors. At the May 1996 meeting we sought permission to enter into contracts and the Governors turned it back. In November 1996, they turned it back a second time. We spent four months preparing for the May 1997 meeting. The night before the Board of Governors' meeting was awful. It was 1:00 a.m. and the EDI Task Force still didn't have a resolution to present for the next morning. We had become so deeply divided ourselves! We voted and split evenly on the recommendation that the ODA should continue working on EDI. I don't remember how we resolved it. I think we brought forward a positive recommendation while noting that there was dissension on the Task Force itself.

"At the Board meeting we had demonstrations of how the system would work. I was 7 hours standing at the podium, explaining EDI, answering questions and fending off the attacks. I had never worked so hard and we were *not* successful in persuading the Governors. A motion was passed that we could continue, but the ODA was not allowed to sign contracts without the Board of Governors' approval. No one stood up to suggest that we are instituting profiling, but it was there. People were also worried about being forced to computerize. It was a situation of high fear/low trust. I don't know where the fear came from. It was the lowest point in my life."

John Roberts, a Senior Staff Member of the ODA

"EDI would be just like the standard claim form, but filed electronically. We figured the insurance companies would save $5.00 per claim in processing costs and there are 15–20 million claims per year in Ontario. We thought the insurance companies should pay; the dentist should not have to bear any cost. More important, we decided that dentistry would manage and control its own business. We did what we needed to do to make this happen.

"We saw this as a utility to our members and their patients. The revenues would cover the costs to our members and insurance carriers could reduce the costs of dental plans to companies and unions. Thus companies would keep buying dental plans

[3]Profiling refers to the possibility of monitoring and identifying patterns in dental practices through computer analysis of patient claims to insurance companies.

to obtain high quality care for their employees. Everyone wins! Unfortunately, most dentists were only marginally aware of EDI."

Negotiations over EDI

"There were 3 sets of negotiations going on at the same time. We asked ourselves, do we create it just for ourselves in Ontario or do we do it at a national level? We went national and that decision cost us a million dollars! The negotiations between the Ontario Dental Association and the Canadian Dental Association (CDA) did not go well.

"Our plan was to sell the data to the insurance carrier. There were two competing companies that offered networks to transact the data, National Data Corporation and Shared Health Network Services. One group of insurance companies aligned themselves with National Data and another group aligned themselves with Shared Health. The CDA supported National Data and we supported Shared Health—two absolute and unyielding commitments. There was a fight about the standards, about what information would be provided. All of the issues between the ODA, CDA, and insurers eventually got resolved.

"The CDA and ODA involved one set of negotiations. The dental profession and the insurance industry involved yet another set of negotiations. The final and most difficult set of negotiations was between the ODA leadership and the Board of Governors. So many things were happening simultaneously, it got out of control!"

Discussions with the Board of Governors

"We were taking contracts back to a large body which only met every 6 months. The Governors would take the contracts to their lawyers who would find some problem with the wording. There was no fixed base from which to operate. There was a group that was totally opposed to what we were doing and some of the opposition went up or down with the tide. There was no agreement on the policy objective, on what we were trying to accomplish with EDI. About 40% saw it as a benefit to the members, 40% didn't and said let's not do it at all, and 20% shifted either way. The 20% occupying the middle ground didn't understand the issues. One common element is that dentists who don't understand will still vote. A neighbour is more authoritative than someone from ODA headquarters! We eventually outlasted them. We used up their resources. Each obstacle they put up, we were able to satisfy the people who vote. They eventually ran out of obstacles. It was a war of attrition."

Richard Krychek, a Member of the EDI Task Force

"I began my involvement in ODA politics by becoming active in my dental fraternity at university. I was put on an ad hoc 'Issues Management' working group. I was to report what was going on in Toronto. In 1995 I was put on the EDI Task Force as a representative from Toronto. There were representatives who were rural, urban, multi-practice, single practice and so forth. However, we *never* got involved in cutting the deal, the Chair did that.

"The Canadian Dental Association and the Ontario Dental Association clashed from the outset. The CDA was looking for someone to transact the data and chose National Data. The ODA really liked Shared Health. National Data led us around the bush with the notion that you could use a swipe card to send the claim. This was lie #1. No one bothered to say, 'Show me the technology!' You told the profession that they could use a point-of-sale swipe card. The little dentist in Toronto thought he didn't need a computer for EDI. What they described never existed. I discovered for myself that the point-of-sale cards didn't exist. The CDA thought National Data was better but I went to their office one day to check them out and it was virtually empty! I asked about the swipe card system for dental offices and the guy said that doesn't exist, but maybe in 5 years it will! That meant every dentist would have to buy a computer to use EDI but in 1995 only 15% of dentists in Ontario were computerized. The person who was advising us from the ODA should have been on top of this but he didn't sweat the details and everything was in the details."

Discussions with the Board of Governors

"Every month or two we would get a little bit of an update from Steve Smith, who was doing most of the negotiations. About this time, in 1996, I was elected to the Board of Governors as a representative from Toronto. The ODA and CDA claimed that there would be no cost to the dentist, we would make money from EDI transactions, we would control the data, and we could use the data for analysis. I was getting concerned about how much this was costing us. We asked, 'How much are you going to spend?' They didn't know! This thing was sucking money out of the Association like you wouldn't believe! Even worse, we couldn't see the contracts! *We* were the EDI Task Force! There were contracts being drafted between the CDA and ODA, with National Data and Shared Health, and with the insurers but we weren't involved. Show us the contracts boys, because we don't trust you!"

Issues in Conflict

"There were obvious benefits to the insurers: They could dump data entry and that would save them millions. Are we doing the work of the insurers? The Association would get just 15 cents per claim. Members were getting absolutely nothing from this deal. I was one of those who worked on the 10 points of concern drafted by a group of dental societies (see Exhibit 2). We wanted to be assured that there was going to be a pilot project. A group of us felt that EDI would affect the organization of our offices and we had questions we wanted answered. What sort of glitches would you encounter with this new system? We saw this as poorly managed.

"On the Task Force, it was like talking to a brick wall. In my opinion, they weren't focussed on the best interests of the members, the 7,000 dentists of Ontario. We beat the insurance companies on capitation. We never dealt with the insurance companies from a position of strength on EDI. The ODA gave away so much. They should have said to the insurance companies, 'If you don't meet our conditions we walk.' Instead, they saw the possibility of National Data setting up its own system, of losing control, of profiling.... My vision of the ODA didn't match what was going on. We were getting stonewalled. They spent $1 million of our money, which they will never recover.

"I believe in the ODA, but this was brutal. The ODA wants to keep information close to the vest. They are very weak at handling opposition; they don't know what to do with opposing views. The more you get ignored, the more you get your back up!"

Peter Hall, a Member of the Board of Governors

"I joined the Board of Governors from Toronto at about the same time as the controversy over EDI erupted. I was totally green. The Executive Council made recommendations

exhibit 2 Position of the Executives of the Greater Toronto Dental Societies

The discussion and debates at the May Board of Governors' meeting have brought to light once again our concerns about the EDI programme. Our group represents a significant cross-section of ODA members. Consultation and discussion with ODA members have affirmed that an EDI programme in Ontario MUST encompass, at a minimum, the following points:

1. EDI is a system to enhance patient reimbursement in the province of Ontario. Following the principles and guidelines of the ODA, it MUST be run on a non-assignment basis exclusively.
2. All contractual agreements involving ODA, CDA, subscribing dentists, data transmitters (e.g. National Data or Shared Health) and insurance carriers must be submitted for review plus revision to all ODA Governors and other concerned members.
3. Before commencement of the pilot project in Ontario, the parameters, method of analysis and research regimen must be submitted to all ODA Governors for review. Consideration must be given to studying the impact of an EDI system in our members' offices. Data, both qualitative and quantitative, as well as the final draft of the report must be reviewed by all ODA Governors and other concerned members before publication.
4. Since an EDI system is only a means of patient reimbursement, the role of our members is in transmitting claims and predetermination. Our ODA members will only be involved in verifying that the claim was sent and not in explaining payment of benefits or the receipt of the claim by the insurance carrier or the data transmitter. Written notification of this must appear on all hard copy, including any swipe cards, or their equivalents, and patient education materials. A contact telephone number and address of the insurance carrier must appear on all hard copy given to our patients.
5. Patient eligibility for coverage under a dental plan will not be part of an EDI system in Ontario. It should remain the responsibility of the patient.
6. There will be no charge for claims transmission, predetermination or any patient dental insurance information.
7. Standards of claims transmission and predetermination MUST follow Dental Practices Advisory Committee guidelines, as they presently exist without changes or modifications.
8. No guarantees can be made to the insurance carriers of the projected volume of claims.
9. It must be ODA policy that ALL marketing information and materials destined for our patients and our member dentists first be submitted to the Dental Practices Advisory Committee of the ODA for review before dissemination.
10. All parties involved in the EDI system must realize that the dentist has the least to gain from involvement in EDI. With this fact in mind, the ODA must make sure that there are royalty payments provided directly to the dentist for involvement and continuing participation. In order to help defray the cost of hardware and software purchases, the ODA must work on behalf of its member dentists to secure the best possible pricing or rebate.

One theme that has been dominant in our discussion is that the ODA is the best vehicle to develop an EDI system in Ontario that is beneficial to both our member dentists and our patients.

The purpose for conveying our message to ODA Management, Executive Council and the EDI Task Force at this time is to let you know our position. We wish to elaborate this position with you and we feel that input to the development of an EDI programme in Ontario is best handled at this juncture rather than at the November Board Meeting.

---

and gave direction, and the Board basically rubber-stamped those directives. They had a 'Father Knows Best' attitude and there was simply no discussion of issues."

Discussions with the Board of Governors

"The ODA Executive had meetings outside of the authority of the Board of Governors. They decided together that EDI is a good thing for dentistry. This was the Executive working totally on its own. EDI contracts were not shown to anyone, not even to

EDI Task Force members! They expected it to be passed at the November 1996 Board meeting. The Governors had a lot of questions, but we didn't get any answers. Stonewalled! This didn't originate from the grass roots at all. It originated in the hierarchy of the Association.

"They felt that they had to rush it. They wanted to put it to the Board in November and get it going in January. I started to think about it: How is it going to impact the office? Is there a pilot? We began talking about it at a meeting of our dental society (Toronto). We felt that they didn't know what they were doing. We were told that you didn't need a computer for EDI, that you could use swipe technology to process claims. They said it would be $800 for the whole system! There was never an attempt to get a cheap system, we were lied to. We were told that you didn't need a special telephone line, but we eventually found out that you did need a dedicated line for EDI. The fellow advising the ODA didn't have a good grasp of the technology.

"The Toronto Dental Society was always a problem for the leaders of the ODA; we were a thorn in their side. We finally got to see the contracts before the November Board meeting. At the EDI Task Force they got to see them for two hours, one time only! I don't know why! When we got the contracts, there were pages missing, it was an abridged version. We brought them to our lawyers and they weren't happy. The Greater Toronto dental societies started working together on this.

"Governors from Toronto also started pairing off with other Governors. We started branching out, talking to people in Durham, in Essex. Hamilton said to us, we're seen as troublemakers too! They divide and conquer us. We sent out letters of concern to our fellow Governors. At no time did we say EDI was bad, but we weren't getting answers in a timely fashion. We started getting better at organizing. We sent our dental society newsletter to every single dentist in Ontario. Steve Smith wrote an article in the newsletter explaining EDI. On our side, we also put down what we wanted, and we printed it in the newsletter (see Exhibit 2)."

Board of Governors' Meeting

"The Board meeting in May, 1997, was mayhem. There was tension in the air, you could feel it. We had a series of presentations on EDI and then the questions started, about the pilot project, about the costs, about what was in it for dentistry. During coffee breaks there was lobbying going on. A person from the Executive comes up to me and says, 'Don't you trust us!' All of a sudden, it's not the issues; it's a matter of trust. It was a very *hot* lunch, with groups of people negotiating. We came to a compromise after lunch. There was an amended motion. They could continue discussions, but the contracts would come back to the Board in November. It was half-baked, and they were saying 'trust us' many times.

"Supposedly, there were benefits to the patients. There were no benefits for the dentist that I could see. There were three huge issues, the first being *assignment of insured dental benefits* from the patient to the dentist. There are dentists who take assignment, although it is a strict policy of the ODA that we are against assignment. EDI would benefit dentists using assignment because they would get their money faster from insurance companies, so EDI was seen as pro-assignment. Second, the big insurance companies could also *profile* you with EDI, giving them even more power. Third, there was *money* to be made with each transmission, big dollars with millions and millions of transactions. With this money going to the ODA, insurance companies would hold the purse strings over the ODA. The membership becomes less important, if the ODA is beholding to the insurance companies. They were bending over backwards to the insurance companies; whatever they wanted, they got! The whole system was being tailored to the insurance companies. The ODA is supposed to be for the members!"

HOW DO WE RESOLVE THIS?

As he left the city and travelled through the rolling farmland on his way home, Steve Smith thought about everything that had led up to the Board meeting. Could he make sense of what caused ODA members to be so strongly opposed to EDI, and to express that opposition in such a deeply emotional manner? Most important, he told himself, was to figure out what he should do before the next Board of Governors' meeting in November.

DISCUSSION QUESTIONS

1. What are the problem(s) facing Dr. Steve Smith and the Ontario Dental Association? Are there short-term and long-term problems in this situation? Who has major responsibility for solving these problems?
2. What are the major arguments advanced by the proponents of EDI? What are the major arguments and concerns advanced by the dissenting voices?
3. What are the major causes and contributing factors to these problems?
4. What criteria or standards do you wish to apply as you consider potential solutions? That is, what characteristics should a good solution possess?
5. What are the reasonable alternative solutions? Applying the criteria you identified, what are the advantages and disadvantages of each alternative?
6. What is your recommended solution, what is the rationale for this solution, and how would you propose to implement it? Do you have a contingency plan?
7. What should the ODA do to "heal the wounds" caused by the conflict over EDI, so that the proponents and opponents of EDI may work together to advance dentistry in Ontario?

case 18 Western Prairie: The Greenfield Start-up

As he left the office for the day, Brian Boydell felt pleased with himself. Everything seemed to be going well at last. The eight plant operators were back from Holland and Texas and were now writing training manuals. He felt proud of the way the operators were developing as a team. "I've done my best to be open and above board with them," he thought. "It's been hard work but I think we finally have the relationship we need to make the team concept work."

PLANT BACKGROUND

As Brian recalled the past year, he remembered how apprehensive and excited he'd been when he accepted his new post in the fall. Pat Irving, project manager, had asked him to join a group of people who were devising a training program for the operators of Western Prairie Ltd.'s new plant in Carseland. He knew then that he would be the management person working with the developing operations. Western Prairie, specializing in ammonia–urea fertilizer production, was opening the new \$370-million plant 40 kilometres east of Calgary in September of next year. It was to be highly automated, with a total operating group of eight workers on each of the five shifts, and 20 maintenance people on a day shift. Its capacity would be 430,000 tonnes of ammonia or 475,000 tonnes of urea per year. Initially, the consulting engineers would be responsible for the start-up of the operation, but the operating teams would take over the running of the plant after the plant had been checked out.

The new plant would use a well-known process to produce ammonia and urea. Natural gas fuelstock and nitrogen would be converted into ammonia in a high temperature, high pressure continuous flow process. Ammonia would then be combined with carbon dioxide to produce urea.

The competitive advantage of the new plant would result from the scale of the operation and the efficiency of production. The latter would depend primarily on fine-tuning a complex set of interdependent processes and upon the elimination of "downtime"—the period of time when the plant computer was not functioning. Estimates of the cost of downtime were based on the cost of lost production. Contribution per tonne of ammonia was estimated at \$150 per tonne. Refining the process would allow for an increase in production tonnage. There was generally no product differentiation and, consequently, the price for ammonia and urea was set as a commodity.

The eight operators would be expected to play an important role in diagnosing problems in the plant and eliminating downtime. In theory, the computer was supposed to run the plant. However, if something did go wrong, it would be up to the operators to take action—from manually adjusting valves and the production flows to shutting down the plant if the automatic controls failed. Plans had been made to have the operators periodically take over control of the plant from the computer in order to sharpen their skills. In a similar plant in Holland, virtually all problems were handled by the computer and operators did not get the chance to control the plant under normal conditions.

TEAM CONCEPT

The new plant was to be run on the basis of "team concept." There were to be no supervisors. Elected, unpaid team representatives would be responsible for voicing concerns, jobs would rotate on a periodic basis, salaries would be based on knowledge and training, not on job position, and there would be training provided in team building.

Pat Irving had really sold Brian on the concepts, saying that the traditional styles of management were passé in the late '90s. Pat was fond of reiterating four questions he'd picked up from some management course at an Eastern business school:

1. What are we trying to do?
2. What is my part in it?
3. What is keeping me from doing better?
4. What am I doing about it?

Brian agreed that these questions seemed to keep everyone on track and he agreed with Pat that leaders in an organization should be "first among equals." The new "servant leadership" approach to management, as Pat described it, meant that while those with ability should lead, leadership should become a service to others. Under such a system, traditional hierarchies would be eliminated.

The new plant was to be organized without supervisors and Brian sincerely felt that the team was making progress towards self-management. The team concept could only be beneficial to the employees, he mused. Pat had expressed the opinion that the employees had a claim on the business, along with the shareholders, the customers and the community. If any group was shortchanged, it would act to increase its share of return. The team concept was an attempt to give the employees a fair share of the pie.

So far, Brian had been pleased at how well the team building was going. He knew that the training team or "core" team (see Exhibit 1) hadn't met with the operators as often as he would have liked, but everyone was very busy working on the technical side of the new plant. Except for the last few weeks, he'd had frequent contact with the operators. It would be good when Bruce Floyd and the rest of the core team were together in one location. Bruce had been a central figure in the project for several years and frequently was away on technical matters. It would be the end of August before he moved to Calgary.

The first team building session held in Banff last May had produced the Employee Relations Document (see Exhibit 2 for excerpts). It had been developed by both the members of the operating team and the core team and expanded on Pat's ideas. "How many drafts did we work through?" Brian asked himself. "Was it four or five? We really put a lot of effort into that document. Thank heavens, head office in Vancouver approved it." And the organization development people had put on a good program. Normally, he didn't trust those guys. They were too "touchy-feely" for him. The operators had liked the opportunity to work on the issues. During the week they had focused on Pat Irving's four questions as well as engaging in team building exercises. Brian had been worried when only a few of the core team could attend but that did not seem to matter now. The after-hours socializing that week seemed to strengthen the group and make everything more fun (see Exhibit 3 for the training schedule for operators).

One thing did bother Brian slightly. It was four months since they had hired the first eight operators and gone through the team building session and it would be difficult to start again. "The cost alone is scary," thought Brian. "I wish we had some guarantee that things would work out. The training is my responsibility, so the $3-million program had better pay off. Not using the team concept would have saved us a lot of money and meant that we could have started training later." (See Exhibit 4 for a breakdown of the training costs developed in July of the previous year.)

Brian also thought that the operators' trips to Holland and Texas had been a little unnerving. Four operators had travelled overseas for three weeks and four had visited the U.S. for four weeks to observe plants similar to the new Carseland operation. "I wonder how much they got out of the three weeks there?" Brian reflected. "Three weeks is a long time away from home and we had hoped they wouldn't party so much. It was surprising that Jim Cuttle and Mike Irving, who also went, hadn't ensured that they worked harder. The group doing the instructing didn't seem to help much either." Several of the operators had mentioned that the trip to the States could have been shortened since there was nothing to do at night in Borger, where the Texas plant was located. However, the Texas group had indicated they had learned a lot about ammonia production on the trip.

Brian congratulated himself and the core team on getting the operators involved—they seemed to be caught up in working out the technical details of the new plant. Brian had been pleased when Bill Gillies had asked Craig Taraday, the instrumentation expert, to bring in the computer person from head office to talk to the operators. And the operators had liked being a part of the recent recruiting process to hire 18 more operators. They had provided a major source of information since 36 of the 42 applicants were personally known to them. In fact, many operators with steam certification in Alberta knew each other because there were so few in the province. Four of the eight operators hired had come from the same company and knew each other well (see Exhibit 5 for a brief description of the operators).

Brian also believed that the operators' role in decision-making was expanding. Doug Ames, one of the eight, had suggested moving everyone from the team room where they had been working to the empty offices upstairs. (The group was sharing the building with the Calgary operators until the Carseland buildings were ready in December.) The team room led to a lot of group cooperations but it was crowded and those operators who were trying to write their manuals were easily disturbed by the others. Brian wondered if too much group interaction was dangerous. He knew that the operators had developed the habit of going drinking together on occasion and was concerned that the group might become socially rather than work oriented.

BRIAN BOYDELL'S PLANS

Brian was aware that he would have to get to work on the new salary schedules. The "pay for knowledge" concept was a good idea but it created difficulty in establishing rates, as there were no comparable jobs. Usually compensation was tied to a particular job. Estimates were made of the job's difficulty, its skill and education requirements, and the working conditions involved. A salary would be determined accordingly. Under the "pay for knowledge" plan, an operator was paid for the amount of training and knowledge he or she had, regardless of the job performed. Thus a low-skill job would provide a high salary for a trained individual. This plan increased flexibility, as people could be switched quite easily from one job to another. At the same time, it allowed the operators to earn more money through their own efforts.

"It looks as if we will have to pay more money if we want to hire good people in September," Brian mused, "especially if we hope to get 18 more. Who knows what the pay will be when we hire the final 14 in December? Wages really seem to be getting out of hand. I'll be glad when the October 1 raise comes through. It will make my job of hiring easier. Setting the pay schedule for these operators took from last December until April before we got approval from head office. I wonder if the reorganization announced last week will speed up the process. Ron Holmes, the new VP, has a reputation of being a hard-nosed but fair and extremely competent manager. He must be, to be where he is at 44. I hope he knows what we're trying to do but I'll bet he doesn't, considering his background at General Coal Co., with its strong union. I guess I'll find out when I meet with him next week on the suggestion that we review salaries three times rather than twice a year."

As Brian left the building, he noticed a car coming towards him. It was one of the operators. Brian was surprised to see him, as most of the operators had been on a writing course at the Southern Alberta Institute of Technology (SAIT). The writing course was designed to help the operators develop the skills needed to write the training and operating manuals and was held at the other end of town. Pat and Brian believed that by having the operators write their own manuals, the final product would be intelligible to other operators and would encourage everyone to be more committed to the project.

When the car pulled up the operator handed Brian two envelopes, saying, "I've been delegated to hand these to you." One envelope was addressed to him and the other to Pat Irving. As he read the letter (see Exhibit 6 for a copy of the letter), Brian's feeling of dismay turned to anger: "How could they do this to me? They aren't following the team concept at all! What are they trying to pull off anyway?"

exhibit 1 Western Prairie Ltd.—The Carseland Plant: Training and Operating Staff

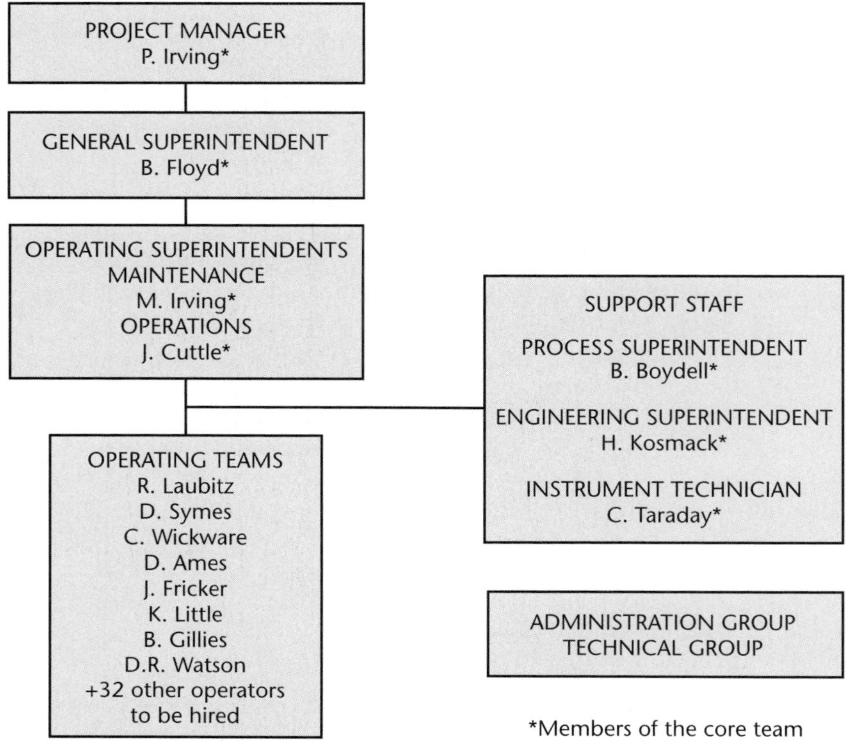

exhibit 2 Western Prairie Ltd.—Extracts from Employee Relations Document

GENERAL

Objective

The basic objective of the employee relations system is to ensure safe, highly efficient and uninterrupted operations with an integrated approach to the management of human resources. The system must respond to the needs, interests and aspirations of people.

Management Philosophy

The following statement of management philosophy represents the type of environment and relationships for which we are striving:

> company competitors differ from each other in the degree of creativity and initiative shown by their employees. Each person has an obligation to use all his or her capacities and those of his or her colleagues in contributing to the growth and betterment of the company's operations at Carseland.

Management has an obligation to provide an environment in which each person has freedom to develop and to use all his or her capacities.

Management Style

All levels of management will be expected to operate on a team basis and to support an integrated approach within and among teams, while encouraging personal initiative and responsibility.

continued

exhibit 2 Western Prairie Ltd.—Extracts from Employee Relations Document (*continued*)

A high value will be placed on obtaining sound creative decisions through understanding and agreement by team members. Decision-making will take place by those who are close to the source of the problem and have the appropriate know-how. Ideas, opinions and attitudes of people will be sought out in the continuing process of improving operating and administrative techniques. When conflict arises, every effort will be made to deal with it in an open manner, and to identify and resolve its underlying causes. Emphasis will be placed on developing talent and potential and encouraging, by example, a high degree of effort and participation. Openness, courtesy and respect will be expected in all interpersonal relationships.

PERSONNEL POLICIES AND PROGRAMS

Organization

The organization will be designed in such a way as to establish a relationship among jobs which promotes flexible, integrated work teams. This goal will be achieved in the Carseland organization by means of the following:

(1) The number of authority levels will be kept at a minimum.
(2) All employees will be encouraged to develop their job-related skills.
(3) Versatility of operating and maintenance people is considered essential and will be encouraged by such innovations as block training, job rotation, and cross-trades training.

exhibit 3 Western Prairie Ltd.—Training Schedule for Operators

April 1	Hire first eight operators	
April	Introduction to the company Training techniques Team building (Banff Springs Hotel) Ammonia familiarization	1 week 1 week 1 week 1 week
May	Urea familiarization Specialty training—ammonia or urea (4 operators for each specialty)	1 week 3 weeks
June	Visits to Geleen, Holland and Borger, Texas	3–4 weeks
July	Return home Writing of training and operating manuals begins	
August September	Writing of training and operating manuals	6–8 weeks
September October	Begin training other operators	8 weeks

exhibit 4 Western Prairie Ltd.

Pat Irving's Memo of January 28—The Carseland Plant: Training Costs

January 28

Memorandum

To: Vice President, Pacific Region, Vancouver
From: Manager, Operations
Subject: Appropriation of Pre-Production Expenses

This is a request for funds to carry on with pre-production training.

The amount requested is $3 million as outlined in my memo of July 24, attached. We are negotiating with the Alberta Department of Manpower and Labour to share this cost. We, therefore, request that $3 million be appropriated and $2.0 million be authorized at this time.

A budget is being prepared and monthly control statements will be issued.

P.W. Irving: mb
Enc.
c.c. B. Floyd
B. Boydell
J. Homes
P. W. Irving

Pat Irving's Memo of July 24—The Carseland Plant: Training Costs

July 24

Memorandum

Subject: Training Costs

It is important that those people who will be operating the new plants receive adequate training. Any operating errors will be extremely costly. The cost of this training should be carried as a separate cost centre to allow proper control.

The operators now involved—Irving, Floyd, Kilborn, Boydell, Hind and Mintsberg—are not taken into account here. The cost of pre-production training at the plant is also not included in this estimate.

The estimated breakdown is:

For 24 months:		
1 Supervisor @ $5,000/month	$120,000	
Expenses and travel $3,000/month	$ 72,000	
	$192,000	
For 21 months:		
6 shift supervisors @ $57,000/year	$598,500	
3 maintenance supervisors @ $52,000/year	$273,000	
1 assistant supervisor @ $52,000/year	$ 91,000	
	$962,500	
Expenses @ 52%	500,000	$1,462,500
Total staff		$1,654,500
Air fares		50,000
		$1,704,500

continued

exhibit 4 Western Prairie Ltd. (*continued*)

Purchase of 2 Carmody trainers (simulators) has been included in the capital estimates.

Programming of trainers	$ 20,000	
Labour of Murray Williams (trainer)		
4 months @ $4,000/month	$ 16,000	
Training films, tapes, etc.	$ 20,000	
Total training equipment		$ 56,000
4 junior engineers		
6 months @ $50,000/year		$ 100,000
Operator Training:		
10 operators		
1 year @ $40,000/year	$400,000	
20 operators		
6 months @ $40,000/year	$400,000	
Steam engineer training	$ 60,000	
Total operator training		$ 860,000
Total		$2,664,500
Unaccounted and contingency		335,500
		$3,000,000

P.W. Irving:ft

cc: F.A. Moore, Vancouver

B. Floyd, Head Office

exhibit 5 Western Prairie Ltd.—Operator Profiles

Doug Ames
- Married, two children
- Third Class Certificate
- District manager of distillery sales for two years
- Operator and shift supervisor of Calgary ammonia plant for seven years
- Plant operator for 11 years
- Hobbies: hockey, golf, curling, fastball
- Member of Fraternal Order of Eagles

Keith Little
- Married, two children
- Second Class Certificate; St. John's First Aid Certificate
- Plant operator for 5 years
- Previous supervisory experience
- Hobbies: ball, golf, curling, swimming

Joe Fricker
- Married, one child
- Second Class Certificate, SAIT Power Engineering Diploma; one year university
- Operator of two different thermal power electrical generating stations for four years
- Hobbies: curling, badminton, mechanics

Dave Symes
- Married, two children
- Second Class Certificate; one year university
- Operator of ammonia plant for four years, including gas and steam plants (Calgary)
- Worked as salesman for Western Canada Steel (summer job)
- Machine operator on railroad tie gang and signal helper for three summers
- Hobbies: tropical fish, astronomy, oil painting, cave exploring
- Member of Moose Lodge

Rob Laubitz
- Married, two children
- Third Class Certificate; Part A, Second Class, NAIT Gas Technology Diploma; St. John's First Aid Certificate
- Operator in steam, and process of sulfur recovery and gas processing plant at Okotoks for three years
- Engineering technologist with oil company for three years
- Hobbies: woodworking

Chris Wickware
- Married, two children
- Operator for eight years
- Millwright at Edmonton Steel Mill for five years
- Hobbies: hiking, fishing
- Member: Women in Technology Advisory Council
- Union steward of several years

Don R. Watson
- Married, three children
- Third Class Certificate; two years university engineering
- Operator of fertilizer plants in Calgary for five years
- Hobbies: skiing, snowshoeing, motorcycling, Member of YMCA

Bill Gillies
- Married, two children
- Second Class Certificate
- Operator and relief shift supervisor in Calgary ammonia plant for ten years
- Operator in Fort Saskatchewan ammonia plant for three years
- Hobbies: hunting, football, carpentry, mechanics
- Member of Western Coop Social Club, and Canton Meadows Community Association

exhibit 6 Western Prairie Ltd.—Brian Boydell's Letter

July 21

Dear Mr. Irving:

During the latter part of June and early July, in response to our earlier request, Brian Boydell indicated the possibility of a July pay raise. However, this morning, Brian indicated that a raise in July would be impossible.

We, of the operator training team, respectfully submit this letter of discontent regarding the negative feedback to our request.

The reasons for the raise are as follows:

(1) All of us took wage cuts to come to the company.
(2) The cost of living has escalated substantially.
(3) We are receiving lower wages than competition staff for similar jobs.
(4) We have a desire to maintain a *strong* and *loyal* team.

We also note that a 37.3 hour work week has been adopted by numerous companies. We believe that Western Prairie should not be among the exceptions.

We feel confident that you will give this letter your every consideration.

Sincerely,
The Operating Team
Doug Ames
Chris Wickware
Don R. Watson
Joe Fricker
Dave Symes
Keith Little
Rob Laubitz
Bill Gillies
c.c. Mr. Brian Boydell

case 19 Christine Carmichael

Tony Dunlop, the new president of Roselawn Manufacturing Ltd., was very concerned. He had been hired to "turn the company around" and reverse the declining customer service levels and profitability which had resulted from the disastrous implementation of new enterprise resource software, which integrated all of the company's existing systems and used one underlying data base. Roselawn Manufacturing was 30 years old, had 35 employees at its Scarborough headquarters, and just over 200 manufacturing workers at its plant in Oshawa.

The Board of Directors had suspected for some time that employee morale was a major problem. These suspicions had been confirmed last week when a group of employees went to the Ontario Human Rights Commission and accused Tony's predecessor, John Morgan, of creating a "poisoned environment" for employees, particularly females. Tony had just finished a long discussion with Christine Carmichael, a recently departed employee, and now was convinced that changes had to be made in the way employees were treated. He decided to review what Christine had told him about how her motivation had been destroyed during the year she worked at Roselawn Manufacturing and try to identify specific problems that needed to be addressed.

GREAT EXPECTATIONS

Upon completing her university degree in Business Administration, Christine Carmichael applied for numerous positions she found on the Internet, in the local newspaper, and at her university's career service department. She knew it would be difficult to land her "dream job" in human resources management, as she was just starting out and had a limited network of contacts in that profession. In August, Christine applied for a management trainee position at a local company, Roselawn Manufacturing Ltd. This position appealed to her because a large component of the work was training staff on the new enterprise resource software that the company was about to implement. Also, Christine was to be groomed for a management position once one became available. Although the position had relatively low pay for a university graduate, Christine wanted to gain experience and hoped that with hard work, she would be compensated equitably.

Christine started working the first week of September, during the pilot project for the new system. Her boss, Mel, was the Accounting Supervisor. Mel was friendly and helpful, but very busy. During her first week, she was present for all training sessions on the new software, which was expected to go live on November 1. Suddenly, it was decided that the software would not be implemented until the following summer. This dramatically changed the position for which Christine was hired. Optimistically, she hoped to learn more about Roselawn Manufacturing and more about the software, and then help to train other employees before they started using it.

Christine spent the next few weeks assisting in the preparation for the new software by converting data from the old system to the new. She was given conflicting instructions by her boss (Mel), the general manager (Bill), and the Vice President of Finance (Andy). She found it difficult to complete tasks because each person acted as though they were in charge. This confusion continued through the entire duration of the project. Christine started to wonder if the delays were a result of this method of organization.

THE STAFF PARTY

Christine noticed that many of the staff seemed afraid of the new software. They seemed to have adopted the opinion that if they avoid it, they could prolong the time until they would have to start using it. Perhaps as a result of the other employees' discomfort with the idea of learning new software, Christine found it very hard to fit in at her new job. People did not welcome her because they did not welcome the purpose for which she was hired. She was ignored in the social atmosphere and looked down upon by those who feared change. Two weeks after she began her new job, the company had its annual staff party, and she was not invited. It was the talk of the office both before and after the party, which added insult to injury and made Christine feel like an outsider.

REALITY BITES

After all the data conversion was completed, Christine began working for the general manager, Bill. She worked hard and frequently stayed late in order to learn the business. About three months after she started, a new manager was hired from outside to head up the accounting group that handled ordering and invoicing for large national customers. Christine was discouraged to hear that although the new manager, Phil, had just completed his business degree and was the same age as her, he was not placed in the management trainee program as she had been, but was hired as a manager immediately. One of the more experienced female staff members pointed out that all managers and executives in the company were male, and that this was not likely to change. Christine did not believe this until later when one of the managers was fired. The assistant manager, Anna, was assigned all of the former manager's duties, but received no pay increase, and had her title changed to "Department Coordinator." After a long fight with senior management, Anna ended up getting a mere $1,000 raise in annual pay.

Christine began to get discouraged when the president, John, called her into his office one morning. He said that he and the other executives had just met and decided that because Phil, the new manager, was having trouble adjusting, Christine would be moved to his group to help get him "up to speed." Christine was flattered to be a valuable member of the company that the management could depend on, but she wondered why she had to work under someone who had equal experience and education, but could not handle his own responsibilities.

Thus Christine was reduced to a member of the clerical staff. In Phil's group, she was trained for one hour on how to invoice customers, and then put to work. She had some difficulties but had little guidance as her supervisor, Phil, had no experience either. She had worked in Phil's group for three days when the company's year-end occurred.

INTERROGATION BY THE PRESIDENT

The previous problems with invoicing came to a halt as the entire staff had to conduct the inventory count required at year-end. Christine and the others worked as best they could on the items they were asked to inventory, but in the end, their count did not balance with the amount on the books. Christine was shocked when she, but not Phil, was asked to meet with John and Andy. They asked her questions for two hours about how she was trained and why she thought she could do the invoicing job and the inventory after only one hour of instruction. They put her in an awkward position by asking questions about the operations of the department and who gave instructions to do what. She was grilled long enough to bring tears to her eyes. John had a condescending way of asking questions, one that made Christine second guess every word she said.

After that incident, Christine noticed that every time John spoke to any member of his staff, it was to provide negative feedback. Employees cringed whenever he entered their workspace and feared speaking to him. He enjoyed this power, which was evident when he approached another new employee and asked whether she had been "warned" about him yet. As a result of this management style, every employee was more concerned with passing blame than solving problems. Departments were segregated and did not function well as a team with a common goal.

THE SCHOOL OF HARD KNOCKS

One of Christine's coworkers, Mary, was responsible for ordering raw materials. Mary called in sick repeatedly. Christine was responsible for doing Mary's work when she was away, and Phil and the rest of the department did little to help her. In January, Mary went on stress leave. Christine then formally took on Mary's responsibilities for ordering without any increase in pay or any recognition.

The busy spring season rapidly approached and Christine's job responsibilities had totally changed since she was hired. She spent her days working in operations when she wanted to be in a staff function—training. John promised that she would soon be relieved of her invoicing and ordering duties, so that she could concentrate full time on the new system. Finally, Jill was hired to take over Christine's invoicing work. She was trained by Christine to perform the invoicing function while Christine concentrated on ordering as well as acting as an assistant manager to Phil. At the beginning, Jill worked hard because of the example set by Christine. However, as time went by, Jill began to follow the other members of the group, doing as little as possible, knowing that Christine would pick up the slack. Again Christine was not promoted and never received any reward for her hard work.

STABBED IN THE BACK

The invoicing activities were now running much more smoothly than when Phil took over, which Christine believed was a direct result of her own hard work. It became clear that Phil wanted authority, but not accountability, when Christine had some difficulty with a supplier who overcharged on an invoice. Phil expressed his disappointment in Christine's inability to renegotiate pricing with the supplier. He called the supplier in a rage, demanded lower prices, ruined the working relationship with the supplier, and in the end, came out no further ahead than Christine had. To make matters worse, Phil took credit for the outcome Christine had obtained, in order to prove to John that the poor treatment of the supplier actually accomplished something. In addition, he had belittled her for her method of dealing with the situation, then took matters into his own hands and made the situation worse.

One day Phil received a letter from a member of the sales staff. The letter complimented Christine for her rapid service and friendly manner. Phil sent a copy of the letter to Christine through email with the title "A Reverse Complaint." Again, Christine was hurt because the supervisor refused to tell her that she was doing a good job. She became increasingly depressed and lost all drive to exert effort as she felt she was being taken advantage of.

BACK TO THE FUTURE

In July, as the end of the busy season approached, Christine's original boss, Mel, approached Phil about Christine returning part-time to her duties on the new enterprise resource software, as it was to be implemented in six weeks. Christine was pleased about going back to the work she was initially hired for, but suspected it was too good to be true. Her workload had eased a little, but every time she tried to work on the system, Phil would give her more work. Mel criticized her for not dedicating time to the system. She was angry that the other members of the department were slacking more than ever and her hard work continued to go unappreciated.

Christine was fed up, and she started looking for a new job. Through a combination of networking and good luck, she was fortunate enough to find an entry-level job in a human resources consulting firm. She was thrilled and rejuvenated at the prospect of this new opportunity. She left Roselawn Manufacturing one week before the implementation of the new software.

* * *

Tony Dunlop realized that with Christine's departure, the company had lost a hard working, knowledgeable employee who had been very important to the successful implementation of the new software. Others who left at the same time had told him similar stories, and it was clear that managers had to change their style in dealing with employees. He decided to try to remember some of the motivation theories he had studied in his business school days—maybe something there could help him figure out what to do.

case 20 Oliver Davis's Entrepreneurial Success Story: No Lost Clients, No Employee Terminations, No Debt

Oliver Davis, founder and owner of Green Meadows Lawn Services in Ottawa, was wrapping up his eighth season in the outdoor lawn maintenance business. Through those eight seasons, Oliver sustained his enviable record of no lost clients, no employee terminations, and no debt. His revenues had continued to grow and, as a university student, he was pleased that the gross revenue for his summer job was six figures. The previous year marked another accomplishment for the young entrepreneur. Oliver was awarded the 2003 CIBC Student Entrepreneur of the Year for his company, Green Meadows. It had been a great summer but now the lawn care season was coming to an end and Oliver was becoming increasingly preoccupied with the future. The challenge of sustaining his personal commitment to growing the company while not losing touch with his employees, his clients and his values weighed on his mind. As he headed to the coffee shop to meet his crew at the end of the day, he knew that the changing seasons signaled a need to focus on a plan for the future.

THE COMPANY

In the summer of 1996, Oliver Davis had just finished grade 8 and, like a lot of his friends, was at loose ends. He was not old enough to have a "real" paying job but he wanted to earn some money. His father suggested that Oliver offer to cut their neighbour's lawn—the idea appealed to Oliver. So, with a $300 loan from his father, Oliver purchased his first lawn mower and started Green Meadows. Through word of mouth, Oliver found that his work snowballed. Within a few weeks, Oliver was cutting his neighbour's lawn, the lawn of a friend of the neighbour's and then a friend of that friend. Because Oliver was too young to drive, his father drove him and his lawn mower to the various homes. The summers through high school found Oliver's little grass cutting business growing steadily. His reputation for courteous, reliable and thorough service spread. By the end of high school, Oliver had a crew of three employees working for him.

In the spring of 2001 Oliver doubled his number of lawn care clients. John Simpson,[1] the owner of a local lawn care company, was selling his business. Oliver bought out all the contracts (40 to 50 contracts in total) from Simpson, whom Oliver describes as a "born entrepreneur." Oliver first met Simpson at a McDonald's and, as Oliver says, "we just got chatting." Over the months, their paths crossed on a fairly regular basis at a variety of coffee and fast food shops favoured by the lawn care crews working in the area. Crews on break were easy to spot—pick-up trucks with trailers loaded with lawn mowers, rakes, and assorted garden equipment. Oliver's baby blue trucks were especially noticeable. Oliver's signature baby blue trucks became Green Meadows' primary form of promotion. On occasion, Simpson would ask Oliver if he would take a job that his crews were too busy to service and vice versa. After some months, Oliver learned that Simpson was interested in selling out his contracts but only to someone who would look after his customers the way he had done over the years. Oliver felt that the two companies were very similar. They both strove for excellence in customer service, and treated their crews fairly and equitably. What started as a casual coffee shop conversation developed into a win-win situation for both men: for Simpson who was looking to sell to someone who would look after his clients with the same care and attention to detail that his customers had come to expect, and for Oliver who valued the growth opportunity. Oliver's chance encounter led to his successful buyout of his competition with a doubling of his lawn care contracts.

Oliver prides himself on his company's reputation for customer service. He would often "go the extra mile for clients." Oliver credits his father with instilling the "do what it takes" attitude. Oliver found that "doing the job until the customer is satisfied" paid off in spades. In one instance, a customer was removing patio stones in order to install interlocking brick. A friend of the customer wanted the stones for his own property. Green Meadows removed the stones and delivered them to the customer's friend—free of charge. Green Meadows had also developed a reputation for community service. A local seniors' complex was in need of lawn care service and Green Meadows provided that service free of charge for the complex.

Much of Oliver's day sees him at job sites and talking with his customers. He found that an increasing number of his customers were either installing or inquiring about interlocking patios, walkways and driveways. Sensing a growth opportunity for Green Meadows, Oliver was determined to expand his services to include the design and installation of interlocking bricks. He knew that with some training he could provide as

[1]The owner's name has been disguised.

good, if not better, interlock design and installation for his valued clients. To Oliver each lost interlocking opportunity was simply lost revenue for his company. Green Meadows expanded into the interlock market in 2001. Within two summers, the interlock side of his business (listed as "other services" under revenues) exceeded the lawn care side of his operations. Green Meadows' 2003 gross revenues also showed an impressive increase from 2002 (see Exhibit A for the 2002 and 2003 Income Statements).

exhibit A Green Meadows 2002 and 2003 Income Statements (January 1st to December 31st)

	2002	2003
REVENUE		
Lawn Mowing	50,262.41	55,155.55
Dethatch & Fertilizer	3,223.30	2,035.00
Other Services	41,768.55	80,173.33
GST Quick Method	1,905.09	2,706.57
Total Revenue	97,159.35	140,070.45
TOTAL REVENUE	97,159.35	140,070.45
EXPENSE		
Payroll Expenses		
Wages & Salaries	18,859.61	22,665.32
EI Expense	601.34	642.04
CPP Expense	708.50	885.27
WCB Expense	1,477.67	1,149.13
Total Payroll Expense	21,647.12	25,341.76
Operating Expenses		
Liability Insurance	1,296.00	1,834.62
Advertising & Promotions	463.46	1,429.93
Bad Debts	0	190.91
Supplies	10,338.25	18,721.07
License Fees	222.00	328.00
Credit Card Charges	11.25	149.09
Amortization	2,707.00	1,896.00
Interest & Bank Charges	130.90	81.45
Office Supplies	1,170.08	939.00
Equipment—Fuel & Oil	912.09	48.74
Equipment—Repairs & Maintenance	701.55	1,733.35
Small Equipment Purchases	1,591.07	4,888.76
Rent	286.40	278.20
Miscellaneous	167.41	284.44
Cellular Telephone	1,340.95	1,810.58
Travel & Entertainment	221.78	257.60
Vehicle—Fuel & Oil	2,351.00	3,021.44
Vehicle—Repairs & Maintenance	647.24	2,205.48
Vehicle—Insurance	1,621.01	1,457.49
Total Operating Expenses	25,893.04	41,277.95
TOTAL EXPENSE	47,540.16	66,619.71
NET INCOME	49,619.19	73,450.74

Oliver takes customer service very seriously. At the end of every season, Oliver distributes a "Customer Report Card" for his clients to evaluate his company's performance (Exhibit B). Oliver firmly believes that his strong customer focus is central to Green Meadows' continued revenue growth. After a little research, Oliver found that between 2000 and 2002 Green Meadows' growth consistently outpaced that of the landscape industry (Exhibit C). The company's mission states that:

> Green Meadows provides customers with a sense of pride and satisfaction in their home landscape. Green Meadows provides employees with the opportunity to be creative and achieve personal growth. Green Meadows has a strong focus when it comes to the community, customers, work quality, and employees.

Oliver's financial strategy has been to "grow the business from existing cash flow, with the intent of growing the business for long term stability rather than growing the business quickly at all costs" (Davis, Company Report, 2003). Oliver prides himself on keeping costs down whenever possible. Both of the company's trademark blue trucks were bought used—well used. In the off-season, Oliver has them serviced in the high school auto shop program where his father teaches. New, $60,000 trucks are just not a luxury that Oliver feels he can afford. He would rather offer his employees a higher wage rate than spend his company's money on depreciating assets. In comparison with other local lawn care companies, Green Meadows' pay scales are above average. Oliver does insist, however, on the purchase of top-of-the-line lawn care and interlock equipment. To Oliver, downtime from unreliable and inferior equipment is an unnecessary cost.

Oliver cites a mentor relationship with Thomas Wright,[2] a local corporate executive, as invaluable in helping him develop his business skills. Like his relationship with Simpson, this connection started from an impromptu conversation in a local restaurant. While dining out one evening, Wright overheard Oliver talking about his business and he became intrigued by the young man who was running his own business. Oliver soon learned that Wright was an accountant and Chief Financial Officer in a large corporation. Wright offered to manage the books for Oliver's company.

exhibit B Customer Satisfaction Report Card—2002 Season

#	Question (1 = Poor, 10 = Excellent)	Score
1	Was your property cut often enough	8.8
2	Was your grass cut at an appropriate length	8.7
3	Were you satisfied with the trimming around gardens and flower beds	8.2
4	Were you satisfied with the cleanup of grass clippings—lawn, walkways, and driveways	8.3
5	Would you recommend us to a neighbour	8.6
6	Was your lawn furniture etc. left in order	8.6
7	Were you happy with our courteous service	8.7
	Total	8.5

Source: Oliver Davis, Company Report Prepared for CIBC Student Entrepreneurship Presentation (2003).

[2]Name has been disguised.

exhibit C Comparative Growth Rates

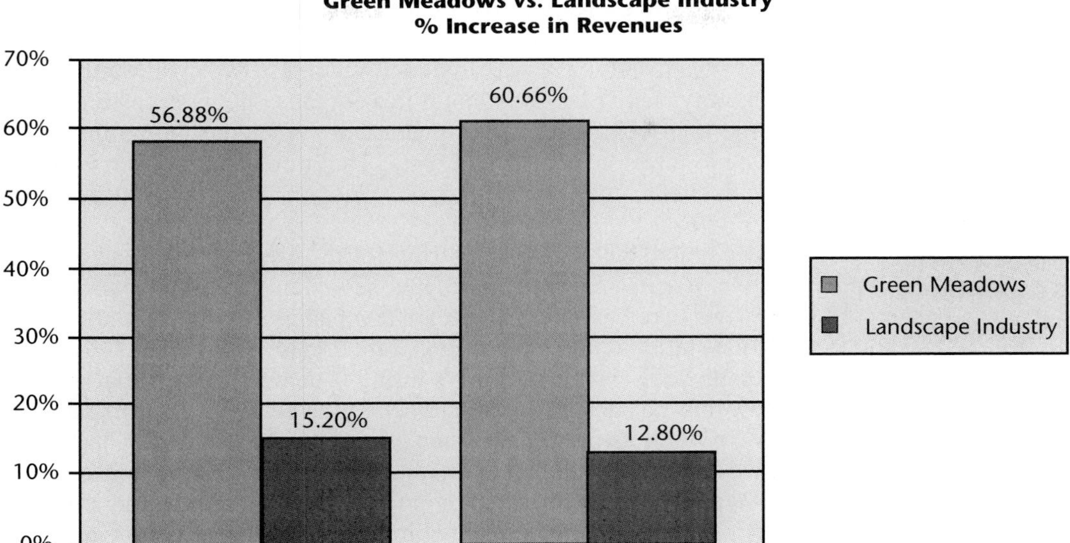

According to Oliver, Wright "is excellent for just sitting around and chatting. He shares lots of life's lessons with me." Recently, however, Wright's schedule was involving an increasing amount of out of country travel and was generally taking up almost all his time. Oliver sensed that the day would soon come that the CFO would simply not be available for Green Meadows.

Oliver's typical 15-hour days see him working from 7:30 a.m. to 10:30 p.m., and according to Oliver, it has been that way for at least the past three seasons. It was only recently that Oliver took the occasional weekend off work, just to bring some respite to his demanding schedule. "I could probably step out of working but I enjoy it. I often wake up in the middle of the night thinking about business. I find myself thinking about other projects…what else I could do. How else I could expand the business? The opportunities and possibilities are just so exciting that I can't sleep; it keeps me up at night."

Oliver incurred a frightening injury on a job site a couple of summers ago. While he was operating a gas powered hedge trimmer, he had a momentary lapse of attention and nearly completely severed off one of his fingers. Because Oliver was unable to get back to the jobsites for several days, his Dad helped manage the crews. For Oliver, "That type of thing, which could take me away from my company, scares me, scares me, really, really scares me. I know my Dad and Bob could step in, but…."

THE CREWS

In the two years since the buyout, Oliver's company had grown to include two crews: a lawn maintenance crew and a garden/patio (interlock) design crew. The lawn maintenance crew looks after routine lawn maintenance of over 120 properties across four towns. The activities of this crew include grass cutting, de-thatching, aerating, organic fertilizing, top dressing (Green Meadows Company Information Sheet, 2003). The second, four man crew looks after garden design and maintenance, the design of interlocking brick driveways and patios, garden walls and retaining walls (Green Meadows Company Information Sheet, 2003). Although crew members work primarily on one type of job there was frequent rotation between crews. Lawn cutting jobs could take anywhere from 30 minutes to a couple of hours depending on the size of the property. Interlocking jobs were much more time consuming. Installation often involves up to three or four days of work. That time is in addition to the consultation time with clients, the time needed to develop the design and place orders with suppliers.

In the four years since he started hiring for the crews, Oliver had never had an employee leave, nor had he terminated anyone—a unique and remarkable staffing record in the lawn care business. Lawn care companies are usually staffed with temporary, seasonal staff and marked by significant employee turnover. Oliver was cautious in his employee selection—always hiring someone for an initial probationary period. If they didn't have the attention to detail, the desire to do an excellent job, or a willingness to work as part of the team, they did not get to stay past week one. Most potential employees, however, made the initial screening and continued on with Green Meadows. Oliver's selection process disregarded the old axiom of "not hiring friends." In fact, so far he has only hired people that he knew or who were recommended by friends. He looked for employees with a work ethic and customer service orientation similar to his own.

Among Oliver's staff, six of his seven employees were connections from high school. Like Oliver, they attended university or college and wanted to work outdoors in the summertime. Oliver's seventh employee, Bob, is a forty-something expert in the design and installation of interlocking brick. Like most of Oliver's other business relationships, Oliver's association with Bob started with a chance meeting at one of his job sites. As Oliver recalled, Bob stopped by one of Oliver's job sites and asked Oliver if he needed some help. Oliver quickly realized that Bob had skills in the design and installation of interlocking bricks—skills that could help Oliver grow the interlocking side of the business. Bob's easy-going style, twinned with his strong work ethic and customer service focus, was an ideal match for Green Meadows. Oliver invited Bob to join the company. Two summers later, Bob was still employed full-time during the outdoor maintenance season (typically April to November). As Oliver notes, "Bob knows a lot of the tricks of the trade. He knows how to talk to the customers." On the job site, Bob and the crews started referring to Oliver as "boss," something which makes Oliver both chuckle and wince. The owner/employee relationship between Oliver and Bob has gradually evolved into one where Bob frequently joins Oliver for a beer after work and has became a sort of confidant, advisor and sounding board for business ideas.

As with many of his other relationships, his connection with Bob, his most senior employee, started informally. As Bob recalls:

> I had just finished with a company and I was out walking in my neighbourhood and I saw some young lads working on interlock and I said something like, "Gee, you probably need some help. Where's your boss? Who's your boss?" Then we saw him coming down the road. I said to him, "I think you need some more help." He agreed and I asked him, "When do I start?" It was a quick handshake, nothing formal. It's been as easy as that ever since...very easy.

To Bob, an employee with twenty-plus years of industry experience:

> Ollie treats us all pretty damned good. If someone didn't have a lunch, Ollie brings him a sandwich and a drink. I'm 49 years old and the rest are 22. Ollie's the boss but I can show him ways to do interlock jobs more efficiently because of my years of experience. That's good for the job, that's good for the company and good for all of us. I do his layout, start to finish and make sure it's done right…I execute it. Ollie does all the legwork, the hard work. He's often out visiting clients until 10:30 at night, getting the clients and dealing with people is something that's very stressful.
>
> This kid's a pleasure to work for. He's very easy going. He's not cocky or pushy or anything. He never gets mad, he never gets rattled. Sometimes I say to him, "JC, Ollie why don't you scream a little once in a while?"

Oliver's days usually start and end with a coffee shop meeting with his crews. Over coffee, the day is plotted out or reviewed. During the day, Oliver is always available on his cell phone and spends most of his time split between the two job sites. In managing his teams, Oliver says that:

> I want an empowered workforce. They're important, the employees are important for sure. I'm not into yelling at the guys or getting on their backs and I don't have to with my crews. How would I feel if someone was yelling at me? I don't yell. There's no point. Some of the work is pretty tedious, so you don't need someone yelling at you. When we go to a job site, we're laughing when we hear all the yelling that goes on with some of the crews. You'd be surprised how many people in this business rant and rave at their employees. It's just treating people the same that you would want to be treated. Bob told me that he had worked for 23 years for another employer and then took one day off when his wife had a baby. He was back at work the next day. Bob's former boss actually phoned the homeowner to see if was working the day after the birth—Bob quit two days later.
>
> I want all my guys doing everything. I'll talk to them about the jobs. Like, if I'm unsure about the best course of action, I'll say, "I don't like the look of this, come over here, what do you think?" I think that four heads are always better than one. I always try to get their input, definitely…but obviously my decision stands. They've starting calling me "Boss" now. That's the joke now.
>
> I like to keep my guys happy. We all do all the work. Some of it is grunt work and we all do it. How can someone be happy if they are the one who does all the grunt work, all the time? That's not a team. I have built a team over the years. I'm into constant team building. Brett came over last year; he is a friend of one of the other employees, Paul. Brett's a great guy and we just hang out. As I said, we're into constant team building. We get together after work and we go out at the end of the year.

Oliver has also been able to offer his seasonal employees Christmas bonuses and, during the off season, has taken his crews to Senators' hockey games. During busy periods, Oliver's crew will expand to include his father who helps out with the grass cutting side of the business. Oliver credits his father with providing the foundation for his belief system. In talking about his father, a retired police officer and currently a teacher, Oliver says, "Oh yeah, my Dad's super. We do things the same way."

CLIENT RELATIONS

The customer is at the centre of Green Meadows Lawn Care. In describing his clients and the way he manages them, Oliver says:

> I don't screw anyone around. If I say I'm going to do something I do it. We do a good job. Doing good and being nice and kind are the foundations of what we do…. Just be-

> ing kind to clients, just helping people out if they're in a jam. One of our clients fractured her ankle last winter. She phoned when I was home on Christmas break so I went with one of the guys to shovel her walk. That's just the kind of relationship I have with the clients. It's the little things, if clients want something done, it usually only takes one hour, I ask them just pay me for cost or don't even worry about it. That's probably how your name gets passed on.

Oliver's client focus has resulted in the extraordinary record of never having lost a client—a unique record in his industry. Getting clients is tough in the industry—retaining them is key to his success. Oliver estimates that for every 20 quotes, he secures 2 contracts. Typically working Monday to Friday from 7 a.m. to 3:30 p.m. with the crews, evenings and weekends are spent visiting potential clients and preparing quotes. As Oliver says, "I can't get to the cottage as much as I'd like." As mentioned earlier, in 2003, for the first time in a long time, Oliver started taking the occasional weekend off.

To build his business, Oliver has also actively built a network of relationships with contractors and suppliers in the area. One local contractor had some extra gravel aggregate (GA) building compound left over from a job. He had no need for it but Oliver knew that he could use it for one of his sites. The contractor, who knew Oliver, told him to take as much as he wanted. Oliver's willingness to haul the GA away from the construction site saved the contractor the cost of removal.

Comments from two of Oliver's clients describe Oliver as his clients see him. Anna Smith, a Green Meadows client for the past five years, says that Oliver

> ...has a really friendly attitude. It's not so much that he develops a business relationship with his clients but it's the relationship you develop with him as a person. You can call the company at any time. There is a strong service orientation. He's not too big but I hope he doesn't get too big. I think his father's a big component. It's a family thing. Costing too, it's a good service at a reasonable price.
>
> I would absolutely recommend him. He's such a nice kid. You have to appreciate that he was a kid when he started. So, we've sort of watched Oliver grow up. He had a vision, which is crucial. He has defined his business and anything else that he has expanded into has been a natural fit that has allowed him to keep control and the quality. He's such an amiable person. He's got charm and charisma. He's come so far for someone so young. He's got a lot of emotional intelligence.

Diane Miller, whose family has been a client of Oliver's for over five years, says:

> He has the perfect personality for business. He's so professional, yet in a way, he's laid back, therefore he just puts you at ease. Our family has gotten quite close to Oliver. He will just pop in for a coffee. He's just a real, nice young man. We couldn't be happier. He presents himself always as very clean despite the business he's in. He has the whole package. You just like him when you meet him. My Dad has referred him to others. We would never change. As long as he's here and we're here, we would never change!

LOOKING AHEAD

On his way back to the coffee shop, Oliver drove his baby blue truck to a newly built, upscale neighbourhood where his interlocking crew was just finishing up for the day. Getting out of his truck to talk to the crew, he was pleased to see the crew doing the routine end of the day job site clean-up. Bob was hosing down the white garage door to remove the reddish stone dust residue that was kicked up while cutting the interlocking stones. The other three crew members were reloading the truck, sweeping the driveway and washing down the front door of the house. Leaving the job site clean and organized for the client's return at the end of the work day was one of the trademarks of a Green Meadows job. Leaving the job site in immaculate condition was not only for the benefit of the client but for the company as well. As Oliver reminds his crews, "the neighbours are watching!"

Getting back in the truck to meet the other crew at the coffee shop, Oliver found himself thinking about the next stage in Green Meadows' evolution. For Oliver, entrepreneurship and sole proprietorship had been financially and personally rewarding and now, with his University studies half finished (as was the case for many of his crew), the goal was to plan for the future. As Oliver says, "For me, five years is the short term. I plan to just keep going as hard as I can. In the long term, I think there are endless opportunities. I can integrate things vertically so that I could supply my business. I want to grow, keep it profitable but I want to still be able to control it. I just need another me."

case 21 Northmar Distributors

On a dreary afternoon in March, George Dubroy,[1] Director, Wholesale Operations, Northmar Distributors, was reviewing the variety of rather unpleasant tasks facing him. George had just hung up from a call with his boss, Yvan Cournoyer, Vice-President, Distribution for Alliance Inc. (Northmar's parent company), where he and Phil (his Warehouse Manager and longtime friend) had learned that the decision had been confirmed to close their long-standing profitable operation. Alliance corporate had found another way to generate greater profits from the distribution function of their convenience store sales company. One of the results of this decision was that not only George and Phil were going to be affected personally, but also all of Northmar's employees (see Exhibit 1 for an organization chart), many of whom George considered to be his friends.

Now that the closure decision had finally been confirmed by Alliance, George began wondering what operational and personnel challenges he needed to prepare himself for as the closing process began. George knew that negotiations on severance packages (see Exhibit 2) between his friends and co-workers and his soon-to-be-former employer would need to be a part of the process, and he began to ponder where his ultimate loyalties should lie.

THE CONVENIENCE STORE INDUSTRY

Within Ontario there are approximately 11,000 convenience stores, 20% of which are controlled by major chains. Alliance's chain, Gerry's Convenience, consists of 600 stores located throughout Ontario. Outside of Ontario, Alliance owns and operates 900 other convenience stores under the names of KwikStop, Clark's Mart and Easy Treats.

[1]The authors are grateful for the support of George Dubroy and Nipissing University in preparation of this manuscript. The authors may have disguised certain names and other identifying information to protect confidentiality.

exhibit 1 Northmar Organization Chart

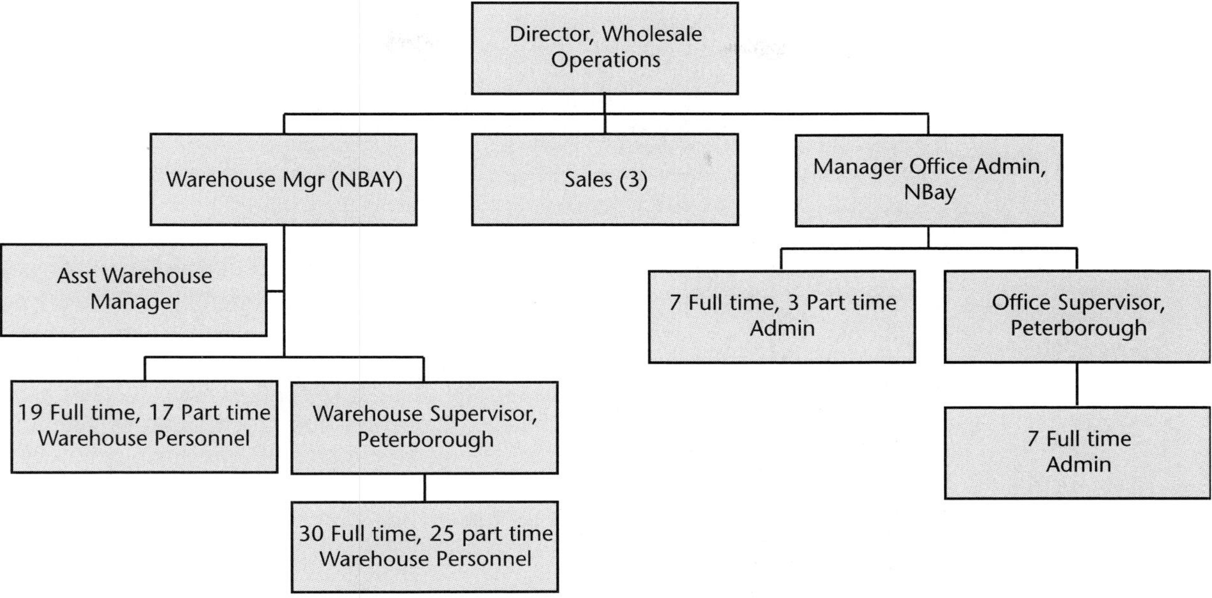

Convenience stores operate on the premise that customers are willing to pay additional margins for everyday products in exchange for added convenience. Small stores (with very accessible parking) are often located in high traffic and residential areas. Product inventories are quite small (due to the restriction in store size) but aggressively managed. Studies had shown that 45% of convenience store sales are impulse purchases, and as a result, stock-out of any product truly results in lost sales. Margins in convenience stores often approach 30%, as opposed to grocery stores that more typically achieve 20% margins. Consequently, convenience store operators look for wholesale suppliers who can provide small, frequent, accurate shipments, at a good price.

exhibit 2 Severance Package Information

Financial Termination Package		
	Average Package (000's)	Package Range (000's)
North Bay Warehouse		
Admin.	37	4–165
Full-time Union	14	7–23
Part-time Union	2	0–4
Peterborough Warehouse		
Admin.	8	2–27
Full-time Non-union	7	4–16
Part-time Non-union	2	0–2

THE DISTRIBUTION FUNCTION

Within the convenience store chains, the advent of computerized inventory control and electronic ordering allowed convenience store operators to more aggressively manage their inventory. The most forward-thinking wholesale suppliers responded with sophisticated complementary software systems and ever-larger warehouses with integrated, automated picking systems. Stock-outs have become rarer for convenience store owners and they have begun to expect higher levels of service from their wholesalers. Also, as a result of the automation of the wholesaler's systems, the "cents per pick" variable costs decreased for the wholesaler.

ALLIANCE'S DISTRIBUTION STRATEGY

In Quebec, and the more thinly distributed Western Canadian market, Alliance had historically contracted the distribution function to a third party wholesaler. For the Quebec market, a recent decision had been made to bring the distribution function in-house. Alliance corporate had committed $12 million to the construction of a state-of-the-art distribution centre in suburban Montreal.

Up to the time of the case, Alliance had been mainly using their wholly owned wholesaler, Northmar Distributors, to service the Ontario market. They did this from two locations: Peterborough for the greater Toronto area, and North Bay for central and northern Ontario. Even though Alliance controlled the bulk of distribution for Gerry's Convenience stores in Ontario, it didn't reduce their need to accommodate the increased service requirements the convenience store industry demanded from the distribution function. As a consequence, Alliance began looking at how they could improve the distribution service levels (and profit generation) from their distribution division for the Ontario market.

EXISTING ONTARIO DISTRIBUTION—NORTHMAR DISTRIBUTORS

Northmar is a wholly owned subsidiary of Alliance Inc. that wholesales food, snack items, drink items, tobacco products and any other confectionery products that can be sold to convenience stores. Northmar sells the bulk of their products to the 600 Gerry's Convenience locations, with the remaining sales to the "Mom and Pop" corner stores located throughout Northern Ontario. Northmar purchases products directly from manufacturers through ITWALL, the largest confection-buying group in Canada. In addition, Northmar negotiates and purchases directly from other manufacturers not affiliated with ITWALL.

Once the products are received from the manufacturers, Northmar then stores the pallets of products in their warehouse until individual orders are transmitted electronically by the individual convenience stores to the order desk. At this point, a Northmar-designed fourteen-year-old information system generates a pick ticket, a manifest and a routing list for delivery directly to each individual convenience store. These deliveries occur weekly to each store. A contract shipper, who specializes in the convenience store trade and understands the need for timeliness and low loss shipments, handles shipping and delivery to individual stores.

NORTHMAR'S PROFITS

Northmar generates its profits from two sources, the "up charge" (or markup) and the "O&A" account.

In order to maximize the up charge, Northmar is continually trying to knock down supplier prices and negotiate internally with Alliance's Gerry's Convenience stores for improved selling prices. When combined with the Mom & Pop sales, the up charge roughly covers the ongoing overhead expenditures and "cents per pick" costs (the only substantial variable costs in the operation) and allows Northmar to break even.

The Over and Above account, or "O&A," makes up the bulk of the profits for Northmar. This account comes from multiple sources but basically consists of three major components:

1. Sharing in ITWALL volume discounts,
2. Volume-based rebates from the tobacco industry (a common industry-wide practice), and
3. Proprietary deals between Northmar and suppliers based on the volume Northmar sells to the Gerry's Convenience stores.

NORTHMAR CORPORATE HISTORY

Northmar started out as McDonald Beverages and Wholesale Services in 1928 at its current location on 2 acres close to the Lake Nipissing waterfront in North Bay, Ontario. Over the years, the building had been expanded to 25,000 square feet, employment grew to 53 full and part-time employees and a subsidiary of approximately the same size had been acquired in Peterborough, another small city about 200 km closer to the major southern Ontario retail markets.

Three years ago, Alliance Inc. became the latest in a series of owners of the Northmar operation, all of which seemed to follow a policy of minimizing additional investments in Northmar. The one constant throughout the years had been the local employment base, resulting in average full-time employee tenure of about 10 years (see Exhibit 3 for a breakdown). George had been with the Northmar operation 20 years and had been "in the trenches" during three similar acquisitions of their operation.

Ten years earlier, the Northmar warehouse employees had voted to unionize. The warehouse personnel joined the Retail, Wholesale and Department Store Union (RWDSU). Three years later, there had been a one-week, somewhat bitter labour disruption over wages. Other typical management/union strains occurred over the remaining years. One example of the union's typical approach to these issues occurred when management moved to reduce shipping costs and outsourcing of shipping was one of the options being considered. Management approached the union to jointly problem-solve the shipping cost issue, but the union didn't actively respond until the decision was finalized to outsource shipping. Labour relations at the time of the case ranged from strained to good, depending upon the employee. In summary, management characterized the union executive as primarily reactionary and not particularly forward-thinking.

exhibit 3 Workforce Characteristics

Workforce Characteristics			
	No.	**Average Service**	**Job Titles**
North Bay Warehouse			
Admin	14	9.4	Director, Commission Sales, Office Manager, Purchasing, Office Clerks
Full-time Union	19	10.6	Lead Hand, Picker/Packer, Shipper/Receiver
Part-time Union	20	0.9	Picker/Packers
Peterborough Warehouse			
Admin.	9	3.8	Supervisor/Clerks
Full-time Non-union	30	3	Lead Hand, Picker/Packer, Shipper/Receiver
Part-time Non-union	25	1	Groc and Cig Pickers
Totals	117		

ALLIANCE'S ONTARIO OPPORTUNITY

Toronto-based Johnson's Brothers is a growing third party wholesaler that serves a parallel market, the small convenience item kiosks located at gas bars. They are constantly looking for more volume to support the significant investments they have made in their wholesale operations.

Late last summer, Johnson's Brothers approached Alliance corporate with a very attractive offer. Johnson's offered to assume the convenience store business handled by Northmar at similar price levels, while passing on efficiency savings in "cents per pick" and the bulk of any improvement in "volume discounts" attributable to Alliance's additional volume. About the time Alliance received this "no investment," "guaranteed" savings offer, Alliance was in the process of evaluating the capital requirements to rebuild the Northmar infrastructure to more modern standards.

Upon receiving the Johnson offer, management at Alliance didn't hesitate to begin negotiating an agreement for Johnson's to assume Northmar's volume. At the time of the case, these negotiations had resulted in Alliance and Johnson's producing a memorandum of understanding on a more formal agreement to follow later.

GEORGE'S DILEMMA

George, and a few of the other senior people at Northmar, had worked on an alternative distribution center proposal (based on the strategy employed by Alliance in Quebec) over the last year. If their efforts had been successful, it would have meant they had more control over what happens to themselves and their people. George had presented the proposal to Alliance's management but it was turned down in favor of the Johnson's Brothers proposal. George had thought the closure of Northmar was likely coming, but now that it was real, he needed a little time to let it all sink in. He knew he faced some really unpleasant tasks over the next few months and Alliance made it very clear that he was being held responsible to execute a smooth transition of Northmar's volume to Johnson's Brothers. Besides all of this, George knew that a wind down of operations would take between 4 and 6 months. A smooth transition to Johnson's would be paramount for Alliance to hang onto its Mom and Pop accounts.

First thing the next morning, George had a visit from his friend Phil who was visibly upset. Phil had been doing his homework in case the closure of Northmar became inevitable and he had successfully acquired a job offer (in a medical warehousing operation in North Bay) that looked like it would carry him through to his planned retirement in 6 years. Phil was upset because he had started going through the Company's severance policy and it looked like if he took the job he stood to lose as much as $36,000 of the $76,000 he had expected to receive upon termination (see Exhibit 4 for the calculation).

Once Phil left his office (after George promised to look into his situation), George began taking a long hard look at the termination policies Alliance had used when they recently closed a dairy operation in Southern Ontario. He knew that there had been some ugly backlash incidents resulting from that closure. George knew that Alliance's existing severance policy (see Appendix 1 for relevant excerpts) would be especially troublesome for his North Bay employees and friends. Given the poor economic situation in North Bay, he suspected many of his long term warehouse workers would have real difficulties making ends meet with the type of minimum wage jobs that might become available in North Bay. In particular, the severance payment claw back provision (see below) was expected to be troublesome as already demonstrated by the discussion with Phil.

Excerpt from Alliance corporate severance policy:

3.2.6 It is the normal practice of the Company to provide payment on a regular pay basis (every two weeks) until such time as the terms of pay for termination have been completed.

In the event an individual secures alternative employment, or mitigates loss of income derived from Alliance in any other way, prior to the completion of the period covered by the additional Company payments, the Company will make a lump sum payment equivalent to 50% of the balance of these additional Company payments.

exhibit 4 Phil's Termination Payment Calculations

Phil's employment statistics

Years of employment—26

Salary level—15—$55,000/yr

Option A—Don't take the new job

Weeks of termination = 26 × 4 = 104—reduced to 72 weeks according to section 3.2.2.

Rate of pay/week = 55,000/52 = $1,057.70

Termination payments over next 72 weeks = $76,154.40

Option B—Phil starts the new job in 4 weeks.

Weeks of termination = 26 × 4 = 104—reduced to 72 weeks according to section 3.2.2.

Rate of pay/week = 55,000/52 = $1,057.70

Termination payments over next 4 weeks = $4,230.80

Lump sum payment = 50% of (Total termination possible—termination payments made)

= 50% × (72 × 1,057.70 – 4,230.80)

= 50% × (76,154.40 – 4,230.80)

= 50% × (71,932.60)

= $35,916.80

On the other hand, when George reviewed some of the estimates of closing costs for the corporation (Exhibit 5), he quickly realized that these costs would likely eat up a significant portion of last year's profits. He knew Alliance would undoubtedly include closing costs in the calculation of his personal bonus/termination package. In addition, George had other personal factors to consider. He was 52 years old, and even though he was financially comfortable through some prudent real estate investing, he wasn't ready to retire. At the same time, he had a comfortable lifestyle in North Bay and he wasn't enamored of the thought of moving to head office in Toronto. On the other hand, if his original proposal had been accepted, he would have willingly moved to the new Distribution Center location (which would have likely ended up somewhere in the greater Toronto area), so he wasn't completely tied to North Bay, if the right opportunity came along.

He also knew that if he wanted to avoid the ugliness that happened with the dairy operation closure, and the potential for sabotage which always existed in the food supply industry, he needed to think clearly and quickly about how he was going to share the news with the rest of his co-workers.

exhibit 5 Corporate Costs as per Current Policy (forecasting 25% re-employment rate)

	Corporate Costs (000s)			
	Notice Costs	**Severance as per Policy**	**Stay-on Bonus**	**Totals**
North Bay Warehouse				
Admin	113	366	47	527
Full-time Union	90	185	0	275
Part-time Union	35	0	0	35
Peterborough Warehouse				
Admin.	30	35	5	70
Full-time Non-union	109	87	0	196
Part-time Non-union	41	0	0	41
Totals	418	673	52	1,144

appendix 1 Relevant Excerpts from Alliance's Termination Policy

Purpose:

The policy of Alliance is to provide a period of salary continuance in the event that the employment of an individual is terminated by the Company, or by mutual agreement, for any reasons other than for cause or inability to perform normal job responsibilities. This policy outlines the terms and provisions for determining the level of payment that the individual would receive in the event that the Company terminates employment.

This policy is a material term of your contract of employment

3.0 Payment on Termination of Employment

Alliance Limited will make payments to an individual employee where the employment contract is terminated as a result of a management decision (other than for cause or inability to perform normal job responsibilities). It is the policy of Alliance Limited to pay an individual for a period of time, which in all instances includes the minimum period, defined by relevant legislation. The Company payment program exceeds the requirement defined in relevant legislation.

3.1 The company is not required to make any payments if the employment contract is terminated during the probationary period (as defined as 90 days from the start date with the Company).

3.2 In the event the Company wishes to terminate employment of an individual that has completed the probationary period for any reason other than cause or inability to perform normal job responsibilities, the following payment policy will apply:

3.2.1 The terms of the termination payment will be determined based on the salary level of the position that the individual whose employment is being terminated currently occupies.

3.2.2 For the purpose of calculating the period of salary continuance, the following payment schedule will be used;

Salary Level

1–5, two weeks pay for each year of completed service (to a maximum of 36 weeks of pay)

6–18, four weeks of pay for each year of completed service (to a maximum of 72 weeks of pay)

3.2.3 The number of years of completed service is calculated by subtracting the date of termination from the start date, and rounding up to the next quarter of a year.

3.2.4 For the purpose of calculating weekly base salary, the Company will use the annual base salary for the individual divided by 52.

3.2.5 (Not relevant to the case)

3.2.6 It is the normal practice of the Company to provide payment on a regular pay basis (every two weeks) until such time as the terms of pay for termination have been completed.

In the event an individual secures alternative employment, or mitigates loss of income derived from Alliance in any other way, prior to the completion of the period covered by the additional Company payments, the Company will make a lump sum payment equivalent to 50% of the balance of these additional Company payments.

case 22 Team Ontario (A)

Bill Bowker put the phone down and leaned back in his chair. He had just been selected as Head Coach of Ontario's women's hockey team for the upcoming Canada Winter Games. It was a great honour to be named coach and at the same time the biggest challenge of his coaching career. The Games were part of Canada's High Performance Hockey Program and were intended to identify and prepare athletes who could succeed at the international level, such as the forthcoming Winter Olympics at Salt Lake City in 2002.

Bowker knew that the expectations of him were very high. Ontario had lost to Quebec in the gold medal final at the last Winter Games and it was hoped that this time Ontario would be victorious. Bowker was also aware that doing a good job as coach would increase his chances of advancing to more senior coaching levels in Canada's program. The previous coach of Team Ontario, Karen Hughes, was subsequently appointed Head Coach of the National Women's Under-22 Hockey Team and Assistant Coach to the National Women's Hockey Team.

The challenge facing him was daunting. He had to select the best players from across Ontario and mould them into a team in a relatively short period of time. He knew that this was the experience of a lifetime for many of these young athletes. As good as they were, perhaps one or two from his team would eventually make it to Canada's National Team. How could they win *and* make this a great experience for these young women?

THE GAME

Hockey is Canada's national game. Although Canadians love to play many sports, hockey resides deep within the Canadian soul. All winter long the game is played in thousands of arenas, neighbourhood and backyard rinks, and frozen ponds, in every province and territory of Canada. Each year a new generation of young boys, and increasingly young girls, takes to the ice to learn this great game. What attracts them to hockey is the speed and intensity of the action, the continuous flow from one play to the next, and the fellowship of the team.

Women's hockey differs from men's, in that there is less reliance on size and strength. By contrast, the women's game emphasizes skating, passing, and controlling the puck. The rules of the game also emphasize skill over brawn. Unlike the men's game, body checking is not allowed, although some body contact is permissible when there is an attempt to play the puck first.

Many people view hockey as a man's game, perhaps because of its association with aggressive play on the ice. Nothing could be further from the truth. Women have been playing hockey since the 1890s in Canada and until the 1940s hockey was considered a game for both sexes.

At the turn of the 20th Century women were playing in teams across Canada. By the 1920s women's university teams had been formed at Toronto, McGill and Queen's, and competed in the Women's Collegiate Ice Hockey League. Some of the players and teams during this era were truly remarkable. Bobbie Rosenfeld of the Toronto Pats was an outstanding player of the 1920s. This gifted athlete was also a member of the 1928 Olympic track and field team, and won a gold medal in world record time in swimming. The Preston Rivulettes, led by Hilda Ranscombe, won 348 games and lost just 2, and won 6 national championships during the 1930s. Other great women's teams of this era were the Edmonton Monarchs, Winnipeg Olympics, Ottawa Alerts, Montreal Maroons, and the Roverines of Newfoundland.

Men appear to have been largely indifferent to women's hockey during this time, although some were clearly more skeptical of the notion of women participating in the sport. The latter view is captured in an article entitled, "Girls Shouldn't Do It," written by Andy Lytle in *Chatelaine* magazine in 1933:

> Ice hockey is a game, fortunately indulged in by comparatively few girls teams, even as in lacrosse, for which the soft yielding flesh with which Nature equips the sex, makes them wholly unsuited, to say nothing of the general unwisdom of arming members of the more impassioned gender with clubs to be bent over beautiful heads that were surely created for more entrancing purposes.

The women's game suffered during the 1940s and 1950s when women were discouraged from playing all sports, including hockey. A revival in the women's game began in the 1960s, reflecting broader support for women's participation in athletics. During the 1970s teams were formed across Canada, the United States and Europe. In 1975 women's hockey took a huge step forward with the formation of the Ontario Women's Hockey Association. The OWHA promoted the game based on the values of: "Fair play, fun, excellence, good citizenship, integrity and honesty, and equity."

The initial move toward international competition occurred when the World Invitational Tournament took place in Toronto in 1987. The International Ice Hockey Federation sanctioned the first Women's World Championship in Ottawa in 1990 with eight teams competing. Canada won the first and all subsequent world championships, with the United States taking silver each time. The rivalry between these two teams is intense and attracts considerable interest from hockey fans in both countries.

The profile of women's hockey has risen dramatically since its inclusion as a medal sport in the 1998 Nagano Olympics. The American team upset the favoured Canadians to take the gold medal. The following two years saw a 50% increase in the number of girls and women playing with Hockey USA. The growth in the sport in Canada has been phenomenal. In 1990, just 6,000 girls and women in Ontario played this sport; by 2000, close to 30,000 were playing. It would be difficult to overstate the dedication of many of these players. Practices and games can be as many as 120–140 times per year.

BILL BOWKER, HEAD COACH

"I was brought up in a home that believed in sport, which believed in the value of the life skills learned in sports. I feel I am very fortunate to have that background. My Dad was a huge influence on my athletic interests as a child. He was a baseball player who was offered a contract with the Cincinnati Reds as a catcher. Agents from the Reds went to his home in Grandby, Quebec and things were going well until my grandfather heard that some games were played on Sundays. He ripped up the contract and told them to get out.

"I was good at a number of sports. In 1964, at the age of 15, I won the Junior Men's Canadian Archery Championship. I also represented Canada at the World Archery Championships in Watkins Glen, New York that year. I was shooting 4, 5, and 6 hours a day. I got burned out and stopped shooting the next year.

"I had taken up baseball in 1962 and played pitcher and third base. There was outstanding baseball in Quebec at that time, the best in the country. I went on to have a great baseball career in Quebec. I played Junior A ball and was the leading hitter in the league and made first team all star 3 times. I probably would have been among the top 4–5 players in the country at that time. I was an all-around athlete and played pretty much every sport. I was the quarterback of my high school football team, and on the swimming and basketball teams. I loved sports and the outdoors.

"But one sport was my favorite—hockey! The game of hockey is based on values. If you instill them now, they last for the rest of their lives. I started playing with a team called Black Magic in Montreal and we had tournaments that lasted through the night. Then I went to Junior B hockey, which was very structured and a huge jump from shinny hockey. After that, I went to Junior A with the Lachine Maroons of the Quebec Major Junior League, which was part of the Montreal Canadiens' farm system. I then went to the Verdun Maple Leafs and that was a step up in my development. I had two tryouts with the Montreal Junior Canadiens, the main feeder team for the Canadiens.

"Hockey was the most important thing in my life at this time and my goal was to make the Canadiens. I hadn't gone to school in a year. I was totally committed to conditioning and skill development, and I was working out non-stop. I was shooting 500 five-pound steel pucks a day. It was a great period in my life. I couldn't wait to get out of bed in the morning to go running and to the gym. I grew 10 inches in one year. I was a pretty big person and played a physical game. I was determined to stay drug free, but other players were starting on steroids.

"I didn't make Montreal's program and was released in 1969. I didn't have the skill to play there. I knew it was coming but I was devastated. I had blown out my knee, which sure didn't help. They didn't have the medical technology in those days to deal with my injury. I worked hard at trying to rehabilitate my knee. I went to the New York Rangers training camp as a free agent and played in their farm system in Guelph, Ontario. From 1970 to 1975 I played pro hockey with a team called the Embrun Panthers. All of us knew that our careers were over, but you always think that maybe you'll be the one to make a comeback. At that point, hockey was over for me." (Bowker's career in business over the next 20 years is described in Exhibit 1.)

"I came back to hockey years later when I started coaching my kids. I hadn't realized how much I missed the rink. It was great to be back! I had the playing background but I needed to get a coaching education through the National Coaching Certification Program. It didn't take long to move through the academics of hockey. I became certified to coach at the national level in 1994. I had a winning record and kids entrusted to me started to become outstanding at the game. I coached from 1994–96 at a very high level in boys' hockey. This was in an Ottawa Senators' satellite development program called Shooting Stars, for the best academic hockey players. You had to have great marks to be part of it. The parents believed in the value of what I was bringing to the game. I was building people more than building hockey players. For 90% of coaches winning is everything. That value by itself is a mistake.

"I took a job as Head Coach at Carleton University with the men's hockey program for the next 3 years. At the same time, I was coaching my daughter's hockey team and we won 3 provincial championships. I was starting to get noticed. I got invited to the Olympic evaluation camp and helped to select the Women's National Team for the Nagano Olympics.

"I believe in solid foundations, in team building, and in the work ethic. These beliefs are based on my experiences as a player and a coach." Coach Bowker's philosophy of coaching may be found in Exhibit 2.

ANGELA JAMES AND JEAN VAILLANCOURT, ASSISTANT COACHES

Angela James and Jean Vaillancourt were appointed as Assistant Coaches to Team Ontario. Each brought unique skills to the coaching team. Bowker described Angela James as the Wayne Gretzky of women's hockey, as the finest hockey player ever. She had enormous credibility with players as a result of her remarkable career in hockey. Although she had a depth of experience as a player, she did not have much experience at coaching. Jean Vaillancourt did not have the playing experience but had tremendous organizational skills. Together they had the potential to be a great coaching team.

Angela James grew up in a housing project in Toronto and from an early age sports was central to her life. "I loved sports, loved being competitive. Sport brings so much to a person's life—involvement, friendships. It doesn't matter what sport. I played hockey, softball, soccer, roller hockey, field hockey, and basketball. I played softball at the provincial and national levels. I was on the National Women's Hockey Team for 10 years."

James had an outstanding career on the national team. At the first World Championship in 1990, she led the Canadian team with 11 goals and 2 assists. She was a team captain and a key player in Team Canada's subsequent victories at the World Championships in '92, '94, '96, and '97.

"They came and asked me to be Assistant Coach once Bill went in as Head Coach. I had experience playing in short term competitions where a team must pull together in a very short time." Of her philosophy of coaching, she responded, "Experience tells you what to do, but confidence allows you to do it."

THE PLAYERS

Bowker and his coaches had to choose the best 20 players from across the province to represent Team Ontario. The age and eligibility requirements specified that the players had to be under the age of 18 as of December 31, 1999, and that they be Canadian citizens or have Landed Immigrant status in Canada. A total of 720 young women tried out for the team at evaluation camps held across the huge province of Ontario. A group of 10 evaluators from the OWHA helped Bowker select the players to represent Ontario. "The logistics of putting all of this together was a huge undertaking." The players Bowker and his team selected ranged in age from 14 to 17. Several players described how they became interested in hockey, their experiences at the evaluation camps, and their initial reactions at the first training camp of Team Ontario.

Katie Germain, Goalie

"I've been playing hockey as far back as I can remember. My Dad played for 11 years in the International Hockey League and my brother also played hockey. I started playing in the backyard and by 10 or 11 I had joined a team for my age group in Sarnia. I also played soccer, basketball, volleyball and tennis.

"There were regional tryout camps across the province for Team Ontario. The camps lasted the whole weekend. There were speakers on health and nutrition for the athletes. There were evaluation drills and scrimmages at the end of the camp. You were selected to move on to the final 2 or 3 camps. At that level they had round-robin tournaments to compare players. After the final camp everyone got a phone call from Bill Bowker as to whether they had made it or not. I had set a goal for myself a year earlier to make the team. When I heard that I had made the team I went jumping through the kitchen and did a lap around the house.

"Going to the first training camp was pretty nerve-wracking. It was a little intimidating because these were the best players in Ontario. Three other players from my team also made Team Ontario, so we were a group at the first camp. I noticed that other players were also in their own groups of people they knew."

Cheryl Muranko, Forward

"Mom took me to the rink to skate when I was young and I would stay to watch the hockey games. I loved the fast-paced intensity of the game. I started playing hockey when I was 6 years old. I played all competitive sports at school, including soccer, basketball, and volleyball. When I was in Grade 3 I was doing a project on ice hockey and my teacher knew Hilda Ranscombe. I went to see her at the retirement home where she lived and we talked about hockey. When I was 8 or 9 I went to Kitchener to see the National Team and met Margot Page. When I met her I knew there was something for me to strive for.

"There were a huge number of girls at the first evaluation camp. Everyone who wanted to try-out was there. There was not a lot of room to do your stuff. Players could almost get overlooked. It was a pretty intense and competitive atmosphere. I knew a lot of the players, but I'm not going to let her get the puck just because she's my friend.

"I had been on Team Ontario in 1997 for the Midget Nationals, so I knew what it was all about. I felt pretty confident going to camp that I would make the team. However, in any situation where someone is going to say 'you make it and you don't,' you will feel some tension. When I made it, I thought, 'Great, another step toward where I want to be.'

"When I arrived at the training camp, I knew everyone. Some I had played with on different teams, some I had played against. There were some people I really disliked. We didn't have a lot of time together. We had very different personalities, different skills. Oh my goodness, we had to become a team!"

Meghan Hunter, Forward

"I started playing hockey when I was 8 years old, probably because my brothers were playing hockey. My dad also played junior hockey and my uncle played in the NHL.

"An incredible number of people turned out for the evaluation camps. It was a bit intimidating. There were people evaluating us from the stands. I was shocked when I was selected and very grateful. Just to be a member of the team was awesome.

"I was very excited when we got together at the first training camp. I found that I knew a lot of the people when I arrived. I had been part of Team Ontario for the Midget Nationals in 1997. Bill was an Assistant Coach for the Team in 1997, so I knew him a bit but not very well."

Cherie Piper, Forward

"I started playing hockey at 8. I had 2 older brothers who played hockey. I played pretty much all the sports, including soccer and baseball for the last 8 or 9 years.

"The tryouts were good: Very intense and very organized. I was happy and excited to be selected to Team Ontario. This was my second under-18 experience, as I played for Team Ontario in 1997. I had played with a lot of the girls before. Everyone knows Angela James. I had watched AJ play over the years. I was also playing with the Beatrice Aeros and had met her through that program. I was comfortable talking to the coaches. All of us played on different clubs and were used to different systems, so the coaches had to get us on the same page."

THE COMPETITION

More than 3,500 athletes would be competing at the Canada Winter Games during the last week of February and the first week of March in Corner Brook, Newfoundland. Over 6,000 volunteers had been working for 3 years to prepare for the Games. The athletes representing each of the 10 provinces would be competing in 23 different sports over this two-week period. There were Opening and Closing Ceremonies for the Games, as well as pep rallies for Team Ontario. The athletes had specially designed Team Ontario clothing, including jackets, hats, vests, and sweatshirts. The major national sports network, TSN, had dedicated 50 hours of coverage for the Games. In the case of women's hockey, the semi-final and final games would be broadcast nationally. The hockey arena would be sold-out for the final match and watched by more than 6,000 people. Athletes were prepared for television interviews with TSN. In the stands for the Games would also be scouts from Canadian and U.S. universities. Strong performance at the Games could mean a full athletic scholarship at a prestigious U.S. school.

Hockey teams were grouped into two pools of 5 provinces each for the preliminary competition. The two top teams in each pool after round-robin competition would then play off for medals. For the semifinal game the first-place team in each pool played the second-place team in the other pool. The winners of the semi-final games then met in the final to determine the gold and silver medal winners. The two losing teams from the semi-final games met to decide the bronze medal winner.

Ontario and Quebec were considered the two powerhouses for the women's hockey competition and they competed in separate pools for the preliminary competition.

Ontario competed against Manitoba, Alberta, Nova Scotia, and Prince Edward Island in its pool. The four games for each team in the preliminaries, and the semi-final and final games were scheduled on consecutive days. The tournament would be physically demanding and played at a higher level than these players had ever encountered in the past. (An overview of the game of hockey and a glossary of rules and terms may be found in Exhibit 3.)

THE CHALLENGE

Bowker faced an enormous challenge: "Once the team was set, we had 5 weekend camps to bring them together, a very small window! These young people are the best players on their teams. Because of their immense talent, these players are used to being out on the ice for most of the game. You have to deal with their egos. How are we going to mould them into a team?"

James saw the challenge in a similar way: "These players are all-stars from their teams. They need to understand that not everyone can be the best at this level. They also have to learn new positions and understand how the system works at a higher level. Some will be unhappy, some will be homesick."

The players on Team Ontario were moving to new levels of skill and competition. Many had never played at a national level, had never competed against players who were the best from across Canada. The skills and plays that had made them all-stars in their respective leagues would not be enough at this level. Players had to push themselves to develop new skills and learn new plays. Some players would make this transition easily, but many would not. Bowker thought about how he should help manage the emotions these players would experience as they met this challenge.

He didn't have to wait long for an opportunity. His talented goalie had a bad game at one of the first training camps. In her words, "If a goalie makes a mistake, it's a huge deal. At one camp I was scored on several times. I was down and upset at how I had played. I wanted do so well with this team." Bowker could see that she was devastated by the experience. How should he respond to her, and to the many other players who would suffer similar setbacks as they stepped up to this challenge?

Bowker was searching for ways of building these players into a confident, skilful team. More than that, he wanted the lessons learned from this experience to be ones that these young people would carry with them all their lives.

QUESTIONS

1. What goals should Coach Bowker have for Team Ontario at the Canada Winter Games? Do you agree with his statement that this is about "building people more than building hockey players"?
2. What are the challenges facing Coach Bowker and the other coaches as they prepare Team Ontario to compete in the Canada Winter Games?
3. What alternatives seem reasonable? Which would you recommend and how would you implement these?
4. What values and personality characteristics seem to describe Coach Bowker and the other members of Team Ontario? Do you think these attributes will enable them to be successful in their careers after hockey?

5. What are the attitudes and skills that can be learned in team sport which help prepare us for life and for a career? Are there attitudes learned in sport that may prove troublesome later in life?
6. What lessons from managing a team in sport may be particularly useful in building and developing teams in business?
7. What strategies have other successful coaches used?

exhibit 1 Coach Bowker's Career in Business

I had no education when my hockey days were over. I still had high school left to finish. I had met my wife in 1973 and she was a settling factor in my life. I went back to school and took the engineering and refrigeration program at Algonquin College. After that, I went to the University of Guelph and graduated from the 5 year Program in Arena Management. I then worked as Arena Manager in charge of a recreation complex in Kanata, outside Ottawa. I stayed in arena management for about 7 years but finally I just got sick of it.

I was very good with mechanical things and so I bought a service station in Kanata. As luck would have it, the highway was changed and we went from being this dumpy little station to being the #1 gas station in eastern Ontario. This put us on our feet financially. I didn't like it that much as I was working 12–14 hours a day and everything smelled of gas. We received an offer for the station and we took it. We then moved to Midland, Ontario, for a job as Assistant Arena Manager and Parks Superintendent. What a mistake! The Arena Manager was 500 years old in his thinking and I reported to him. I hated my job and I had just moved my whole family there.

RCA had a big plant with 1,000 people in Midland and they hired me as a team leader. I dealt with production problems on the assembly line. My job at RCA was very demanding. The plant ran around the clock with 3 shifts. You spent 2 weeks on each shift. I enjoyed it but the hours were absolutely ridiculous.

I then went back to Ottawa as a sales representative for United Auto Parts. I worked as a sales rep for 5 years and increased the sales in my territory from $5 to $30 million. The company was opening many new stores and we bought a franchise for our own store. Over 5 years, we became the #1 store for UAP. Our annual sales increased from less than a half a million to two and a half million and we went from 4 to 22 employees.

I was back to working 100-hour weeks. The store became huge and you had to sell a lot of auto parts to make payroll. I was never home with the kids. I sold the store back to UAP and had to sign a contract not to open a competing store. I took two years off work to re-establish things at home. I had missed the hockey and baseball games with my family. I then took a job with an auto parts company to straighten out their inventory. I was with them for 7 years and was very successful. I used the team concept to develop the sales staff. I also had the opportunity to set my own hours. It gave me the chance to get involved in coaching with my kids.

exhibit 2 Coaching Philosophy

A hockey coach is a multitude of things to different people. To some he is a dictator, to some an authority figure, to others a psychologist, to still others a big brother, and to some an extension of a parent figure or a replacement for a mom or dad. However, a coach is first and foremost, a teacher to every one of his/her players. You are a teacher whose job it is to instruct and reinforce in your players the skills that are necessary to compete in the greatest game in the world, Hockey.

There are many people who are qualified to teach the skills that are required to compete. There are many people who teach, plain and simply, the skills involved in our game of hockey. They join together to make up a very large percentage of those involved in the coaching profession.

Occasionally, or sometimes only once in a lifetime, an athlete comes in contact with a truly great coach, a coach they will never forget. This is a coach who teaches the same basic skills taught by other coaches, yet is one who teaches something special. He teaches a player how to win, and how to be successful. He teaches the intangible aspects that are the substance of a winner. He is the coach who stresses, and who exemplifies in his own life, the qualities, the attributes, and the characteristics that allow the athlete the opportunity to improve not only as a hockey player, but more importantly as a human being. He is the coach who makes a lasting contribution to the lives of his players.

In my opinion coaching is a privilege, an honour, and a way of life that few people are fortunate enough to experience. I welcome the opportunity, and accept the challenge to be the kind of coach a player meets only once in a lifetime.

exhibit 3 Hockey Glossary

THE GAME

Period: The 60 minute game is divided into three 20-minute periods.

Intermission: An intermission of 15 minutes occurs after the first and second periods, at which time the ice is resurfaced.

Overtime: If at the end of the three 20-minute regulation periods the score is tied, play shall continue for a 10-minute overtime period, with the first goal ending the game in "sudden victory."

THE RINK

Attacking zone: The zone between the opponent's blue line and the goal line.

Blue lines: Two blue lines divide the rink into 3 zones, a defensive zone, a neutral zone, and an attacking zone.

Boards: A fibreglass white barrier that surrounds the rink to a height of at least 4 feet and is topped by Plexiglass to protect the audience from errant pucks.

Crease: A blue, semicircular area in front of the goal. A referee may disallow a goal if an attacker is in the crease when a goal is scored.

Defensive zone: The zone between the defending team's goal line and blue line.

Goal line: The red line at either end of the ice (13 feet from the end boards) that is used to determine if a goal has been scored or if icing has occurred.

Neutral zone: The zone between the two blue lines. Player changes take place within this zone.

The point: The spot just inside the defending team's blue line near the boards.

continued

exhibit 3 Hockey Glossary (*continued*)

PLAYERS

There are never more than 6 players (including the goaltender) on the ice for each team at any time. Players are substituted during play and when there is a stoppage in play.

Centre: The player responsible for leading the offence and taking the face-offs.

Forwards: The centre, left and right wing offensive positions on the team.

Defence: The two positions responsible for preventing the other team from scoring.

Goalie: The player who guards the net to prevent the other team from scoring.

PLAYS

Backcheck: When forwards cover an opponent as play returns to the defensive zone.

Breakaway: When a player with the puck skates in alone on the opposing goaltender.

Breakout: When a team moves out of the defensive zone with the puck.

Changing on the fly: Players on the bench replace players on ice as the game continues.

Cycling the puck: A series of short passes in the offensive zone used to control the puck.

Deke: A feint by a player with the puck to trick a defender or goalie.

Face-off: A referee starts play at the beginning of each period by dropping the puck between two opposing players and restarts play in the same manner after an infraction has stopped play.

Forechecking: When the defending team puts pressure on the attacking team in the latter's defensive or the neutral zone.

Freezing the puck: A player uses her skates or stick to hold the puck against the boards, or a goalie uses her glove to cover the puck, in order to get a stoppage in play.

Poke check: To take the puck away from an opponent using a short jab with the blade of the stick.

Power play: When a team has the advantage of more players on the ice than another team because of penalties.

Pull the goalie: When a team removes their goalie to add another forward in the game.

SHOTS

Backhand shot: When the puck is shot from the backside of the stick. A shot that is difficult for a goalie to anticipate where the puck will go.

Blocked shot: When a player on the defending team stops a shot with her body before it reaches the goal. A courageous and exceedingly painful action on the part of a defender.

Slap shot: When a player takes a high back swing before striking the puck. This is a powerful, but difficult shot to control.

Snap shot: A quick, accurate shot.

Wrist shot: When a player leans into her stick and uses her wrist to shoot the puck.

SCORING

Assist: The last two offensive players who touch the puck before the player scoring a goal are awarded assists.

Goal: A goal is scored when a puck completely crosses the goal line between the two goalposts and below the crossbar of the net.

Hat trick: When a player scores 3 goals in one game.

continued

exhibit 3 Hockey Glossary (*continued*)

PENALTIES

Body checking: When a player uses the hip or shoulder to impede the progress of an opponent. Not allowed in women's hockey but permissible in men's.

Charging: When a player body checks an opponent after taking two or more strides or steps.

Crosschecking: When a player hits an opponent with the shaft of the stick that is held between the player's hands.

Delayed penalty: When a player commits a penalty but the other team is in possession of the puck. The referee will not stop play until the offending team is in possession of the puck.

Elbowing: When a player uses her elbow to hit an opponent.

High sticking: When a player strikes an opponent above the waist with her stick.

Hooking: When a player impedes an opponent's progress with the blade or shaft of the stick.

Interference: When a player makes intentional body contact and impedes the progress of an opponent who doesn't possess the puck.

Major penalty: A five-minute penalty given to players for spearing, fighting and checking from behind.

Match penalty: A five-minute penalty and ejection from the game when a player deliberately injures an opponent.

Minor penalty: A two-minute penalty given to players for less serious actions, such as elbowing, high sticking and interference.

Misconduct: A 10-minute penalty given to a player who verbally abuses an official. The player's team does not have to play shorthanded during the penalty.

Penalty shot: When a player denies an opponent a scoring opportunity through hooking or tripping, the opponent is given the puck at centre ice and skates in alone on the goalie.

Roughing: When a player pushes or shoves an opponent.

Slashing: When a player hits an opponent with a chopping motion using the blade or shaft of the stick.

Spearing: When a player strikes an opponent with the tip of the stick blade.

INFRACTIONS

Icing: Icing occurs when a player shoots the puck from her team's half of the ice past an opponent's goal line. Play is stopped and a face-off will take place in the offending team's defensive zone. Icing will not be called if the offending player's team has a player off the ice serving a penalty.

Offside: An offside occurs when a player enters the offensive zone with both skates before the puck arrives. Play is stopped and a face-off occurs in the neutral zone where the infraction took place.

case 23 Alberta Energy Company and the Ethics of Operation Kabriole

It is September 1998. Gwyn Morgan, President and CEO of Alberta Energy Company (AEC), is quietly sitting in his Calgary office staring out the window towards the Rocky Mountains. He has a difficult decision to make that could affect his company immensely. He had been approached by the Alberta RCMP with a proposal that may finally put an end to the period of industrial sabotage that had plagued not only his company, but also the entire oil and gas industry. The terrorism had been costly and had intimidated company staff. The RCMP was proposing that AEC property be bombed to secure cover for an undercover agent. Worse yet, for this operation to work, only a select few individuals will be allowed to know the truth. The sting was to be known as the "Operation Kabriole."[1] How will he explain his actions to the company's directors and shareholders after the fact? How would they react? How would the industry react? How would the media respond? How would the nearby residents and communities feel? He wondered how things had gotten to this point.

INDUSTRY BACKGROUND

In 1998, the oil and gas industry in Alberta had grown to a $26-billion a year industry and now comprised 20% of Alberta's Gross Provincial Product. The industry is regulated by the Alberta Energy and Utilities Board (EUB), established in 1995 through the amalgamation of the Energy Resources Conservation Board and the Public Utilities Board. The EUB, an independent, quasi-judicial agency of the Government of Alberta,

[1]Note about "Kabriole": If spelled with a "c" instead of a "k," the word refers to a curved, tapered leg, often with a decorative foot, characteristic of Chippendale and Queen Anne furniture and named after its resemblance to the leg of a leaping animal.

is mandated to adjudicate issues relating to the operation of utilities in Alberta and to ensure that development, transportation, and monitoring of these resources is in the public interest. Companies wishing to explore or develop new oil and gas sites, such as wells, plants, and pipelines, or to make changes to existing sites, must apply to the EUB for approval.

The oil and gas industry in Alberta grew rapidly during the late 1980s and throughout the 1990s. In 1998, the EUB received approximately 25,500 applications for development and related activities for the oil and gas industry. This was up from 12,800 in 1990. The number of oil and gas companies also rose from 70 in 1970 to approximately 1,200 in 1998. During this time the EUB had 90 field surveillance staff working out of eight field centers. Surveillance staff was responsible for monitoring Alberta's growing infrastructure of 264,000 km of pipeline, 75,080 operating wells, 33,791 inactive wells, and 644 gas plants, in addition to investigating 1,354 accidental spills or releases of gas and oil and responding to public complaints. This extensive infrastructure placed severe limits on the EUB's ability to adequately perform its monitoring functions.

THE ALBERTA ENERGY COMPANY (AEC)

AEC was created by the Alberta Government, through the AEC Act in 1975, "to provide Albertans and other Canadians with a special opportunity to participate, through share ownership, in the industrial and energy-related growth in the province of Alberta."

Over the years, the company expanded into areas other than oil and gas, including forestry, pipelines, petrochemicals, coal and steel. In 1992 it began to refocus activities toward the oil and gas industry through divestiture of other divisions and expansion of its oil and gas activities. At the same time, the Alberta Government was selling off its shares in the company and the company was fully privatized in 1994.

The company is traded on the Toronto Stock Exchange (Symbol "AEC") and the New York Stock Exchange (Symbol "AOG") with major institutional investors owning a large portion of AEC's shares. Financial highlights are given in Exhibit 1.

exhibit 1 Financial Highlights—Alberta Energy Company Ltd.

	1997	1996
Revenues, net of royalties ($ millions)	1,208.6	932.6
Cash Flow ($ millions)	544.7	411.9
Net Earnings ($ millions)	21.7	68.0
Net Earnings per Share ($, fully diluted)	0.23	0.65
Dividend ($ per Common Share)	0.40	0.40
Common Shares Outstanding (millions)	112.1	111.5
Direct Capital Investment ($ millions)	824.9	2,028.9
Long-Term Direct Debt ($ millions)	1,006.8	968.3
Debt-to-Capitalization Ratio	29:71	32:68
Interest Coverage	12.4x	8.8x

Source: Alberta Energy Company Ltd., *1998 Annual Report.*

In 1998, AEC activities were focused on two aspects of the petroleum business: four upstream operations in natural gas and oil exploration and production, and two midstream operations in natural gas storage, pipelines and natural gas liquids processing. The company operates in a decentralized manner with six semi-autonomous, entrepreneurial business units outlined in Exhibit 2.

AEC AND THE COMMUNITY

Over the years, AEC developed a strong reputation in Alberta communities as both a socially and environmentally responsible company through its operations practices, for example, sponsorship and donation activities. AEC is a founding sponsor of the Imagine philosophy that encourages corporate support of charitable organizations across Canada. AEC supports over 300 initiatives and programs and annually contributes at least 1% of its pre-tax profits (based on a three-year rolling average), or about $1.2 million. Part of this allocation includes matching employee donations to any Canadian charity.

Contributions are made to a variety of organizations, but there is a focus on health and education. Assistance is provided to traditional and complementary health and wellness organizations consistent with a corporate value to encourage healthy

exhibit 2 Summary of Operations—Alberta Energy Company Ltd.

AEC East (Upstream)	Shallow gas and oil exploration and development in the plains area of the Western Canadian Sedimentary Basin. 1997 operating statistics include: production of 325 million cubic feet/day of natural gas and 17,389 barrels/day of conventional oil, proven and probable reserves of 1,543 billion cubic feet of natural gas and 65.8 million barrels of conventional oil, and 55 exploration and 209 development wells.
AEC West (Upstream)	Exploration and production of natural gas in the West Peace River Arch. 1997 operating statistics include: production of 263 million cubic feet/day of natural gas and 11,421 barrels/day of liquids, proven and probable reserves of 2,142 billion cubic feet of natural gas and 51.7 million barrels of oil and natural gas liquids, and 90 exploration and 123 development wells.
AEC International (Upstream)	1.8 million acres of exploration lands in large blocks of Australia and Argentina. 1997 operating statistics include: 1,683 barrels/day of conventional oil, 4.2 million barrels of proven and probable of conventional oil, and 4 exploration and 7 development wells.
AEC Syncrude (Upstream)	Second-largest owner of the Syncrude Project, the single largest source of oil production in Canada, and the world's largest producer of oil sands–based light, sweet oil. Ownership interests are 13.75% interest in the joint venture and 5.0% gross overriding royalty on an additional 6.25%. In 1997, sales were 28,447 barrels/per of oil.
AEC Storage and Hub Services (Midstream)	Operated AECO, North America's largest independent natural gas storage and trading facility. Assets included: 85-billion cubic foot gas storage reservoir in Alberta, 14-billion cubic foot Wild Goose Gas Storage in California, and contracts with terms varying from one to 15 years.
AEC Pipelines and Gas Processing (Midstream)	Alberta's largest intra-provincial oil transporter and owns natural gas liquids extraction assets. Assets include: 70% ownership of AEC Pipelines, L.P., 35% interest in Empress Straddle Plant, and 33% interest in Alberta Ethane Gathering System.

Source: Alberta Energy Company Ltd., *1998 Annual Report*, pages 13–23.

and balanced lifestyles. Educational and sport programs are considered to provide skills and information that benefit young people throughout their lives. Examples of initiatives supported are:

- Assistance for the purchase of a magnetic resonance imager (MRI) for the Grande Prairie Mistahia Regional Hospital.
- Support for DARE, a province-wide drug awareness program for Grade 6 students.
- A major community partner in The National Sport Centre–Calgary and its Youth Education Through Sport (YES).
- Support for annual fundraising telethons for the Medicine Hat Public School Foundation and Medicine Hat Regional Health Foundation.
- Support for women's emergency shelters in AEC-based communities.
- Sponsorship of Junior Achievement in major areas of operation.

AEC is also involved in Aboriginal communities in Alberta through investments in the development of programs aimed at improving the capacity of local people to help themselves. These programs include awarding contracts to Aboriginal-owned companies, and through providing on-the-job training and scholarships for Aboriginal students pursuing oil and gas related studies.

Another of AEC's basic values and most ardent commitments is to the environment. The company strives to safeguard the beauty and balance of the environment in which it operates and is pursing initiatives to reduce emissions by improving production efficiency. It is also working with the Tree Canada Foundation on a "carbon sink" pilot tree-planting program intended to decrease the amount of carbon dioxide in the air.

The production and processing of natural gas and oil involves substantial risk for the environment. The potential for adverse impact of their operations on the environment is a major challenge for the company.

THE FLARING PROBLEM

In Alberta, most farmers own only the top six inches (15 cm) of topsoil, but what is underneath remains the property of the provincial government (with the exception of gravel deposits). The government leases this land to the oil and gas companies, who, in turn, explore and drill for oil and gas. Should an oil company find oil and/or gas beneath the topsoil owned by a farmer, they are permitted (by the EUB) to erect oil and gas wells on that site regardless of whether it is in the middle of the farmer's crops, pastures, corrals, or even front yard. Petroleum companies work with landowners to minimize any adverse impact, and they pay approximately $5,000 per year for loss of land use. This arrangement has been in place for many years, but as the number of wells increased a minority of farmers began to complain of the ill effects the wells had on their crops, cattle, and families.

The cause of the farmers' concern is the flare stacks associated with well sites. Flaring is routinely used in the energy industry throughout Alberta and the world. A typical application occurs when oil is being produced and the solution gas (gas which bubbles out of the oil as it is brought to surface pressure) is uneconomical to recover and is flared (burned) near the well site. In 1996, Alberta alone had more than 5,200 solution gas flares operating. These account for approximately 1.8 billion m^3 of flared gas per year. The theory is that through flaring, substances in the gas are converted to their safest form possible. For example, hydrogen sulfide (H_2S), a highly toxic chemical, is converted to sulfur dioxide, a less dangerous chemical. Unfortunately, the ability of flare stacks to accomplish this task is affected by conditions such as:

- Composition of the flare stream
- Flow rate of flare gases
- Wind velocity
- Ambient turbulence
- Presence of hydrocarbon droplets in the flare stream
- Presence of water droplets in the flare stream

The flaring process releases some 250 compounds. The fact that these flares are not able to convert all the chemicals to safe forms means that some toxins may be released into the environment surrounding the flare stack. Farmers believe it is these toxins that are the cause of health problems occurring in their families, livestock, and crops.

In fact, studies have supported the farmers' claims. A 1996 Finnish study comparing two communities (one with sour gas pollution, one without) found that members of the polluted community suffered from more headaches, respiratory infections and coughing than the non-polluted community. Another study found that H_2S in low doses might cause persistent neurological dysfunction, for example, memory loss. A retrospective study performed by the Alberta and Federal Governments, which looked at 630,000 dairy and beef cattle near 231 sour gas plants, found delays in first births and delays between births in areas of highest exposure to sour gas emissions.

FARMER FRUSTRATIONS

Because of the research evidence, farmers have become increasingly vocal and active regarding the effects of pollution on their families and farms. Health problems alleged to be associated with flaring include asthma, coughing, headaches, aching muscles, shortness of breath, and memory loss. Illness in cattle and poor crops has also been attributed to the pollution. There is a growing perception among farmers that their concerns are not being taken seriously. Many reports of these problems appeared in newspapers and other media. The stories claimed that farmers could not get help from government or through the legal channels such as the EUB Environmental Appeals Board set up to deal with farmers' concerns.

Hundreds of rural dwellers claimed that the increasing oil and gas developments, poor regulations, and lack of government interest compromised their livelihoods, livestock, and health. There were some controls on the number of wells, batteries, pipelines or gas plants that could be situated in one area, yet they claimed that the government either ignored the protests or failed to enforce the regulations that did exist. The EUB received about 800 complaints annually, but its ability to respond was limited. The Alberta Government reduced its funding by 28% between 1992 and 1998 despite a fourfold increase in drilled wells. The EUB lost its capacity to provide a meaningful level of auditing or inspection of petroleum industry activities. Farmers, environmentalists, and industry spokespersons felt that insufficient scientific evidence existed. The difficulty was that studies performed were not conclusive of the harm caused especially when low doses of chemicals were involved. Many farmers did not know whether they should complain to a government department or local municipal districts about the spills, leaks, dead cattle or bad land deals. It was alleged some farmers signed compensation agreements that bound them to secrecy, while others were afraid to speak out.

The situation became volatile with acts of terrorism occurring against the oil and gas industry. In February 1998, a particularly violent event occurred near Bowden, Alberta when a beef farmer shot and killed an oil and gas company vice-president supervising the cleanup of a well site on his farm. A petroleum company that previously operated the site had caused the pollution. The farmer had been attempting to get the well cleaned up for two and one half years and apparently broke down over all the frustrations at getting the clean up done.

The eco-terrorism also occurred in AEC West's area of operations in northwest Alberta, especially in the Peace River area. In the mid 1990's, the vandalism of petroleum installations began and continued during 1997 and into 1998. Over one hundred acts of terrorism had occurred since mid-1996 and the major acts are listed in Exhibit 3. Property damage was running in the millions of dollars, and there was concern for the safety of field workers and neighbors. Some employees had received threats of harm. The RMCP had not charged anyone with responsibility for the acts. The police force was experiencing a shortage of staff and limited resources to devote to the terrorism. The petroleum industry's concern for its property and for employees and neighbors plus the inability of the police to address the problem resulted in cooperative efforts between the industry and the police.

POLICE/INDUSTRY COOPERATION

Throughout 1998, the police and industry representatives cooperated in a variety of ways in an effort to address the vandalism problem. On March 27, 1998, a meeting was held between senior police officers and officials of AEC and other petroleum companies. The companies recognized the police force's lack of resources and discussed the possibility of contributing financial and other resources.

exhibit 3 Chronology of Selected Terrorist Activities

Date	Event
1996	Nails thrown on remote roads on land leased by oil companies. Power lines cut down. Shots fired through offices of two gas plants near Hythe, Alta.
December, 1997	Fire at Norcen Energy well south of Hythe, Alta. Cement studded with shotgun shells is found in fire.
April 25, 1998	Three shots fired at AEC well site building
June 16, 1998	AEC pipeline is hit with homemade projectile bomb.
July 31, 1998	AEC sweet gas well at Goodfare, Alta. bombed.
Aug. 2, 1998	Sour gas well near Demmitt, Alta. bombed.
Aug. 24, 1998	Suncor Energy oil well south of Hinton, Alta. is bombed.

The industry officials decided instead to support the South Peace Crime Prevention Society (SPCPS), a local organization. The SPCPS was a dormant local community organization that was revived through the combined efforts of AEC, other petroleum companies and local business people. Industry would support the Society, which in turn would provide assistance to the RCMP. Security Management Consulting Inc., a private security firm working for AEC and several other companies, suggested this approach. AEC donated $25,000 to SPCPS out of a total of $188,000 raised from industry. The industry assistance enabled the RCMP to obtain additional resources to address the vandalism, for example, to support a Rural Crime Watch program and to purchase all-terrain vehicles for accessing marshy areas. AEC also donated a computer, appropriate software, and technical staff support to SPCPS, near to where much of the vandalism had occurred.

AEC offered a $50,000 reward for information resulting in the arrest of the persons responsible for the vandalism. The company approached Crime Stoppers to act as custodian of the funds with the RCMP to determine who received the reward. Crime Stoppers was limited to allocating $2,000 to the reward and AEC contacted other companies for donations bringing the total to about $125,000.

REV. WIEBO LUDWIG

Rev. Wiebo Ludwig, leader of the Church of the Shepherd King sect of the Christian Reform Church, along with his friend, Richard Boonstra, felt strongly that flaring was responsible for a range of human and animal birth deformities and stillbirths. Ludwig had become widely known as an outspoken critic of the petroleum industry and flaring in particular.

Although several companies had operations in the area, only AEC officials contacted Ludwig and his family regarding possible damage as a result of flaring near their farm, known as Trickle Creek Farm, at Hythe, Alberta. The company had offered to monitor air quality and conduct soil and water analyses. These offers were declined. Ludwig had met with AEC's President and CEO, Gwyn Morgan, in January 1998 when he railed about the damage to his family and property from flaring. He suggested that AEC should pay conciliatory compensation for the hardships imposed on his family.

From March through July 1998, AEC officials negotiated with Ludwig to purchase the Trickle Creek Farm. The farm was appraised at $438,000 to $450,000 and in negotiations with AEC Ludwig demanded as much as $1.5 million for the property. On July 29, Ludwig was offered $800,000. AEC's rationale for purchasing the farm at an inflated price was based on a belief that Ludwig was behind much of the vandalism and the company wanted him removed from the area before someone got hurt or even killed.

A few days later, Ludwig refused the offer, as he did not agree with the clauses added at the last moment by AEC to the sale agreement. The clauses included a restrictive confidentiality clause relating to the terms of the agreement, a standard waiver clause in real estate transactions proclaiming that the land was free of environmental problems, and three variations relating to the time before the family could reside in the area.

At this time, the acts of vandalism resumed (refer to Exhibit 3).

OPERATION "KABRIOLE" AND THE STING

The petroleum industry, the police, and the communities in the area were increasingly concerned about the vandalism. In late summer 1998, the RCMP put together a special initiative labeled "Operation Kabriole" to focus on the petroleum vandalism problem, and asked the industry for assistance. The operation was targeted at Ludwig, and he and his supporters were to be under 24-hour ground and airplane surveillance. The operation's budget was $354,750, but before it was over, the operation would cost $750,000.

Ed McGillivary, AEC's director of environment, health, and safety, received a call from Robert Wraight, a friend of Ludwig's. Wraight offered his services as an undercover agent if AEC would purchase his land for $109,000. AEC flew Wraight, at their expense, to Calgary and set up a meeting with the RCMP.

After discussions with the RCMP, Wraight agreed to become a paid agent and attempt to gather evidence for a case against Ludwig. The evidence gathering included wearing a concealed tape recorder when visiting the Ludwig farm. As an informant, Wraight was given a $10,000 signing bonus and placed on the payroll at $475 per week. Later the police picked up $14,000 in other expenses that he incurred. AEC did not purchase Wraight's farm.

The RCMP approached AEC for their cooperation and the company agreed to provide resources if it would help solve the vandalism problem. The company offered to supply high-tech night vision equipment from its private security firm. This offer was refused, as it was not consistent with RCMP policy. The security firm was to provide tips to the RCMP on Ludwig's movements, something that many other organizations and individuals were doing.

In order to enhance Wraight's credibility, it was proposed by the RCMP that a petroleum installation be deliberately vandalized. The RCMP proposed blowing up an old vehicle that they were willing to purchase from AEC for $8,000. Gwyn Morgan objected to this as he felt that it would cause stress among employees who feared that their vehicles might be vandalized. Instead, it was agreed that an abandoned, remote petroleum site building would be bombed. No date was set for the bombing but it was agreed that the sooner the better.

In mid-September, County officials and AEC discussed and agreed to co-sponsor two town hall style meetings to help the community deal with the increasing vandalism. In an effort to increase dialogue between the company and concerned stakeholders, AEC offered to hire professional facilitators to conduct the meetings. The meetings were set for October 20 and 21. There was no attempt to coordinate the timing of the bombing and the meetings.

GWYN MORGAN'S MORAL DILEMMA

Gwyn Morgan was being asked to approve an act of vandalism and the company would not be able to disclose its involvement in the near future. All through the planning of the sting, he expressed that he wanted a complete disclosure of the context for AEC's cooperation. He knew that this might be difficult given the process through which charges are laid and the timing of court proceedings.

Morgan was concerned that the vandalism was escalating into life-threatening sabotage. The direct and indirect costs to AEC were now over two million dollars, but there were more serious concerns. Putting explosive devices on wellheads, pipelines, and gas production facilities was dangerous to employees and potentially dangerous to surrounding residents. Employees had received anonymous death threats creating stress for them and their families.

Morgan had many thoughts floating around in his head as he considered the decision. He was concerned about how the public would react to being deceived. Although the RCMP had assured him that the explosion would be safely discharged, he still worried about the success of the clandestine operation. He agonized over the level of co-operation between AEC and the RCMP even though the RCMP assured him that such cooperation would be helpful in preventing extremely serious crimes. Only four others at AEC knew of the operation, and he wondered how shareholders, the directors, and other employees would react when the event was disclosed.

He was aware that injury or death could be avoided and thought that to do nothing by being a bystander would be the easy way out. Furthermore, the company was cooperating with an organization that society relies upon for law and order. Despite this, he anticipated that it might be viewed differently in the future as the media and the public questioned the close relationship between the company and the RCMP. The public might perceive that the line between corporate interests of the oil industry and law enforcement had become blurred. Moreover, they may not appreciate the company having been less than forthcoming about the staged bombing.

He knew that he and the company would be held accountable in any judicial process if the eco-terrorists were caught and charged. The public may not consider it appropriate for business to supply money and other resources to a police force. Thinking back over the events of the preceding months, he wondered if cooperating with the RCMP had been wise or appropriate. AEC's security firm, Ed McGillivary and himself had been in contact with the police force.

The dilemma for Morgan meant agonizing over compliance with the RCMP sting or being a bystander resisting any further involvement with police attempts to catch those responsible. He had to balance the protection of individuals from harm and the inclination to cooperate with the police against the consequent requirement to be less than forthcoming in corporate announcements. He was President and CEO and it was his decision to make. Looking out the window again, he noticed that storm clouds had moved in and that the Rocky Mountains were no longer visible.

DISCUSSION QUESTIONS

1. Should Morgan cooperate with the RCMP sting operation involving the bombing of an abandoned well site? State why or why not, and provide your rationale.
2. Who are the important stakeholders that will be influenced by the decision and/or that can influence the company in relation to the decision?
3. Which of the ten ethical principles is most appropriate or helpful in resolving the dilemma: self-interests, personal virtues, religious injunctions, government requirements, utilitarian benefits, universal rules, individual rights, economic efficiency, distributive justice, and contributing liberty? Why?
4. Based on the principle(s) chosen above, how are the harms and/or benefits of the decision distributed among the key stakeholders?
5. After answering Questions 2, 3, and 4, is your answer to Question 1 the same? Why or why not?

case 24 A Midsummer Day's Nightmare

I started work at a nationally known fast food restaurant when I was seventeen. I had had other jobs, but none of them was as much fun as this one. I reported for my first shift at the beginning of February and was introduced to a new atmosphere that was unlike anything I had experienced before.

One of the first things I learned was that having fun was really encouraged. Smiles were the norm, and were, in fact, expected. This friendly environment led to a lot of fast friendships with my co-workers, especially since we all went to neighbouring high schools. Our employer encouraged these ties and would organize activities for us outside of work.

We enjoyed these outings, but the best "perk" by far was the food, which was half price to employees, even outside of scheduled shifts! We could even informally extend this discount to friends once in a while, which made it an even more enviable privilege.

I loved my job and worked very hard at it. After fourteen months I got my first promotion. Six months later I was promoted again to a junior management position along with two of my co-workers.

We received very little preparation to deal with this move up to management. We were given a workbook covering topics such as food safety, employee relations, shift planning, scheduling, etc., and were supposed to get time on the job to work through it and then go to classes. But that never happened. However, we were all told immediately about the importance of management always presenting a united front. Most of our training was on the job—we were given a different color shirt, a new nametag, and encouraged to do our best. My first shift as a manager I was left alone to supervise a busy dinner hour.

My promotions brought me into more frequent contact with Michael Roberts, area manager for the district. Michael was a scary figure to all store employees because whenever he came in he found faults. Heaven help you if your personal grooming wasn't perfect, if you didn't have your nametag on, or even if you weren't using the prescribed pattern to mop the floor!

Now that I was in a management position, Michael knew me by name, and made a point of talking to me every time he came in. I suddenly had to develop a working relationship with him and meet his high standards.

There were many benefits to this promotion though, the best of which was now, *free* food! The expensive items on the menu were now always available to us. We would take advantage of this whenever we could, sometimes eating three meals a day at our restaurant! We now also had the authority to reward our subordinates with free food.

Because we were a small branch, we rarely had more than one manager working at a time, which left me completely in charge during my shift. This meant that it was up to me to ensure that company standards were met and that all customers were satisfied, as well as to deal with any complaints. I also had to make sure everything was in place for the next shift; if there was something that I wasn't able to finish, I had to communicate it clearly to the manager of the next shift.

I also became privy to more knowledge about our store. I quickly learned that we had trouble making a profit because the restaurant was so small. As a result we had to be very careful about expenses, especially food wastage. We would order \$5,000 to \$6,000 of supplies every week to ten days, and try to be careful to order only what we would need. As a result sometimes we would run out of something, or several things, before the next order. I hated when that happened.

If it was just a little thing, like milk or tomatoes, we would buy some at retail to tide us over, although this was not encouraged. For more basic items, like hamburger patties and buns, I had to phone around to other outlets and "beg" to "borrow" some supplies. This was a real hassle, and irritating to the other managers too. Furthermore, we often had only two or three employees working at a time, so it was a huge inconvenience to send one to pick up supplies—that is, provided I could convince someone with a driver's licence and gas in their car to go. I once had to go myself on a busy Saturday during Christmas season to pick up eighty trays of buns. It took me three hours and my mom's SUV.

Most of the equipment in our restaurant was old and in bad repair. We couldn't get authorization to replace it, so we had to make do. When I complained, I was told to use the manuals and try to fix it myself! I had absolutely no idea how to service these temperamental machines that would often act up, especially when we were busy. I once had an ice cream machine explode goo all over me for my trouble trying to fix it.

The air conditioning didn't always work either, but the grills were by far the most troublesome. They would stop heating properly in the middle of the day and not cook the food thoroughly.

I got to know several repairmen on a first-name basis, and we spent many hours going over this problem together.

Nevertheless I persevered, and over the next ten months I gained valuable experience, and completed all the necessary steps to be promoted again. Towards the end of this period I met with my restaurant manager several times, and she assured me that a promotion was in the works, subject to the approval of the area manager.

I was really looking forward to that...it would mean I would no longer have to wear a hat on the job!

ONE SUMMER DAY...

One summer day I came in to open the restaurant after a day off. It was 6:00 a.m. and already warm outside, even more so inside the store because the air conditioning didn't work well. I started getting the computer systems up and counting the cash, and sent the opening staff person, Jason, to start making the muffins and getting the tables ready for our 7:00 a.m. opening.

As I was counting the cash, Jason called to me from the back. He was young and somewhat excitable, so I didn't think anything of it as I went over to see what was the matter.

Jason gestured excitedly and directed me towards the large walk-in freezer, insisting I look inside. I went into the freezer to take a look. I didn't like going in there because it was always so cold. But not today!

The freezer was room temperature! It must have been off overnight!

"*Oh NO*!" I thought, as I looked in an open box of chicken and picked up a piece. It was warm and squishy; the coating crumbled off on my hand. I opened a box of hamburger patties and touched one on top. It felt mushy, and was beginning to lose its shape. I leaned over and opened a box in the middle. It was cool, and the meat in the center of the box seemed still frozen.

My mind started racing. I ran to the phone to call my restaurant manager; I knew she was opening at another location that morning. It was about 6:30 a.m. Pat picked up the phone after several rings.

> "Hi Pat, it's me … umm … I have a really big problem. You see ... uh..."

> "Jennifer, I'm really busy! Hurry up!" she snapped.

> "I came in this morning and the freezer has been off for hours. Everything is goopy and gross and I don't know what to do. It's disgusting!"

> "WHAT! You've got to be kidding. Who the hell was working yesterday?! I just don't believe this. Damn! I'm too busy to deal with this now. Call Mike." Click—she hung up.

I looked at my watch; it was 6:35 a.m. I had to call Michael at home.

> "Hi Michael, it's Jennifer from 82nd West … Pat told me to call you!" I blurted out. "Sorry about this, but I have a big problem. Our freezer has been off for several hours, the food's gross and mushy. I don't know what to do."

There was a brief pause as Michael woke up.

> "What? Are you joking? Why is the freezer off? Is it broken? Is it unplugged?"

> "Umm … I don't really know."

In a panic I ran to the back room to figure out why the freezer wasn't on. The answer was at the fuse box, where I discovered the freezer circuits were in the "off" position. Quickly I reset them. I knew we had received a supply order the day before. In order to save energy in the heat of the day, the freezer was likely shut off while the order was carried in. This wouldn't have been a problem ... if only someone had remembered to turn it back on.

> "The fuses were shut off, probably when we got our order yesterday."

I could tell Michael was seething, but he controlled it well.

> "OK, as long as all the cooking temperatures are met, the food will be all right. You can still use everything there."

> He went on, "It's important that we don't cause a panic about this. Don't talk about it in the restaurant and make sure food temperatures are met. Everything will be OK. Continue your shift Jennifer."

> "Uh ... OK ... umm ..."

I hung up the phone in a daze. I couldn't quite bring myself to carry out those instructions right away. I felt confused and upset, as I stood lost in my thoughts searching for some instruction or part of my training for guidance. I knew what to do if there was a bomb threat, but nothing had prepared me for this.

I had about twenty minutes worth of food in our small freezers up front. Jason was waiting for my instructions. I looked at my watch—it was 6:45 a.m.

exhibit I Excerpts from the Food and Drug Act and Food and Drug Regulations, as Administered by Health Canada

Interpretation

"Unsanitary conditions" means such conditions or circumstances as might contaminate with dirt or filth, or render injurious to health, a food, drug or cosmetic.

Food

4. No person shall sell an article of food that
   a) has in or on it any poisonous or harmful substance;
   b) is unfit for human consumption;
   c) consists in whole or in part of any filthy, putrid, disgusting, rotten, composed or diseased animal or vegetable substance;
   d) is adulterated;
   e) or was manufactured, prepared, preserved, packaged or stored under unsanitary conditions.

Sale of Barbecued, Roasted or Broiled Meat or Meat By-Products

B.14.072 No person shall sell meat or a meat by-product that has been barbecued, roasted or broiled and is ready for consumption unless the cooked meat or meat by-product

(a) at all times
   (i) has a temperature of 40°F (4.4°C) or lower, or 140°F (60°C) or higher, or
   (ii) has been stored at an ambient temperature of 40°F (4.4°C) or lower, or 140°F (60°C) or higher

(b) carries on the principal display panel of the label a statement to the effect that the food must be stored at a temperature of 40°F (4.4°C) or lower, or 140°F (60°C) or higher.

case 25 A Gift from the Web (A)

Brian rested his head in hands as he read over the finance group assignment that Professor Rong had distributed today to all students in the third year financial management classes of the undergraduate business program at University of Ontario. Already feeling overwhelmed with his current middle-of-the-term workload, Brian wondered how he would find the time and energy to work with one more group on yet another case study. At least this one was only worth 10% of his final finance mark.

"Well, maybe I'll check my email," thought Brian, looking for a distraction from his current frame of mind. Then suddenly an idea popped into his head as he looked at his Yahoo entry portal; he stared at the search engine briefly, then thought, "Why not?" and entered the title of the case "Sink or Swim" into the search field. "What are the chances anyway?" he muttered. He quickly scanned the search results and, to his surprise and pleasure, found an entry entitled "Sink or Swim—Instructor's Key." "No way!" he exclaimed under his breath and quickly navigated the weblink, which brought him to another university's webpage, where a professor had posted the answer key to the identical case for her students. Brian rapidly downloaded the file, printed it out, and compared it to the assignment in front of him. "Unbelievable! It's identical!" he laughed. "Talk about a time-saver!"

As Brian reached for his phone to give his group members the exciting news, he stopped to consider what he was about to do. Either the professor was not aware that the answer key was so readily available, or he could be testing them to see how they would handle this situation. "Either way," thought Brian, "How could I not use this lucky find? I am just being resourceful! Seriously, how could a third year student really be expected to pass this up given the workload and pressures? How could I possibly resist? This will just help us be more efficient. And if I don't tell my group, I'll end up having to take the credit for coming up with the perfect solution, which would be dishonest. Besides, I can't resist sharing the wealth!"

"Guess what, Rima?" Brian asked breathlessly over the phone. "I've found a gift from the Web—an unbelievable time-saver for us. I hold in my hand the answers to our finance assignment."

"What?" exclaimed Rima. "Where in the world did you get that?"

"Let's just say Yahoo is more resourceful than I thought," laughed Brian.

"You haven't told anyone else, have you?" asked Rima.

"No, just you so far," said Brian. "Why?"

"Well, isn't this cheating? I mean, I guess it'd be one thing for our group to compare our answers with it since it's our 'find,' but we're not going to let the other groups know, are we? That seems too much like a conspiracy!" exclaimed Rima.

"I don't know. I haven't thought that far yet," said Brian. "Look, there's no way our group's not going to use this! That would be stupid—we all have too much else to do! Besides, if it's on the internet, it's a public document that I'm entitled to. It's not as if I cracked into the Prof's hard-drive or anything; I was just being resourceful! Let's call a group meeting this afternoon and figure out what we should do from here."

case 26 Whooo's Wise Enough to Save the Owl?

Kathleen felt a thrill of excitement as she watched the snowy owl beat massive wings, rising high into the clear October sky. It circled the field once, then headed for the shelter of the trees bordering the field. Kathleen heaved a sigh as she headed back to the field hospital. If the Manitoba Wildlife Rehabilitation Organization didn't get itself straightened out, and soon, there would be no more releases to the wild. And she firmly believed that the wild was where wild animals really belong.

The Manitoba Wildlife Rehabilitation Organization (MWRO) is a registered non-profit volunteer organization. It was formed in 1984 in response to the public's call for assistance to help injured and orphaned wildlife. With membership of over 500, and an active base of volunteers, the MWRO provides direct care to over 1,000 native birds and mammals every year. MWRO is currently the only organization in the province which is legally permitted to handle and rehabilitate injured wildlife.

MANITOBA'S NEED

In 1996, MWRO received over 7,000 telephone enquiries from citizens from across the province requesting advice or assistance in responding to what appears to be an injured or orphaned animal. This compares to 6,000 phone calls in 1995. In many cases, the call can be resolved by simply answering a question or by asking callers to take simple action like replacing a baby bird that has fallen from a nest. At other times, the call may be about a bird or mammal that is legitimately orphaned or injured. In these instances, the caller is asked to bring the animal to MWRO.

Every year approximately 1,000 animals are admitted to MWRO (see Figure 1 for 1996 information). These animals range from Ruby-Throated Hummingbirds to Great Blue Herons, from Grey Squirrels to Red Foxes, from Cedar Waxwings to a full-grown snowy owl with a broken wing. When animals are admitted to MWRO, their medical conditions are assessed immediately. MWRO volunteers work closely with veterinarians across the province to determine the extent of injuries, and implement a treatment protocol. The aim of all rehabilitation is to ensure that the animal in care remains wild.

figure 1 MWRO Resolution Summary for 1996

Animal Type	Admitted	Released	Shipped	Ongoing	DOA/Died	Euthanized
Birds						
Ducks	134	65	13	7	18	31
Hummingbirds	2				1	1
Gulls, etc.	18	4			3	11
Doves	50	16			10	24
Hawks	95	28	3	12	13	39
Robins	113	27			22	64
Grackles	43	6			10	27
Sparrows, etc.	166	41	3		45	77
Woodpeckers	19	6			8	5
Owls	47	9	1	7	11	19
Others	59	19	3		17	20
Total Birds	746	221	23	26	158	318
Mammals						
Mink/raccoon/red fox	10	1			4	5
Rabbits	91	43		1	17	30
Gray squirrel	45	21			6	18
Red squirrel	50	33			3	14
Other	18	6	1	2	3	6
Total Mammals	214	104	1	3	33	73
Reptiles (turtle)	1					1
Grand total	**961**	**325**	**24**	**29**	**191**	**392**

Source: Notes for April 5, 1997 MWRO Annual General Meeting

Injured or abandoned animals are medically cared for until they can be released back into the wild. This often involves extensive preparation for release: animals must be fully capable of an independent life in the wild. Pre-release training is done to ensure the animals are able to recognize, capture, and consume their natural food; can handle weather conditions; and have sufficient muscle strength for life in the wild (particularly important for birds that migrate). Releases are often done publicly for education and publicity purposes.

Animals not suitable to return to the wild are used for education, or are transferred to breeding programs or to other educational facilities. Transfers are done under permit from the provincial government Department of Natural Resources.

Education is a major focus of MWRO, to promote public awareness and responsibility for preserving wildlife. This takes the form of presentations to school classes and community groups, and booths at community events such as the Boat Show and community fairs and in shopping malls. A major part of the education program has been to tell people that "orphaned" baby animal infants are rarely that—in most cases, the infant has been left for a few hours, with mother returning to keep an eye on things. This part of the program had been very successful.

MWRO HISTORY

MWRO is an organization that "just evolved," according to Jean, who has been associated with the organization from the beginning.

> We started, like so many other people, when my daughter took in one injured robin and nursed it back to health. Then we just started rehabilitating other birds. We decided that we wouldn't take mammals, since it was all done in our own home, but we found another person in the area who was taking mammals, so that worked out. This developed into a sort of network of people who worked at rehabilitating wild animals so they could be released back into the wild.
>
> Then around 1983 or 1984, my daughter started working with Dr. Nero on some owl studies. He was with the Department of Natural Resources, and he was the one who pushed us into becoming a formal organization. We got a Board and a charitable number, and some assistance. Then it got beyond just a few people, we got a phone system and an answering machine, then other people agreed to answer the phone and so on. And it just kept growing.
>
> Then someone sat down and got us organized. We got committees for phones, for runners to pick up the animals, for medical, for convalescent care, and for rural volunteers. It was always changing, especially with volunteers coming and going. There was a coordinator for each area. All the care was still done in people's houses.
>
> The idea for building the Centre [MWRO's animal hospital] just grew. We went to some conferences in the U.S. with other rehabilitation organizations, and talked to them about how they were doing. Then we raised some money, and finally got to build it. Finally, we had a place we could rehabilitate the animals, not in someone's home.
>
> The education program just grew too. We started speaking at a few places, then it grew into a program because one volunteer can't do everything.
>
> There were always financial constraints. At first, we just paid for it ourselves, or used what we could get, begging a bit. Then we moved to something a bit more formal. There were people in the Department of Natural Resources in the background always helping.

PERSONNEL

MWRO is a volunteer organization. An extensive province-wide rural network of volunteers work in conjunction with volunteers in the city of Winnipeg. Volunteers do everything from feeding infant birds with an eyedropper every 15 minutes dawn to dusk, to cleaning cages several times a day, to making presentations to school children. There is intensive training, and incremental volunteer responsibilities. There are about 50 active volunteers, a mixture of ages and backgrounds, but all with a desire to help wildlife.

Volunteers perform the rehabilitation and administration work of the organization. One volunteer veterinarian acts as the main liaison to the Manitoba Veterinary Association; other vets donate time. Volunteers work within a committee structure under the leadership of coordinators. Volunteer activities are organized as follows: volunteer coordination; public relations; fund raising; Centre development; membership coordination; and rehabilitation (medical; orphan care; convalescent care; telephone answering; animal transportation; records keeping). See Figure 2 for a current organizational structure. However, everyone is ready to pitch in and help out with whatever needs to be done.

Until recently, there were two salaried employees of MWRO: a full-time Executive Director responsible for the Centre's development, plus a salaried Rehabilitation

figure 2 Organizational Structure of MWRO at October 1997

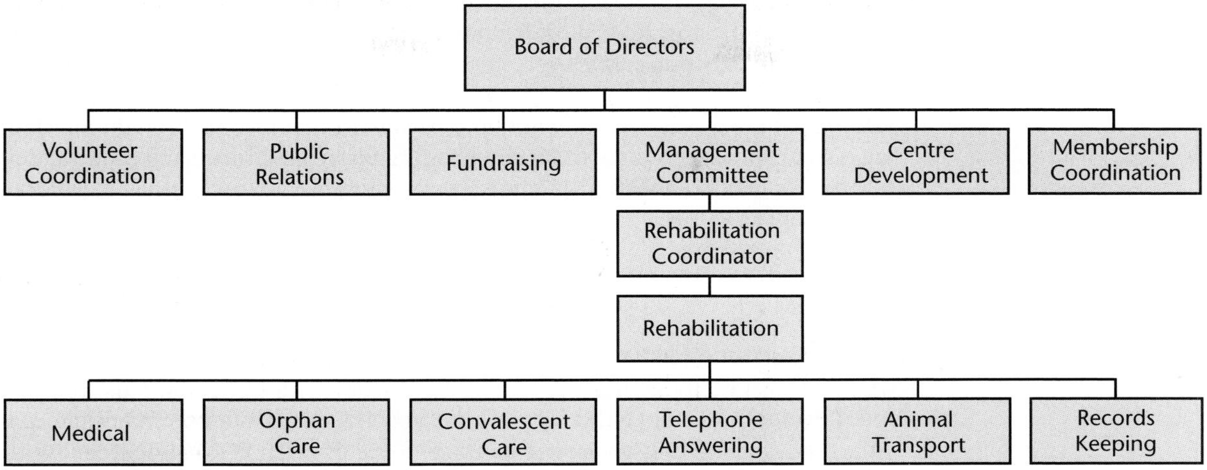

Director responsible for all admissions. Currently, there is only one paid staff member, a Rehabilitation Supervisor, who is on a six month contract. The Board, which has overall responsibility for MWRO, and the Management Committee, responsible for day-to-day operations, are composed of volunteers.

THE CENTRE

In 1993, MWRO opened the province's only Wildlife Rehabilitation Centre on land leased from the University of Manitoba at the Glenlea Research Station, 14 km south of Winnipeg on Highway 75. It consists of two connected buildings: reception/administration offices and a treatment hospital. A variety of flight and holding cages have been constructed on the property. The largest flight cage is 40 metres (110 feet) long to permit flight conditioning for large raptors such as hawks and owls. The Centre also houses a reference library on wildlife rehabilitation and a computerized database which is used for record keeping, treatment information, and research purposes.

Before the Centre was built, animals were cared for in volunteers' homes and back yards. This required a heavy time commitment, and was emotionally draining. All treatment now takes place at the Centre. As well as facilitating record keeping and work coordination, this is easier on the volunteers, who usually work 4 hour shifts at the Centre rather than having 24 hours a day responsibility for a few animals at home. Accidental domestication of the wild animals is more easily prevented when treatment is not in a home setting. Training and monitoring volunteers is also easier (supervision was almost impossible under the old distributed system). All volunteers who work directly with wildlife are trained in proper handling and treatment procedures, and work closely with provincial veterinarians and wildlife authorities.

FUNDING

Funding for the MWRO is from four main sources: membership fees, private donations, corporate sponsorships, and government grants (see Figure 3 for 1996 income statement). Corporate sponsorships seem to be falling off, and government grants are harder to get.

Membership fees are important not only because of the income brought in. Members are also the primary source of income from fundraising efforts such as raffle tickets and the fundraising dinner. Membership over the last few years has steadied at about 450 people.

FOCUS

Prior to 1995, all wild animals were considered to be under the mandate of MWRO, although appropriate rehabilitation sites limited work with larger animals. In 1995, the Board decided to change the focus: some species would not be rehabilitated. In particular, raccoons would no longer be treated due to costs of treatment and problems of release sites and volunteer availability (orphaned raccoon babies have to be overwintered, so a baby raccoon must be tended by a volunteer for a year and a half,

figure 3 Manitoba Wildlife Rehabilitation Organization—Statement of Operations

Year Ended December 31, 1996 (with comparative figures for 1995)		
	1996	1995
Revenue		
Membership fees and donations	46,294	30,884
Government grants	9,668	5,536
Grants	2,021	10,000
Fund raising	41,384	15,666
Interest income	836	1,547
	100,203	63,633
Expenses		
Capital expenditure	4,242	7,242
Land lease	2,085	2,000
Salaries and benefits	64,062	47,112
Printing, stationery & postage	4,460	3,209
Telephones	2,446	2,979
Hydro	544	638
Insurance	1,675	1,596
Fund raising	31,123	7,231
Rehabilitation costs	8,929	6,394
Miscellaneous	9,857	4,376
	129,423	82,777
Operating income (deficit)	–29,220	–19,144

Source: Notes for April 5, 1997 MWRO Annual General Meeting

while maintaining its "wildness"). In addition, many members of the public consider them major pests, and question the credibility of an organization that fosters them. In addition, white tailed deer would not be treated because they need large areas to graze in, there was a lack of rural volunteers with large area available, they tame extremely easily, and they're not indigenous to Manitoba.

Further work on narrowing species to be treated was halted when the Winnipeg Humane Society came to MWRO in Spring 1997 and asked them to take *all* wildlife turned over to the Humane Society. In return, they would provide a steady payment of $500 per month. MWRO had decided to discontinue treatment of pigeons and starlings in 1996, but this was too good an opportunity to turn down. In light of the financial situation, MWRO changed its position and accepted the Humane Society's offer.

CURRENT CRISIS

One of the big problems facing MWRO is volunteer burnout. Everyone believes in what MWRO is doing, and is willing to pitch in and help out. No-one has ever said "it's not my job." Having the Centre has reduced volunteer burnout due to direct care of animals, but everyone is concerned about what will happen to the organization in the near future. The burden on the Board in particular is very heavy.

The biggest concern for MWRO is financial. Income is flattening out. Grants have been falling off, and private donations are at risk due to competition for donations. Corporate sponsorship for specific purposes is still available, but not to cover operating expenses (see Figure 3).

WHAT'S BEEN DONE

MWRO sent out a special appeal to the public for funds in March 1997. Basically, the message was that MWRO needed money or would have to temporarily close the Centre. This appeal was moderately successful—enough money was raised to keep the Centre going through the spring busy season. Hopefully, other measures will take over and this kind of emergency appeal will not be necessary again. It made the volunteers very concerned and cast some doubt on the long-term viability of the organization.

In spring 1997, MWRO received a special one-time grant from the Winnipeg Foundation of $20,000. This cannot be counted on to be repeated in the future.

Attention has been paid to new fundraising schemes. In addition to an annual raffle which has been held for several years, and a fancy annual fundraising dinner, MWRO is now selling bird seed, and acting as agents for Robert Taylor's new coffee table book on the Great Grey Owl. An endowment fund is in the process of being set up, and a program of planned giving has just been organized. There is concern that it is the same people giving and giving, and competition for donations is extremely fierce in current times.

Attention has also been paid to expenditures. Salaries have been cut as far as possible (instead of two paid employees, the work is done by one paid employee at a lower salary plus volunteers). All expenditures that can be delayed, have been delayed. But this can't go on forever.

THE QUESTIONS

Kathleen, like all the Board members, knows that something needs to be done, and it should be done soon.

Maybe MWRO should stop tending some more species, such as pigeons or starlings—but then they would have problems retaining the Humane Society contribution of $500 per month which really helps cover the operating costs. MWRO no longer treats big animals such as bears and deer because of lack of rural volunteers with space to nurse them, but how much further should MWRO narrow its focus? It could eventually look at becoming a centre for birds-of-prey (raptors), or specializing in song birds, or only in endangered species. The problem with any sort of specialization is the potential of alienating and thus losing both volunteers and contributors.

The most pressing question is how to get the finances under control. Maybe the Centre shouldn't have been built—it's expensive to run, but it's done now. Where can they get money to cover operating costs? There is less of a problem to get corporate donations for one-time special projects like bird cages, specific education programs, etc., but it's hard to get someone to pay for hydro and the phone bill. Salaries, pared as far as possible, also have to be covered.

Kathleen has been involved with the MWRO for 6 years, as a volunteer, a board member and as education coordinator. She isn't about to let it fold. And as she thinks back to that snowy owl, soaring free as it was born to do, she knows that there must be a way.

case 27 Atlantic Health Center

It was January 2004, and Jim Cormier was reviewing the last year's results of his business concern. Jim, 35, had extensive experience in various small and medium size businesses, both as an employee and as an entrepreneur. While working full-time he had studied on a part-time basis and earned a bachelor's degree in business administration. The Atlantic Health Center, his latest venture, had undergone a major expansion over the last five years. Jim was worried: was the business moving in the right direction, or did he need to make significant operational or strategic modifications to ensure its viability in the long run?

STARTING THE HEALTH CENTER

After working for various companies for about 15 years, Jim had opened a small health club in 1999 in Barnes, Nova Scotia, a town of about 40,000 people. Over the following three-year period, he gradually expanded the business from three employees to five as revenues, memberships, assets, and profitability increased. The balance sheet and income statements can be found in Appendix 1 and 2. As a hands-on owner/operator of a small business, he identified and rectified quickly any issues as they arose. The employees wore many "hats," and assisted with each other's responsibilities. Jim maintained the leadership role and looked after behind-the-scenes management of the business, but he also helped the employees with any task as needed, from front desk reception, personal training, marketing material, administration, to cleaning the washrooms. Duties and responsibilities were defined on a daily, weekly, and monthly basis. Employees worked on a two-shifts a day schedule—from 6 a.m. to 2 p.m. or from 2 p.m. to 10 p.m.

In 2002, an opportunity had come up for a major expansion. His 3-year lease was expiring when the landlord offered him a much larger space nearby that had become available due to the previous tenant having built and moved into its own new location. The landscape of the Canadian health, fitness, and recreation industry was changing rapidly, and Jim knew that to survive in this changing environment, health and fitness providers had to deal with numerous challenges. (Appendix 3 gives some

This case describes real events but some details have been changed.

information about trends in the industry based on reports collected by the industry association.)

Until about 2000, health clubs typically offered just the basic exercise facilities. But the focus had begun to shift towards health clubs becoming health "centers," expanding their service offerings to better accommodate the growing demands of an increasingly sophisticated market. Jim saw some similarities to what had already happened in the grocery industry with one-stop supermarkets replacing the traditional corner grocery store. The bigger health clubs began doing the same thing—they did not wish to restrict themselves to exercise equipment, but began to offer members a complete lifestyle and wellness centre. Jim believed that the future success of health clubs would not come from focusing all their efforts on recruiting new members, but from increasing the revenue per member from sources other than the monthly or annual dues.

The main components of a total health-oriented lifestyle are physical, mental, and social well-being. The expansion strategy Jim decided on was to continue with the health club for physical well-being; to add a full service Day Spa (including a Hair Salon) for mental well-being and relaxation; and a restaurant/lounge for social well-being. Jim saw various advantages to his expansion plans. He felt that with the broadening of the facilities he could obtain

- Economies of Scale
- Economies of Scope
- A Sustainable Competitive Advantage
- Increased Client Loyalty and Retention
- Increased Promotional Opportunities
- Complementary Cash Flows

MISSION STATEMENT

With the expansion strategy, Jim felt it necessary to create a new mission statement. For the first three years of operation in the smaller location, the mission statement was posted near the entrance of the facility, and it read as follows:

Our Mission Statement:

- To be the best health and fitness facility provider in the community based on our commitment to service
- To never lose a great member
- To never lose a great employee
- To be the best in all that we do

With his decision to offer a day spa/hair salon and a restaurant/lounge in addition to the improved exercise equipment, Jim prepared a new mission statement as follows:

- To provide the best services and products at reasonable rates
- To ensure the future growth of our business based on our reputation for great service
- To ensure a high retention of our clients by reinvesting into the business to adhere to market changes and providing great service

- To promote excellence in our employees in providing the necessary tools to perform at the highest level of service

EXPANSION STRATEGY

Over an 18-month period starting in 2002, Jim negotiated a $250,000 small business loan from his bank; a $250,000 forgivable grant from a government economic development agency to create 25 new full time positions; and a $500,000 leasehold improvement investment to be financed by the landlord over the term of a 10-year lease. A mentor had once told him that the secret to success was using other people's money. So Jim focused on the growth of his business with $1,000,000 of other people's money.

With his strategy of expansion, Jim gave some thought to the internal relationship between the three aspects of the new health center. From a financial perspective, each of the three business units was to be responsible for contributing revenues, while common area expenses were allocated on a square footage basis. In essence there were three profit centers—the Health Club, the Day Spa, and the Restaurant/Bar.

The following charts outline the overall management structure as well as the organizational structures of the three business units.

Management Structure:

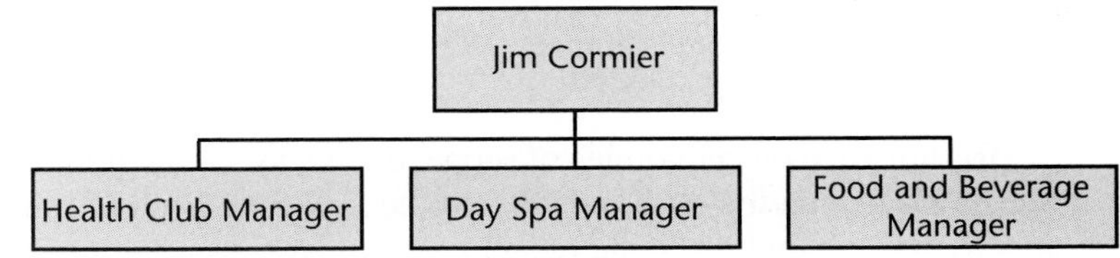

Health Club:

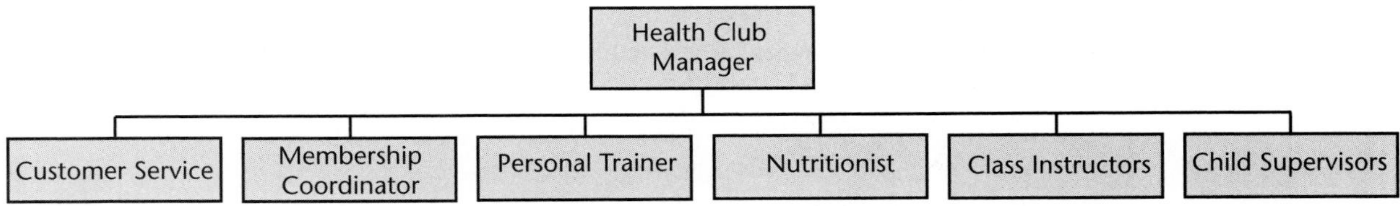

Day Spa:

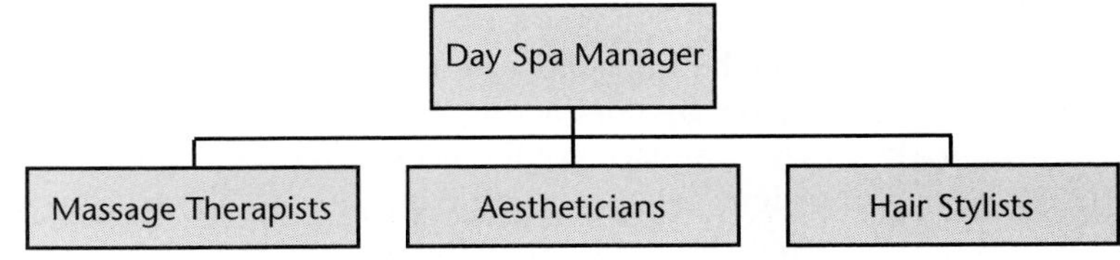

Restaurant / Bar:

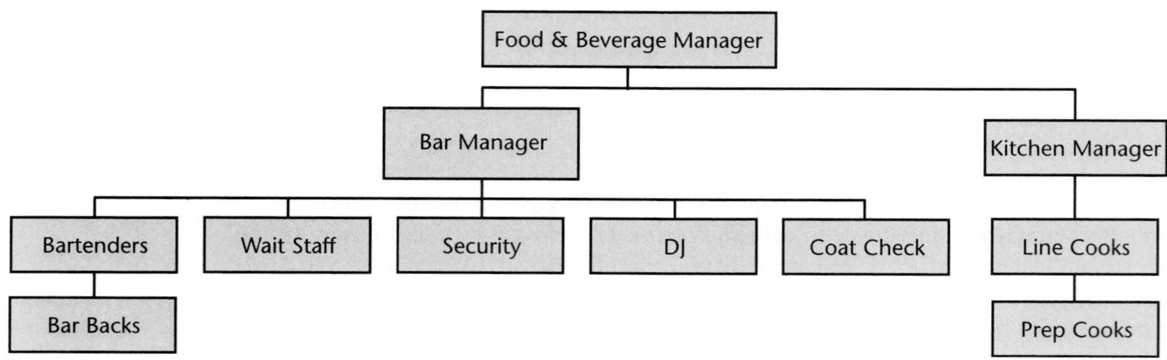

To take advantage of opportunities for synergy, the health club's promotion was tied to the two new units in various ways:

- All health club members were given promotional booklets with gift certificates for nutritional counselling, personal training, spa services, and restaurant meals.
- Daily "Healthy Xpress Lunch Specials" were offered to members when they checked in at the health club. Members would check the appropriate lunch special, the time required, and whether they preferred to eat in or take out.
- Spa "Packages" also included complimentary healthy choice menu items from the restaurant to be provided between services in the Day Spa.
- Membership Packages and Spa Packages were also promoted in the restaurant for non–health club members.

To capitalize on economies of scope, there was an integration of the customer service staff between the Health Club and the Day Spa. Both of these strategic business units (SBUs) shared the same reception area. However, the health club manager was responsible for assignment of duties and responsibilities. If the Spa Manager should have an issue with any of the customer service representatives, the problem was to be first directed to the Health Club Manager. (This policy was implemented after customer service representatives felt that they were being pulled in two directions since they were supervised by both the Health Club and Day Spa Managers.)

OPERATIONAL ISSUES

With the addition of the spa and the restaurant segments, the number of staff had increased rapidly from 5 to 40, and this had created some difficulties as illustrated by the customer service representatives being supervised by two different managers. Jim was not satisfied with the current structure and was searching for new approaches to deal with the challenges facing him as the owner-manager.

For a year and a half the expansion was planned from a financial and equipment utilization perspective by conducting extensive research into the industries. Jim attended trade shows, seminars, conferences, and even contracted for the services of industry specific design consultants. Utilizing industry journals on profiles of success, he was able to determine the appropriate financial measurements and appropriate ratios in measuring financial performance. For example, he discovered that attrition rates in the health club industry average between 30–35%, food costs should be no more than 32% of revenue, and spa services should be operating at an 80% utilization rate before expanding.

The Day Spa had limiting factors based on service providers and room availability. Specific rooms were equipped to perform specialized services. An example would be when a person booked a "Spa Package." A Spa Package usually entailed a minimum of two treatments that usually coincided sequentially. The Customer Service representative would have to book the treatment based on the limiting factors. If on one day there was only one opening available for a massage (room and therapist), then the spa treatments would have to be scheduled around that time slot. Scheduling rooms, therapists, and treatments became difficult at the best of times but Jim had resolved this challenge creatively. The Day Spa was designed with a lounge area and a private steam bath. If delays or a scheduling mistake occurred, the client could relax in the quiet lounge area, and be given a complimentary snack and beverage from the menu, or have a complimentary steam bath until the logistics problem had been corrected. Fortunately when this did occur, clients usually perceived it as a value-added service and not a scheduling mistake on the health center's part. The customer received better service while at the same time it alleviated stress among the employees by having a "buffer zone."

MANAGEMENT OF EMPLOYEES

With the exception of the Registered Massage Therapists, licensed aestheticians, the kinesiologist (personal trainer), and the nutritionist, the bulk of the employees required neither formal training nor education to complete their assigned jobs. This was the case, for example, with most of the restaurant employees. These employees were low wage earners who were there for a pay cheque and not for a career—the restaurant industry is seen as providing low paying wages and experiences high turnover.

All the employees requiring technical qualifications were hired based on their experience in the industry and/or their certifications. Each employee was given a copy of his/her responsibilities and duties and a policy handbook to be read and signed-off on upon employment. This served as a summary of job duties. As for skills, effort, and competencies, these were addressed in the interview process. Jim looked after all the hiring for the Health Club and the Day Spa while the Food & Beverage Manager was responsible for the hiring of all the Restaurant/Bar Staff. During the interview expectations were agreed upon as well as remuneration.

Training

As a member of the International Health, Racquet and Sports-club Association (IHRSA), Jim was able to purchase industry specific training videos and guides. These were utilized when training health club employees in a one-day training session upon their employment. The training was task specific whether it be customer service, membership sales, or developing a personal training clientele. For the Day Spa employees and customer service representatives, a one-week on-site training program was established. The vendor of the Day Spa equipment flew in a representative from

Toronto for one week to train all the relevant staff in the correct use of all the equipment and products to be used during the services and for retail sales. As for the restaurant, the training was limited to the utilization of the Point of Sale (POS) system, its capabilities, and reporting structure.

Compensation

There were several different compensation schemes used depending on where the employees worked (restaurant, health club, spa), and their level in the organization.

The Restaurant

The Restaurant/Bar employees (with the exception of the Food & Beverage Manager) were paid an hourly wage and kept any tips for themselves.

The Food & Beverage Manager received a salary and a profit share bonus. The profit sharing plan was based on meeting defined financial objectives, which revolved around controlling costs. These objectives were established because in the food and beverage industry, controlling costs is the key to success. The profit-sharing scheme for the food and beverage manager was structured as follows:

- Must maintain monthly beverage costs below 35%
- Must maintain monthly food costs below 32%
- Monthly payroll must not exceed 25% of monthly sales
- To receive monthly bonus—monthly actual results must meet budgets and the previous three targets must be met
- If the above criteria were met, then the monthly profit share would be 15% of EBIT (earnings before interest and taxes).

The Spa

The Day Spa employees also worked under a quantifiable compensation plan. In order to build an established clientele in a new business, Jim agreed to pay a base hourly wage of $10 to the spa employees, whether the services were booked or not. In addition to the base wage, the spa employee received 15% of the fee charged to the client. This was the norm in the Spa industry. Thus at the breakeven point, 85% of the revenue from services would contribute to the bottom line.

In addition to the above, a 15% commission was included for all spa retail items sold to the client. When a customer came in solely to purchase retail items, however, this led to a conflict as to who would receive the commission. The front-end computer system was utilized to alleviate this issue. When a client received a service, the service provider was assigned as the sales person for that customer. Any future purchases by that client would be credited to the therapist and show on a sales summary report. If there was no record of the purchaser having been a client, then the customer service representative who logged the sale would be given credit for the 15% commission.

The Spa employees also received the following additional benefits:

- 50% co-pay on insurance plan after 6 months of employment
- One week training seminar on Spa services, products, and equipment usage prior to opening

- Free health club membership
- 50% discount on menu items in the restaurant during work hours and 20% at all other times
- Free use of the baby-sitting service in the health club when required
- Two free Spa services per month

The Health Club

In the health club industry, monitoring and controlling retention rates is critical to profitable operation. The positions of personal trainers and the membership coordinator were measured strictly on achieving the quantifiable objectives. The performance standards for these positions were written down and signed by the employees and Jim as the agreed upon terms for the compensation structure. The signed forms were then maintained in the employee file.

The Personal Trainers

The personal trainers were paid an hourly wage for complimentary training sessions for all new members. This provided a value-added service to all new members and provided the personal trainer the opportunity to sell personal training packages. Other than the wage for the complimentary sessions, the personal trainer was compensated on the following scale during each 2-week pay period.

- $0–$750 revenue (fees charged to the clients)—40% of revenue
- $751–$1499 revenue—50% of revenue
- $1500+ in revenue—60% of revenue

Jim saw this as a good compensation system because the objectives were quantifiable, measurable, understood by all parties involved, and required little, if any, effort other than the administrative time necessary to keep track of all the quantifiable items.

The Membership Coordinator

The Membership Coordinator was paid:

- A base salary
- 35% of the registration fee for new members
- 4% of clients' monthly dues if those dues met or exceeded the previous month's results
- 2% of clients' monthly dues if those dues were below the previous month's results

The customer service representatives and other Day Spa staff received a base wage and 15% commission on retail sales as mentioned earlier. The nutritionist was compensated based on bi-weekly revenue volume (higher percentage commission for higher volume sales per pay period).

Non-monetary Rewards

A part of Jim's mission statement was "To promote excellence in our employees." Jim believed that non-monetary and intrinsic rewards were just as important to achieve this as monetary rewards. Thus he introduced the following features:

Social Rewards

- Every Sunday after closing at 9 p.m., there was a movie night for all staff from each of the three business units, and their family members. The movie was shown on a 12 by 10 foot projection screen with free finger food and "Happy Hour" prices for drinks.
- Staff had opportunity to participate in team events during charity functions
- Every employee received a birthday cake on their birthday with an informal gathering in the restaurant usually during downtime in the afternoon.

Intrinsic Job Rewards

- The spa staff had considerable job autonomy because they could arrange their own schedule to a great extent.
- The jobs of the spa employees were further enriched by allowing one of the staff to be responsible for scheduling, one to be responsible for inventory management, and one to be responsible for monitoring services and retail sales and allocating the credits to the appropriate personnel.
- Staff received quarterly review and feedback.

OVERALL ASSESSMENT OF THE BUSINESS AND CONCLUSION

Jim assessed the overall performance of each unit every month based on income statements, inventory levels, and attainment of cost control objectives. The performance of the restaurant was reviewed by Jim and the F&B Manager, and they "micro-managed" any problems that needed to be addressed. The remainder of the restaurant staff was involved in monthly meetings on the first Monday of every month. As for the Health Club, the membership coordinator, the health club manager and Jim sat down on the first Tuesday of every month and reviewed the membership revenues from new members, and attrition proportions of members who did not renew their memberships. Similarly Jim met each month with the Day Spa manager to review revenues and expenses generated by the Spa, and the rest of the spa/hair salon staff was given the opportunity to offer their suggestions and comments in a monthly staff meeting.

There were several things that Jim was concerned about regarding the results achieved in the first year after the expansion. He had created the fixed wage plus commission structure for the trainers and spa employees so that employees could depend on getting some income even when the business was slow. This worked fine when the utilization rate was around 20% in the first three months and the staff were not doing a lot of work. But when the utilization rate increased to 80% in some months, staff complained that they were "only" getting $19 from the $60 fee charged to each client ($10 base wage plus 15% of $60 or $9) although they were getting 31.67% of the fee collected. As mentioned earlier, there had also been conflicts over who was to get the commission when a client walked in and purchased something from the Spa or when the client had both a massage and a facial. The staff also seemed to abuse the flextime system put in for their benefit.

Jim expressed his overall feeling of frustration in these words: "In short, I tried to create a non-intimidating and pleasant work environment for all employees, hoping that it would be effective in encouraging good performance. Within a year, I had a 100% turnover in staff! Two of the staff left and opened a small business on their own. The hair stylist also opened his own hair salon. The staff repeatedly complained about how hard they had been working, the perceived unfairness of the amounts earned by employees in each of the three units in comparison to each other, and especially about who got how much commission for which kind of sales. At the same time, I was working seven days a week, often 12 or more hours each day, and yet the income I derived from the business seemed very small in relation to that of the employees, in spite of the fact that I was the only one taking all the financial risks as the owner."

appendix 1 Balance Sheet, as of March 31, 2003

Assets		
Current Assets		
Petty Cash	2,000	
Bank—Operating	–9,556	
Total Cash		–7,556
Accounts Receivable		8,281
Health Club Inventory	4,906	
Day Spa Inventory	3,149	
Restaurant/ Bar Inventory		
Food	7,320	
Beverage	6,436	
Total Inventory		21,811
Total Current Assets		22,536
Equipment & Leaseholds		
Equipment	683,485	
Accum. Depreciation	–159,685	
Equipment: Net		523,800
Leaseholds*	329,777	
Accum. Depreciation	–24,485	
Leaseholds: Net		305,292
Total Assets		**874,164**

continued

appendix 1 Balance Sheet, as of March 31, 2003 (*continued*)

Liabilities		
Current Portion		
Small Business Loan #1		11,390
Small Business Loan #2		15,661
Lease #1		9,191
Lease #2		1,898
Lease #3		6,278
Lease #4		18,203
Lease #5		953
Deferred Revenue		2,668
Accounts Payable		223,547
UI Payable	4,327	
CPP Payable	3,939	
Income Tax Payable	8,053	
Receiver General Payable		16,319
Vacation Payable		5,377
WCB Payable		2,156
HST Collected on Sales	253,262	
HST Paid on Purchases	–244,884	
ITC Adjustments	–3,686	
HST Owing (Refund)		4,692
Total Current Liabilities		318,333
Long Term Portion		
Small Business Loan #1		36,070
Small Business Loan #2		129,203
Lease #1		14,866
Lease #2		2,375
Lease #3		9,417
Lease #4		27,305
Lease #5		1,588
Angel Money		45,000
Total Long Term Liabilities		265,824
Total Liabilities		**584,157**
Equity/Share Capital		
Government Grant	250,000	
Retained Earnings	27,546	
Current Earnings	12,461	
Total Equity		**290,007**
Total Liabilities & Equity		**874,164**

* Leaseholds—does not include the $500,000 in leaseholds financed by the landlord in the term of the lease

appendix 2 Consolidated Income Statement for the Month Ending March 31, 2003

REVENUES		
Health Club Revenue		
Monthly Membership Dues	21,322.39	
Membership in Full	2,957.56	
Supplements	2,879.67	
Accessories	358.31	
Personal Training	2,100.00	
Nutrition Counselling	1,600.00	
Tanning	2,550.73	
Total Health Club Revenue		33,768.66
Day Spa Revenue		
Massage Therapy	4,705.50	
Aesthetic Services	3,882.90	
Hair Services	3,689.50	
Spa Retail	1,347.58	
Total Day Spa Revenue		13,625.48
Restaurant/Bar Revenue		
Beverage Sales	41,788.63	
Food Sales	22,131.34	
Total Restaurant/Bar Revenue		63,919.97
Total Revenue		**111,314.11**

EXPENSES		
Health Club COGS		
Supplements	1,180.39	
Accessories	175.43	
Tanning	127.86	
Total Health Club COGS		1,483.68
Day Spa COGS		
Spa Back Bar	119.07	
Spa Retail	558.07	
Total Spa COGS		677.14
Restaurant/Bar COGS		
Beverage COGS	14,312.62	
Food COGS	7,614.63	
Total Restaurant/Bar COGS		21,927.25
Freight	546.05	
Total COGS		24,088.07

continued

appendix 2 Consolidated Income Statement for the Month Ending March 31, 2003 (*continued*)

Payroll Expenses		
Wages Health Club	15,837.27	
Wages Day Spa	8,231.10	
Wages Restaurant/Bar	22,925.53	
UI Expense	1,575.53	
CPP Expense	1,406.76	
WCB Expense	384.35	
Vacation Pay Expense	857.22	
Benefits	127.16	
Total Payroll Expense		51,344.92
Advertising & Promotion Expenses		
Radio	2,250.00	
Newspaper	1,250.00	
Yellow Pages	125.00	
Direct Mail	197.56	
Promotion	500.00	
Total Advertising & Promotion Expense		4,322.56
General Administration		
Professional Fees	125.00	
EFT Fees	356.00	
Business Occupancy Tax	146.52	
POS Interac/Visa Discount Fees	987.56	
Travel	249.65	
Meals & Entertainment	137.56	
Vehicle	543.14	
Vehicle Insurance	207.72	
Vehicle Maintenance	162.99	
Courier & Transport Costs	147.81	
Insurance	642.17	
Bank Interest	1,857.06	
Bank Charges	657.42	
Interest Expense	1,204.01 *	
Rent	12,500.00 **	
Repairs & Maintenance	432.56	
Cleaning & Supplies	681.56	
Garbage Removal	150.00	
Telephone	1,454.33	
Satellite	189.25	
Power	3,867.71	
Propane	1,873.97	
Total General Administration Expenses		28,573.99
Total Expenses		**108,329.54**
Net Income		**2,984.57**

Notes: * Includes Interest Expense from Payables and Equipment Leases

** Rent includes $500,000 investment for leaseholds from the landlord financed over the 10-year term of the lease

appendix 3 Expansion Plans

The following information represents a sample of findings from research reports from the International Health, Racquet, and Sports-club Association (IHRSA).

The column titled '2000' indicates percentage of clubs that added the listed facility in 2000. The other column indicates percentage of clubs planning to add a given facility in the next 24 months.

Club Facilities	2000 %	Next 24 months %
Cardiovascular Equipment	26.5	24.9
Resistance Equipment	21.0	23.8
Aerobics/Dance Studio	19.3	16.0
Free Weight Area	18.8	23.8
Office Space	15.5	14.4
Locker Rooms	13.8	19.3
Pro Shop	12.2	8.8
Child Care Area	11.6	13.8
Front Desk	11.6	8.3
Food & Beverage	11.0	8.3
Day Spa/Rehabilitation	8.8	15.5
Meeting Rooms	8.3	7.2
Children's Rec. Area	6.1	9.4
Indoor Pool	4.4	5.0
Lounges	3.9	7.2
Gymnasium	3.9	5.0

case 28 EDS Systemhouse (Revised)

In late Spring, 1999, Sheelagh Whittaker, CEO of EDS Systemhouse,[1] considered the situation facing her.

EDS Systemhouse was a newly merged information technology (IT) services company with Canadian revenue of well over $1,000 million.[2] The first stage of the integration between EDS Canada and SHL Systemhouse (SHL) had just been completed, and the framework for the new organization was in place. EDS Systemhouse now needed to create a supporting organizational structure that would incorporate SHL's Canadian operations with EDS.

"What I want now," Whittaker thought, "is an organizational structure for EDS Systemhouse that will support our goal of becoming the undisputed leader in IT services in Canada. In the past we have kept our focus by using a key target account model.[3] But we need to make sure that it works for all the business we do. And we need to create a coherent strategy for e-commerce."

THE INFORMATION TECHNOLOGY SERVICES INDUSTRY

Spending on IT in Canada was more than $33 billion in 1998 and is forecasted to grow to more than $53.3 billion by 2003.[4] The compound annual growth rate was forecast to be around 10% per year.[5] IT services included management consulting, IT consulting services, implementation services, operational services, support and maintenance services and training and education services.[6] The largest firms (by

By Ken Harling and Tupper Cawsey

[1]Biography of Sheelagh Whittaker can be found in Attachment 1.

[2]All currency is in Canadian funds except as noted.

[3]A discussion of the "key account target model" can be found later in the case.

[4]Source: International Data Corp., Report#20182: Canadian Professional Services Markets and Trends, 1998–2003.

[5]Source: International Data Corp., Canadian Professional Services Markets and Trends, 1998–2003, pg. 7, Table 2.

[6]Source: International Data Corp., Canadian Professional Services Markets and Trends, 1998–2003, pg. 9, Table 3.

revenue) in 1998 were IBM Global Services, SHL Systemhouse, EDS Canada, CGI Group and DMR Group. The top 10 IT Service Firms held over 30% of the market in Canada.[7]

One recent trend was for companies to outsource their IT business to specialists such as EDS and IBM Global Services. When IT services are outsourced, price is the dominant concern. However, other considerations lead to organizations buying "solutions." These considerations are:

- Leading edge, innovative technology that will give the client a competitive advantage.
- IT solutions specifically tailored to a company's culture, needs and situation.
- Full, "start-to-finish" services that will solve all a company's IT needs in one package.
- Broad geographic coverage in many markets to ensure consistent service in all markets. (This is particularly important to firms expanding into new markets.)

The most significant change to the IT business in recent times has been the emergence of e-commerce. Whittaker believes that Internet and electronic services will drive IT growth in the next few years.

ORGANIZATIONAL STRUCTURE OF INFORMATION TECHNOLOGY SUPPLIERS

Large IT service companies are often structured along the lines of industry, geography, or services (technology) offered. EDS Canada, for example, is a geographical unit (so it can adapt to such factors as Canadian governmental regulations, market size, and culture). It has an internal industry structure (e.g. government services, manufacturing, financial services, etc.). Regardless of how the service company organizes itself, however, some of the company structure is dictated by its technical infrastructure and major capital investments (such as centralized data processing centres).

A developing concern of IT suppliers is in the area of knowledge management. IT suppliers recognize that they develop expertise and knowledge when they solve client problems. Capturing and transferring this expertise and knowledge to other clients without violating client relationships is a major challenge. For example, EDS Worldwide may develop solutions in the transportation industry. How should EDS Systemhouse be organized to capture this knowledge so it can be used in a Canadian setting?

A critical organizing choice is whether services are organized by projects or by customers. Some service companies have a separate team leader for each project while others have the same team leader for all projects with the same customer. Using the latter approach presents a consistent image to the client and avoids, in the worst cases, having different teams competing with each other for the same business; using the former means the individual with the most suitable skills for a specific project or situation directs that project.

---

[7]Source: IDC Report #20182: Canadian Professional Services Markets and Trends, 1998–2003.

EDS CANADA, SPRING 1999

History and Performance

EDS Corporation (EDS) was incorporated in Texas in 1962. It was acquired by General Motors in October 1984 and subsequently split off again in June 1996. EDS Canada, a wholly owned subsidiary of EDS, was formed in 1985.

In August, 1998, long-time Chairman Lester Alberthal resigned, and was replaced in December 1998 by Richard Brown. Brown had a reputation for focusing on profits and earnings, rather than growth or development. According to *Fortune* Magazine, when he took over Cable and Wireless in 1996, he replaced more than half of the top 100 managers, signed 21 deals worth over $20 billion and doubled the share price.

Performance

In 1998, EDS had a consolidated revenue of US$17 billion and net income of US$73 million (see Table 1). Sixty-one percent of its revenue was generated in the United States, 11% in the United Kingdom, and 28% elsewhere.

EDS Canada had revenues of $592 million in 1998. Client coverage organized along industry lines. Exhibit 1 shows the operating statement broken down by industry. Regionally, Ottawa accounted for 41% of revenues, the Western region for 30%, the Central region for 20% and Quebec for 9%.

Strategy

The services provided by EDS Canada can be divided into three main categories:[8]

- Systems and Technology Services includes systems development, systems integration, systems management, desktop services, Year 2000 conversions and enterprise applications. This business accounted for 63% of revenues and 64% of gross profits in 1998.
- Business Process Management Services encompasses transaction processing services such as remittance processing, procurement logistics, enterprise customer management, customer service and training and operating functional processes which have been outsourced. This business accounted for 19% of revenues and 18% of gross profits in 1998.

table 1 EDS Consolidated Financial Highlights (in millions of US$, except earnings per share)

	1994	1995	1996	1997	1998
Revenues	$9,960	$12,422	$14,221	$15,235	$16,891
Net Income	821	938	431	730	743
Earnings per Share	1.69	1.94	0.88	1.48	1.50

[8]Percentages have been altered to protect confidential information.

- Electronic Business Services covers interactive marketing and payment services, Internet and online services and advertising, electronic commerce, EDI (electronic data interchange), smart cards, multimedia and home shopping and the design, development, implementation and operation of Internet websites, corporate Intranets and Extranets. This business accounted for 12% of revenues and 12% of gross profits in 1998.

In 1998, 50% of EDS Canada's revenue was related to systems integration work, 29% to outsourcing work, and 21% to other types of work.

EDS Canada supplemented its service capabilities through alliances with a wide variety of companies (such as Microsoft, Computer Associates, Hewlett Packard and Sun). However, it had no exclusive alliances because it did not want to compromise its selling point of being independent of IT vendors.

EDS Canada focussed on selling "solutions" to large companies, rather than "commodity-type" services. The company's competency in serving large companies started with General Motors Canada, and many of the skills developed through that relationship were then used with other large clients. The company worked to understand what the CEO or CIO of a key target account wants, then aimed to provide them with business solutions, not just technical services.

Structure

EDS Canada had approximately 3,800 employees: 2,974 in Ontario, 475 in Quebec, 84 in British Columbia, 46 in Manitoba, 23 in Alberta and 36 in the Maritimes.

EDS Canada was a Strategic Business Unit (SBU) which operated within EDS Worldwide. The reporting relationships within EDS Canada varied by unit. The industry divisions, excluding the General Motors account, reported directly to EDS Canada but also on a dotted line basis to the EDS Worldwide industry units. The General Motors account and EDS Canada's technical infrastructure and corporate support groups had "double solid line" reporting relationships. That is, they reported both to EDS Canada and to EDS Worldwide. The double solid line reporting relationships were complex. For example, each unit within the Canadian technical infrastructure unit reported to the Canadian infrastructure leader, to a similar unit in the U.S. and to a global infrastructure team. Exhibit 2 shows the direct reporting relationships in EDS Canada.

The degree of influence exerted by EDS' global units on the Canadian units depended upon business conditions, the Canadian unit's performance and the individual leading the units. The senior leadership team at EDS Canada had to balance the requirements of the non-Canadian structure with the requirements of EDS Canada.

Within this structure, EDS Canada business managers had a great deal of latitude providing they produced satisfactory financial results while keeping their employees and customers satisfied. Business managers were required to develop business plans showing how they would develop business with their clients over the next three to four years.

In June 1999, EDS Systemhouse was restructured to incorporate SHL into the new organization. Exhibit 3 is the temporary organizational chart. This new structure continued the key target account and industry focus of EDS while broadening the target range within Canada. Each of the industry groups was to be run as a separate business unit, led by an Executive Vice President of the unit who held responsibility for revenues and costs.

Technical Infrastructure (TI) was a cost centre within EDS Canada. Normally, business units contract with TI for its services; alternatively they could hire outside technical expertise or provide the technical services for themselves by building the capability within their unit. When a unit provided its own technical resources, it received the benefits of owning those resources; however, it also assumed the risk and responsibility for redeploying those resources if business lessened.

SHL SYSTEMHOUSE, AN MCI COMPANY (SHL), SPRING 1999

History and Performance

SHL was founded in Ottawa, Canada in 1974. In 1995 MCI Communications Corp. acquired and renamed it MCI Systemhouse. SHL became the sole IT services operation in MCI. In 1998 MCI Corp merged with WorldCom to become MCI WorldCom. In late 1998 MCI WorldCom decided to sell its MCI Systemhouse unit to EDS Worldwide. SHL had worldwide revenue of $1.8 billion in 1998 with 12,000 employees, of which 5,500 were in Canada. The international operations of MCI Systemhouse (Canada, the United Kingdom and others) were run out of Ottawa, Ontario while the U.S. operations were run out of Atlanta, Georgia.

SHL was one of North America's leading systems integration firms and had considerable international operations, although it was not in the top 25 companies globally. It was the second largest service provider in Canada in 1998. Revenues from business done in Canada provided over half of SHL's revenue and EBIT on this business was 11% versus 4.7% for SHL as a whole.[9]

In 1998, SHL's Canadian revenue was $530 million. It focussed on government work and energy, and manufacturing and financial sectors. IBM offered fierce competition in the financial area. Exhibit 4 presents the operating statement for Canadian operations.

Strategy

SHL provided its Canadian clients with four services:

- System Integration (SI) services involves linking together various hardware and software components to form one system.
- Outsourcing includes data processing, the provision of help desk services and the management of networks.
- Technical Services and Deployment includes helping the client to decide on systems and equipment, to procure, install and maintain them.
- Education involves training people to work with hardware and software. (Included under SI for reporting purposes.)

In 1998 SHL reconfigured and extended its services, creating a set of global practices based on specific technologies, most of which were still in the formative stages. These provided product solutions in the following areas:

---

[9]Figures have been altered to protect confidential information.

1. Corporate Administrative Solutions (CAS): financial, material and human resource solutions as well as Enterprise Resource Planning (ERP) software
2. Internet Productivity Solutions (IPS): Internet strategy, managing documents and access to them, messaging and workgroup collaboration and strategic consulting on the Internet
3. Consumer Interactive Solutions: call centres and customer service solutions
4. Electronic Commerce Solutions: Internet procurement solutions, supply chain automation and merchant services
5. Systems and Enterprise Management (SEM): network and systems management, network operations and enterprise help desk

SHL's strategy was supported by a strong alliance program that had been ranked number one by the consulting firm G2R as the "best-in-class." The alliance program had more than 75 major partners who worked with hardware, software and services, and joint ventures supplemented the alliance programs, extending SHL's global reach and network enterprise offerings.

The company was increasing its activity in Toronto and Quebec, and management believed that these regions offered significant growth opportunities for the future. It also had strong presence in the Prairie Provinces: it purchased Sage Consulting Group in Regina in 1994, and was one of the prime IT suppliers to Alberta oil companies.

SHL had 300 active SI clients in Canada, many of them in smaller markets. It had over 70 outsourcing customers, encompassing over 180,000 end users, more than 3,200 mid-range devices and servers, and over 6,600 network devices (routers, hubs, PBXs, etc.). SHL's enterprise help desk dealt with more than 125,000 end user calls per month. Its top 35 accounts represented 75% of total revenues. The value of contracts outstanding in 1998 was two times revenues for that year.

SHL called itself the "network enterprise," differentiating itself from the competition by arguing that the combination of its computing capabilities (IT services) and the network capabilities of MCI WorldCom, a telecommunications provider, made it a single provider that could meet converging client needs in computing and telecommunications.

Structure

In Canada, SHL had 48 locations and 579 subcontractors. Most of SHL's employees—2,757—were in Ontario; Alberta had 1,067, Manitoba 446, British Columbia 353 and Saskatchewan 187; Quebec had 502 employees, while the Maritimes had 383.

51% of employees were Systems Integration, 25% in Outsourcing and Deployment Services, 5% in Sales and Marketing and 19% in General & Administration and Management (including finance, legal, human resources, recruiting and executive). The subcontractors worked on systems integration.

SHL had been organized on a geographic basis, with operations in Canada divided into four regions: Western, Central, Ottawa-Atlantic, and Quebec. Each geographic region had its own support staff for finance, human resources and marketing. Sales and delivery units would cooperate on proposals and sign off on price and costs. SHL thus operated in a fairly centralized manner, with no indirect and overhead costs included in profit and loss (P&L) statements below the regional level. The Global Delivery Services (GDS) unit, the Strategy and Marketing Services unit and some of the industry units operated in Canada, but were part of the U.S. Global Delivery Services and Strategy and Marketing Services units respectively.

In 1998, following its acquisition by MCI, SHL was reorganized. In the new structure, geographic and industry units had the prime responsibility for selling products and services. The industry units were responsible for specific "named" accounts. The geographic units were responsible for all accounts and for personnel and infrastructure not specifically allocated to industry units. Each unit was a profit centre, but only revenues and costs associated with systems integration work were attributed to it; other costs were allocated. See Exhibit 5.

The Global Delivery Services unit delivered services through its Outsourcing and Technical Deployment Services (TDS) units. Outsourcing Services provided processing, help desk support and the management of computer networks. TDS helped clients buy, deploy and maintain desktop and network hardware and software. TDS was a profit centre with its own sales people selling its services to customers. As a result it tended to focus on selling rather than providing services.

Resources were based at the regional level and allocated to projects as needed. A comprehensive system tracked the capabilities and availability of technical personnel at all times, and calculated the hours employees allocated to each project. Under this approach, all labour costs other than direct labour for an account were charged at the regional level. The profitability of accounts was judged by revenue minus the direct cost of the labour.

COMPARISONS OF EDS CANADA AND SYSTEMHOUSE CANADA

Prior to the merger, EDS Canada and Systemhouse Canada had differences in the amount of decentralization. For example, their cost control systems were quite different. As one executive stated:

> SHL is organized geographically and their technical infrastructure is independent of the clients. If they lose a client from the Calgary data centre, everyone gets charged more as the overhead is reallocated. EDS, on the other hand, does not allocate infrastructure costs. An account is responsible for redeploying resources as required. The technical infrastructure organization can usually reallocate them to other business opportunities because it has a global focus. That way it absorbs the fluctuations in business volume in specific geographic areas.
>
> SHL Global Delivery Services, therefore, has a different focus from the regions. However, the outsourcing organization in SHL is more aware of market forces than that of EDS.

Differences in centralization showed up in the structure of their sales forces as well. In EDS, the sales function was buried within the industry teams. In EDS, no sales people are evident because they are located within the structure organized by industry. A big account manager may have a sales person reporting to her/him, or a sales person may be at the sub-industry or industry level depending on demand and need. EDS would have 20 sales people designated as such.

This allows EDS to maintain an industry focus and fits with the longer-term relationship that EDS wishes to develop with its clients. SHL is able to move people resources (programmers) from project to project easily with their structure. However, this lacks the customer focus that EDS can have. The EDS structure is shown below.

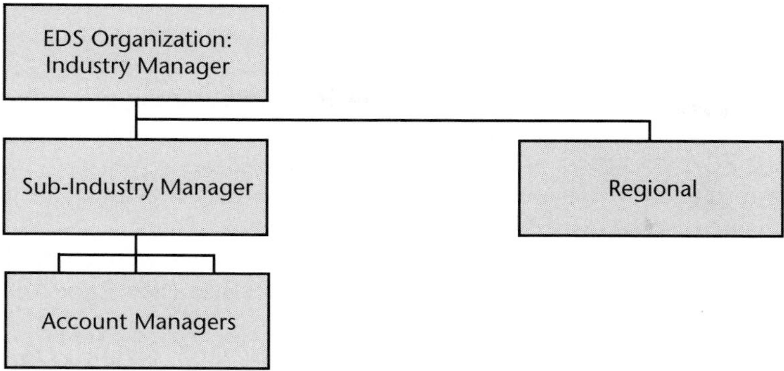

SHL on the other hand has approximately 300 sales people, 200 in product resale and 100 in solutions. The sales people are titled "client managers." Client Managers sell to customers and manage the relationship with the customer. They have no delivery responsibility, although they invoice the customer. They have P&L responsibility but it simply includes revenue and cost of goods sold—indirect costs are not allocated to them. These are charged at the regional level.

Sales Specialists have specialized knowledge on topics such as "enterprise solutions" or "electronic commerce." Delivery Managers source the delivery of all products and services. For example, all programmers will be located here in a pool relationship assigned to projects. The SHL structure is shown below.

KEY TARGET ACCOUNTS

One of the differences between EDS and SHL was in their focus on client size. Whittaker developed the concept of Key Target Accounts (KTAs) as the way to focus the organization on clients. Potential KTAs had several characteristics:

- Canadian-controlled
- change-oriented industry leaders with a minimum of $200 million in sales revenue
- IT important to their business
- IT challenges aligned with EDS's offerings
- no entrenched service supplier
- pre-existing client relationship with EDS Canada

Using these criteria, the top management team estimated that 73 per cent of EDS Canada's global and domestic accounts fit these requirements at the time of the acquisition. Of its domestic accounts, 96 per cent could be classified as KTAs.[10]

Business with a KTA was to be developed over time, starting as a prospect and finishing as a mature client with EDS Systemhouse acting as a strategic partner and providing the KTA with most of its IT needs (see Table 2).

The performance of business units would be evaluated against the maturity model, to ensure that the relationships were developing as planned, investments being made in developing the business were paying off, services were being delivered on and that the team working on the account was effective. (See Appendix 1 for a more detailed explanations of the KTA concept.)

The concept of the KTA created significant controversy within EDS Systemhouse. Believers in KTAs argued that this allowed the company to concentrate its efforts on large accounts with high value-added activities. One executive said,

> First we look at the customer. We start with those that are big enough to be KTAs. The second stage is to look for the emerging players that will be future winners. Then we look at our position in that market and ask what it takes to grow above the industry average. This helps us identify opportunities.
>
> We are big in Toronto, Calgary and Montreal, and we will focus on these locations. We will resource the top ten KTAs and then identify the next top five and move on. However, there are some markets where there is not enough business to support the KTA approach though there is profitable business there. We have to look at the SHL and learn how to adapt our approach to these regions. But if the market will not sustain a KTA, I would exit that market.
>
> I don't want to invest limited resources trying to develop the market in a way that won't work. If the market is not sustainable, exit the market.

table 2 A Maturation Model for Key Target Accounts

Key Elements	Prospect	Infancy	Adolescence	Maturity
Duration	Identify KTA Define and refine strategy to capture it	1–3 years of business with the KTA	2–5 years of business with the KTA	3 years and more of business with the KTA
Volume of IT business sold to the KTA	None	\$0.5 to \$5.0 M/yr. with the likelihood that it would lead to a minimum \$1 M/yr.	\$3.0 to 10M/yr minimum revenue	1% of the customer's revenue outsourced to EDS-S
Mix (Project VS Stream)		80/20	50/50	20/80

Source: EDS "Key to the Future" KTA presentation (item #4)

[10]If EDS Worldwide had a client with Canadian subsidiaries, EDS Canada would sometimes service those subsidiaries even though they did not fit the KTA definition.

Another Executive VP offered a different view:

> Some large markets, such as Ottawa, will support the KTA concept. Other markets—Victoria, the Prairies, Quebec and Atlantic Canada—can't support it. In these we will have to develop a hybrid to get enough business.
>
> KTAs are good but they are not the full solution. We will have to let revenue dip and accept variability. If we want to sustain the KTA idea, we will have to fill in with other business like SHL did. No one owns a single KTA: they own a group, so they can move among KTAs to where the action is. And they can add some smaller clients to the mix.

THE ACQUISITION OF SHL BY EDS

In the second half of 1998 MCI WorldCom decided that the SHL operations did not fit with the company's strategic direction. In February 1999, EDS purchased SHL for US$1.65 billion in cash and established significant outsourcing contracts with MCI that would capitalize on the strengths of each parent company.

During the merger, the management at EDS Canada sought to combine its own experience with acquisitions with that of other companies. For example, it approved of G.E. Capital's model of four merger phases: pre-acquisition, foundation building, rapid integration and assimilation.[11]

Actions to Date

After the merger, Whittaker set up the task force teams to ensure the new company enjoyed the best features of the two original businesses. Town hall meetings were held in April to reassure employees, address their concerns, and ultimately decrease turnover during the merger. At those meetings, Whittaker outlined a 90-day timetable for the merger, during which a high-level organizational structure would be announced and the initial phases of integration would be complete. The executives also explicitly described the differences between the two organizations, and the problems that might result (see Table 3).

table 3 A Comparison of SHL and EDS

SHL	EDS Canada
A large number of clients	A small number of clients
A broad spectrum of markets and clients	Large clients in large markets
Sales and delivery units separate	Profit and loss responsibility with units
A technology approach	A business approach

[11]Ashkenas, Ronald et al. "Making the Deal Real: How GE Capital Integrates Acquisitions," *Harvard Business Review*. Jan–Feb, 1998, pp. 165–178.

The new structure, announced in May, organized the company along industry lines. Whittaker named Executive Vice Presidents for financial services, manufacturing, government services, communications and energy, and created a Vice President for alliances. The Canadian Infrastructure unit was split into Solution Centres and Technical Infrastructure, with both units reporting to Whittaker. Finally, a new E-Solutions unit was linked to EDS' newly formed E-Solutions unit.

Issues Arising from the Acquisition

Several executives commented on the issues that needed to be resolved as a result of the integration of EDS Canada with SHL. The first executive stated the following:

> The real risk is that, because of the changes and uncertainty, we will lose people—both sales people and programmers—to competitors. In Ottawa there is some overlap in the sales force and headquarters functions. We need to sort out our strategy and communicate it because both sides are worried.
>
> EDS is organized by industry. In effect, we run separate business units. Managers have responsibility for revenues and costs and make decisions based on those. With SHL many costs are allocated.
>
> EDS is better than SHL at providing technical support; with EDS the issue is one of cost control because they are a cost centre. Theoretically, we could go elsewhere for service, but what we really do is say, "Look guys, I can't bid on this contract without costs in this range." Our technical people just don't have the incentive to control costs in the same way. I often think that our technical guys should be a profit centre, but that would create the same client interface problems that SHL has.

A second described the situation as:

> I think there is some confusion over merger and acquisition. This is an acquisition. It is not a merger of equals. So there probably are some instances where we aren't moving quickly enough. It might sound ruthless but it works.
>
> In the merger, you can expect one third of the employees to be on side, one third off-side and one third on the fence. If you move quickly, you can swing those on the fence. My division will be integrated in six months although nine months will probably be okay. Some of the systems will be slower but I can operate.
>
> With the IT infrastructure, I would convert the systems. The notion that you can pick the best of both is fallacious. We have to integrate with EDS worldwide and, unless there is a compelling competitive reason, I would convert.
>
> The most successful mergers do it quickly and follow the retail model where every operation works the same (e.g. Home Depot). Canadian Tire failed with Whites in the U.S. because they never integrated into one model. G.E., the most successful acquirer, says the faster the better. Make your decisions, get 80% of them right and then fix the 20% you missed. When you have two of everything you just chase the customers away.

Finally, a third executive outlined the issues:

> SHL is organized on a regional basis. They sell technology solutions, including lots of PC's, programming services, C++ programmers. They are more commodity-oriented and aim at the CIO and lower. EDS has an industry focus: government, banking (finance), manufacturing and energy, telecommunications and transportation. We try to sell business solutions, not technological solutions. We are oriented to look at the business problem, to understand the drivers of the industry, their cost structure. With an industry focus

we can do this. We try to work at the CEO, CFO and CIO levels. Sometimes, for example, when we deal with outsourcing, we are working against the CIO!

EDS wants to establish longer-term relationships with clients and do more custom work where the margins are higher but the volume is lower. SHL tends to do more project work with higher volumes and more of a commodity service. For example, SHL would suggest using e-commerce where they can build the IS. EDS would work on a business solution that might use e-commerce.

EDS assigns both direct and indirect costs as far down in the organizational hierarchy as possible. We pay for everything we use. If I connect one of my people to a LAN, I have to pay for the connect costs. The same holds for phones, cell phones, space—everything. We push accountability as low as possible to make people responsible and have them understand how to affect their costs.

At SHL, financial management is done at a collective level. Costs of overhead are distributed on an allocation basis. This means lower levels cannot control their operations because they don't really know their real costs. At EDS over 50 people would have the information to worry about profits. At SHL, only the four regional VP's would have profit responsibility.

On the other hand, SHL is much better than EDS at controlling its resources. Every employee has a time sheet and the time is allocated to a project or to overhead. They can track everyone and reallocate people easily from project to project. They use "Protrack" and "BOS" tools to track employee information. Because of their smaller projects, SHL needs to reallocate people from project to project as the projects are completed. We hope to learn from them how to use these tools as we integrate the systems across organizations.

The challenge is to figure out which system will lead to the highest bottom-line profits. If there are many projects, the EDS system is too cumbersome! If the projects are lengthy, SHL can't control the costs properly and the allocation produces misleading information.

The reports in the media about the culture are wrong. In SHL every decision has to go to the top because of the financial structure. At EDS we are able to make many more decisions at a lower level. EDS Systemhouse will be left alone as long as we make our numbers. With SHL, the Canadian operation was one half of SHL; so Canada was too big to be left alone. There might be a "sons of Ottawa" phenomenon with SHL because that is where their roots are.

EDS doesn't have anyone in Western Canada. Integration works better with two groups of equal size. How will we transform SHL in the West to EDS? We don't have a great deal of customer or geography overlap, even in Toronto. Ottawa, Quebec City and the provincial government have some overlap, but even there we deal with different departments.

There are probably not a lot of synergies in terms of cost, except in the overhead structure: you only need one accounts receivable manager, one president, etc. Otherwise we need the people. From a business point of view, the number of people drives the volume of business we can do.

SHL has a larger client base of smaller clients. We hope to grow with them as they move from $2 to $3 million to $10 to $15 million. We will be able to rely on our U.S. experience to find solutions and transfer that knowledge to our Canadian operation.

There is some client overlap. For example, a client both EDS and SHL were chasing put out two contracts and six work packages. We won one contract and SHL the other. When we came together at the time of the merger, SHL thought EDS' business was a disaster and that they were blowing us away. Their delivery and sales people thought they were doing a great job because they kept business flowing. They were surprised to learn that EDS was getting three to four times the revenue, was making a lot more money than they were and had the government telling us that it wanted us to run the whole thing.

Whittaker's Problem

Whittaker summarized the complexity of the problems facing her.

> Each business (EDS Canada and SHL Systemhouse) is a product of its history and market experience. Putting the two together requires more than changing the formal structure and reporting relationships. We have to appreciate the way each company really works and then integrate them so that we work in a common way. Redefining who our customers are means redefining management structure and processes.
>
> What I am looking for are some principles for how to organize the business. These principles include a vision of the company, how to approach the market, how to divide and align accounts, and how this relates to what the clients expect and are willing to buy.

Several issues were on Whittaker's mind. The KTA approach seemed to be an effective way of allocating EDS Systemhouse's scarce business development resources. However, the approach would not be applicable for all clients: coverage of small markets was contrary to the KTA philosophy because no clients would qualify. One of Whittaker's requirements was that no sales be lost with the reorganization. What would be the new organization's "go to market strategy"? How would the organization integrate the overlapping lines of business and the different strategies from old SHL and old EDS Canada?

Whittaker was also concerned that the organization be able to support the push into e-commerce that EDS was promoting. "I wonder how we should approach e-commerce, which is more important to some businesses than others," she said.

attachment 1 Biography of Sheelagh Whittaker

EXECUTIVE PROFILE

Sheelagh D. Whittaker

Chair, President and CEO

EDS Systemhouse Inc.

Born in Ottawa, Ms. Whittaker holds the degrees of Bachelor of Science from the University of Alberta and Bachelor of Arts from the University of Toronto.

Upon receiving her MBA in Finance and Economics from York University (Dean's Honour List), Ms. Whittaker began her career as a Combines Investigation Officer for the Department of Consumer and Corporate Affairs.

During eight subsequent years with The Canada Consulting Group (now the Boston Consulting Group), where she became a Director and Partner, one of Ms. Whittaker's many accomplishments was leading the successful application by the Cantel group to operate Canada's first national cellphone network.

In 1986, Ms. Whittaker was appointed Vice President, Planning and Corporate Affairs, at the Canadian Broadcasting Corporation where she played a crucial role in winning the competition against other broadcasters for the license to create Canada's first 24-hour television news channel, now known as CBC Newsworld.

In March of 1988, Ms. Whittaker joined Canadian Satellite Communications Inc. (Cancom) as Senior Vice President and Chief Financial Officer and in April, 1989, was appointed President and Chief Executive Officer.

In November of 1993, Ms. Whittaker joined EDS Canada as President and is now Chair, President and Chief Executive Officer of EDS Systemhouse Inc., the leading pure provider of IT services in Canada.

Ms. Whittaker serves on the Boards of the Royal Bank of Canada, Royal Trust Corporation, Imperial Oil Limited, Donohue Inc. and CanWest Global Communications Corp. Chosen as Woman of the Year by Canadian Women in Radio and Television in 1992, Ms. Whittaker has since received the Outstanding Executive Leadership Award from York University and an Honorary Fellowship from Ryerson Polytechnical Institute as well as being included by *Maclean's* Magazine in its Honor Roll of outstanding Canadians. She and her husband, William Morgan, have a blended family of six.

appendix 1 Key Target Account Development

EDS Systemhouse's strategy was to develop and grow relationships with client organizations over time. Developing a KTA relationship started with "winning" a major contract, but such a contract did not necessarily imply a long-term relationship. Growing the relationship with the KTA was a complex process. The following examples show relationships with KTAs in various stages of development.

An Example of a "Mature" KTA

EDS Systemhouse provided IT facilities management for one mature KTA in the automotive sector. The core business for EDS included the following:

- Ongoing support for many systems including materials management, production control, engineering, purchasing, finance and administrative systems.
- Network and desktop support, including a consistent office environment program.
- Hardware and technical support for mainframe, mid-range and client server systems.
- Additional shorter-term projects as required.

EDS had been working onsite at this client's location for 12 to 13 years. Over this time, the systems supported by EDS had evolved to meet the client's specific business requirements. The EDS personnel on site determined what the client was planning, offered the client advice and competed for the client's projects. EDS' key competitive advantage came from providing products and services tailored to the client's specific requirements.

The EDS account team worked closely with EDS' Solution Centre, which provided training and had experience with technology that was key to the client's business.

The team was aligned with the client's functional areas. The manager of each area was responsible for a P&L, workload management, identification of potential opportunities, and reporting on the status of various initiatives within his/her functional assignment.

A mature KTA entailed several challenges. First, growth had to be managed. This meant planning for three time horizons: the immediate (what is needed in order to sustain the core business?), near term (what factors are likely to emerge within the next 8 to 12 months?), and longer-term developments (what factors are likely to emerge in two years or so?). EDS sought information from the client for all three horizons so that it could propose projects that would improve the client's business. Second, investments had to be made in such a way that EDS would have the resources required to deliver services across the three horizons. Third, the team had to maintain its financial performance so that it could make these investments supporting future business. Fourth, the team had to respond quickly to the opportunities it identified, and deliver as promised.

As IT became more of a commodity business, it was important that EDS demonstrated the ability to provide value in other areas of the client's business.

An Example of an "Adolescent" KTA

EDS had a less-developed, five-year relationship with one of North America's leading financial institutions. This firm offered retail and wholesale financial products and services through its electronic banking network, branches and offices throughout North America and the rest of the world. EDS Systemhouse provided it with electronic commerce, systems management, facilities management, systems development, systems integration and technical consulting. Approximately 60 to 70 per cent of the business was project-oriented, while 30 to 40 per cent was long term/contractual.

continued

appendix 1 Key Target Account Development (*continued*)

EDS Systemhouse had persuaded the client's leaders of its value, but wished to expand its influence to middle and lower management. This was important to the evolution of the relationship because middle managers both influenced and recommended which services the institution bought.

A KTA leader was dedicated to the account because of the volume of business and the maturity of the business relationship. This individual was responsible for the overall account performance and client relationship, specifically for P&L, customer satisfaction, new growth and organic growth, and strategy. Four account managers were assigned specific contracts with specific customers in the client's organization. The account managers worked very closely with the KTA leader on the overall account strategy and sought assistance from EDS' sales organization as required, although each was responsible for P&L and the growth of his/her account.

Project managers were responsible for specific projects with the client. As projects were completed and services became maintenance-oriented, responsibility was passed over to the account manager.

Building the business relationship with this type of account was always challenging. Often competitors had significant relationships with senior levels in the client's organization, so EDS had to demonstrate results superior to those provided by competitors. This meant that projects had to be immediately successful and service delivery excellent. While doing this, EDS had to develop a positive relationship with the in-house IT organization.

An Example of an "Infant" KTA

One of EDS Systemhouse's new clients was one of the largest and oldest financial institutions in North America. It had over US$100 billion in assets, more than 30,000 employees, and both U.S. and Canadian operations.

EDS Systemhouse assisted this organization with applications support, systems management and an electronic commerce initiative providing electronic bill presentment. Approximately 90 per cent of the services provided by EDS Systemhouse were longer-term, contracted revenue services.

EDS Systemhouse provided the account with a KTA leader, part of an account manager's time, a sales executive and sales support. The overall delivery and client relationship approach was similar to that described in the prior example.

The challenges faced by "infant" KTA accounts were similar to "adolescent" KTAs. Often competitors who had long-term relationships with senior executives were entrenched in these accounts. Also, the in-house IT organization needed to be turned into an ally, since it saw organizations such as EDS Systemhouse as competitors trying to replace them. Client education about the value of EDS' services was important.

exhibit 1 EDS Canada Operating Statement: Actual for 1998 (in millions of dollars)*

	Actual 1998			Planned 1999		
	Revenue	**COGS**	**G. M.**	**Revenue**	**COGS**	**G. M.**
Vertical						
Communications & Trans.	$ 30	24	6	$ 36	28	8
Government & Health	237	200	37	260	220	40
Manufacturing	127	107	20	135	110	25
Energy & Crowns	47	41	6	55	48	7
Financial	151	115	36	160	117	43
Other	—	—	—	—	—	—
Total Vertical	**592**	487	**105**	**646**	523	**123**
Overhead		(6)		(7)		
SBU Total	**$ 592**		**99**	**$ 646**		**116**

* Financial figures have been altered.

exhibit 2 Organizational Chart of EDS Canada, Spring 1999

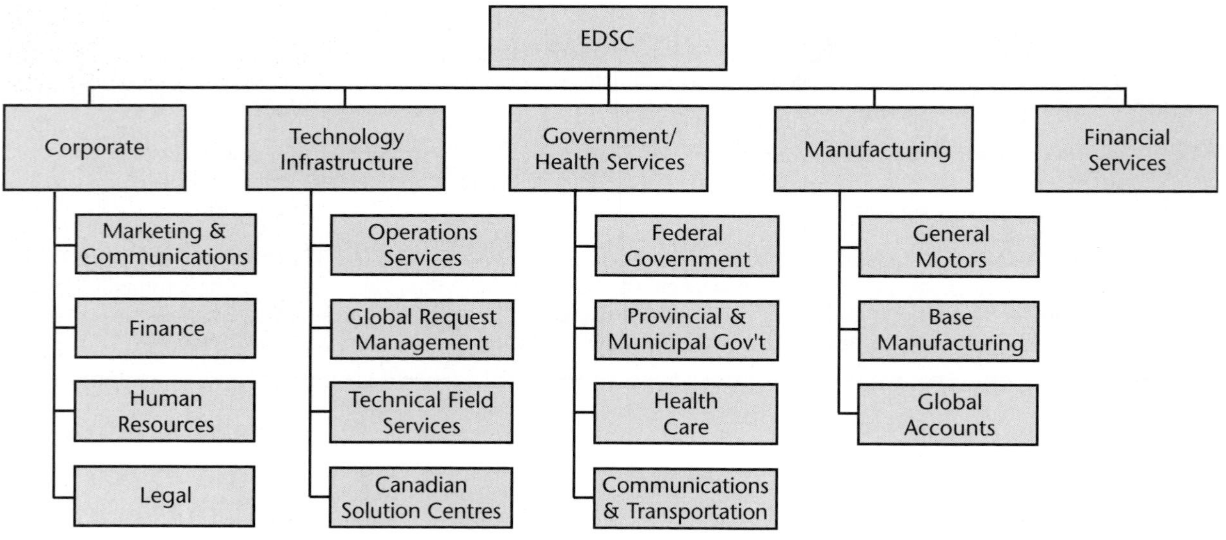

exhibit 3 Organizational Chart of EDS Systemhouse, June 1999

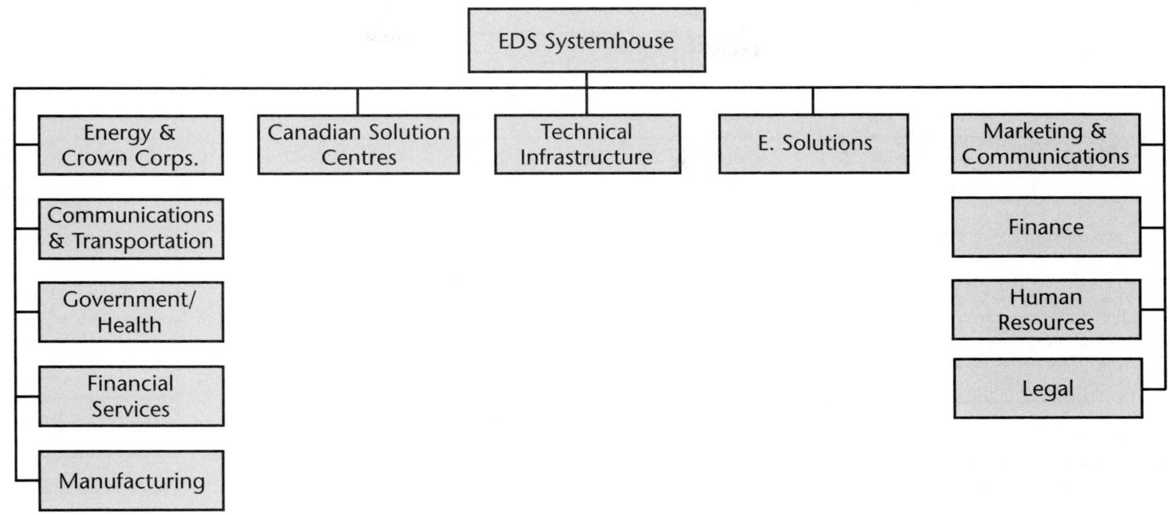

exhibit 4 SHL Operating Budget for Canada by Region; 1998 Actual and 1999 Budget (in millions of dollars)*

	1998 Actual					1999 Budget				
	Quebec	Ottawa	Central	West	Total	Quebec	Ottawa	Central	West	Total
Revenue (SI & OS)										
SI	$25	85	52	100		$33	115	71	118	
OS	6	102	6	40		8	105	14	51	
Other	14	33	46	21		7	34	40	11	
Total Revenue	**$45**	**220**	**104**	**161**	**$530**	**$48**	**254**	**125**	**180**	**$607**
Cost of Goods Sold										
SI	$23	66	59	56		$ 22	74	62	62	
OS	5	75	3	31		6	87	12	47	
Total COGS	**28**	**141**	**62**	**87**		**28**	**161**	**74**	**109**	
Operating & Administration	16	30	25	45		18	42	29	55	
Depreciation & Amortization	1	3	2	2		1	4	2	3	
Total Costs	**$45**	**174**	**89**	**134**	**$442**	**$47**	**207**	**105**	**167**	**$526**
EBIT	**$—**	**46**	**15**	**27**	**$ 88**	**$ 1**	**47**	**20**	**13**	**$ 81**

* Financial figures have been altered.

exhibit 5 Organizational Chart of MCI Systemhouse Corporation, Canadian Operation, Spring 1999

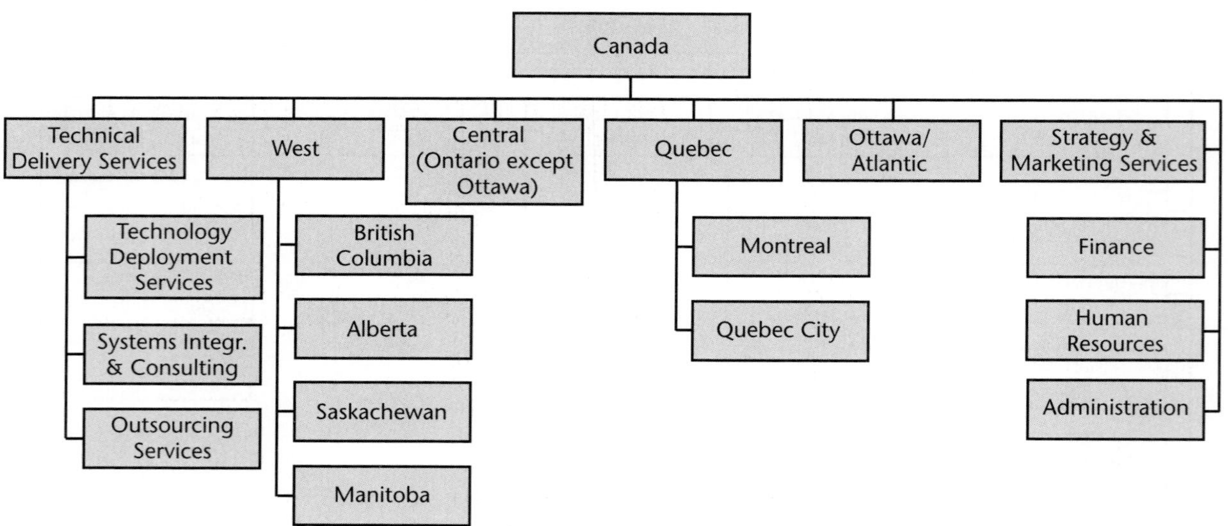

case 29 Jessica Casserra's Taskforce: Hospital Integration in the Region of Erie

Jessica Casserra stretched back from the monitor and rubbed her eyes. Technology had made it possible to be home in the evenings with her family, but as they pointed out, that didn't mean they saw much of her. For the past two months, most evenings and weekends had been spent poring over internal reports, briefs, governmental documents, spreadsheets, and consulting studies concerning the integration of hospital services in the Region of Erie.

The taxpayers of the Region had received far more than their fair share of her time, but she wasn't sure that was translating into added value. Budgeting, control, program integration, human resource and organization design issues had not been resolved—they had only festered as senior hospital management, board members and key stakeholder groups squabbled and continued to avoid making difficult decisions.

Nonetheless, the formal organizational integration of Metropolitan with five smaller hospitals and ancillary services (e.g., laundry, food services) was required to be agreed to and set in motion within ten months. The Ministry of Health had fixed the timing. It was extremely unlikely the provincial governing party would back down from the start date, given the political heat they had taken throughout the review process that resulted in their decision to regionalize hospital services. Jessica knew they would not want to give integration opponents additional opportunities to mobilize resistance or any hope that decisions might be reversed. They would also want this matter long past prior to the next provincial election.

HOSPITAL SERVICES IN THE REGION AND THEIR RESPONSE TO INTEGRATION

The combined hospital services in the southeast region of the Province responded to the needs of 250,000 people in their catchment area of approximately 30 kilometres by

60 kilometres. Metropolitan Hospital was, by far, the largest facility, with 150 beds and 700 employees or 493 full-time equivalents. Metropolitan specialized in primary care and offered a fairly full range of hospital services, from emergency to surgical, basic cancer care and dialysis. The specific services offered varied depending upon the medical specialists they were able to attract to their area at any particular point in time. However specialized needs in such areas as neonatal, advanced trauma, MRI and more complex cardiac and cancer care interventions were transferred to a larger hospital.

Metropolitan was located in the major urban area (population = 90,000) in the region. It was surrounded by agricultural and tourist areas and a number of smaller municipalities. Five of these towns hosted 20 to 50 bed hospitals, offering limited services to residents in the immediate area.

Each of the hospitals in the region had strong local support and a good reputation for the quality of care and services they provided. In recent years this support had been tested as waiting periods for medical procedures increased, and emergency care lineups lengthened. Shortages of funds and health care workers (nurses, specialists and general practitioners) were stressing the system and there was a growing concern over the future of public health care in the region.

For several years the Province had been involved in efforts directed towards reining in escalating healthcare costs through initiatives aimed at improving the efficiency and effectiveness of the hospital health care delivery system. This had led to provincially initiated studies of how best to rationalize and deploy services. In the southeast region of the Province, this had translated into the provincially mandated integration of Metropolitan with the five rural hospitals and related ancillary services in the area.

The specific terms and conditions of the merger were yet to be determined, but the default position was clear. If the parties were unable to come to an agreement, the Province would appoint an administrator who would impose the terms and conditions of the merger. In addition, de-facto penalties would be imposed upon the hospitals in the region, because they would be responsible for all integration costs and would lose access to provincial transitional funding support—sums that could run to $10–20 million over the next two to five years.

The prospects of the forced integration had not been met with open arms. While the Metropolitan Board was largely supportive of the idea, the boards of the other five hospitals had all opposed the move. They saw it as usurping local control and as code language for the maintenance and enhancement of urban services at the expense of local services. They believed it would lead to service degradation in rural areas, culminating in the closure of some of the facilities they had worked so hard to develop and sustain. In addition, four of the five rural hospitals perceived this to be a blatant cash grab on the part of the Province and Metropolitan hospital. These four had all managed to save significant funds over the years, due to fundraising and fiscal prudence. Metropolitan, however, found itself with a modest operating deficit ($250,000 on a $42 million operating budget). It also had an accumulated debt of $3.3 million. The smaller hospitals were free of debt.

Board members of the four hospitals with significant surpluses saw the budgetary situation as an example of urban mismanagement, whereas Metropolitan board members saw it as the result of years of over-funding of rural hospitals, combined with the fact that Metropolitan inherited the more expensive and difficult to manage patients.

JESSICA CASSERRA'S APPOINTMENT

Following the decision of the Ministry of Health to require the realignment of hospital service in the southeast region, Jessica Casserra was approached to lead the initiative by the chief administrative officers of three of the hospitals involved (including Metropolitan). Jessica was a former nurse with a Masters in Health Administration and she was a Certified Management Accountant. She was the head of Finance, Administration, and Ancillary Services at Metropolitan. She was 47 years old and had a stellar reputation as an honest and creative hospital administrator who understood the health care issues of the region. When approached privately, most senior administrators at all six hospitals admitted that Jessica had, by far, the best chance of any administrator in the area of managing the integration successfully. In addition to her technical and managerial talent, she was politically astute and in possession of excellent facilitation skills.

At first Jessica had rejected the overtures. She knew this would be a very difficult assignment, she worried about the level of local support she could expect from medical and hospital staff in the region, and she doubted whether the Province had the will to see it through to its conclusion. Moreover, Jessica wondered whether she had the organization skills to take on this task. Once Jessica became convinced there would be no provincial backsliding, her professional sense of responsibility, combined with her commitment to the quality of health care in the region, moved her to agree to head the hospital integration taskforce.

To maintain her legitimacy in the region, she retained her responsibilities at Metropolitan. Additional help was recruited at both the hospital and taskforce levels to assist her with her new responsibilities, but Jessica soon found herself working 55 to 65 hours per week. This was not unexpected, but it was tiring and stressful. She was now two months into this assignment, with ten months to go to the deadline. If agreements could be achieved by that point, she recognized that she would likely retain significant responsibilities for integration activities that would run for at least the next two to three years. If agreements could not be reached, Jessica would step down from her taskforce role and a provincial administrator would be appointed. What would happen then was far from clear.

THE TASKFORCE DESIGN

When Jessica agreed to chair the taskforce, the Ministry of Health had already decided upon its membership structure. In addition to the chair (formally appointed by the Ministry of Health), each hospital nominated three members, the local physician's association nominated 3 members, the nurses' association nominated 2 members, and the member communities each nominated 1 member of the public. Further, the Ministry of Health appointed 2 non-voting, ex-officio members to represent its interests. In addition to the chair, the taskforce had 29 voting members and two non-voting members. The taskforce was expected to seek consensus and act in an advisory role to the involved hospitals and the Province. In addition to those from health care professions, about a third of the taskforce members came from other walks of life (e.g., 2 farmers, 1 engineer, 2 lawyers, 1 pastor, 2 business owners, 2 accountants). Jessica remembered when members had been told by the Province at the first meeting that service on the taskforce would not unduly impair their capacity to meet their regular responsibilities. Jessica reckoned that since that first meeting, taskforce duties had taken 20 to 30 hours per week of her time and about 10 hours per week of the time of other members.

The taskforce had adequate funds to hire professional staff, consultants, and support personnel to help them in their deliberations. They had a full-time staff of 8 including two hospital planners, an information systems specialist, a human resource specialist, a financial specialist, and 3 staff supports. These employees were hired directly by the taskforce through the efforts of Jessica and her staff sub-committee. In addition, consultants had received contracts from the taskforce to assist in the needed background work and analysis. They included two well-respected retired hospital CEO's who were contracted to investigate service structure and delivery options. Once implementation of the plan became the focus, an implementation taskforce would be formed. It was anticipated that most implementation taskforce members would be drawn from the existing hospital staff, but it had yet to be designed.

The staff of the taskforce was housed in office space supplied by the Region of Erie and the taskforce used Erie's council chamber for its meetings. In addition, there was temporary office space and a board room available to taskforce members, and Jessica had permanent office space available to her there.

Following the initial taskforce meeting a month and a half ago (a session hosted by the Ministry of Health), the taskforce had been meeting one day per week and working fairly well on exploratory matters, but they had not yet had to face difficult questions. Once the more contentious strategic and operational questions came to the table, Jessica was concerned that they might simply defer to the public positions of the various groups that had selected them for membership. This was not a recipe for success. If they were going to really add value, she believed that they had to seize this unique opportunity to reinvent hospital service delivery in the region—a tough concept to sell. Board members and representatives of other stakeholders were quick to point fingers at who needed to improve. To this point most taskforce members were not prepared to publicly argue that the current system was in crisis. The preference of members seemed to be for targeted analysis and solutions that intervened in ways that preserved and enhanced the position of the stakeholder group that was recommending the tinkering.

Jessica wondered what she should do to increase the chances of taskforce success. How should the taskforce be managed and what things should she be doing outside of the formal taskforce meetings? Jessica had developed a good working knowledge of the medical and managerial talent available in the hospital system in the southeast region and she had fairly good knowledge of the various stakeholders involved. She was also a respected administrator who had developed a reputation for being a fair minded and independent thinker who understood and cared about healthcare. She knew her capacities in these areas would be taxed to the utmost.

THE STRATEGIC QUESTIONS

From a strategic perspective, Jessica continued to ponder what would be the best way to integrate hospital services and configure their management and governance structures, systems, and supports. There were a range of options, but all came with strings attached.

When thinking about the integration challenge, Jessica was very aware of the fact that Metropolitan had a well-developed strategic plan that had already contemplated some of these questions. However, she also believed these documents would likely be more of an impediment than an aid at this time. Two of the smaller hospitals had made some attempt at developing a strategic plan for themselves while the other three had spent little time engaged in such activity. However, virtually all the hospital CEO's and their senior managers seemed to believe that they were skilled strategists who knew what the region needed. If the services offered by a newly constructed regional hospital delivery system were to be as effective and efficient as possible, Jessica knew that the hospitals would have to depart dramatically from the way they had organized themselves in the past. At present, Jessica did not have a strong sense of the strategic focus or skill set of most taskforce members, but it was her belief that many would be tempted to defer to the various groups that had nominated them.

INTEGRATION OPTIONS

Option A

From the perspective of the Board and CEO of Metropolitan, full integration was the preferred way to approach hospital integration. This approach would rationalize services and lead to higher levels of resource use. This would mean moving to a single board and CEO, a consolidated budget and governance structure, a complete realignment of services and roles, control over all ancillary services, access to accumulated surpluses and contingency funds, and the possible consolidation of all hospital foundations into one for the entire region. This approach was seen to minimize organization risk in the sense that all major management functions would be centralized. The fundraising foundations were supposedly independent but most were effectively controlled by the hospital that they were focused on. The smaller hospital foundations had combined savings of $17 million. Metropolitan's foundation controlled $15 million. In addition, the accumulated reserves and contingency funds held by the smaller hospitals themselves totaled $16 million.

The Metropolitan Board salivated at the thought of what they could do with this money, but Jessica knew that any integration that was viewed by the smaller hospitals as a frontal attack would lead to protracted court battles, particularly over the control of the assets managed by the fundraising foundations. She was told that there was a 60% chance Metropolitan would be successful, but it could take up to five years to conclude the legal wrangling and the financial and organizational costs would be substantial.

She also knew that it could have a profoundly negative effect on future fundraising activities in these communities and she anticipated that most staff and volunteers in the smaller hospitals would view the approach very negatively. Staff resistance would likely come in the form of absenteeism, less willingness to work overtime and extra shifts, and resignations by nurses and physicians. Only the staff at Metropolitan, most of the medical specialists and some of the GP's would be likely to view this option positively, due to their beliefs concerning the need for the infusion of funds to shore up their ability to supply new and higher quality leading edge medical care to citizens in the region.

Option B

At the other end of the integration continuum was a model that would allow all hospitals to retain their independent structures and boards, with member hospitals each nominating representatives to a supra Board that would act as a planning and coordinating body. This was the option that was favored by the smaller hospitals and towns, because it allowed continued local access and control of the institutions that the smaller communities had been instrumental in developing and supporting. Neither Metropolitan nor the Province viewed this model favorably, because it seemed likely to perpetuate fairly siloed operations and did not seem likely to result in significant savings from consolidation and increased efficiency. These potential savings were thought to be in the order of at least $4 to $6 million per year. Given the position of the Province, this would leave Metropolitan scrambling to find ways to fund an operating deficit likely to grow by $100,000 to $350,000 per year over the next few years as the population aged and the smaller hospitals continued downloading their more difficult and expensive cases.

Between these two extremes there were many other possibilities and Jessica knew that these needed to be narrowed, developed and assessed. In addition, there was the wild card issue of how to best handle chronic, long-term care in the region, but taskforce members and the Province seemed prepared to set this issue aside for the present.

COMPETITION

Competition was becoming more intense—somewhat surprising because this was not supposed to happen in a publicly funded system. Competition came from several sources. Private clinics had opened in or near the southeast region and were offering a number of services that had previously been supplied by Metropolitan.

Hospitals had found that these specific services were financially attractive to supply because they were relatively easy to perform, in many cases patients (or insurers) paid for the service themselves, and in other cases the provincial reimbursement rate greatly exceeded the costs of supplying the services. Cosmetic surgery, routine hernia treatment, rehabilitation services, CT services, and diet and lifestyle counseling were the types of services that were coming under increased competitive pressure.

In addition, residents in the area could easily access private medical facilities by crossing into the United States. A number of these facilities were actively marketing their services to Canadians and it was not unusual to find Canadian physicians affiliated in some way with these U.S. facilities. Jessica noted that the Provincial government was willing to pay U.S. suppliers the provincially mandated rates for insured services. Individual patients were responsible for any differences, but for procedures such as CT's and MRI's, the provincial payments covered the majority of the bill.

ANCILLARY SERVICES

Ancillary services represented both a competitive opportunity and a threat. Metropolitan Hospital, in particular, was in the catering, vehicle repair, fundraising, payroll services, security, housekeeping/cleaning, hazardous material handling, homecare and laundry businesses, to name just a few. These were services that they could potentially commercialize and/or privatize and spin off. While Jessica had only begun inspecting these opportunities, she already knew that some were fairly efficient and effective operations—laundry, payroll services, and food services, in particular. Others (custodial/cleaning services and homecare) were less efficient and cost effective than private sector competitors at the present. It was not clear how she should go about structuring and evaluating these opportunities and risks. Several Board members looked at such initiatives very favorably, because they saw them as a way to address deficit problems and provide funding for mainstream medical care delivery. However, a minority continued to have serious concerns about the commercialization of hospital services.

Equipment and physical plant were, on the whole, in a fairly good state of repair in the region. Equipment was never as modern or as abundant as staff would like, but overall the hospitals had managed maintenance programs well.

Jessica recognized that some of the commercialization opportunities would require significant investments in order to realize their potential. For example, the laundry facility required an investment of $13 million to allow it to take advantage of the commercialization opportunities in the area (supplying hospitals, nursing homes, the University and Community College, and others in need of institutional laundry services). While the laundry, in particular, seemed to have solid economic potential, she recognized that some would argue that the resources were needed to fund hospital plant and equipment needs that more directly served the delivery of medical services.

CONTROL AND INFORMATION SYSTEMS

With the exceptions of Metropolitan's computerized accounting and payroll systems, computer information systems represented a serious point of concern. Each hospital had its own system or systems and the systems did not communicate with each other. Some of these were clearly antiquated and even within Metropolitan there was duplication of information entry, difficulties with information flow, and far too much reliance on paper.

Jessica knew that the issues in the areas of control system design extended well beyond software and computer concerns. Ministry of Health and Ministry of Finance requirements drove much of the activity in this area, but Jessica felt that this would be an ideal time to sort through and establish the management control information that could really benefit managers and the organization. For example, there was little to no consistency in the boundary, belief, diagnostic or interactive control systems in operation in the various hospitals. Metropolitan's system was the most developed, but even here Jessica believed improvement was needed with both its design and use. She believed the new organization would be well served if it approached the design of the control system with an open mind and then ensured that their managers were literate in the effective use of the information emanating from it.

The critical questions concerning the control system were what the system should be designed to do and how its implementation should be approached. Jessica believed these would be impossible to determine in a definitive way until the fundamental strategy questions had been answered. She knew that gaining interest and approval for control system initiatives (other than those required by statute) would be a challenge. However, building the business case for control processes that went beyond historical reporting requirements would get progressively more difficult as time passed and resources tightened.

PEOPLE

Managing hospital employees during the transition represented a key point of risk. Hospitals in the region were already short of nurses and the area had been classified as under-serviced by general practitioners and specialists. Little in the way of strategy had guided hospital activities, with the exception of Metropolitan that had a fairly well developed strategic plan. For example, three years earlier Metropolitan had developed detailed and sophisticated initiatives aimed at attracting and retaining general practitioners and specialists. They had also developed initiatives to improve management practices and employee satisfaction and performance by moving to team-based management. Their efforts had met with some limited success in the areas of attraction, retention, and satisfaction, but Jessica still believed they relied far too much on hierarchy and traditional management practices. Team members still deferred to managers and physicians and engaged in few of the self-management behaviors Jessica had hoped to see.

Once integration was undertaken, the human resource challenges would escalate. Each hospital and ancillary service had their own bargaining units and each represented a unique culture, with its own approach to financial, physical plant and human resource management. For example, two of the smaller hospitals had served as exemplars for Metropolitan when they had begun investigating team management. They had achieved high degrees of success with the approach and were viewed as extremely well managed.

At the other end of the continuum was one small hospital that was believed to be in fairly serious difficulty with respect to their management practices. Turnover and absenteeism were high, satisfaction was reported to be low, and efficiency and effectiveness were both well below national norms. Nonetheless, the Board of that hospital was highly supportive of its practices and the performance of its senior managers. They attributed observed shortfalls to unique issues in their catchment area, but Jessica felt that this assessment didn't stand up to closer scrutiny. The fact that the hospital CEO and the head of nursing were respectively 62 and 60 years old might make change easier to manage at this site, if they should choose to retire early.

Jessica knew that integration activities would occasion job insecurity, with its magnitude dependent upon what integration approach was adopted. At present, this fear was most pronounced in middle and senior management levels, but unions had already voiced concerns about possible job losses caused by service rationalization, contracting out, and/or privatization. Until the post integration roles of the various hospitals were clarified, staff uncertainty and anxiety were bound to escalate.

NEXT STEPS

Jessica mulled over her options but then stopped and laughed. For many years she had been a vocal advocate of strategic thinking, accompanied by action, execution, supportive management, measurement and learning. Here she was, three months into her taskforce assignment, bogged down by tactical and operational concerns. Maybe it was time to step back and do some strategic planning for herself, but she was unclear about how best to proceed.